Minor Mlabri
A Hunter-Gatherer Language
of Northern Indochina

in memory of
Søren Egerod

Minor Mlabri
A Hunter-Gatherer Language
of Northern Indochina

by Jørgen Rischel

Museum Tusculanum Press
University of Copenhagen 1995

Minor Mlabri

© Jørgen Rischel & Museum Tusculanum Press 1995
Set in Palatino by Jørgen Rischel
Cover design by Thora Fisker
Cover photos by Jørgen Rischel
Printed in Denmark by AiO Tryk, Odense

ISBN 87 7289 294 3

The front cover photo shows Mr. Top, the first speaker of β-Mlabri encountered by the author.
The back cover photo shows Mrs. Lat, also a speaker of this variety of Mlabri. Both of these persons died some years ago.

Published with the support of
The Carlsberg Foundation

MUSEUM TUSCULANUM PRESS
University of Copenhagen
Njalsgade 92
DK-2300 Copenhagen S

CONTENTS

INTRODUCTION	8
Part I: Description	19
CHAPTER 1: THE LANGUAGE AND ITS SPEAKERS	21
1.1 What is Mlabri?	21
Mlabri-like tribes and ethnonyms 24	
1.2 Minor Mlabri	25
Two kinds of Mlabri 27 – Male and female speech 28 – Mlabri dialects or "ethnolects" 30	
1.3 The Social Situation of the Mlabri	32
1.4 Minor Mlabri and "Yumbri"	35
CHAPTER 2: THE LINGUISTIC SCENARIO	41
2.1 Diachronic, Areal and Sociolinguistic Aspects	41
2.1.1 Mlabri from a Comparative Perspective	42
2.1.2 Linguistic Contact Phenomena	46
2.1.3 Bilingualism and Language Norms	54
2.2 The Origin of Mlabri Lexical Material	58
A digression on relative calendary terms 61	
CHAPTER 3: A PHONOLOGICAL SKETCH	63
3.1 Segmental Phonology	63
Vowels 64 – Diphthongs 67 – Consonants: Initial conss. 70 – One or two phonemes? 72 – Syllabicity 74 – Final consonants 75	
3.2 Prosody	77
Syllables-types 77 – Vowel quantity 77 – Stress and tone 78	
3.3 The Phonology of Sentence Types	79
CHAPTER 4: THE MLABRI WORD	82
4.1 Morphology	83
4.1.1 Infixation	84

Phonological generalizations about infixation 87

4.1.2 Prefixation 89
Causative formation 90 – Voicing dissimilation between prefix and stem 90

4.1.3 Reduplication 92
Expressives 92 – Reduplicatives as fossils 94 – Symbolic function 94 – Predominant patterns of reduplication 96 – Echoing with ablaut 98 – Elaborate expressions 98

4.1.4 Compounding 99
4.1.5 Inflection 99
4.2 Word Semantics 100
Polysemy, metaphors, metonyms 100 – Synonymy, antinymy, semantic fields 103 – Expressions of time 105

4.2.1 Negation 107
4.2.2 Eating, Drinking and Smoking 111
4.2.3 Colour Terminology 112
4.2.4 Kinship Terminology 116
Lineage: relative generation 118 – Lineal vs. collateral relationship 118 – Relative age 119 – The concepts of "first" and "last" 119 – Sex (gender) 120 – Proximity of relatedness 121 – Consanguineal and affinal relatedness 122 – Blood relatives 126 – Point of reference 127 – Address terms 128 – Spheres of usage 129 – Primary and secondary dimensions 129 – Terminology to do with age 130 – The use of titles with personal names 130 – Name-sharing 131 – Proper names 131

CHAPTER 5: SYNTAX 133
5.1 Phrasal Syntax 134
5.1.1 Noun Phrases and Pronominal Constructions ... 134
Possessive constructions 140 – Verbs as descriptive modifiers 141 – Specifying and quantifying parts – Classifiers 143 – Determiner function 144 – Downgrading of referentiality 145 – Numerical quantification 146 – Deixis and anaphoric reference 148 – Personal pronouns 149 – Possessive pronouns 151 – Definite article 152

5.1.2 Adverbial Phrases 154
Prepositions 157

5.1.3 Verb Phrases	158
Explicative verb complements 161 – Serialization 164	
5.2 Sentence Syntax	167
Sentence-types 168 – Constituency 170	
5.2.1 The status and Order of Sentence Constituents	171
Subjecthood 172, Constituent order, topicalization and focus 174 – Indirect object and direct object 176 – The position of adverbial phrases 180	
5.2.2 Clause-mates With Connectives	183
Coordinating conjunctions 183 – Comparison 185 – Other connectives 186	
5.2.3 Clause-mates Without Connectives	190
Comparison 191 – Subordination 192	
5.3. Samples of Connected Speech	194

Part II: Lexicon 199

CHAPTER 6: THE SELECTION OF LEXICAL INFORMATION	201
6.1 Simple and Complex Lexical Entries	202
6.2 Phonemic Notation and Alphabetic Ordering	203
Pretonic syllables 204 – Syllabification 205 – Rhythm 206	
6.3 Phonological Variation	206
6.4 Morphology and Alphabetization	211
6.5 Word-class Membership	212
6.6 Homonymy and Polysemy	213
6.7 Spheres of Usage and Reliability of Information	214
Restricted use of vocabulary 215 – Adequacy and degree of coverage of the lexicon 216	
CHAPTER 7: MLABRI-ENGLISH DICTIONARY	219
CHAPTER 8: ENGLISH-MLABRI WORD INDEX	343
REFERENCES	363

INTRODUCTION

The language described in this monograph is spoken by a small hilltribe in northern Indochina. Its existence has attracted considerable attention because of the legendary and intriguing primitiveness of the Mlabri or "Spirits of the Yellow Leaves", as they are traditionally called, but reliable information about the cultural heritage and particularly the language of the Mlabri is sparse (cf. the concise and excellent statement in Smalley 1994, p. 272-274). This is true in particular of an ethnic subgroup whose culture and language are now close to extinction: the group which I here refer to as the "Minor Mlabri".

There are thousands of languages in the world which are insufficiently documented or even practically unknown. Several languages disappear without ever being thoroughly investigated. Languages which exist only as spoken vernaculars, seldom evoke much public attention by their dying out, but the scientific community is aware of the resulting loss, and there is now much concern about so-called endangered languages.

Languages exist in cultural settings. In the case of the Mlabri we see a *tribal society* in the sense of a small, holistic and relatively static society in which there is little or no stratification into different social ranks of the community members. There is, on the other hand, a cross-classificational network of subdivisions ("vertical cuts") between subgroups of different kinds such as families, sexes, and also ethnic subgroups exhibiting strong polarization and mutual animosity. It is an interesting objective in itself to study a tribal language from the perspective of this sociolinguistic scenario.

From a somewhat different perspective, the language is the medium of preservation and transmission of a spiritual culture. Only by gaining considerable insight into the language can one start to understand the myths and other oral traditions of the tribe. It is, for example, becoming more and more clear that the

Mlabri (of both ethnic groups) possess their own cosmogonic tradition, which is still alive in the memories of some middle-aged or elderly men, but which may not survive for long. The present volume does not deal with Mlabri myths as such (although some brief passages are presented in section 5.3 below for illustration of connected speech), but I think that I have provided some of the information necessary for the study of oral texts.

The death of a language, however "small", is not only a loss to the people speaking that language but also an impoverishment of global human culture. And from the point of view of linguistic sciences it is an irreparable loss of future access to information about rare linguistic "species". The insights one can gain from an almost extinct language are always relevant to general and comparative linguistics. The phenomena which one observes may occasionally be quite novel; in other cases they may at least corroborate the genetic or typological evidence available from the study of other languages and cultures.

This monograph is based on field notes from the year 1988 and later years, in which I have had occasion to visit the "Minor Mlabri" ("β-Mlabri"). They are a couple of small families who keep to themselves and do not associate with the more well-known Mlabri in Thailand (here referred to as "Major Mlabri" or "α-Mlabri"), and they belong to the few indigenous peoples of Indochina that have remained in little contact with civilization.

The Mlabri are traditionally hunter-gatherers and seem to have been so for a long time (although it is an unsettled issue whether this is their original culture). Until recently, this was also more or less the lifestyle of the small group under study here. They now associate with Hmongs in remote villages because they were for several years trapped in the war zone between Thailand and Laos, and the few survivors of the β-Mlabri families had to settle down in safer environments. Deforestation has made it increasingly difficult for them to live their traditional life in the area where they belong. They often stay in villages. Still, the Mlabri of both groups prefer to eat and sleep in uncultivated areas outside the village.

It is my guess that it will not be long before the language variety used by this tiny group ceases to be used in daily communication. The few youngsters are fluent both in Thai and Hmong, and they are motivated to use Mlabri only to the extent that the elders make a point of doing so. There is an obvious conflict between the traditional ethnicity and language loyalty of these people and the fact that their way of speaking (like their whole identity) has the very lowest social status among hilltribe people in the area. The special variety of Mlabri dealt with here is now spoken by less than a dozen people who do not even all stay in the same place. Thus this variety is in imminent danger of *language death*, whereas the other variety (whose phonology and grammar differ very little from the present description) stands a much better chance of survival for some time to come.

The Mlabri language (in all of its varieties) has been virtually unknown up to now; the material accessible to Mon-Khmer scholars does not go much beyond a few word lists. The present monograph is the first attempt at a comprehensive description of any kind of Mlabri, although it represents only a small step in the direction recommended in James Matisoff's programmatic remark about Southeast Asian linguistics (Matisoff 1983, p. 79):

> One key desideratum is that there should be exhaustive studies of the grammars and lexicons of individual non-literary or 'tribal' languages, going beyond the mere word-lists and sketchy grammatical descriptions, which were all we had to go on for dozens of languages in the past.

Still, scholars outside the field of Mon-Khmer studies may perhaps question the relevance of Mlabri for general linguistics. There is an enormous variation in the extent to which linguists take the typological and social diversity of the world's languages into consideration when they make their theoretical claims, and a similarly enormous variation in the responsibility with which linguistic evidence from more or less reliable sources is used to support such claims. The Mlabri language is interesting from several perspectives, both because of its inherent properties and because of the rather unique cultural setting in which it is spoken in its different varieties. This language is slowly but steadily revealing itself. I hope that Mlabri will enter the general linguistic scene and that it will do so without suffering the fate depicted in Matisoff's harsh observation:

> Too often data from 'exotic' languages have been used in a slipshod and meaningless way by 'theoretical' linguists anxious to prove some pet point of general theory, but not too concerned about getting their facts straight in the first place (Matisoff 1983, *ibid.*).

I have seen as my major tasks to present organized raw data and to make the most basic generalizations about the ways in which morphemes, words, phrases, and clauses are combined to encode various types of meanings. It has been my intention to present such information in as much detail as is warranted by my data. This immediately raises a fundamental question: to what degree and in what sense is a language adequately represented by the kind of data to be presented below? I must emphasize that the present work is neither a sociolinguistic study of Minor Mlabri nor an analysis of natural Mlabri discourse. Most of the sentences and other language specimens presented here stem from settings in which the Mlabri speakers were aware that I was gathering linguistic information, and even in the case of more spontaneous talk and story-telling my presence has probably influenced the speakers' linguistic performance (except perhaps in the case of long narrative texts such as cosmogonic myths).

The present work does not focus on the question of normative versus actual language use. The information presented in the various chapters is to a considerable extent coloured by or even dependent upon statements *about* linguistic usage furnished by the Mlabri persons whom I judge to be the most competent speakers. This is true in particular of two major aspects of lexical variation: male versus female vocabulary and obsolescent versus current vocabulary, for which I have had to depend mostly on metalinguistic information (this issue is taken up in chapter 6, section 6.7). As for idiolectal variation the dictionary (= chapter 7) contains numerous cross-references between variant forms (also see chapter 6, section 6.3), but both the delimitation of the vocabulary and the selection of head entries are somewhat arbitrary. I am aware that the account of the language which I give here may be misconstrued as reflecting some kind of existing norm, be it a *consensus* among speakers about their language or *the most common usage* as observed in actual speech. I have found no evidence for a single norm of the former kind, and as for the latter I have not been able to define what is "prevailing" usage. (It is part of the picture that there were only eight fluent speakers of Minor Mlabri left when I first met these people; they were scattered over a considerable area and some of them probably had to speak other languages much more often than Mlabri.)

Although chapters 1, 2 and 6 deal with various aspects of language use, the information given on these matters is highly incomplete and often just anecdotal. The bulk of this monograph, i.e. chapters 3-5, is a descriptive account of various characteristics of Mlabri phonology, semantics and grammar. These chapters are all rather heterogeneous. In the survey of Contents above I have included page references to several paragraphs which might otherwise be difficult to locate, as they are not marked as numbered main sections or subsections in the text although they contain information about specific topics. (This rather extensive listing of paragraphs, together with cross-referencing within the text, takes the place of a subject-matter index.)

The Lexicon (= Part II, chapter 7) is of course first and foremost a documentation of Mlabri vocabulary (with the English-Mlabri Index = Chapter 8 as a key to lexical entries). It is, however, an essential feature of the lexicon below that it contains numerous collocations and illustrative examples, although these appear as isolated (and often truncated) linguistic specimens.

All through this monograph I have strived to keep both the degree of grammatical formalization and the use of theory-specific terminology at a very low level, compared to the high degree of sophistication that is characteristic of much contemporary work in linguistics. There are various reasons for this which have to do both with the nature of the data and with the overall purpose of the monograph.

When one deals with a virtually unknown language spoken in a little-known culture, one faces a gamut of phenomena all calling for analysis and explanation. These phenomena range from topics which normally form the core of descriptive and comparative linguistics to topics which are interdisciplinary or belong to cultural and social anthropology in a wide sense. The study of such a language is an all-encompassing enterprise which requires the integration of all kinds of available information (although it is possible *afterwards* to abstract certain structural phenomena of the language and look at these from a typological or comparative perspective). At the same time, thorough understanding of the language is a prerequisite to in-depth study of the culture of such a tribal group. This is not just a matter of understanding oral traditions (cf. my mention of myths above); the indigenous language underlies the establishment of cultural patterns and social institutions of all kinds and on all levels.

It is therefore my conviction that a language documentation such as the present one should be designed in such a way that it is applicable as a tool in anthropological and linguistic studies alike. It is often the immediate linguistic data, rather than sophisticated *a posteriori* analyses and formalizations, that turn out to have the most lasting relevance. That is one reason why I have chosen a "non-technical" format of presentation and have strived to remain faithful to immediately observable language data.

Another consideration is that the linguistic study of Mlabri – as of several other minority languages of northern Indochina – is still pretty much in the "discovery phase" (to use the jargon of classic structuralism). This is true of syntax in particular. Moreover, the evidence on which one may attempt to posit syntactic structures in these languages is to a great extent semantic and pragmatic rather than morphosyntactic. If viewed in isolation, a string of Mlabri words often seems ambiguous as regards the possibilities of syntactic parsing. I cannot, however, help feeling that such formal ambiguity may arise as a pseudo-problem generated by the choice of a rigid descriptive framework. That is an additional reason for choosing a non-technical format of presentation at the present level of understanding.

As is rather customary in European linguistic work, I have used the IPA conventions for the transcription of speech sounds.

This means that there are certain deviations from the symbols used in much of the literature on Mon-Khmer languages.

Although Mlabri phonology is treated in some detail in chapters 3 and 6 below, it may be expedient to point to some major notational discrepancies here (equivalent symbols which may occur in other sources are given in quotation marks in parentheses). (i) As for *palatal consonants*, the symbol /ch/ is used to denote an aspirated stop, affricate or sibilant (= "ś"); the unaspirated voiceless stop is rendered as /c/ (= "č"), its voiced counterpart as /ɟ/ (= "j", "ǰ"), the corresponding nasal as /ɲ/ (= "ñ"), and the voiced glide as /j/ (= "y"); likewise, I use /jh/ to denote a (syllable-final) voiceless/aspirated glide or fricative (= "yh", "ç"). (ii) As for *back unrounded vowels*, the symbols used for the two highest vowels are /ɯ/ (= "ɨ", "ï", "ü", "y") and /ɤ/ (= "ə", "ë").

Within linguistics proper, the most immediate use of a documentation of the kind I have attempted here (and earlier with Søren Egerod), may be in comparative Austroasiatic study. Mlabri has, among other noteworthy features, a robust derivational morphology and a conservative phonology, which in combination with the presence of several chronological layers of loanwords makes genetic comparison interesting and sometimes baffling.

The origin of the Mlabri tribe and the genetic affiliation(s) of their language are still in question. As mentioned earlier, they are traditionally hunter-gatherers (or, in the case of the Minor Mlabri, rather just gatherers), unlike the other hilltribes of the area. Their folklore (so far little known and unpublished) seems to contain both elements shared with neighbouring peoples and elements of a different origin. Their language has obvious affinities to languages classified as *Northern Mon-Khmer*; Mlabri is generally regarded as belonging to a "Khmuic" sub-branch. The genetic relationship of Mlabri to Northern Mon-Khmer is anything but straightforward, however.

The description of an endangered language and culture need not have the character of a collection of debris from a crumbling ruin. On the contrary, I hope the data presented here will demonstrate that a language spoken only within a couple of households need not be in a state of disintegration. This is a fully functional language which can be used – and still is used – in all kinds of conversation and narration, as I know from my experience as a more or less participant observer.

Minor Mlabri is in a state of flux, however, and exhibits the type of variation that may lead to linguistic change if the language survives long enough.

Because of difficulties in using standard fieldwork techniques, Mlabri is not an easy language to work with. My colleague Theraphan L. Thongkum, who has been working with the other variety of Mlabri, strongly warns putative future researchers about the difficulties one may encounter. She makes the following blunt statement (Tongkum 1992, p. 57):

> I myself have a great deal of experience in field work but when working with the Mlabri I found myself quite frustrated, almost giving up on several occasions.

Things come to look different, however, when one has been in fairly close contact with the people and their language over several years: although some basic "technical" problems remain in spite of highly improved communication, the frustrations are now easily outweighed by the positive aspects of the field sessions.

It was my own ambition from the start to make the communicative situation as "natural" as possible and therefore to work without the presence of an interpreter, but that was sometimes very difficult. On every occasion the Mlabri have been most willing to assist me, e.g. by providing paraphrases and explanations in a kind of Northern Thai, but unfortunately I often had difficulties understanding what exactly they were saying when using that vernacular. Looking at the situation in retrospect, I realize that my poor command of their variety of the highlanders' lingua franca has been an impediment from the very start. (I suppose that all researchers studying minority languages and cultures in this area should give high priority to an extensive knowledge of Northern Thai and Lao, both for communicative purposes and because of the significance of borrowing from both into the minority languages.)

On later occasions I have been able to profit more from the speakers' eagerness to converse in Mlabri and to demonstrate things or processes while speaking their own language. The fieldwork, however, was not made any easier by the fact that the most sophisticated speaker of this variety of Mlabri has impaired hearing and tends to speak very rapidly and indistinctly except when dictating words or phrases.

The relationship between the two varieties of Mlabri is enigmatic. On my first encounter with speakers of Minor Mlabri, I was intrigued by the paradoxical situation that a large proportion of the words they used in everyday communication were totally unknown to me although they clearly spoke the very language I had been studying for several years together with my colleagues. I was further intrigued by finding that there was virtually no difference in segmental phonology between the two varieties of Mlabri although they differed strikingly in prosody (rhythm and intonation) as well as lexicon.

The present monograph deals exclusively with what I call Minor Mlabri or β-Mlabri. A separate documentation of the other language variety (i.e., in my terminology, α-Mlabri) for which the lexical raw data have recently been updated and were being edited by my deceased colleague Søren Egerod and myself, will be published separately.

My fieldwork in Thailand over the years has been made possible by funding from Scandinavian sources, viz. from the Carlsberg Foundation, the DANIDA Foundation, the Nordic Institute of Asian Studies (NIAS) and Einar Hansens Forskningsfond. I gratefully acknowledge this financial support.

I wish to acknowledge my indebtedness to The National Research Council of Thailand for the permits which I have obtained to study Mlabri and other Khmuic languages in Thailand ever since 1982, and for the practical assistance I have received from the Research Council in conjunction with the Tribal Welfare and Development Centre of Nan Province.

In connection with the present monograph, I also wish to acknowledge the scholarly or practical assistance I have received from several fellow scholars, in particular: Theraphan L. Thongkum (Chulalongkorn University), Nipatwet Suaebsaeng (Chiangmai University), Frank Proschan (Indiana University), Kristina Lindell, Jan-Olof Svantesson and Damrong Tayanin (all at

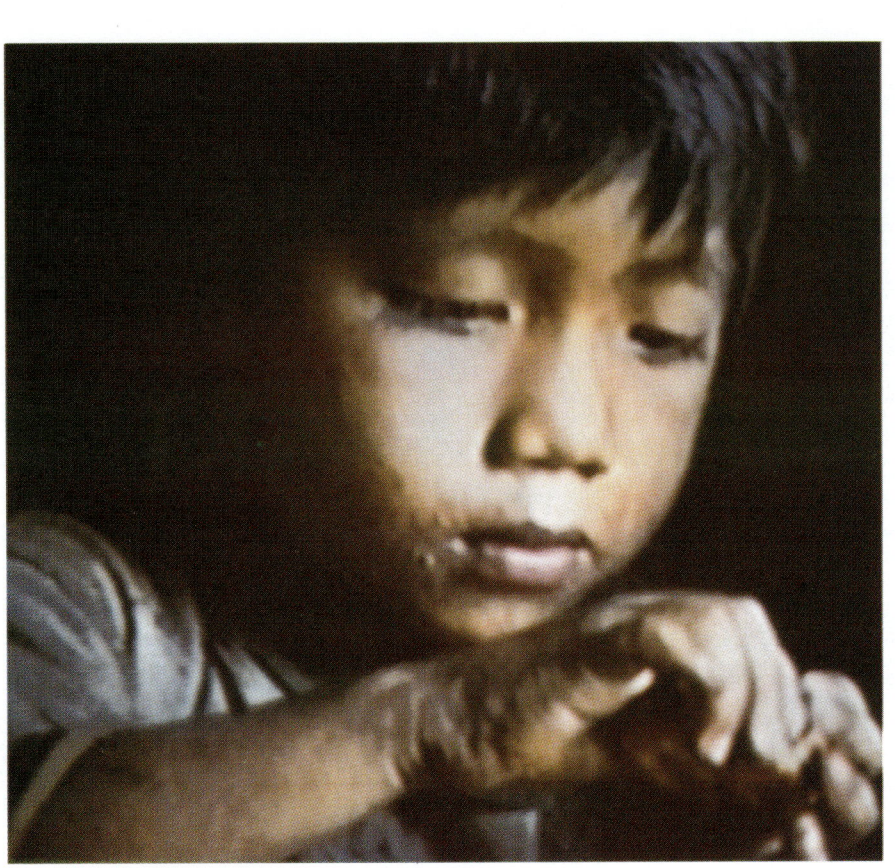

the University of Lund), and Jesper Trier (Moesgaard Museum). I have also profited from discussions with my linguistics students at the University of Copenhagen.

The material on Mlabri is sparse, and independent collections of data are of great importance. There actually exists a (fairly short and unpublished) word list of β-Mlabri which Michel Ferlus (C.N.R.S.) made in Laos as early as 1964. Dr. Ferlus has shown much scholarly generosity by putting this list at my disposal for comparison with my own data.

Above all, I am indebted to Søren Egerod, who invited me to become involved with Mlabri studies in 1982, when he embarked on a linguistic project which initially included Dr. Theraphan as well. The objective was the then known variety: α-Mlabri. Although we concentrated our joint efforts on lexicon from the start and did not get so far as to work out an explicit grammatical description, many paragraphs of the present monograph draw on basic insights about Mlabri which emerged from our extensive fieldwork in the eighties. – Dr. Egerod read a manuscript version of my text a few months before his death and gave many helpful comments. I take sole responsibility both for the overall contents and the descriptive format, however.

The appearance of this monograph in its present form is due to an initiative taken by the Publishers and a subsequent grant from the Carlsberg Foundation, which I gratefully acknowledge. – My colleague Peter Holtse provided me with the technical tools necessary to bring the manuscript typographically into shape. My present and former students Leah Wingard and David Lipscomb read the text and made many suggestions on how I could improve my style. I regret that I have not been able to follow their good advice on all points.

In this connection I must apologize to readers who take offense with one particular piece of terminology: throughout the monograph I have used the word *sex* rather than *gender* (as was generally done until quite recently even by the most non-sexist scholars) whenever the conceptual distinction 'female' versus 'male' has seemed linguistically relevant. Perhaps because of my lack of native competence in English I have been more concerned about the risk of confusion with a firmly established grammatical term, and I have permitted myself to keep the former word as an expedient though conservative technical term.

It may be added that notwithstanding the appropriateness of discussing "female" vs. "male"-based linguistic conventions with reference to institutionalized *social roles*, these roles seem firmly anchored in the biological sex distinction in traditional Mlabri culture. The conceptualization of that specific dichotomy plays a prominent role in Mlabri semantics (in metaphorical usage, etc.).

As stated already this monograph is, in its entirety, a presentation of material which stems from fairly recent work in the "field". Ultimately, the credit for the linguistic data presented here goes to the β-Mlabri speakers who have attempted to teach me Mlabri and who have patiently and willingly supplied all kinds of information about their language, life and culture.

It may be suitable to conclude this preface with a quotation from the oldest surviving member of the β-Mlabri group, a passage which is remarkable both as a specimen of poetic style and because of the way it depicts the hardships of life (the Mlabri have a vivid recollection of a chaotic situation of warfare with people fighting, fleeing and starving in the forest area along the Thailand-Laos border):

– jɤɤm dok jɤɤm jen, hɤɤj,
met ɓj boŋ thɛh boŋ mɤk, ɟak nɛŋ mɛɛʔ nɛŋ mɤj

which I think can be paraphrased as: "... living under the most miserable conditions, indeed, having nothing good and healthy to eat, rambling in rain and tempest ...".

The tone of this ritual-like passage is in a strange contrast with the tranquil happiness which the Mlabri can still enjoy if they sit in the sunny forest with enough to eat and with no enemies around. It is to be hoped that that situation will prevail for some time to come.

Part I
Description

Chapter 1

The Language and Its Speakers

The language dealt with in this monograph is a spoken vernacular. It is neither the bearer of written literature nor the reflex of an ancient civilization (as far as we know) but just a tribal language close to extinction. Nevertheless, it has survived up to now in an apparently well-preserved form characterized by its expressive possibilities and its interesting structural features. It also possesses a rather extensive lexicon. The latter gives ample etymological attestation of words which have sources in at least two different language-families. Several of these words occur with a very conservative phonology and may have been part of this language for a long time.

1.1 What is Mlabri?

Mlabri is the name of a tribe consisting of a small number of families in the mountains of the easternmost part of North Thailand, and it is at the same time the name of their language. At least two distinct varieties are found: "α-Mlabri" and "β-Mlabri" (see 1.2 below). There are, in total, less than 200 speakers in Thailand, who are now almost confined to the Nan and Phrae Provinces in the north, close to the Laotian border. Some of the Mlabri occasionally wander into the province of Phayao (west of Nan).

According to earlier (more or less reliable) sources, the Mlabri used to be scattered over a larger area of North Thailand. There are also records of more or less closely related minority groups in Laos (see below), and it is widely assumed that the Mlabri entered North Thailand from Laos, i.e. from the east, some time in the past. There are further speculations that they originally came from a homeland somewhere in Southern Indochina and travelled north along the mountain ranges of Eastern Indochina. It is a question, however, whether the origin of the Mlabri should be traced along a single path. The present Mlabri may well represent a conflux of groups from different parts of Southeast Asia, and their culture may even reflect *regressions* from more developed stages to a survival culture. When one looks at the language and the oral traditions of the Mlabri from a comparative perspective, it seems advisable to keep a totally open mind on the geographical and ethnic origin(s) of this tribe.

The Mlabri language (also referred to in textbooks as "Mrabri", "Yumbri", or "Phi Tong Luang") has been classified, on somewhat shaky lexical evidence, as belonging to a "Khmuic" branch of Northern Mon-Khmer (cf. discussion and etymological exemplifications in Tongkum 1992, p. 44-45 and 61-65). There are two other minority languages spoken in Nan Province which are classified as belonging to that same branch, namely Kmhmu (Khmu', Kammu) and Tin (T'in), the latter with two rather different sub-branches Mal and Prai (the Tin speakers themselves often prefer the term Lua').

The Mlabri, Kmhmu and Tin are considered to be indigenous inhabitants of the eastern part of Northern Thailand. The other highland minority groups of the area: the Hmong (Miao, Meo) and Mien (Yao), whose languages belong to a different language family, have entered Thailand from China rather recently.

The dominant population of both the lowland and the lower regions of the highlands are the Northern Thais (Khon Muang). Their Northern Thai vernacular (which used to have the status of a language with its own script but is now regarded as a dialect with respect to Standard Thai) is closely related to both Lao (Laotian) and Central Thai (Siamese).

The existence of the Mlabri, an evasive and extremely shy tribe straying in the mountain forests of North Thailand, was first mentioned in the scholarly literature in the twenties. The first Mlabri to be described in any detail were the group that Hugo Bernatzik met on a journey in 1937-38 and referred to as "Yumbri". A different group was encountered by an expedition headed by Kraisri Nimmanhaeminda in the beginning of the sixties; that group was called "Mrabri" by Nimmanhaeminda (the highlights of the research history were mentioned in Rischel and Egerod 1987 and Rischel 1989a). As a member of the latter expedition, Boeles described the tribe as a group of people who have not known a stone age and thus have no pottery, who do not make their own clothing, who do not practice agriculture, who do not build houses, and who do not wear ornaments. He concluded: "It will be difficult to find groups of human beings in this world that live in similar conditions" (Boeles 1963, p. 150).

The Mlabri are to a varying degree in the process of adopting features of the cultures of other highlanders (as for the changing scenario, cf. Vongvipak 1992 dealing with the α-Mlabri). Still, one is struck by the extreme scarcity of their own material culture. The Mlabri lifestyle, which it best preserved among the α-Mlabri families, is regulated by religious constraints. These have had the effect of making the gradual integration of the Mlabri into peasant society a very slow process and of preserving essential features of their traditional culture, such as the absence of stationary settlements. With the few remaining β-Mlabri families, however, this pattern of behaviour is in a process of change.

The Mlabri have a unique status among all ethnic groups of North Thailand in that they are traditionally hunter-gatherers. They have in the past lived on food they could find by moving about in the dense forests of the high mountains without settling for more than a few days in any particular place. Until recently their shyness and ability to hide in the forest has prevented their culture and language from being exposed to outsiders except for a few encounters with expeditions (Bernatzik 1938, Nimmanhaeminda 1961, 1962). For the same reason, the linguistic data available has been limited and much of its quality poor.

Even the name of their tribe: mlaʔ briiʔ, i.e. 'Forest People', which is also the name of their language (more elaborately: chmbɛp mlaʔ briiʔ, 'Lips of the Mlabri'), occurs in distorted form in international reference works up to this day, although it was given correctly as Mla Bri in a Thai-English source (Jerry W. Gainey and Theraphan L. Thongkum's *Language Map of Thailand Handbook*) as early as 1977. As mentioned above, the most widely used names referring to this tribe and its language are "Mrabri", "Yumbri" and particularly "Phi Tong Luang", all of which are inappropriate terms.

There is in fact no such form as "Mrabri"; it is a distortion of "Mlabri" (an unfortunate conjecture due to Kraisri Nimmanhaeminda). Bernatzik's term "Yumbri" is an enigmatic form (its only immediately transparent component is brii? 'forest'); it is not recognized by the Mlabri in Thailand as an ethnonym for their own group(s). As for "Phi Tong Luang", this is a pejorative Thai designation meaning 'Spirits of the Yellow Leaves'; its use is extremely unfortunate since it reinforces the traditional local prejudices against this tribe.

Besides "Mlabri" ("Mla Bri"), there are two Thai-based names which are acceptable to the tribespeople themselves: one is "Khon Pa", which is a direct translation into Thai of mla? brii?; the other, which is being used increasingly, is "Khon Tong Luang" = "Yellow Leaf People" (playing on the traditional Thai designation but avoiding the offensive allusion to ghosts).

Mlabri-like tribes and ethnonyms:

There are various tribal people in Laos and Vietnam whose material culture resembles that of the Mlabri. They are often referred to as Kha Tong Luang, "Yellow Leaf-Tribe" (according to Proschan 1992, p. 15 "Xá Toong Luong" can even refer to the Lahu).

Matisoff (1991, p. 215) in his linguistic survey of endangered languages in Laos makes a distinction between "Mlabri" and "Kha Tong Luang/Phi Tong Luang". The language of the former is classified as Khmuic, and its speakers are said to total 300 (exactly the same statement is made about Mlabri in Thailand, so I suppose that the figure is meant to include speakers in both countries).

The "Kha Tong Luang" or "Phi Tong Luang", however, total 200 speakers of a language of the Viet-Muong group, according to Matisoff. To this I wish to add that in Vietnam as well there is evidence of traditional "Yellow-Leaf People", e.g. the Ruc people speaking a language of the Muong subgroup.

The term "Yumbri" may be an ethnonym, like Mlabri. The only source for the use of this term in Thailand is Bernatzik (1938). The Laotian National Census, as summarized by researchers at the Institute of Ethnology 1985, however, uses "Yumbri" as the name of an ethnic group in Laos with 24 speakers (the survey is given as an appendix in Proschan (1992); according to more recent communications the number of people has diminished since 1985). I do not know whether the ethnonym has been borrowed from Bernatzik simply in order to distinguish the group from the more well-known Mlabri (α-Mlabri) in Thailand.

Finally, the Thai term "Kha Hok", i.e. "Spear Tribe", is sometimes used by the Tin and even by the β-Mlabri to refer to allegedly savage Mlabri who carry spears and have tattoos; according to these attributes the α-Mlabri of Thailand are also Kha Hok, although they have recently discontinued the use of spears. The Kha Hok are widely claimed to be dangerous people, but that is in contradiction to the notorious shyness and meekness of the known α-Mlabri in Thailand. Altogether, it is a very confusing term, like Kha Tong Luang. Proschan (1992, p. 45-46), cites a number of sources for the use of "Kha Hok" to refer to a group of Kmhmu who wear "only loincloths rather than pants", but notes (p. 43, footnote) that the term implies the perspective of an outsider. It is hardly an ethnonym used by any group.

1.2 Minor Mlabri

At least two distinct varieties of the Mlabri language exist in northern Thailand, although only one has been documented so far. This is "Phi Tong Luang", "Mrabri", or (more correctly) Mlabri, as described by Nimmanhaeminda (1963), Egerod and Rischel (1987), and Thongkum (1988). In recent publications (Rischel 19891, 1989b, 1992, 1993) I have referred to that variety as α-Mlabri to distinguish it from the variety I am dealing with here: β-Mlabri. Since the number of known speakers of β-Mlabri is ten times smaller than that of the known α-Mlabri speakers it may be more informative to call the former variety Minor Mlabri (and the latter Major Mlabri), as I have done in the title of the present monograph. For convenience, however, I shall mostly stick to the terms β-Mlabri and α-Mlabri.

The Minor or "β" variety of Mlabri is spoken by a very small group of people living in the border area between North Thailand (Nan Province) and Laos (Sayaburi = Xeignabouri Province). They have no separate ethnonym that I know of.

The members of this Mlabri group say that they used to be more numerous. I have been able to retrieve the names (and family relationships) of some thirty persons. Most of these family members are reported to have been lost as a result of the former long period of warfare in the border area. One female Mlabri is supposed to have married a Northern Thai somewhere, but I have not been able to get any confirmation of this. During the period in which I have known the group, two Mlabri have died. In the same interval, one baby was born.

As of now, I know of only eleven surviving members of the group, eight adults and three children. They constitute at least four households, between which there is some but not much contact. I have met and spoken with all of them but I owe most of my linguistic data to three adult males, who at the time of data gathering were in their forties or fifties, by the names of bɔ chuʌŋ, bɔ tɔp and bɔ khit, and one younger female, ʔi can. These persons all belong to the same family network and they speak essentially the same dialect. I have noted idiolectal differences in the pronunciation of certain words but hardly in the overall phonological system; such variation is indicated in the dictionary (in addition, see 6.3 on Phonological Variation below).

The fact that the Mlabri in Thailand form two ethnic subgroups is surprising considering the small overall number of Mlabri. It is tempting to speculate whether they represent two different strands of almost extinct peoples who have associated with each other because of their forest life and their migration into the same area in the past. The Mlabri, however, are obviously closely related both with respect to language and spiritual culture and they know this themselves, in spite of their mutual animosity. Speakers of both groups confirm that they are all "Mlabri", i.e. 'people of the forest', and it is part of their cultural tradition that they consider the different groups of Mlabri to be all speakers of one language: chmbɛp mlaʔ briiʔ ('the lips of the Mlabri').

The concept of Mlabri or "Phi Tong Luang" in Thailand-Laos is based mainly on their traditional life as hunter-gatherers building lean-to bivouaks in the forest. Because of varying degrees of association with villages, however, the traditional material culture

is not as dominant as it used to be, especially not among the
β-Mlabri. Moreover, some features of Mlabri material culture are
not unique – although they might seem to be so. The use of the
lean-to has counterparts among other traditional forest-dwellers
e.g. in northern Vietnam, and although the Mlabri have been characterized as possessors of a pre-stone-age "bamboo culture", most
types of implements which the Mlabri use in daily life, are known
either from Kmhmu culture or from other groups.

Structurally, the two kinds of Mlabri are so extremely close
that one may speak of sub-dialects of one dialect. The two varieties have almost the same phonology and morphology, and to the
extent that lexical material is shared, it occurs in largely the same
phonological shape (cf. Rischel 1989c and forthcoming). *Prosodically*, β-Mlabri differs from α-Mlabri by having much less of the
final lengthening and strongly falling terminal pitch which is one
of the most striking characteristics of α-Mlabri. There are *segmental* differences between α-Mlabri and β-Mlabri in the pronunciation of several words, but there is also idiolectal variation within
each variety of Mlabri. On the whole, the appearance of the shared
wordforms is uniform for all Mlabri.

In other respects, however, the two varieties are very different. Take an arbitrary sample of commonly used words:

	β	α
speak	glaʔ	tʌɲ
sit	jɤɤm	hŋuh
drink	ɟrʌʌk	wɤɤk
dog	chɔɔʔ	braɲ
day	tawɪn	taal

Although it is possibly to make up short sentences that contain the
same words in α-Mlabri and β-Mlabri, such lexical equivalence is
certainly the exception. The typical case is for a sentence to contain several words which are usable only in one or the other variety of Mlabri, cf. β-Mlabri ʔitɯ mlaʔ ʔa pruk 'who is coming?' vs.
its α-Mlabri equivalent ʔa leh tɯʔ mlaʔ ɲʌʌ.

The lexical differences may have at least three different
causes. They may in some cases reflect the existence of

synonymous (or near-synonymous) word pairs in Old Mlabri. Synonymy was then lost as one variety retained only one word, and the other variety retained only the other synonym: i.e. a split. In several cases one of the language varieties has borrowed a term from a neighbouring language and discarded the genuine Mlabri term. Then again there are several instances where one variety of Mlabri has an ordinary Mon-Khmer etymon whereas the other variety has a word exhibiting peculiar features, suggesting that it is a deliberate innovation.

The need for creating new words may stem from a stigmatization of the old word: a word may have become undesirable (within one group of Mlabri or within the other group) because of taboo, for example. But there is little evidence to support claims of this kind. Why, for example, do β-Mlabri speakers use the Khmuic loanword chɔɔʔ for 'dog' (a word known also from conservative α-Mlabri), whereas α-Mlabri speakers now use a word braɲʔ (The latter may be an innovation based on braŋ 'horse', cf. the similarity between words for 'horse' and 'dog' in Thai.)

Often a word used in one variety is known but considered obsolete or stigmatized by speakers of the other variety. In several instances speakers even deny any knowledge of a word used by the other group. The linguistic attitudes towards lexical material is a complex issue. Male β-Mlabri speakers, when confronted with an α-Mlabri word, may claim that the word is *used in female speech but not in male speech*. An example is leh 'come', which is neutral in α-Mlabri but considered a female word in β-Mlabri; β-Mlabri men are supposed to say pruk instead, although I have heard some of these speakers say leh themselves (see further discussion in 6.7 below).

The case of leh is typical. In the vast majority of instances, α-Mlabri and β-Mlabri do not seem to agree on the labelling of words as male or female speech, although the existence of such a distinction is recognized in both language varieties. Occasionally, however, they agree. A case in point is a word for 'hair': borthor (in α-Mlabri burthol/burthor), which in both varieties is said to be used by women only, although there is no similar agreement with respect to the corresponding "male" word (in β-Mlabri it is mujmuj, in α-Mlabri either klmuj, as a collective term, or riwoj when referring to single hairs on the body).

In some instances, speakers of one group discard a word used by the other group as being not real Mlabri but Kmhmu, Tin or Northern Thai. As a matter of fact, it is often the case that one variety has a seemingly old Mlabri word where the other variety has a recent loanword. Thus the α-Mlabri word for 'meat' is a loanword ciin, whereas β-Mlabri uses the old Mon-Khmer word thʌc, and conversely the β-Mlabri word for 'skin' is a loanword naŋ, whereas α-Mlabri uses a Mon-Khmer looking word: goguh. In both cases the loanword is from (Northern) Thai.

The differences in lexicon are so great that one would not expect easy intercommunication between the two groups, especially in the case of young people who have not learned (and will probably never learn) the more or less obsolete words shared by the two language varieties. This assumption was corroborated when on one occasion I let two young α-Mlabri speakers listen to a β-Mlabri mythological narrative. It was apparent that they recognized several words and vaguely accepted the speaker's performance as a kind of Mlabri. When I asked them to recapitulate what had been said, however, they just picked a couple of phrases from the narrative which happened to be lexically very similar to α-Mlabri and repeated them several times, although these particular phrases gave no clue to the overall contents of the story.

This lexical divergence, as contrasted with the structural similarity of the two varieties of Mlabri, must be recent but is so strong that it suggests an effort to mark the distinction between the α- and the β-Mlabri. The Mlabri society is not stratified, but there are very conspicuous differences in linguistic usage which reflect subgroupings according to such criteria as (1) *ethnicity* (α-Mlabri versus β-Mlabri and possibly other varieties), (2) *female versus male, and (3) age.*

A brief comment on the age parameter is appropriate here: in β-Mlabri I have come across some apparent innovations and loanwords in the speech of adolescents. One such word is hlek 'there is none' (α-Mlabri has hlaak with that meaning), which was used spontaneously by a young man but was emphatically discarded by his father, who is the most knowledgeable speaker of the language but who did not at all recognize that word as Mlabri (the word is not included in the vocabulary in chapter 7 below).

By and large, the lexical difference between present generations of β-Mlabri speakers seems to be that young persons have a much poorer command of the Mlabri lexicon than their parents. This unidirectional process of decline and decay is anything but surprising, considering that the youngsters are *much too few* to form a separate stratum of Mlabri-speakers: they can enter a network of young people only by associating with their own age-group in the Hmong villages and speaking Hmong instead of Mlabri (see more on the importance of peer languages in section 2.1.3).

Major Mlabri or α-Mlabri is viable as a language variety because of its active use among the youngest generations. If, however, one compares the lexicon in current use among young people with the words which were used by the parents of the oldest Mlabri speakers (according to their capacity to remember), then change is conspicuous. But although this process of change involves a considerable loss of traditional Mlabri words (often old words shared with β-Mlabri, so that the process contributes to an increasing distance between the two varieties), it leaves α-Mlabri fully functional as a vernacular. It seems that the α-Mlabri children are mainly exposed to Mlabri in their infancy and thus learn to speak their mother-tongue fluently, at least within the limits of everyday domestic conversation. The use of β-Mlabri among children, on the other hand, must compete with other much more powerful languages, inevitably with Mlabri as the loser.

Persons from the two groups of Mlabri avoid each other. One β-Mlabri told me that on one occasion his parents had encountered somebody from the other group in the forest; the two parties exchanged some words and discovered that they spoke the same language, but they then realized that they belonged to two mutually hostile groups and fled in opposite directions. They never met again.

In view of the ethnic separation and strong mutual repulsion between the groups, I have earlier referred to their language varities as *clan* sociolects. It may, however, be more precise to speak of *ethnolects*.

Considering both the great differences in lexicon and the whole sociolinguistic situation, I find it appropriate to keep the

β-Mlabri material carefully separate from the α-Mlabri material gathered by Søren Egerod, Theraphan L. Thongkum and myself. This is motivated also by significant differences between α-Mlabri and β-Mlabri in the use of grammatical words and specific syntactic constructions. There is also a lack of uniformity in our data collection: neither lexically nor grammatically does the work on one variety of Mlabri cover the same ground as the work on the other. Hence this is a separate monograph on β-Mlabri. (A thorough updating of our more extensive α-Mlabri lexicon has been made in 1988 and 1994, and a separate publication by Egerod and myself is planned for the near future.)

So far, it has not been possible to trace the history of the Mlabri to see if the different groups were at one time clans of the same population kept together by regular social contact. The β-Mlabri whom I have met do not keep track of their ancestors more than three generations back; they claim that they have forgotten because most of the kinsmen died so long ago. I have managed to learn the names and family relationships of thirty-one β-Mlabri, and several of those seem to be only vague memories (mlaʔ prɨm 'people of the past') for those alive today.

The genealogical information which I have been able to retrieve does not suggest any genealogical interrelations with the α-Mlabri (nor with Bernatzik's "Yumbri", cf. below). The contemporary β-Mlabri consider it to be absolutely impossible to intermarry with the α-Mlabri. They do not consider associating with Mlabri people in Laos either; they insist that there are none of their own group there any longer. The β-Mlabri in Thailand are fully aware that their group cannot possibly be continued as an ethnically unmixed group since nearly all surviving members of the group are closely related (which prohibits marriage). For several years now the β-Mlabri have in some cases taken Tin spouses.

1.3 The Social Situation of the Mlabri

Since the Mlabri associate with Hmong villages in remote areas, they also come into contact with phenomena which enter these villages from the ambient Thai society. There has been a very active policy over the last several years with the objective that village children of all ethnic groups should have access to a local school (teaching in Thai only), and there are now schools even in villages high up in the mountains and far removed from the district townships. The β-Mlabri are confronted with the existence of this institution, and one Mlabri, bɔ khit, told me that they have their own words both for "hooŋhian", i.e. 'school' (allegedly bɯrwɛɛc in Mlabri), and for "khuu", i.e. 'teacher' (allegedly tiin briin in Mlabri)! This is typical of the paradoxical cultural situation in which the β-Mlabri have survived.

The future for the survival of Mlabri culture and ethnicity is dismal, especially in the case of the β-Mlabri. It seems unavoidable that their variety of the language will succumb to *language death* within one or two decades (see further discussion in section 2.1.3 below). The α-Mlabri may, however, survive as a group with a distinct language for several decades; this very much depends on the official policy of the local and national authorities, e.g. the attitude toward such controversial issues as (i) compulsory settlement or even compulsory displacement, (ii) compulsory school training, (iii) tourism directed toward unspoiled tribal areas and (iv) protection of the Mlabri against exploitation and abuse.

Although the relationship between the Mlabri and other inhabitants of Thailand is discussed in many places in the present work, it may be useful to make a longer and coherent comment on the four issues raised above (hopefully, this comment will not be understood by local authorities as a one-sided criticism; it is, in fact, meant as an appreciation of the very complex problems facing both officials and others who are dealing with the Mlabri).

re (i) above: The authorities appear to be unhappy about the existence of tribal people who have no permanent settlement. One aspect of this is the question of survival: how can the Mlabri sustain their life in the shrinking and increasingly empty forest? What kinds of support from the local administration does that require? Another issue is the current emphasis on the registration of inhabitants, locally and for the purpose of the national census. Both of these considerations are unfavourable to the continuation of a nomadic life on the part of the Mlabri. As far as I know, there is no ideal official solution in sight. A resettling of the Mlabri, giving them employment in a developmental rural area, was seriously discussed not very many years ago. At one point there was also considerable political debate over a suggestion to establish a national forest as a reservation for the Mlabri.

On the other hand, it is being increasingly realized that the existence of original (indigenous) ethnic groups who preserve traditional culture, is an asset, although opinions differ as to the nature of this asset (cf. item iii on tourism below). Still, there does not seem to be any general appreciation within the local Northern Thai community of the cultural value associated with the existence of such a minority group; the prevailing prejudices seem to be stronger than the fascination. Hopefully, this is gradually changing with the increasing focus on the Mlabri in Thai media.

In recent years international attention has been directed toward the survival of such small tribes with their unique preservation of essential features of traditional hunter-gatherer culture. The fate of the Mlabri and their culture and language should no longer be a problem for Thailand (and Laos) alone; it deserves being looked upon as an international concern of the same nature as the protection of rare species.

re (ii): Compulsory schooling for everybody is a very important ambition in Thailand, and even in remote areas the program is close to being entirely effective. The case of the Mlabri stands out as an exception: public schooling has not so far been enforced in the case of Mlabri children, for whom a hasty initiative in this direction might create a cultural disaster. The policy may change any time, however. Hopefully, future political initiatives in this area will proceed at a slow pace so as not to be entirely out of rhythm with the inevitable general adjustment of the Mlabri to modern society.

re (iii): There are conflicting opinions as to whether money and other gifts from visitors to the Mlabri families themselves is something good or something harmful. A related issue is whether the Mlabri have a future as manufacturers and sellers of handicraft to tourists, like other hilltribes. Might this source of income eventually be so essential to the survival of the (α-)Mlabri as an ethnic group that its advantages would outweigh the drawbacks of having tourism directed toward so small a group?

What relevance Mlabri-related tourism has to the outside society is a very different question: whether it will ever attract so many visitors that it makes much difference to the overall economy of the provinces in question. Tourism in the northern provinces of Thailand is a somewhat paradoxical issue. These provinces are (understandably) promoting tourism at the same time as one of the qualities that have attracted outsiders, the unspoiled landscape, is rapidly changing. The colourful ethnic diversity is another major attraction; so far, it has survived much better than the surrounding nature. Many of these groups are found in other provinces of North Thailand, however; in fact, most of the tourism to mountain villages occurs in areas other than those in which the Mlabri are found. As for the latter, some α-Mlabri families, who tend to stay close to Hmong villages, are visited by small groups of "trekking" tourists, but the extensive deforestation and the gradual decrease in number of wild animals and birds will inevitably change the traditional lifestyle of these people.

re (iv): This issue is particularly sensitive. One aspect of it is the variable treatment of the Mlabri by other hilltribe peoples, above all the Hmong. Visitors may feel it as particularly offensive that one must often pay a Hmong farmer in order to gain access to a Mlabri family, as if the latter were the property of the former. The situation is unacceptable from an ethical point of view although it is not quite as preposterous as it sounds, since it reflects the existence of (unwritten) labour contracts between the Mabri and the Hmong. The main problem with such contracts is that the Mlabri often do not foresee the consequences of the deal and cannot keep track of the balance between work and payment. On the other hand, they are very dependent on their symbiosis with the Hmong, and some Hmong farmers are quite hospitable and helpful to the Mlabri whom they take care of.

Another important consideration is the existence of illegal activities such as poppy cultivation, extensive burning of forest by local people and organized illegal logging by outsiders in some areas. All of this may obviously be harmful to the Mlabri.

A third consideration is, unfortunately, that there exist cases of misuse of power or certainly of ill-judgment on the part of low-level officials in remote areas. To mention one result of this, Mlabri persons, from adolescents to grown-ups, have sometimes been invited or even "bought" to appear on shows in local marketplaces. Among the most popular local events are festivals where all the different ethnic groups of a province appear in their costumes and perform in some fashion. This is a problematic kind of initiative in the case of the Mlabri, however, and it is worse, of course, if Mlabri persons are brought to town just for advertisement or entertainment purposes *without* being part of an official event. The Mlabri are easy to lure into such arrangements by offering them some forward payment. There have been reports of unfortunate events of this kind.

It must be emphasized that it is the official policy of Thailand to take large-scale measures in order to support and integrate minority groups through a network of hilltribe welfare and development centres as well as schools. The administrations of the northern provinces pay attention to the special situation of the Mlabri, but it is difficult to predict what will be the future of this tribe in Thai society.

1.4 Minor Mlabri and "Yumbri"

The externally documented history of the β-Mlabri goes back some thirty years. In 1964, Michel Ferlus recorded a short list of Mlabri words in a village in westernmost Laos (this is mentioned in passing in Ferlus 1974). The speakers referred to their language as Kam Lua' (i.e., Tin), but Ferlus found it to be what is now referred to as Mlabri and he further noted that their vocabulary was closer to Bernatzik's "Yumbri" than Kraisri Nimmanhaeminda's "Mrabri" (i.e. α-Mlabri). Dr. Ferlus' material, which he has kindly put at my disposal, clearly belongs to the type of Mlabri that I refer to as β-Mlabri.

There is direct confirmation of the link between Ferlus' speakers and my β-Mlabri since one of the persons whom Ferlus met and photographed could be identified as the former, deceased wife of an elderly informant of mine. Thus my linguistic data would be expected to represent more or less the same linguistic usage as his. In fact, out of 126 entries on Ferlus' list only three cannot be immediately identified as words (or phrases) occurring also in my β-Mlabri material. Although there are several differences between Ferlus' transcriptions and my own data they are generally very minor differences, and I am quite sure that most of them are merely notational. It goes without saying that Ferlus' material, which dates back some thirty years, must be considered in the comparative and historical study of Mlabri which will hopefully be possible once the vocabularies of all attested Mlabri dialects and sociolects have been recorded as fully as possible.

It is not strange at all that Ferlus met people from the same group in westernmost Laos back in 1964. The Mlabri used to live in a very large area comprising contiguous parts of North Thailand and Laos, south of northeastern Burma. This is a very mountainous area, and until recently the hills were all covered by large forests (this is still the case on the Laotian side) with no permanent settlements, since the hilltribe peasants were using the slash-burn technique which requires a certain amount of moving around. Over the centuries the national borders between Burma, Thailand, and Laos have been shifting around but this was probably of little consequence in the high areas.

Both α-Mlabri and β-Mlabri speakers have been able to migrate over vast expanses without having to pay attention to provincial or national boundaries. It is only quite recently that it has become an issue to define the national affiliation of hilltribe people, even in such a case where the solution may be arbitrary. I see no reason to define the β-Mlabri to be traditionally a "Laotian" group in contradistinction to the α-Mlabri. This is not supported by linguistic evidence; on the contrary there are traces of Lao influence on α-Mlabri which are not shared by β-Mlabri, e.g. the word for 'tomorrow': α-Mlabri has the Lao word maʔɯɯn whereas β-Mlabri has an old word ɟrɯw (which is also a part of the expression for 'morning': tak ɟrɯw).

The adult β-Mlabri say that they themselves and almost all of their children were born in the wild forest. They are, however, rapidly adjusting to peasant life since it is becoming impossible to sustain life on the things they can gather in the forest. The α-Mlabri, on the other hand, still prefer to stay in the forest as much as possible in an attempt to survive as part-time hunter-gatherers.

This closes the survey of the presently known Mlabri groups in Thailand. It remains an intriguing problem how these relate to the "Yumbri" people encountered in the same province by Bernatzik in the thirties. Some twenty-five years later, Kraisri

Nimmanhaeminda compared the material published by Bernatzik with his own "Mrabri" (= α-Mlabri) word list and made an important statement (Nimmanhaeminda 1963, p. 181-2):

> (...) out of another list of 187 words prepared by Dr. Hugo Bernatzik (...), said to be the language of the Yumbri, 41 words have close similarity with the Mrabri words. I am, therefore, inclined to believe that the Yumbri and Mrabri are the same people.

Smalley (1963), however, considered the linguistic specimens in Bernatzik's book to represent a language different from Nimmanhaeminda's "Mrabri".

The research group studying Mlabri since 1982 has always tended to side with Bernatzik, and at one point a fieldwork session was devoted to the specific task of attempting to identify all of Bernatzik's forms as either correct or corrupt Mlabri data (i.e. as data belonging to the type of Mlabri known to us from Nimmanhaeminda's expedition and above all from our own fieldwork). This was a rather bold undertaking since Bernatzik had presented his word list in a very unconventional notation which is difficult to interpret. By 1987 much more was known about Mlabri phonetics and phonology than when Smalley made his comparison with "Yumbri", so that both Bernatzik's and Nimmanhaeminda's transcriptions could now be seen in a new light. In our ensuing paper (Rischel and Egerod 1987), which was written without any knowledge of β-Mlabri, we rather exaggerated the similarity between α-Mlabri and "Yumbri" but the main conclusion stands: that Mlabri and "Yumbri" should be classified together as varieties of one language.

It was only half a year after we had published the paper on Bernatzik's material that I first established contact with speakers of β-Mlabri. My first conclusion was that it was *their* language variety, rather than the one we had been studying previously, which was the continuation of Bernatzik's "Yumbri". When Michel Ferlus gave me a copy of his old field notes from Laos, it immediately became apparent that his data represented the kind of Mlabri that I have referred to as β-Mlabri; Ferlus had much earlier taken note of its similarity with "Yumbri" (Ferlus 1974).

"Yumbri", however, is not just the β-Mlabri of a previous generation. Lexically, it sometimes sides with α-Mlabri against β-Mlabri (cf. Rischel 1989a, Rischel 1989c) and it may be the rather conservative character of β-Mlabri that is responsible for its greater overall similarity with "Yumbri".

The phonological relationship between the three varieties of Mlabri is somewhat unclear, also because of the problems associated with the interpretation of Bernatzik's forms. As far as prosody is concerned, the impressionistic statements in Bernatzik's work show that he heard the conspicuous vowel lengthening combined with high, slowly falling pitch in utterance final position that is characteristic of α-Mlabri. This is remarkable since it is a feature which is almost absent in present-day β-Mlabri. And as far as segmental phonology is concerned, "Yumbri" seems to have sided with α-Mlabri with respect to the only major difference between the two varieties: that β-Mlabri has /ɯ/ in some words which have /a/ in α-Mlabri (e.g. klɯɯr vs. klaar 'sky'). This, more than lexical divergences, weakens the case for considering β-Mlabri to be the present day representative of Bernatzik's "Yumbri". Moreover, its phonology may have differed from both α-Mlabri and β-Mlabri on some points (Bernatzik's notations seem to suggest that "Yumbri" had a final palatal glide in some words where Mlabri otherwise has a lateral with final aspiration, i.e. words such as ʔuulh 'fireplace', but that may be an artefact of his transcription practice).

I think that it now can be concluded on linguistic grounds that the "Yumbri" of half a century ago were not β-Mlabri but spoke a third language variety which formed a link between the other two, a variety which I would call "γ-Mlabri". We still know too little about existing or former varieties of this language, however, to set up a meaningful Stammbaum of dialects; the main obstacle is the absence of linguistic information on the "Yellow Leaf" people which are reported to still exist in Laos.

Bernatzik's account of "Yumbri" culture is largely what one would expect from a description of traditional α-Mlabri, rather than β-Mlabri, people. It may suffice here to mention two characteristic features: the "Yumbri" had spears and holes in their ears.

Not only are these features alien to the contemporary β-Mlabri culture, the members of the small β-Mlabri group actually refer to the use of spears (and of tattoo) as a feature defining the "other" Mlabri.

Bernatzik (1938) contains many interesting statements about the *spiritual culture* of the "Yumbri". Although he must have had severe communication problems – working with interpreters, none of whom spoke "Yumbri" – much of what he says is supported in one way or other by present-day evidence about the Mlabri. Similarly, most of the words in his list can be identified as Mlabri. Much of what he says may be valid generalizations about traditional Mlabri culture and is thus of relevance both to the study of α-Mlabri and β-Mlabri.

The amount of information in Bernatzik's book is impressive. It is, however, necessary to evaluate each of his statements carefully. For example, one forms an erroneous belief in a very poor lexicon from his claim that the "Yumbri" had no terms for plants and animals beyond a distinction between *useful* and *useless* ones. Mlabri lexicon (α-Mlabri as well as β-Mlabri) is actually anything but poor with regard to phenomena of forest life, and I cannot believe that "Yumbri" was any poorer. The truth of the matter is that there is a very important distinction between species that are *relevant* to traditional Mlabri life and species that are not relevant. A species may be relevant either because it is useful or because it is harmful.

It seems true of the Mlabri lexicon in general (i.e., both "Yumbri", α-Mlabri, and β-Mlabri) that it is highly differentiated with regard to relevant species but it may be much more restricted when it comes to species which do no good or no harm (an observation which is so expected in such a culture as to be almost trivial). For example, it has never been possible to retrieve more than one or two Mlabri terms for 'butterfly' although there is an abundance of species in the forest: they are to my knowledge irrelevant to daily life (unlike harmful or edible insect species) and are on the whole just referred to by generic terms, irrespective of their different sizes and colour patterns. Monkeys, on the other hand, are important in traditional Mlabri life, so there are names for several species but apparently no generic term although Thai has such a term (liŋ).

Bernatzik wrote his account as a sweeping statement about "Yumbri" culture. It is fascinating reading but strongly coloured by his whole approach. He was clearly very much inclined to conclude that phenomena about which he had failed to retrieve information did not exist in the culture, and that the Mlabri were not capable of reasoning about matters unless he could persuade them to communicate such thoughts to him.

The general picture of the Mlabri, not as noble savages but as spiritually primitive people, which emerges from Bernatzik's statements, has on the whole been reinforced by later travellers' accounts of encounters with Mlabri groups. There are, however, obviously strong prejudices involved because of imperfect knowledge and imperfect understanding (one international travel guide has it that the Mlabri have "no art, language, religion, or aspirations"). It is my own experience that the Mlabri way of thinking unravels itself slowly: after prolonged contact during which a mutual attitude of confidence is established. In-depth acquisition of spiritual information, such as the complex oral traditions which stem from "people of the remote past", can occur in a culturally intimate and monolingual setting; my own experience with many hours of listening to and recording myths flatly contradicts Bernatzik's impression that such material was largely absent in Mlabri culture.

Chapter 2
The Linguistic Scenario

2.1 Diachronic, Sociolinguistic and Areal Aspects

The Mlabri language is interesting for the comparative and historical study of Mon-Khmer and thus ultimately of Austroasiatic. This is true because of the cultural level and the undoubtedly quite extensive migrations of this people in the past. Such migration is reflected linguistically: there are words in Mlabri which occur in identical or almost identical form in distant Mon-Khmer languages but apparently not in the geographically closest languages, whatever the historical reason (this topic is outside the scope of the present monograph). Mlabri definitely deserves a place as one of the languages to be considered in the reconstruction of Proto-Mon-Khmer.

On the other hand, Mlabri has numerous words which are more or less identical to the form they have (or would have) in Pre-Tin as reconstructed by David Filbeck (1978) and thus suggest that Mlabri is either an offshoot of a common ancestor or has borrowed rather massively from Tin in the remote past (the latter assumption is corroborated by the presence of a great number of words in Mlabri which do not look like Tin or even like Khmuic). Moreover, there are several words which must be considered very recent borrowings from Tin (the relationship of Mlabri to Tin is discussed at length in Rischel 1989b). Finally, there is a very considerable number of words in Mlabri which have identical or almost identical counterparts in Kmhmu; several of these are likely to be quite recent borrowings.

This issue is mentioned, but only briefly and with very little documentation, in a recent paper (Rischel 1993). The degree and age of Kmhmu influence on Mlabri, as compared to the Tin (Lua') influence, certainly deserves closer study. The Kammu-Lao Dictionary by Svantesson, Tayanin, and Lindell (1994) is with its 501 pages the current standard reference work for such cross-language comparison but it appeared too late to be cited in the present monograph.

This complex origin of the lexical material found in present-day Mlabri must be taken into consideration if Mlabri is to be used as a source in comparative Mon-Khmer research.

Mlabri has a very conservative phonology which preserves features which have been lost in many Mon-Khmer languages. The language is also remarkable from a comparative and a typological perspective by its proliferation of "minor syllables" (this phenomenon is discussed in detail in chapters 3, 4, and 6 below). Some of these minor syllables reflect old morphological material that is preserved with less reduction than in other languages of the area. As demonstrated in chapter 5 below, Mlabri also has peculiar features of *syntax* which makes it rather unique as a type of Mon-Khmer language.

Without in any sense outlining the historical phonology of Mlabri (which would be entirely premature) I shall make a rather long digression in order to point to some characteristic features of Mlabri phonology from a comparative perspective. Some of these are conservative features; others are innovations.

2.1.1 Mlabri From a Comparative Perspective

This monograph on β-Mlabri is not the proper place to attempt to define the genetic placement of Mlabri, let alone to account for the diachronic changes underlying present day Mlabri. That is a matter for future research, once all the lexical material on Mlabri in its different varieties has been made generally available with cross-referencing between the varieties. Still, when one considers that this is the first extensive presentation of any kind of Mlabri, it is tempting to say something about the way in which Mlabri presents itself within Mon-Khmer, with reference to some of the more interesting phonological correspondences.

Perhaps the most striking phonological feature of Mlabri is the distinction in final position between an aspirated (partially unvoiced) lateral and an unvoiced alveolopalatal fricative, e.g.

poolh 'barking deer', ʔuulh 'firewood, fireplace' vs. kroojh 'crocodile', gajh 'nine'. Tin and Kmhmu exhibit no corresponding distinction. The aspirated lateral is quite unusual in Mon-Khmer; other languages mostly have a sibilant or /-h/ in the etyma in question. This is amply documented by the words poolh and ʔuulh, which are very widespread in Mon-Khmer.

In addition, Mlabri has two laryngeal consonants /h ʔ/ in final position, as in mɛh 'you', hmɛʔ 'new'. The distribution of these in well-established etyma is sometimes enigmatic; it does not always agree with Tin or Kmhmu, for example.

This whole set of partially or completely unvoiced finals, in Khmuic and in Mlabri in particular, deserves to be given more attention in comparative Mon-Khmer research.

A more widespread, conservative feature is the complete preservation of ancient voicing and glottalization in syllable-initial stops, and of ancient voicelessness/aspiration and glottalization in syllable-initial sonorants (cf. the presentation of the inventory of initials in chapter 3 on Phonology below; also see Rischel 1989b and 1993). Mlabri has not undergone any kind of consonant mutation whereas Tin, for example, has aspirated the old unvoiced stops and devoiced the old voiced stops in initial position, and some dialects of Kmhmu have merged the voiced and unvoiced stops and have become tonal.

The picture is complicated by the Khmuic words in Mlabri which are (or may be) loanwords. For example, recent borrowing from Tin has introduced a considerable number of words with initial aspirated stops, such as khɔt 'spear'.

Needless to say, Mlabri is not just fossilized old Mon-Khmer or fossilized Khmuic. It has numerous characteristic features which do not seem explicable with reference to present comparative knowledge, but it also has some features which are suggestive of regular sound change either in Khmuic or within Mlabri proper.

It is, with the present limited knowledge of Mon-Khmer historical phonology, often difficult to decide what is old and what is new and to decide whether discrepancies between the attested forms of an etymon in different Mon-Khmer languages are due to phonological change or to affixation. For example, some of the words that have initial /h/+nasal in Mlabri have cognates with initial clusters of stop+nasal in Monic, e.g. hnʌm 'year' (cf. Monic *cnaam according to Diffloth 1984, p. 134), hmɛʔ 'new' (cf. Monic *t[ ]miiʔ, where [ ] indicates an uncertain element in the reconstruction, Diffloth 1984, p. 155) and hmaaj 'wife' (*'widow', also occurring in Thai; cf. Monic *k( )maay, where ( ) indicates an optional element in the reconstruction, Diffloth 1984, p. 117).

Monic is not necessarily close to Proto-Mon-Khmer, of course, but similar stops occur in such a distant branch of Mon-Khmer as Katuic (examples in Dorothy Thomas 1976, also cf. Sriwises 1978, p. 128 for */tm-/ in 'new'). This makes it plausible that the stop consonants before nasals in these words belong to Proto-Mon-Khmer. Mlabri does not have the initial cluster type *stop+nasal* at all. As for the surrounding Northern Mon-Khmer languages, we often find a plain nasal or /h/ plus nasal in the words in question (I have recorded the word 'new', for example, in a conservative dialect of Tin in exactly the same form hmɛʔ as in Mlabri). Thus Mlabri sides with its neighbouring languages on this point, but it is so far an open question whether this is because all the words in question just happen to be borrowings from Tin or from some other language of the area, or whether it also reflects something that has been characteristic of early Mlabri proper.

There is occasionally a confusing but informative variation with respect to the laryngeal features of initial consonants in my Mlabri data, also in the case of words shared with Thai. An interesting case is kan 'if, when', which in nearly all of my data has been taken down with the same voiceless unaspirated initial as the corresponding Northern Thai conjunction. When I asked a Mlabri speaker to repeat a long-winded expression containing clause-initial kan, and to say it very distinctly, he pronounced the word as gan with a fully voiced stop and insisted on that as the proper Mlabri pronunciation. The Northern Thai traditional spelling and pronunciation actually point to etymological *gan.

A related type of variation, though affecting the feature of aspiration in this case, is found with hmiʌŋ versus miʌŋ, two idiolectal pronunciations of the word for 'fermented tea'. The form hmiʌŋ sides with the Northern Thai (Lanna) spelling of this etymon and supports the etymological validity of that spelling; miʌŋ happens to side with the Standard Central Thai spelling, but I suppose that it simply reflects a recent adaptation to contemporary (Northern as well as Central) Thai pronunciation on the part of some speakers.

There is a rather specific consonant change which I think must have taken place *within Mlabri proper:* Mon-Khmer initial */s-/ > /th-/. It is well attested, e.g. by β-Mlabri thaŋaap 'to yawn' (Diffloth 1984, p. 210 reconstructs Proto-Mon *sŋʔaap), or thawaaʔ 'macaque (monkey)' (Shorto 1976, p. 1062 reconstructs Proto-Mon-Khmer *swaaʔ 'monkey'; Tin Mal has swaa across the dialects according to Filbeck 1978, p. 39).

The Mlabri development */s-/ > /th-/ raises the question what is the origin of the entity /ch-/ in Mlabri. It is a palatoalveolar consonant, which vacillates between more affricated and more sibilant pronunciations. It occurs in several loanwords in which it reflects Thai /s-/, e.g. chuʌn 'dry field', but also in numerous words which are not of Thai origin. It makes sense to assume that these words in Mlabri represent a Khmuic stratum and may even be of recent Tin origin.

Unlike the very conservative consonant system, the rich vowel system of Mlabri presents a complex picture when seen from a comparative Mon-Khmer perspective. Without going into any detail here I shall just mention two characteristic features which set Mlabri off from Proto-Mon-Khmer and, in the case of loanwords from Thai, from Proto-Thai:

– (1) Mlabri regularly exhibits /ɛɛ/ which corresponds to Proto-Mon-Khmer */aa/, e.g. in such words as bɛɛr 'two', gɛɛŋ 'house'. The joint Mon-Khmer and even Austroasiatic evidence indisputably points to an old low vowel in such forms. It has undergone diphthongization to /ia/ ([iʌ]) in Tin and some other Khmuic languages *not* including Kmhmu, and I think that there is some evidence for assuming that Mlabri ɛɛ stems from a monophthongization of such an intermediate diphthong ia (the evidence will be presented and discussed elsewhere).

– (2) Several loanwords which have a diphthong in some dialects of Thai including Central Thai, occur in monophthongized form in Mlabri, as they do in certain Thai dialects spoken north of the central Thai area. The most conspicuous regularity of this kind is that Mlabri regularly has /ɯɯ/ as against Central Thai /ɯa/, e.g. in hlɯɯ 'leftover' (this word also illustrates the preservation of old "high" continuants, which have lost their aspiration in Thai). This is hardly a specific Mlabri development; it rather reflects the phonology of an intermediate lending language.

The remarks in this digression on comparative and diachronic phonology have all been rather inconclusive. So far, virtually nothing is known about the genetic placement of Mlabri. The comparative work on Mlabri and on Khmuic in general, which is needed in order to make well-founded statements in this area, is still non-existent, and the prehistory of Mlabri is certainly no more transparent than that of other Mon-Khmer languages, even though Mlabri phonology is in many ways remarkably conservative. – The remainder of this chapter takes a broader geographical and historical view.

2.1.2 Linguistic Contact Phenomena

Mlabri seems to have received linguistic input from several sources and may therefore have a very complex language history. This is relevant for comparative linguistic studies in a wider framework, since the old loanwords often appear with very conservative phonology and thus may help attest reconstructed forms in Mon-Khmer or in Ancient Thai. As stated above, Mlabri has preserved old distinctions with respect to manner of laryngeal articulation in consonants. This is true also of old loanwords which are of Thai origin or at least occur also in Old Siamese, such as hlek 'iron', hmɯk 'tattoo', gem 'spicy', all of which agree with the conservative Thai spelling and thus probably with the pronunciation in Old Siamese, although the first two of these words have voiced initial consonants, and the third has an unvoiced aspirated stop in Modern Thai. The so-called "mid" consonants which are voiced stops in modern Thai dialects, occur with strong glottalization in Mlabri, e.g. ʔbɔɔk 'tell'; this phenomenon of glottalization is also known from Thai and was probably a prominent feature of their pronunciation in Old Siamese. Some Mlabri forms are at variance with Thai spelling, however, e.g. ʔjaa 'tobacco' or 'medicine' for expected jaa (actually the pronunciation of this particular word is quite variable, with or sometimes without audible pre-glottalization), but here Mlabri sides with some of the present-day Thai dialects in which the tone seems to presuppose an old "mid" = glottalized rather than "low" = plain voiced initial (cf. Egerod 1961, p. 73 on Southern Thai).

Such preservation of old consonantism is not unknown in Northern Mon-Khmer languages. But Mlabri with its richness of old borrowings certainly occupies a prominent position among the languages that provide live documentation for reconstruction, also with respect to Thai.

On the other hand, prosodic distinctions in Ancient Thai may have been lost on the way to Mlabri without leaving any trace. The β-Mlabri form gɔɔj, for example, has two distinct meanings (cf. the entries in the dictionary below) which suggest that it represents a merger of two different loanwords which correspond to Central Thai khɔɔj and khɔ̂j, respectively (it adds to the complexity that an entirely similar form occurs in α-Mlabri but with a third, distinct meaning: 'always, incessantly').

Another essential feature of the history of Mlabri is that its lexical affinity with Kmhmu and (particularly) Tin may be predominantly or even exclusively a contact phenomenon (cf. Rischel 1989b and forthc.). The implication is that the diachronically innermost core of the Mlabri lexicon: the residue that remains if one attempts to "peel off" all loans from neighbouring languages, may ultimately represent a different branch of Mon-Khmer. One may even ask whether the very deepest layer in the Mlabri language was at all Mon-Khmer. These questions can, in turn, be confronted with other questions concerning the ethnic and racial origin of the Mlabri (cf. section 1.1 above).

The languages of northern Indochina share several characteristics as the result of diffusion from peer languages, above all Lao and Northern Thai. Some of the areal characteristics are shared by Mlabri as well; others are not. This is true of phonology as well as syntax and semantics, as will be apparent from chapters 3-5 below.

Although the Mlabri language has some very conservative features, one can observe that its speakers have been in the area long enough for their language to exhibit the expected mixture of indigenous features with features showing strong external influence. In particular, the language has a variety of old or more recent *loanwords*. These include many "culture words" which were adopted some time in the past as the Mlabri encountered things, technologies and institutions in the villages they visited, but there are also loanwords within the sections of the vocabulary that must have been most basic to Mlabri culture.

Even formulae which one might expect to be very culture-specific sometimes contain words which look like borrowings. An example is the opening formula of the ritual evocation of a spirit (hmaal), a formula which is supposed to call the spirit back (although the Mlabri whom I have consulted are vague about its exact meaning): kuuk hmaal mɯɯ. A priori one might expect this to be very archaic Mlabri, but kuuk (which is often said in a falsetto voice in the Mlabri ritual) has a perfect Northeastern Thai counterpart meaning 'to call out to somebody', and mɯɯ is found in Northern Thai and more widely as mɯa 'to return' (the Thai diphthong /ɯa/ regularly occurs as /ɯɯ/ in Mlabri).

That the meaning of mɯɯ really is 'to return' also in ritual Mlabri is seen from another ritual expression di wʌl di mɯɯ 'do return!', where di is a preverbal connective and wʌl is the ordinary Mlabri verb meaning 'to return' (with a close cognate in Tin Prai). When such constructions with two words in parallel occur in rituals, the words may be expected to be synonyms, and they need not be from the same lexical stratum; in an α-Mlabri ritual I have heard gulgut wɤɤk gulgut naam meaning 'the end of the waterfall' (a place of religious significance), where wɤɤk is the α-Mlabri word for 'water' and naam its Thai synonym (which is not otherwise used as a Mlabri word).

In the study of a mixed vocabulary one might expect loanwords from (or via) neighbouring languages to have essentially the same phonetic form and and the same meaning as in the languages they come from. In the case of loanwords in Mlabri, the phonetic form has generally been adopted without much change. The most pervasive change from Thai is the loss of tones, which must have happened already when the words in question were borrowed into the hilltribe language(s) from which Mlabri later acquired these words. As for semantics, however, loanwords do not always have the expected meaning. In some instances the Mlabri seem to have made somewhat different associations between words and phenomena than those which existed in the lending language. This reveals something about the nature of encounters between the Mlabri and their neighbours in the past – situations characterized by semi-communication. To take a culturally interesting example, one of the words for 'white' in both α- and β-Mlabri is phakhaaw. This word reflects a Thai phrase which means 'white cloth' and thus undoubtedly stems from the Mlabri's acquisition of clothing by engaging in barter trade (see further on colour terms in section 4.2.3 below).

There are some other instances in which the meaning of a word in Mlabri is even more strongly skewed in comparison with the meaning of the same etymon in neighbouring languages. If at the same time we observe a strikingly good fit with respect to phonetic form, there is a strong case for assuming that the Mlabri word is a loanword rather than an "original" Mlabri word.

Such semantically strange loanwords are sometimes of Thai origin but they may also be Mon-Khmer etyma. A good example is the word gnrɛɛ 'curry', which occurs both in α-Mlabri and β-Mlabri, and which is interesting by its very existence (one would not expect advanced cooking in traditional Mlabri culture). The word is likely to reflect a well-established Mon-Khmer etymon which in other languages means 'wooden pestle'. The semantic shift may have occurred when Mlabri visitors observed a villager pounding spices for a curry; it is understandable that they might mix up the terminology used to refer to this process.

To take a more tricky example, the word hmaaj, a Mon-Khmer etymon which occurs in many languages with the meaning of 'widow', is used in β-Mlabri as the standard word for 'wife' (α-Mlabri has instead borrowed the Thai word for 'wife' in the form miɤɤ). It is absolutely certain that Mlabri hmaaj does not mean 'widow': it is used also by a husband speaking about his wife. This semantic mismatch becomes even more conspicuous if we look at the phrasal expressions for 'first wife': β-Mlabri hma(a)j kldɯl, literally 'rump wife', and for 'second wife': hma(a)j tuul, literally 'point wife'. This terminology, which in itself is rather surprising (see remarks on this issue in section 4.2.4 below) may actually represent a semantic restatement which turns the concepts around. I gather from unpublished Kmhmu (Kammu) materials, kindly made available to me by Jan-Olof Svantesson, that the Mlabri data would resemble that language if the meanings 'first wife' and 'second wife' were interchanged (although only tuul has a direct cognate in Kmhmu).

Generally speaking, pinpointing the meaning and function of a word borrowed into Mlabri should not be made via an aprioric transfer of the meaning range or the syntax found in peer languages, especially not if Central Thai is the language of reference. An example is tɛɛ, which in Thai occurs in many different functions including the frequent function as a clause-initial conjunction meaning 'but, however'. This word occurs in β-Mlabri, but so far I have only recorded it in the position after a sentence-initial noun phrase where it seems to add more or less contrastive focus to that noun phrase while establishing it as a new topic. The resulting meaning can be paraphrased as 'with respect to X, on the other hand...' or 'now, as for X...'.

A more difficult situation is found with *negative preverbs* (in this monograph I use the term "Preverb" in the sense of Mary Haas' "Adverb-Auxiliaries"). The α-Mlabri word ki always means 'not' (although kibɔ or kɔbɔ is more frequently used), but in β-Mlabri ki means 'also' except in certain lexicalized phrases where it has negative polarity. The word bɔ is expletive in β-Mlabri (*not* negative as in Northern Thai). Then there are other negative preverbs such as chak, met/mit, which are used to a greater extent in β-Mlabri than in α-Mlabri. – The abundance of negative preverbs in Mlabri (cf. section 4.2.1 on Negation below) is intriguing; it does not appear to be due to recent influence from either Tin or Kmhmu.

It is an equally striking general characteristic of Mlabri and other minority languages of the area that in many cases the meanings and the uses of Thai words, but *not the words themselves*, seem to have been borrowed: there are numerous words of indisputable Mon-Khmer origin which have semantic ranges which closely match those of etymologically unrelated expressions in Thai. This is not just a matter of trivial similarities which might be due to chance; the affinity extends to instances of unpredictable polysemy.

The assumption that we are dealing with contact phenomena is supported even more strongly in the case of phrasal constructions in Mlabri.

One topic of specific linguistic interest is the use of noun classifiers. This category is rather marginal in Mon-Khmer languages, compared to its proliferation e.g. in Thai, but it is different in Northern Mon-Khmer. Tin (Lua') has several classifiers, and the same is true of β-Mlabri (see the Mlabri-English Index: the entry "noun classifier"). These classifiers are, at least for some speakers, cognitive equivalents of classifiers occurring in Thai, though in many cases the etyma are unrelated. A good example is lmbʌr, which as an ordinary noun means 'leaf (on a tree)' and is used as a classifier with largely the same range as Thai baj (likewise with the basic meaning of 'leaf'); one Mlabri speaker explained the use of the classifier to me directly by referring to the fact that "lmbʌr means baj".

The use of classifiers is of course not just a semantic but also a syntactic feature shared with Thai. It is, however, noteworthy that Mlabri does not otherwise show any strong influence from Thai syntax; on the contrary it exhibits constructions and word order regularities that are alien to Thai (see chapter 5 on Mlabri syntax below).

The affinity to Thai or Lao can be observed particularly in the use of "fixed expressions": lexicalized phrases with metonymical or metaphorical meaning, etc. Although it is difficult to distinguish between indigenous and borrowed constructions because Indochina is a linguistic area with features shared by large numbers of languages, there has been an unquestionable external influence on the use of phrasal expressions in Mlabri. In many cases we find a mixed inventory of expressions.

When one looks at expressions for mental moods or states, for example, we find on the one hand klol hot 'heart fall' i.e. 'be startled', which is reminiscent of Thai phraseology. On the other hand klol ɟuur 'heart sink', i.e. 'be happy', is entirely different from Thai usage. The former example, klol hot, is interesting in that its constituent order is different from the corresponding Thai expression, although the combination of concepts is the same. A correspondence on both levels is found between β-Mlabri klol ʔjen and Thai caj jen 'heart cool', i.e. 'be calm'. Mlabri sometimes has a choice between alternative orders of constituents in expressions for mood, e.g. thɛh klol, literally 'good heart' or klol thɛh, literally 'heart good'. These expressions correspond to two Thai expressions, respectively: dii caj with which the Mlabri phrase shares the meaning 'be glad', and caj dii with which the Mlabri phrase shares the meaning 'be good-hearted'. It is my impression, however, that Mlabri does not correlate constituent order with meaning in the same way as Thai: there seems to be overlap in meaning between the two expressions in Mlabri.

Across the lexicon there are several complex expressions which may be calques from Thai or Lao although they are, in part or even completely, made up of genuine Mon-Khmer lexical material. In several instances it is a matter of word-for-word equivalence, e.g. ɟakɟak wʌlwʌl, literally 'go-go, come-come' which corresponds exactly to Thai pajpaj maamaa 'to go (travel) forth and back all the time'.

The question, then, is not just whether such expressions are calques but whether (in the latter case) they have been lexicalized in the native language or just reflect occasional language mixing in a communicative situation. The particular example above seems to be part of the native language code proper. It was offered deliberately as a usable Mlabri phrase by a speaker who is very puristic about his language, as far as vocabulary is concerned, and often discards other people's use of words as being not Mlabri but Thai.

Influence from a peer language may be seen in the syntactic templates, in the semantics of the constituent parts or in the idiomatic meanings of such complex expressions. This may be further exemplified by expressions for natural phenomena: mɛʔ hot 'rain fall' i.e. 'it rains', with Thai syntax and semantics unlike Tin leh miaʔ, literally '(there) appears rain'. The expressions for sunrise, tawɪn pruk or tawɪn leh, and for sunset, tawɪn hot, both correspond nicely to the Thai expressions for 'east' and 'west', and in fact these Mlabri phrases can be extended to denote the directions east and west as in Thai. There are also two expressions which are used when translating the Thai words for 'north' and 'south', respectively: thaŋ nɯɯʔ (consisting of the Thai words for 'direction' and 'north') and tɤj ɟuɤj.

This, of course, does not mean that the concept of "corners of the world" can be applied to Mlabri. I have heard a Mlabri use the two last-mentioned expressions in the remarkable statement: tawɪn pruk ʔat thaŋ nɯɯʔ, hot tɤj ɟuɤj 'the sun rises in the north, it sets in the south' (apparently an old saying which may be falling into oblivion). The orientation is relative: another man on a different occasion claimed that the sun rises in the "south" and sets in the "north".

A very complicated issue is the syntax and semantics of verbs which occur both as full verbs (sentence verbs) and as "coverbs" in serial predicate constructions (cf. chapter 5 on Syntax below). A good example is Mlabri maaʔ, which occurs as an independent verb meaning 'give' like its Thai equivalent hâj, and which matches the syntactic potentials of that word by also occurring in constructions where it does not convey the meaning of 'give' but seems to be entirely grammaticalized. At one point a Mlabri speaker said to me: mɤm maaʔ ʔoh di glaʔ, in word-for-word translation 'father give me for-to speak', which in the situation must be construed to mean 'my father has told me to speak (with you)' (i.e. to serve as a language consultant). Just as in Thai, the same verb also occurs in post-verbal position, where the meaning must be construed differently: β-Mlabri ʔbɔɔk maaʔ 'tell to (somebody)' = Central Thai bɔ̀ɔk hâj. Moreover, β-Mlabri guɯt hɔɔt 'think reach', i.e. 'miss (somebody)' matches the corresponding Thai expression khít thɯ̌ŋ perfectly. In both of these examples the first verb is an old loanword; the second is an ordinary Mlabri verb which is grammaticalized (as a coverb or directional verb), like its Thai equivalents.

It goes beyond the present study to determine for each lexicalization or syntatic construction whether it is indigenous to the Mlabri language or reflects direct or indirect contact with some kind of Thai. In the case of contact phenomena their dating is at issue. The fact that the apparent calques are not all equally distributed in α-Mlabri and β-Mlabri speaks in favour of a short history for some of these constructions.

The proliferation of affinities with Thai is a feature shared by more prestigious minority languages, and the influence from Thai may in many instances have been mediated by one of the other highland languages. Thai words in Mlabri may, however, also reflect the use of Lao or Northern Thai as a *lingua franca* on encounters with the Mlabri. Thai (of whatever kind) has been and is a medium of communication not only with lowlanders but among the highland peoples themselves.

In addition to the fully integrated contact phenomena one often encounters straightforward *language mixing*, as in the following utterance said by a woman to her bashful daughter during a meal: tit klɛj kɔ ʔdɛj, boŋ di thɛh gʌh 'you may be shy but eat properly now!'. Of the words tit klɛj kɔ ʔdɛj all but klɛj 'shy' are Thai spoken with a Mlabri accent. This reflects an ongoing competition between languages in the Mlabri households and thus leads to the topic of bilingualism.

2.1.3 Bilingualism and Language Norms

The contact situation of the Mlabri language of today is also characterized by alternating use of languages. There is a considerable degree of *bilingualism* or even *multilingualism* among the Mlabri, which is reflected in basic communication.

The Mlabri are often rather fluent in a kind of Northern Thai and sometimes also in one or more other languages of the area. One female β-Mlabri speaker impressed me particularly when, within one hour of smalltalk, she switched between four different languages depending on the addressee: (1) Mlabri (spoken to her father), (2) Tin Mal (spoken to her husband who was born a Tin), (3) Hmong (spoken to Hmong villagers entering the hut) and (4) Northern Thai, the lingua franca of the whole area (spoken in a subsequent conversation involving both her father and some Hmong people). In all four instances the conversation was lively and rapid.

Not all Mlabri speakers have equally high bilingual or multilingual proficiency, of course. Most persons above a certain age (be they α-Mlabri or β-Mlabri) do not speak any Hmong, in spite of their close social contact with the Hmong.

When they are together with people of other ethnic affiliations (which happens mostly in Hmong villages), the Mlabri heed to comply with the widespread opinion that not only does their language have a low social status, it is funny or even ridiculous. On one occasion a Mlabri introduced me to a villager with an apologetic side-remark (in Northern Thai): "I have to speak Yellow-Leaf language to him because he does not speak Northern Thai!" Though I cannot claim that the second part of the remark was totally unjustified, I understood the remark rather as a maneuver which licensed the use of Mlabri within a Hmong house.

Mlabri and the specific hilltribe variety of Northern Thai are nowadays used alternately among the Mlabri themselves. There is a tendency to switch between language codes depending on the topic, both in the case of α-Mlabri and β-Mlabri speakers. – As for the β-Mlabri lady mentioned above, she and her Tin husband sometimes speak Mlabri together although his Mlabri sounds somewhat deficient. She could not give me any real cue as to the occasions on which they would prefer to speak Mlabri: "If we like to speak Lua' (Tin) we speak Lua'; if we like to speak Mlabri we speak Mlabri".

On a different occasion I heard the same woman and her sister and their father all speaking Tin together, although her Tin husband suggested several times (in a subdued voice) that they should speak Mlabri instead since I was present (!), which he then did himself. I wanted to record the Mlabri-Tin couple when they conversed in that language, and she agreed and said to her husband: glaʔ mɤʔ mɤm 'speak mother father', i.e. '(now we'll) speak like my parents!'.

In another β-Mlabri household which consists of a middle-aged couple, their four children and a young female relative, everybody can speak Mlabri but the children speak with a restricted vocabulary (a kind of "Basic Mlabri"). On one occasion the male leader of the household aired some harsh comments about his youngest children's poor command of Mlabri: "they know only a few words and they say ɟʌʌt instead of ɟrʌʌk!"

On the other hand, the children are reported by the Hmong to be fluent in the Hmong language. On one occasion, when a Hmong woman came to ask for pain-relieving medicine because she had a sore neck, a Mlabri youngster intervened and acted as an interpreter. He urged me to put my questions to him in Mlabri (not in Northern Thai), which he then translated into Hmong, after which he translated her answers back into Mlabri, and finally provided a seemingly meticulous translation of my clumsy Mlabri instructions about how and when to take pain-killing pills. This worked fine, and it was a singularly strange experience: a symbol of the increasing sophistication and self-confidence of the Mlabri at a time when the existence of the β-Mlabri as an ethnic group is at stake.

Moreover, all members of the household have considerable proficiency in their particular kind of Northern Thai. The middle-aged male Mlabri mentioned above seems to have at his disposal a considerable Northern Thai vocabulary, as I noticed when I was checking the meaning of Mlabri words and often obtained more or less adequate Northern Thai equivalents or paraphrases. The words he then uses (e.g. to name plants) are, however, in some cases characteristic of Lao rather than Northern Thai.

On various occasions I have asked people of the Nan area to listen to tape recordings of Mlabri persons speaking Northern Thai. Their reaction was that this was basically Northern Thai but spoken with an "unclear" pronunciation (one listener aptly characterized the pronunciation as monotonous) and mixed with unintelligible words from some other language.

The Mlabri even have some familiarity with Central Thai. In the Hmong villages virtually all children and adolescents can speak Thai as they attend the local, monolingual Thai school and also listen to the radio (small portable radios are widespread in Hmong villages). Mlabri children, too, are increasingly exposed to Central Thai and often understand that language rather well.

On my encounters with the β-Mlabri the Mlabri language has nevertheless been dominant, even when somebody was talking to the youngest child of the group, a boy who is just beginning to talk. This, however, does not seem to be true of other situations. It is likely that my presence as a participant observer with an interest in their language has reinforced their motivation to speak Mlabri on those occasions. There has been an obvious tendency to switch to their variety of Northern Thai whenever they were not aware that I was around.

It was interesting to overhear one evening (when I was *not* supposed to be listening) how the youngest child of the group, a boy of some three years of age, was trained by his father to say the numerals from 1 to 10. The father first said each numeral in Thai, after which the boy repeated it, often with a better Thai pronunciation than that of his father, which showed that he had already heard the numerals several times as spoken by others. After having reached the numeral 10 in Thai, the father then switched to Mlabri and worked on the numerals mɔɔj, bɛɛr, pɛʔ, pon, etc., with the boy. The latter again repeated carefully but this time without at all reaching the level of performance of his father (some of the final consonants were not articulated properly).

The whole question of old and new multilingualism and of code switching among minority groups in Northern Thailand is of interest both sociolinguistically and from the perspective of historical linguistics. It is a complex issue, however. As for Mlabri, virtually nothing is known about the situation as it was only a few decades ago. The past must be inferred from the present.

As mentioned before, the ethnic Mlabri in Thailand number less than 200 persons, as far as can be determined. The size of the population is so small that the Mlabri language, and particularly its β-variety with only a dozen speakers, must be counted among the most endangered languages of the world. The scarcity of speakers is emphasized by the division of the Mlabri into separate groups which speak different varieties of the language.

The vulnerability of the language and its historical interest are, however, not the only reasons for focussing on the study of Mlabri. The language and its speakers also offer much for sociolinguistic study. In addition to the social split between different groups there is a traditional, strong division between male activities and female activities. There is also a rapid transition from traditional culture to a culture that is increasingly being adopted from that of the surrounding populations.

As a consequence of these changes there is an enormous variation in lexicon over the total population, despite its relatively small size. Firstly, the different groups speak very differently. Secondly, there is (at least within the language variety treated in this monograph) a considerable difference in lexicon between male speech and female speech. Moreover, there is (within each of the two varieties known today) a conspicuous difference between more conservative and more modern lexical usage (often so that a word that is current in one variety of Mlabri is obsolete or even "undesirable" in the other).

Last but not least, the speakers of the Mlabri language represent a rather unique level of material culture combined with very peculiar components of social organization and of spiritual culture. But, as with sociolinguistic information, in depth anthropological-linguistic information is difficult to collect. The Mlabri tend to be timid, and long-term relationships with knowledgeable tribespeople is an essential factor. As a result, the information available in the literature is not always reliable.

2.2 The Origin of Mlabri Lexical Material

It was mentioned above and has been stated repeatedly in previous literature (Egerod and Rischel 1987, p. 36; Rischel 1989b, p. 108-114; Rischel 1989c, p. 106-117; Rischel 1992, p. 159-175; Rischel 1993) that Mlabri has a rather mixed lexicon. This is true of both α-Mlabri and β-Mlabri. In the preceding parts of this chapter the Mlabri language was considered partly from a diachronic point of view and partly from an areal linguistic perspective. In the present section the vocabulary which results from internal development and external influences will be characterized in more detail with respect to its origins (with much recapitulation of information from the preceding sections).

A very large proportion of the words in Mlabri are unmistakably of Mon-Khmer type, and out of these a sizeable proportion have very close or even phonologically identical cognates in languages of the proposed *Khmuic* branch of Mon-Khmer. Accordingly, Mlabri was already classified as belonging with these languages by Nimmanhaeminda (1963).

As stated earlier, there are two Khmuic languages which are spoken by villagers (low-income peasants) in the Nan Province of Thailand and in adjacent Laos, Kmhmu (Kammu, Khmu') and Tin (or Lua'). Mlabri shares very many close cognates with Tin, but in β-Mlabri there are also several words which have close cognates in Kmhmu.

Kmhmu and Tin do not seem generally to be closely related to each other if one looks at the overall lexicon. Within Tin there is much lexical divergence between main dialect groups. Thus, the most striking affinities between Mlabri and Tin, or between Mlabri and Kmhmu must be due to very recent borrowing of lexical items from these languages such as khɔt 'spear' from Tin and trlɔh 'pot' from Kmhmu. Other lexical correspondences may be due to borrowing which took place centuries ago, predominantly from Tin; it is possible that a significant element in the Mlabri language is a direct continuation of Pre-Tin. It is an open question whether this stratum should be used to define the genetic classification of Mlabri, or whether one should search behind it. In any case, Mlabri has a close affinity to the group of languages called Khmuic (see further Rischel 1989b, 1993).

The old numerals (up to 10) of Kmhmu, Tin and Mlabri are so closely related as to confirm the close linguistic affinity among these three languages, although it be a matter of extensive contact, i.e. areal rather than genetic affinity (the numerals themselves were probably borrowed at some point, although the Mlabri often demonstrate the knowledge of these numerals as a feature of Mlabri ethnicity).

There is a significant residue of old Mon-Khmer etyma in Mlabri which do not seem to be from Pre-Tin or even from Khmuic. Several lexical items have no obvious cognates at all, as far as I know. Some of these may be very old words, but others may be recent coinages. It is plausible to assume that many of the words in Mlabri which exhibit sound symbolism of one or another kind (names of animals and birds, words denoting characteristic gestures, words denoting unpleasant sensations etc.) were created within Mlabri. Many such words exhibit reduplication.

Mlabri has many bisyllabic or sesquisyllabic words. It may well be the case that some of the material occurring initially in such words is a Mlabri innovation: an elaboration of monosyllabic Mon-Khmer roots. When faced with "strange" minor syllables in Mlabri, however, one should not disregard the possibility that Mlabri has preserved very old material which has been lost in the languages which otherwise seem most similar to Mlabri.

Then there are the Thai words in Mlabri ("Thai" being here taken in the sense of Southwestern Tai, i.e. comprising also Northern Thai and Lao). Some of these words are very old loans; it is uncertain whether such words were borrowed directly from the "original" source language or via some minority language, such as a language of more prestige than Mlabri which has been in extensive contact with some kind of Thai.

Altogether, there are many words of Thai origin in Mlabri, as in other minority languages of the area. Some are from Lao, others are clearly from Northern Thai (Khammueang) and still others look as if they are from Central Thai. In addition to the old lexical material there are very recent borrowings; these are mostly from Northern Thai but they include Central Thai terms for modern implements which are used all over the area (in some cases Mlabri probably borrowed such terms from the Hmong).

It is often very difficult or even impossible to decide on formal grounds *which* Thai language or dialect is the source, especially since loanwords in Mlabri are likely to have been filtered through the phonology of one or another contact language before entering Mlabri. This may be a more important source of phonological modification than adjustments within Mlabri proper, especially when one considers the conservative nature of Mlabri phonology.

When one traces the origin of a word which seems to have come (directly or indirectly) from some Thai dialect, it is an additional complication that several words in Thai are ultimately of Mon-Khmer origin. All this is well-known from the study of other Mon-Khmer languages. It should, however, be taken into consideration that until recently the Mlabri, with their special lifestyle, have carefully avoided meeting people from the lowlands, i.e., *their* contact with languages such as Thai or Lao has probably been strictly limited to the use of the *lingua franca* in mountain villages whose inhabitants otherwise spoke minority languages.

A digression on relative calendary terms:

Terms for 'today', 'yesterday', 'the day before yesterday', 'tomorrow' and 'the day after tomorrow' all differ between α-Mlabri and β-Mlabri. They are a strange mixture of Mon-Khmer and Lao words. Thus, the α-Mlabri use Lao terms for 'tomorrow' and 'the day after tomorrow', whereas the β-Mlabri use quite different terms: ɟrɯw and paaj. The β-Mlabri continue that series with three more terms: pwɛt 'three days from now', muk 'four days from now' and hrlɔh 'five days from now'; from then on they use phrasal expressions which refer to time spans rather than target days: mɔ tɯŋ 'six days from now', mɔ nɯŋ 'seven days from now' and mɔ nɯk 'eight days from now'.

Knowledge of such terms is probably prestigious; I have been able to hear most of them only by eliciting the series as a totality (in nursery-rhyme style). The terms from 'yesterday' up through 'the day after tomorrow' are well established; as for the higher terms, I doubt that the temporal concepts underlying them have ever been functional within Mlabri culture.

Some words used in Mlabri today are simply Northern Thai forms spoken without tones. The dictionary contains rather few of the (Northern) Thai words that may be heard in Mlabri speech, and only ones that seem to have been fully integrated and are likely to be a stable part of the Mlabri lexicon. This is often a very difficult decision, however; the speakers themselves sometimes disagree on what constitutes proper Mlabri.

Something more or less similar may be observed in other Northern Mon-Khmer languages, including the so-called Khmuic languages such as Tin or Kmhmu. The linguistic prehistory of this sub-branch (if indeed it is a well-defined sub-branch) is, however, unknown. Although it is easy to detect Lao loanwords of varying age in these languages, their lexical development from Proto-Mon-Khmer to the present is an area in which our knowledge is extremely inadequate and will perhaps remain so.

In view of the complexity of the scenario I have preferred *not to mark loanwords at all in the dictionary below,* not even in cases where the source seems obvious. For the scholar using the data for language comparison such information would often be either superfluous or insufficient. It may be altogether more misleading than revealing to give brief indications of a source language for borrowed items since the path of borrowing may be anything but direct.

Chapter 3

A Phonological Sketch

Mlabri phonology conforms largely with the prevailing Mon-Khmer type. It is, however, noteworthy that Mlabri has a very rich inventory of consonant types, with four different manners of articulation in stops and three different manners in glides. The vowel system is also rich: it comprises ten different vowel phonemes (plus some diphthongs), all of which exhibit a contrastive difference between long and short. Mlabri, however, has neither tone nor "register" (in the sense in which this term is used in Southeast Asian linguistics, i.e. a distinction of vowel quality, which may have to do with phonation type or tongue-root articulation). The old differences in manner of articulation which have given rise to distinctive tones or "registers" in many other languages, are preserved intact in Mlabri. It thus stands out as a language with very *conservative* phonology.

3.1 Segmental Phonology

The *segmental phonology* of α-Mlabri was treated in Rischel (1982) and in Egerod and Rischel (1987, p. 36-43). With respect to the phoneme inventory and phonotactics of Mlabri, we find the same overall pattern in the two varieties: "α-Mlabri" and "β-Mlabri". There are minor differences in the inventories of permitted consonant clusters and of diphthongs. These differences are, however, so small that the sound pattern may be regarded as essentially the same in both varieties. It should also be noted that in spite of the similarity in phonological structure, the two varieties sound very differently because of differences in rhythm and sentence intonation.

In the survey of β-Mlabri phonology below the subject-matter is arranged rather differently from previous presentations (cf. Egerod and Rischel 1987).

Vowels:

The vowel system posited for α-Mlabri (Egerod and Rischel 1987, p. 41) comprises ten contrastive vowel qualities, with a front unrounded series, a back unrounded series, and a back rounded series, and with four degrees of openness: high = close, high mid = half-close, low mid = half-open, and low = open:

i	ɯ	u
e	ɤ	o
ɛ	ʌ	ɔ
	a	

This is also more or less the inventory one finds in β-Mlabri; however, the arrangement above exaggerates the phonetic symmetry of the vowel system, in particular the overall significance of a "vertical axis" around which the whole system is symmetrical. As for language-internal criteria there is an abstract-phonological or morphological phenomenon which provides evidence for such a symmetrical arrangement, namely the pattern of *vowel harmony* in which /i ɯ u/ occur as the harmonic copies of vowels from the first, second and third column, respectively (this pattern is prevalent in reduplicatives, see 4.1.3 below for details). This harmony pattern suggests that the Mlabri vowel system is – or at least used to be – strictly symmetric in the sense depicted above, since /ɯ/ occurs in harmony with /a/.

It is somewhat less straightforward, however, how the Mlabri vowels should be tabulated in order for the arrangement to be in maximum agreement with their present-day phonetic manifestations and surface contrasts.

There are three points to be made, of which the first two (which apply to both α-Mlabri and β-Mlabri) are of minor significance, whereas the third totally upsets the apparent symmetry as far as β-Mlabri is concerned:

– (1) The arrangement above gives the impression of an overcrowded *back unrounded* category, with /ʌ/ as the typologically most marked member, and one might expect a tendency for /ʌ/ and /a/ to eventually merge into one phoneme /a/. This is not at all what seems to be happening, however. The relevant correlation is between /ʌ/ and /ɔ/, *not* between /ʌ/ and /a/. In α-Mlabri there seems to be an ongoing diffusion of /ʌ/ into words which have /ɔ/ in the elder generation's speech, young persons saying mɔɔʔ for mʌʌʔ 'python', for example. In β-Mlabri there is a similar, though so far much weaker, tendency for /ʌ/ to vary in the direction of its rounded counterpart /ɔ/. For example, gʌh 'here, this' in rapid speech often sounds like gɔh, but unlike speakers of the other variety of Mlabri, the β-Mlabri speakers preserve the unrounded vowel quality in distinct pronunciation (see further on phonological variation in section 6.3).

– (2) According to my tentative analysis the vowel /a/ has a considerably fronted allophone before palatal consonants (i.e. /c ɟ j ɲ/); it exhibits much more fronting than the vowels /ɯ ɤ ʌ/. When one transcribes words with vowels in such environments, the challenge is not to distinguish /a/ from /ʌ/ but certainly to distinguish /a/ from /ɛ/. This is not unexpected, but it weakens the case for treating /ɯ ɤ ʌ a/ as one close-knit series.

– (3) In β-Mlabri there is a small handful of words, which I have been transcribing alternatively with /i/ and with /e/, vacillating back and forth between the two vowel assignments and for a long time assuming the existence of phonemically different alternative pronunciations. I have finally come to the conclusion that these words contain a vowel which is phonetically rather variable but which represents a phoneme intermediate between /i/ and /e/. This phoneme is transcribed here as /ɪ/. Examples of the vowels /i ɪ e/ are:

/i/: (rooj) mim 'a fly', pin 'to spin', ʔdiŋ 'big'

/ɪ/: prɪm 'old', tawɪn 'day', wɪŋ 'meatus of the ear'

/e/: ʔem 'to sleep', ʔjen 'vein', peɲ 'to shoot'

It seems that the contrast between /ɪ/ and other front vowels (i.e. with /i/ on the one hand and with the lower vowels /e, ɛ/ on the other hand) is strictly limited to *the position before nasals*.

Faced with the combined evidence above I find that a different exposition of the vowel system which refers to the natural parameters of tongue articulation (as inferred from the perceived vowel qualities) does more justice to certain aspects of the patterning. According to the alternative presentation there are two sets of vowels. One set is characterized by the absence of any constriction in the back part of the mouth. These vowels are placed along a "front" trajectory going from a high palatal tongue position over a maximally unconstricted articulation and down toward a low pharyngeal tongue position:

$$/i - ɪ - e - ɛ - a/$$

The other set is, on the contrary, characterized by the presence of some posterior oral constriction. According to the region of maximum approximation between tongue and back wall, these vowels are placed along a "back" trajectory going from a velar over a uvular to a high pharyngeal tongue position, either with concomitant liprounding:

$$/u - o - ɔ/$$

or without liprounding:

$$/ɯ - ɣ - ʌ/$$

Except for /ɪ/, which is always short (and seems to have a very restricted distribution), each vowel phoneme occurs short and long. There is a *quantity contrast* in full syllables (except in the position before final /h/ where only short vowels occur), although it is only under phrase-final stress that length is clearly manifested. – Long vowels are here written as double vowels in order to comply with current practice in Mon-Khmer studies:

/ii ee εε aa ɯɯ ɤɤ ʌʌ uu oo ɔɔ/

Most of the vowel phonemes have phonetic qualities which are rather adequately symbolized by the IPA vowel symbols. Long /ee/, however, is a perceptibly "higher" vowel than short /e/, which is quite close to the Cardinal Vowel [e].

In the material presented in the dictionary below, the words cheeʔ and ʔeeʔ were heard in a couple of cases with vowel shortening in non-final phrase position. Although there is no minimal contrast between shortened /ee/ and short /e/, it is my impression that these may be phonetically different even when the former is shortened. If that is true, it reflects a flaw in the analysis as reflected in the transcription system. Rather than complicating the presentation by choosing a separate symbol for /ee/ (or for /e/) because of this potential contrast I, however, have chosen to symbolize the shortened /ee/ (in the very few instances in which it occurs on my data) by e(e).

Moreover, the vowels /ε ʌ/ are slightly higher (in terms of "auditory height") than the Cardinal Vowels [ε ʌ], and higher than the corresponding vowels in α-Mlabri (it may also be worth mentioning that the β-Mlabri vowel /ɔ/ is closer to the Cardinal Vowel [ɔ] than the open rounded back vowel found in Thai).

There are several phonetic *diphthongs* in Mlabri. Diphthongs with a palatal or velar offglide are interpreted here (as well as in Egerod and Rischel 1987) as sequences of vowel plus /-j/, e.g. rejwej, mɯj, rujkoj, or /-w/, e.g. chεw, mɯw. Not all the theoretically possible combinations have been attested, however; there are obviously restrictions on the cooccurrence of front vowels with /-j/, and of back vowels with /-w/.

The main problem with such diphthongs is that of identifying front vowel qualities before /-j/ as allophones of specific vowel phonemes. In my data, /ej εj aj/ are all attested, and there are near-minimal contrasts: cejdej 'to bend the head down and look backwards between one's legs' versus rɛjwɛj 'fruit fly' versus gɯncaj 'blanket'. There is, however, often variation in the pronunciation of words with these diphthongs, and my interpretation of vowels before /-j/ must be considered very tentative, especially in the case of the diphthong written /ɛj/ (it seems very likely that /aj/ and /ɛj/ vary idiolectally in several of these words). Although gɯncaj has a rather fronted vowel [a] there also occurs a more retracted [ɑ]-sound in the same position before /-j/, e.g. in bla(a)j kwaan 'big'). That sound is a manifestation of the long vowel /aa/, which is shortened by a rhythmic rule but tends to remain phonetically distinct from phonemically short /a/ even when shortened.

It is even more problematic to interpret diphthongs ending in a more open vowel. There are a number of such diphthongs, which I prefer to render (like Egerod and Rischel 1987) as vowel sequences. They are peculiar in that they all end in a non-front unrounded vowel, and in that some of them have a distinctively long second component:

(1) with /ɤ/ as second component: /iɤɤ uɤ uɤɤ/

(2) with /ʌ/ as second component: /iʌ (ɯʌ) uʌ/

(3) with /a/ as second component: /ia iaa ua uaa/

Most of the diphthongs above are sparsely represented in the lexicon; it may be due to incompleteness of my data that there is no short (light) diphthong */iɤ/ to fill out an obvious hole in the pattern. The long (heavy) diphthongs /iɤɤ/ and /iaa/ occur in my data in just two words which happen to form a minimal pair: ciɤɤk 'to grasp' – ciaak 'deer'. I have recorded the long diphthong /uaa/ only in the expression klol luaak 'be out of breath'.

The diphthongs /iʌ/ and /uɤɤ/ occur in loanwords and reflect the Thai diphthongs ia, ua (of which the quality of the second component is in fact not a low vowel). Examples are wiʌŋ, the word for 'city', Thai wiaŋ, and gruɤɤ, a word meaning 'things, personal belongings', cf. Thai khrua. In fact, the few words which I have recorded with the long diphthong /uɤɤ/ are all loanwords from Thai. (There is no regular diphthongal reflex of Thai /ɰa/ as Mlabri sides with northern dialects having /ɰɰ/ < /ɰa/.)

The Mlabri diphthong /ɰʌ/ is of very dubious status as it has been recorded only in two loanwords, both of which have a very strange phonology compared to Thai: hɰʌ ʔbin 'aeroplane' and phalɰʌm (also heard as phaljɰm) 'lightning'. One would not expect diphthongs beginning in /ɰ/ at all; as stated above Thai */ɰa/ occurs as a monophthongal vowel /ɰɰ/ both in old and more recent loanwords.

It is altogether a problem how to deal with syllable nuclei which begin with a high palatal or velar glide. In Mlabri, sonorant initial consonants are rather high pitched like the beginning of the vowel, so it is often very difficult to decide how to interpret syllables in which the initial consonant is followed by a palatal or velar segment plus a vowel of different quality. There may not be any contrastive pairs with glide versus high vowel, but the words in question do not all sound alike in this respect.

Some words, e.g. pjaŋ, definitely have a postconsonantal glide; others, e.g. biʌʌc, certainly sound as if the postconsonantal segment is a vowel rather than a glide. The problem is that several words cannot be easily assigned to one or the other category; this is true of piaaʔ or pjaaʔ, and kuɤj or kwɤj, for example. Perhaps there is an ongoing merger between postconsonantal /j/ and /i/ which results in variation.

I have chosen to make a (possibly spurious) notational distinction by positing postconsonantal /j/ consistently in words which sound more as if they contain the sequence glide + vowel, but postconsonantal /i/ in words which sound more as if they contain real diphthongs. This has been done on a purely impressionistic basis and it has not been possible to be quite consistent in the dictionary entries.

There is a similar problem with syllables containing an initial palatal stop followed by a back vowel. There is sometimes an audible vowel or glide in between; it may be strongly articulated, e.g. [chiʌɲ] or [chjʌɲ], or it may be weak and often absent, e.g. [ɟjooŋ] or [ɟooŋ]. I have interpreted the audible segment as /i/ or as /j/ on an impressionistic basis; variant forms with a simple onset are given in some instances. This, however, could not be done very consistently either.

More or less centralized vowels occur in pretonic (i.e. pre-stress) syllables. In the transcriptions of the dictionary and index below these vowel qualities are mostly – often arbitrarily – assigned to members of the vowel set above. Schwa-like vowels also occur in pretonic syllables; they are noted in the dictionary transcriptions by means of a cover symbol ə. The phonemic status of such schwa-vowels is unclear.

Consonants:

There are very different inventories of contrastive consonantal segments in syllable-initial and syllable-final positions. These will be presented and discussed separately below.

Initial Consonants:

(1) Oral Stops:
(Voiceless) Aspirated: /ph th ch kh/
Voiceless (Unaspirated): /p t c k/
Voiced (Nonglottalized): /b d ɟ g/
Glottalized (and Voiced): /ʔb ʔd/

(2) Nasals:
Partially Voiceless: /hm hn hɲ hŋ/
Fully Voiced: /m n ɲ ŋ/

(3) Oral Glides:
Partially Voiceless: /hw/
Fully Voiced: /w j/

(4) Other Sonorants (i.e. "Liquids"):
Partially Voiceless: /hl (hr)/
Fully Voiced: /l r/
Glottalized (and Voiced): /ʔw ʔj/

(5) Laryngeals:
Aspirate: /h/
Stop: /ʔ/

As is customary in practical descriptive work, the use of articulatory phonetic labels implies (at least) that the *auditory impression* of each speech-sound points to the articulatory property in question.

The entity transcribed as /ch/ in the chart above is variably a palato-alveolar affricate or a sibilant. It is often a slightly palatalized [s] without closure at all, but the transcription "ch" is used consistently in this monograph, as in Egerod and Rischel (1987). The sibilant pronunciation seems to be more predominant in certain recent loanwords from Thai such as sɔɔŋ/chɔɔŋ 'two' (used alongside the traditional Mlabri word bɛɛr) and saj/chaj 'put', and perhaps suuŋ/chuuŋ 'high, tall', but I have found no basis for positing two distinct phonemes.

The entities which are tabulated as "partially voiceless" are manifested with an aspiration-like airstream through the open glottis from the very beginning of the onset but with a voiced transition to the following vowel (i.e. the articulation which one might expect for clusters of /h/ plus underlyingly sonorant, according to the general phonetic mechanism of coarticulation). In some instances these same entities form *minor syllables*; they are then manifested as orally invariant long segments consisting of a voiceless nonsyllabic chunk plus a voiced syllabic chunk of the same consonantal articulation (i.e. as if they were homorganic sequences of "hn+n", "hr+r" etc.; see further on the analysis of minor syllables below).

The entity /hr/ has not been recorded as a syllable onset but only as such a minor syllable. Still, I have entered it in parentheses above because the whole pattern predicts the potential occurrence of /hr/ as a syllable onset.

The entities transcribed as /ʔb ʔd/ sound implosive when pronounced distinctly; /ʔw ʔj/ are preglottalized. These laryngeal characteristics are not always audible, however, and it is sometimes difficult to distinguish /ʔb ʔd ʔw ʔj/ from plain /b d w j/.

As for the inventory of *consonant clusters* in β-Mlabri, these cannot be tabulated without a consideration of the phonemic status of aspirated and glottalized segments. I shall here assume that glottalized consonants and partially voiceless continuants in the chart above are clusters (composed of /ʔ h/ plus a stop, nasal, or oral continuant in accordance with their digraph symbolizations), whereas it seems warranted to claim that the aspirated stops /ph th ch kh/ count as single phonemes.

One or two phonemes?

A priori, the aspirated stops /ph th ch kh/ would seem obvious candidates for a biphonemic representation as clusters of the independently occurring /p t c k/ with /h/. The overall combinatorics and its diachronic origin, however, may suggest an analysis of these complex segments as one phoneme each and, on the contrary, of both /ʔb ʔd ʔw ʔj/ and /hm hn hɲ hŋ hw hl/ as clusters.

From a phonetic point of view this is hardly the most obvious solution, except that /ch/ is often manifested as a sibilant and thus appears phonetically as an indivisible segment. However, the proposed phonemicization reflects a pattern of combinatorics which has more or less obvious *diachronic* explanations. Thus, the continuants which are listed as "partially voiceless" in the chart above are likely to have counted as biphonemic in early Mlabri, cf. that /h/ plus nasal can often be traced to Mon-Khmer clusters of stop plus nasal.

It is different with the aspirated stops: there is no obvious evidence for present or former biphonemic status in the case of /ph th ch kh/. There would be hard evidence of this kind if the process of *infixation after an initial consonant* (see 4.1.1 below) occurred in forms with aspirated stops and divided these into two segments: /t-r-h/, etc., but I know of no such data in Mlabri.

There is, on the contrary, a stratum of words in which initial /th/ (like final lh, see below) clearly has a monophonemic origin, since it is the Mlabri reflex of a Mon-Khmer sibilant */s/. Otherwise, words with aspirated stops are for the most part late loanwords whose aspiration comes from the lending language (mostly Tin or Northern Thai or Lao; there are very few words with word-initial /ph/ and rather few with /kh/, anyway).

Synchronically, the claim that there exist clusters of /h/ plus sonorant is strongly supported by *the structure of minor syllables*. There are words such as hŋkeeʔ 'firewood', hrlɛʔ 'to laugh', where there is first a voiceless section and then a syllabic consonantal section in the minor syllable. In the former word there is partial coarticulation of /h/ and /ŋ/ to form an initial voiceless nasal before the homorganic syllabic nasal. If we do not interpret such sequences as /h/ plus sonorant we must posit /hŋ+ŋ/ (understood as a sequence of two segments differing only in voicing and syllabicity) for hŋkeeʔ, and this kind of homorganic consonant sequences is totally alien to Mlabri.

If, on the other hand, we understand such minor syllables to consist of /h/ plus syllabic /n/, /r/, etc., then these are not combinatorily different in type from such minor syllables as /kn-/ in kndiiŋ 'navel' and /br-/ in brpooŋ 'underneath'.

Under the analysis proposed above it is explicable why such entities as /hm, ʔb/ do not form clusters together with other consonants: they are themselves clusters, and (with one type of marginal exception; see below) syllable onsets in Mlabri consist of at most two consonants. There are constraints on the combinatorics of the laryngeals /ʔ h/. As for glottalized stop onsets, there is a strict limitation to "anterior" (i.e. neither palatal nor velar) articulation although there is no similar constraint on glottalized glides (this is a well-known type of pattern). As for /h/ plus continuant, the observation that /hr hj/ do not occur as onsets reflects a similar tendency to favour anterior articulation in onsets headed by /h/: across the lexicon /hm- hn- hl-/ are the only ones which occur in several lexical items.

In addition to the bisegmental clusters which have been defined above with reference to the consonant chart (i.e. clusters consisting of a laryngeal plus an oral consonant) there are just three types of bisegmental onsets:

(I) stop plus nonnasal continuant, with many well-attested clusters, e.g. /khw- chw- pj- ɟr- gl-/.

(II) nasal plus nonnasal continuant: /ml- mr- ŋw-/.

(III) "liquid" (lateral or trill) plus glide: /lw- rw-/.

The last-mentioned cluster /rw/ is part of the only type of three-consonant cluster which I have found in Mlabri:

(IV) stop plus /rw/; such homosyllabic CCC-clusters are found only with labial and velar initial stops: /brw- khrw- grw-/.

This three-consonant onset type is poorly attested and it may well be unstable. The few words in which I have recorded it have in most cases proved difficult to transcribe, perhaps because of variant manifestation. In this position one might expect /r/ to be syllabic, and in the word grwɛɛc, for example, there is a tendency for the medial consonant to become syllabic so that the cluster is broken up into a minor syllable /gr/ followed by the glide /w/ as onset of the main syllable.

The most remarkable *restriction* on Mlabri phonotactics from a Mon-Khmer perspective is that clusters consisting of *stop plus nasal* are not found at all (as mentioned already, such clusters may have occurred in proto-forms of Mlabri words but have been lost by a regular sound change). There are additional, rather trivial, types of restrictions on the combinatorics of individual consonants, e.g. that /l/ can only be preceded by labial or velar stops and nasals, and that /j/ can only be preceded by labial or palatal stops (the latter type of combination is phonetically variable, and there seems to be much overlap with single palatal stops).

Altogether, however, this language must be said to present a fairly rich variety of initial consonant clusters. Even the palatal stops combine with certain (nonnasal and nonlateral) continuants (cf. chwal, jrʌʌk, ɟwiil). In addition the occurrence of clusters with an initial nasal (cf. lexical items such as mlaaʔ, diŋmrɛɛŋ, ŋwɛʔ) is typologically interesting but not surprising in a Mon-Khmer context.

As for *syllabicity*, the main rule is that consonant complexes which count as clusters of three or more phonemes (according to the interpretation above) cannot occur as phonetic syllable onsets; instead, they are realized as sequences of *minor syllable plus main-syllable onset*. The second consonant then becomes syllabic: hŋ.keeʔ, hr.lɛʔ, kn.diiŋ, br.pooŋ (the dot here marks the end of the minor syllable, the consonant preceding the dot being syllabic).

It is possible that there is a further syllabification rule applying to word initial sequences of sonorant plus non-sonorant consonants, since there are some apparent examples of /r/ *being at the same time syllabic and word-initial*, namely before glottal or oral stops. This, however, is at variance with the canonical structure of all other minor syllables in Mlabri and deserves special consideration.

There are a couple of word forms which seem to have pronunciations with a single initial /r/ before a glottal stop. They are also pronounced with /rə/ in β-Mlabri, however: r.ʔɤk or rə.ʔɤk 'chest', r.ʔʌh or rə.ʔʌh 'soon'. In the dictionary below I have taken the forms with /rə/ as main forms, although this choice is open to dispute.

Another deviant form is rt.lat 'tongue', which appears to have initial and at the same time syllabic /r/ before a dental stop both in α-Mlabri (according to the notes from joint fieldwork by Søren Egerod and myself) and in β-Mlabri (according to my notes; in the word list taken down in Laos by M. Ferlus in 1964, however, the word 'tongue' is monosyllabic and has an initial velar stop: khlat). It has been suggested to me by Egerod that this is actually a reduplicated derivative from the word lat 'to lick'; the expected form would then be *lɯt.lat or *lrt.lat. It seems very plausible that the phonetic form which we hear is a reduced reflex of one of these alternatives.

Finally, there are a couple of forms with /r/ before a labial stop, namely a word for an insect species which in casual speech sounds like [rphɛp] and the word for 'to wash' which in casual speech sounds rather like [rpaːʔ], with a short syllabic /r/ in both cases. Careful listening has revealed that the first syllable is closed, however. In distinct speech it also contains a full vowel in harmony with the vowel of the next syllable (as in reduplicatives, cf. 4.1.3 below): rip.hɛp, rɯp.paaʔ. As plausible phonemicizations of the reduced pronunciations I therefore posit rp.hɛp and rp.paaʔ (i.e. the same structural type as rt.lat).

The combination /hr-/ is recorded only as a minor syllable, not as a main syllable onset. It is possible that this is a flaw of the data, but the same restriction seems to exist in α-Mlabri.

Final Consonants:

Stops: /p t c k/

Nasals: /m n ɲ ŋ/

Oral Continuants:
With final Aspiration: /lh rh jh/
Fully Voiced: /w l r j/

Laryngeals:
Stop: /ʔ/
Aspirate: /h/

There is (as in other Mon-Khmer languages) only one series of stops in final position. These are basically voiceless and become voiced only when in close contact with a following syllable-initial voiced stop (voicing assimilation).

The continuants /lh rh jh/ occur only syllable-finally. The former two are pronounced with a slight devoicing or aspiration at the end; in running speech they are often difficult to distinguish from plain /l r/. The third entity, /jh/, is voiceless and often strident: with alveolopalatal rather than palatal articulation. The entity /lh/ reflects a Mon-Khmer sibilant; the etymological relationship between this entity and /jh/ is interesting in a comparative perspective. The aspirated trill, /rh/, has not yet been shown to exist in α-Mlabri, and it was only recently that I noticed its presence in β-Mlabri in the forms bɯrhralh 'heavy' (with syllable-division /rh.r/) and chɯrhkalh 'the quills of a porcupine' (both words have been carefully rechecked with a good speaker which left no doubt about the presence of /rh/ rather than /r/). It may be that a careful rechecking of suspicious wordforms would reveal more occurrences of this evasive aspirate.

Syllables may end in one of the consonants above or in zero (open syllables). As a sandhi phenomenon in rapid speech, a syllable-final laryngeal tends to vanish before a syllable-initial stop in the same stress-group; in β-Mlabri I have noticed this especially with /h/, ʔoh bɔŋ 'I eat', ʔɤh gɛɛŋ 'build a house' becoming [ʔobɔŋ], [ʔɤgɛːŋ], etc. – This and most other low-level sandhi phenomena have been disregarded in the presentation of transcribed data below because a normalization in the direction of highly distinct pronunciation seemed most informative for comparative and other purposes (a detailed phonetic account of sandhi and other phenomena in Mlabri falls outside the framework of this monograph).

Phonemic consonant clusters do not exist in syllable-final position; /lh rh jh/ count as one segment each. Phonetically, however, I have occasionally heard a stop before a final nasal in very emphatic speech, e.g. on the final predicate ʔa noɲ 'completely' in a statement such as ʔat tiʔ tak jʌk wʌl jʌk ʔbɔɔk maʔ ʔoh ʔa noɲ 'the elders told me just *everything*' (i.e. all about the old traditions). Under strong emphasis, the last syllable noɲ 'exhaustive' may be pronounced [nocːɲ] with a voiceless oral stop followed by a homorganic nasal (although the most frequent emphatic manifestation is [noɲː] with lengthening of the sonorant).

3.2 Prosody

There is practically no information on prosody in earlier papers on α-Mlabri phonology. The remarks below apply to β-Mlabri only although some of the features mentioned are also found in α-Mlabri; in other respects the two varieties differ.

Syllable types: Mlabri has both monosyllabic and disyllabic (in a few cases even trisyllabic) words. The word stress is always on the last syllable, and this is the only syllable which can have a long vowel (except for a few reduplicative compounds and other compound words which exhibit long vowels in non-final syllables). Both the final, stress-bearing syllable and the pretonic (pre-stress) syllables (if there are any) may be open or closed. The maximal syllable structure is CCCVVC, and the minimal structure is CV in pretonic full syllables, CVV or CVC in word final syllables.

Like other languages of the area Mlabri also exhibits the special structural type which (with a term coined by J. A. Matisoff) is often referred to as "sesquisyllabic": a word with a full syllable preceded by something which counts as a syllable without having a full vowel. In Southeast Asian linguistics such pretonic syllabic units are generally called *Minor Syllables* (or *Presyllables*; I prefer the former term since the latter causes ambiguity if it is understood as referring to pretonic syllables in general, including those with a full vowel). With the apparent exception of a few forms with initial /r/ (see above) minor syllables in β-Mlabri contain at least two consonant phonemes of which the second is syllabic.

Vowel quantity: Vowel length is phonemic in closed syllables in β-Mlabri (and in very conservative α-Mlabri speech; this was not clear at the time when Egerod and Rischel (1987) was published, but quantity distinctions will be made in a new edition of the α-Mlabri vocabulary). There are several minimal pairs, but vowel durations are very variable and the phonemic status of a vowel as long or short is not always easy to establish, particularly before /-ʔ/. However, there are minimal pairs with final /-ʔ/: choʔ 'ache' vs. chooʔ 'spade', ʔbuʔ 'slowly' vs. ʔbuuʔ 'close by'.

Open final syllables have a phonetically long vowel which, however, is often shortened if the word occurs in non-final position in a stress-group (see below). Pretonic open syllables have a phonetically short vowel (unless the word is spoken over-distinctly).

Impressionistically, phrases form stress-groups with final stress, and *there is a general tendency for long vowels to be shortened in non-final syllables* within such a stress-group. As mentioned above, some shortened long vowels (/a(a)/ and /e(e)/) may remain qualitatively distinct from true short vowels. The pattern seems to be in a flux, however. All of this presents severe problems both for the phonological analysis of the vowel system and for the consistent transcription of phrasal material (cf. also 6.3 below on phonological variation).

Stress and tone: As stated earlier, Mlabri is not a tonal language nor a register language. There are audible differences in stress (cued by pitch, duration and intensity) between consecutive syllables, but as expected of a Mon-Khmer language, there is no phonemic word stress. The predominant rhythm is iambic: the main prominence is on the last syllable of the word.

Some words, however, are (or may be) spoken with high pitch and prominence on two consecutive syllables, e.g. gɯncaj 'blanket'. The occurrence of this phenomenon in my data may in some instances be due to the elicitation technique (words which I know only from word-by-word elicitation may have been spoken in a kind of dictation style), but there are instances in which this prosodic pattern is always used (by different speakers) when the word is spoken in isolation. I have, therefore, chosen to mark this phenomenon even though its status is unclear (in some cases it may reflect the origin of the wordform as a *compound*). – Søren Egerod and I have noted a similar pattern in α-Mlabri (although this finding is so far unpublished).

In the dictionary entries below, words of this category are marked (arbitrarily) with a *hyphen* after the non-final syllable with high pitch. Otherwise, there is no marking of tone or stress in the notations.

There are certain categories of Mlabri words which tend to be spoken with *expressive* prosody. As in Northern Thai and other languages of the area, high pitch is often used to cue such meanings as 'very, very far away', e.g. on the second syllable of təkʌh 'over/up there, far away'. A related but different type of expressive prosody is the use of excessive lengthening and high-pitched, almost whining voice to signal remoteness in time, as in the second word of tak ʔɤ-hɤɤj 'long since' (this word is in itself an exclamatory particle).

Altogether, however, the pitch movements and vowel lengthening phenomena in β-Mlabri speech are relatively moderate compared to the extreme pitch excursions and final lengthenings which several sources mention as characteristic of α-Mlabri (cf. Egerod and Rischel 1987, p. 36 and 42). This difference in prosodic characteristics is superficially the most noticeable difference between α-Mlabri and β-Mlabri speech.

Words go together rhythmically to form stress-groups with stress on the (final syllable of the) last word. Such unit accentuation of stress-groups (or phonological phrases; I do not know whether a distinction should be made between two such units) serves to cue the syntactic and semantic constituency of clauses.

This iambic pattern occurs in most cases. Directional verbs which occur *after* the main verb, however, may be less prominent than that verb. For example, the phrase rɛɛʔ ɟak 'to move away' + 'to move', i.e. 'to be off, to disappear' may be spoken with lower pitch and less prominence on the last word.

3.3 The Phonology of Sentence Types

The relationship between intonations and sentence types in β-Mlabri has not been systematically investigated; this requires in-depth analysis of the semantic and pragmatic structure and ideally also acoustic-phonetic measurements. The speech material in my possession is quite heterogeneous, however, and it is difficult to apply quantitative, instrumental methods to such material. It may also be linguistically premature to attempt to do so.

In communicative situations or when eliciting sentence-examples, I have observed some apparent regularities. These are all non-systematic and purely impressionistic observations, and they are given here only in order to illustrate what kinds of sentence prosody seem typical of this language:

– (1) In *ordinary statements* the unmarked intonation is somewhat falling at the end (but much less so than in α-Mlabri).

– (2) *Lexically and grammatically unmarked questions* seem to be (always?) said with relatively high-pitched and non-falling intonation. I suppose *facial expression* should also be included in a description of how interrogative meaning is signalled.

– (3) It is still unclear to me what the pattern of intonation in *lexically/grammatically marked questions* is, i.e. questions containing an interrogative pronoun or adverb and questions formed with the final interrogative particle lɛh. The only safe generalization which I can make is that questions ending in lɛh are said with a drop in pitch from the preceding word to this extra-clausal final particle (Søren Egerod and I have also observed this in α-Mlabri).

– (4) *Strongly affirmative answers* which express consent and positive attitude by echoing the main verb of the question are marked intonationally by rising intonation on that word (this prosodic contour is different from that of α-Mlabri). – Sentence-types (3) + (4) can be illustrated by the following exchange of question+answer: mɛh ˆtoc `lɛh – ˇtoc 'Do you want it?' – 'Yes!' (the tonal accent marks give a crude impression of the intonation movements but are of course not to be read as tonemic symbols).

– (5) *Commands or requests* are (at least in some cases) spoken rather rapidly and on a high pitch all the way through the utterance. This may be the only phonetic indication of the status of the utterance as a command. The following two examples illustrate commands said in this fashion: chapat ʔot chjʌɲ 'swat my mosquito (i.e. the one on my back)!', toc kɛp ɲʌʔ prgʌɲ tɔʔ 'take that stone and sharpen the knife!'. – I do not know in what ways (and to what extent) such commands are phonetically or gesturally distinguished from questions of type (2) above.

– (6) *Extra-clausal exclamatory particles* are (otherwise) said in a high pitch; unlike commands, some of these may have excessive vowel lengthening. There are several such particles. Some consist of initial /ʔ/ plus a long or overlong vowel: ʔii, ʔee, ʔɛɛ or ʔɛɛɛ, ʔaa, ʔoo. Others consist of a short vowel + /h/: ʔɯh, ʔɤh, ʔʌh. There is the apparent generalization that the latter series is made up of the three unrounded back vowels /ɯ ɤ ʌ/ whereas the former series comprises most of the remaining vowels; I do not know why this is so. The phonological string ʔɤh also occurs as the first part of various more complex, bisyllabic particles. These (and other) particles seem to convey more or less distinct meanings: expressing surprise or disgust, calling out to somebody etc. (for more detail, see the individual entries in the dictionary and the heading "exclamatory particles" in the index).

There are at least two additional exclamatory particles, both consisting of an overlong nasal: mmm. With strongly falling final intonation this segmental "murmur" may have a confirmatory meaning, whereas it is a spontaneous expression of delight if said on a higher and only slightly falling pitch and perhaps with more excessive lengthening. This is more or less what we may find in other languages as well.

Chapter 4
The Mlabri Word

The *word* is the basic unit in grammatical description. Near-isolating languages like Mlabri do not, on the whole, present severe problems to do with the identification of words and the segmentation of a linguistic string into words, although there are analytical decisions to be made especially with respect to cliticization and compounding (the guidelines followed in this monograph are briefly mentioned in section 6.4 below).

The question of *word-classes* is of course of paramount importance for any treatment of syntax. The problems involved in defining word-classes in Mlabri, however, are hardly essentially different from those encountered in the analysis of other languages of Indochina: the question whether verbs can be effectively distinguished from nouns on syntactic grounds (verbs can be negated, for example), the question how to categorize expressive lexemes of various kinds and so on. These are rather formidable theoretical issues but they are shared with a host of typologically similar languages. I have, therefore, chosen to say very little about these issues in the present monograph, the tacit assumption being that there is a certain consensus on the meaning of such terms as "Noun", "Verb" and "Adverb". Unless otherwise stated, the general understanding of such terms should be used as the "default" interpretation of my terminology (see further 6.5 below).

The present chapter approaches the word in β-Mlabri from two different perspectives: (1) word formation and inflection, i.e. morphology in a broad sense and (2) the semantics of words, with particular reference to the existence of more or less close-knit semantic fields.

4.1 Morphology

Although Mlabri is a predominantly isolating language like other contemporary Mon-Khmer languages it has a rich and in part transparent morphology. These features may give the language an "archaic" flavour and they contribute in some cases to mark a difference between nouns and verbs.

As for word formation mechanisms, one encounters infixation, apparent or real prefixation, reduplication, and apparent or real compounding. Infixation, prefixation and reduplication occur as more or less transparent phenomena in many Mon-Khmer languages. Some of these have a variety of different word formation devices which make for a very complex morphology (whereas others only have traces of fossilized morphology). It may be quite complicated to account for causative formation or nominalization of verbs, for example, if there are several different affixes with related meanings and functions, and not just one causative prefix (with or without allomorphs), one nominalization infix etc. Similarly, it is complicated to account for reduplication in Mon-Khmer languages since there is not just one invariant phonological mechanism. There occur several different patterns, and these different patterns have different implications with respect to the type (and degreee) of phonological similarity between the two syllables of a reduplicative wordform.

Mlabri, I think, is remarkable in that it has both a rather rich morphology (for a language of this type) and a very simple and regular morphology. It seems that there has been a strong tendency in this language to have only one affix for each function and meaning (e.g. one causative prefix). Such an affix then appears as phonologically invariant or (especially if it is the historical reflex of a merger of different affixes) with a simple and regular pattern of variation (allomorphy).

4.1.1 Infixation

Infixation, in the form of insertion of one or more consonants after the stem-initial consonant, occurs on many verb stems. The material inserted varies but is sonorant and comprises at least one tongue-tip consonant (in the instances over which I have been able to make generalizations): /rn/, /r/, /mn/ or /n/. This is a genuine typological characteristic of Mon-Khmer and more generally of Austroasiatic languages, the pattern of infixation found in Mlabri being almost prototypical. In several wordforms it undoubtedly reflects very ancient word formation, but there is often a rather transparent relationship between wordforms with and without infixation so that one might consider recognizing infixation as part of synchronic Mlabri grammar (I do not know whether it is really productive, however).

Like Kmhmu, Mlabri is notable for its transparency of infixation (cf. Ferlus 1977 on the weak traces of the instrumental infix *rn in Vietnamese compared to its transparent representation in Kmhmu). Otherwise, the pattern of infixation is very different between the two languages. In this section I shall deal only with liquid/nasal infixation in Mlabri. This, however, does not exhaust all possible occurrences of historical infixation.

There are some near-synonymous verbs which are suggestive of infixal -ra-: bnliiŋ – braliiŋ 'green', brulh – brarulh 'recede' (kralip.. 'close (the door)' may also be a -ra- formation, though *kralap.. would be a more expected form, cf. knlap.. 'door'). There also also traces of a -p- infix: gwɛɛc 'poke' – gipwɛɛc 'scratch softly'. It affects the pattern of infixation that Mlabri contains words for implements borrowed from languages such as Tin; etymologically, such words often have infixes.

In the following, infixation will be discussed from the *synchronic* point of view although some of the most transparent forms may be very old formations going back to Proto-Mon-Khmer. A case in point is chrɛɛt 'to comb (hair)' – chnrɛɛt 'a comb'.

The Mlabri forms chrɛɛt, chnrɛɛt look like continuations of Proto-Mon-Khmer *craas, *cnraas although they are not direct continuations: their unexpected phonology suggests that this pair of wordforms entered Mlabri as a result of the borrowing of "culture words" from a Khmuic language with secondary aspiration of voiceless initials and with */-s/ > /-t/ (both developments are found in Tin Prai, although there are other complications with this very etymon in Prai). In spite of the complex history and considerable age of the derivational relationship between chrɛɛt and chnrɛɛt, however, this derivation is as transparent in modern Mlabri as any such relationship can possibly be.

The most frequent function of infixation (if at all transparent) is to form deverbal, particularly abstract nouns, e.g. gɯh 'to be ablaze' – grnɯh 'flames', gla? 'to speak' – grla? 'speech, words', kap 'to sing' – krnap 'singing, song', kwɛl 'to be rolled up (said of a snake)' – krwɛl 'spiral', pluut 'to peel' – prluut 'layer'. Infixation creates an expletive adverbial derivation in ɟuur 'to descend' – ɟuur ɟmnuur 'to go downhill'.

There is also ample evidence of infixation used to form instrument nouns: klaap 'to hold something by squeezing it' – krlaap 'forceps of split bamboo', peelh 'to sweep the ground/floor' – prneelh 'a broom', tɛk 'to hit' – trnɛk 'a hammer' (also cf. the example chrɛɛt 'to comb' – chnrɛɛt 'a comb' above). The relationship is, however, sometimes less obvious, cf. gwɛɛc 'to poke' – grwɛɛc 'finger'.

In some instances infixation just creates near-synonyms with no difference in word-class membership, cf. bliiŋ – bnliiŋ, both meaning more or less the same: 'raw, unripe, green (etc.)'.

A wordform may qualify formally and semantically as an instance of infixation although the hypothetical source verb has not been identified. Sometimes this is indirectly confirmed, at other times not. I wish to give an illustrative example of the former. On one occasion I produced a small nail cutter and was immediately told that such an implement has a name in β-Mlabri: krliip. Because we were talking about an instrument, and the word sounded like a form containing an infixal element, I guessed that krliip must be a nominalization of a verb *kliip. I failed to look further into the matter, however, and thus did not track that verb down.

Afterwards, in the α-Mlabri data, I found what is obviously the source verb: klip (recorded in that language variety with a short vowel). The tricky thing is the semantics of this verb. On hearing the word krliip I had immediately associated it with the notion of 'cutting', because I thought of nail cutters as something in the category of knives and scissors (in Mlabri there are different words for cutting depending on whether one cuts by chopping or by sliding a knife back and forth and so on). The α-Mlabri word klip does not, however, encode that notion; I have recorded it in a context where it clearly meant (and was explained to me as meaning) 'to hurt one's finger by its being squeezed between two sharp edges'. This is certainly what the nail cutter does to the nail. The identification of this verb as the true source of 'nail cutter' is corroborated if one considers that the word-pair kli(i)p - krliip stands in an ablaut relationship to the word pair klaap – krlaap (which occurs in both varieties of Mlabri). The nominalization with /aa/ denotes a fairly large forceps, i.e. the "krliip" is simply a small-size "krlaap", in beautiful accordance with general sound-symbolic principles.

Now to the strictly morphological and phonological aspects of infixation in Mlabri. As seen from the examples above, infixation consists in adding a sonorant cluster (either /rn/ or /mn/) or a single consonant (/r/ or /n/) just after the initial consonant of the underlying stem. If the underived stem has a single initial consonant, the infix consists of two consonants: /rn/ or /mn/. If the underived stem has an initial cluster, the infix consists of only a single consonant inserted between the two consonants of the stem onset. The underived stem of the latter type must of course be in accordance with the general well-formedness constraints in Mlabri phonology, i.e. if the subtraction of apparently infixal material /n, r, rn, mn/ would yield a stem with an impermissible onset cluster (such as clusters with an aspirated or glottalized consonant as the first member or with an aspirated sonorant in either position), it does not make sense to search for a stem underlying infixation in Mlabri. If such a wordform is morphologically complex, it is rather a matter of *prefixation not infixation*.

In all instances of infixation the resulting form begins with three consonants in a row. Such syllable-initial structures are impermissible and thus require restructuring of the wordform in terms of a bisyllabic structure. This happens irrespective of the origin of the second and the third consonant of the cluster. The third consonant always ends up as the onset of the resulting main syllable, whereas the first two consonants generally go together to form a pretonic "minor syllable" and thus come to look like a kind of prefix, e.g. /bn/ in bnliiŋ (i.e. bn.liiŋ if the syllable boundary is indicated for clarity). Idiolectally, the minor syllable may be inforced by insertion of a parasitic vowel between the two consonants (girwɛɛc = grwɛɛc, etc.) which makes the mechanism of consonant infixation somewhat less transparent.

If one looks at the phonological shape of the infix material, it is off-hand tempting to regard -rn- and -r- as variants, and similarly to regard -mn- and -n- as variants; moreover, -n- might be a variant of -rn- as well. The mechanical choice between infixal CC and C, together with the lack of any consistent difference in meaning between the four kinds of infixal material, suggests that these may all be allomorphs of one infix morpheme in contemporary Mlabri. This synchronic hypothesis is corroborated by the finding that there are no instances of alternative infixal forms (at least that I know of) except klaap 'squeeze' - krlaap 'forceps' vs. the semantically remote knlap (hntor/hook) 'door'.

It must be emphasized, however, that this is a synchronic phenomenon; the diachronic scenario may be different. Comparative evidence suggests that the various infixal consonants and consonant clusters now occurring in Mlabri may have different origins (-mn-, for example, is a typical feature of Khmer but unknown in some other branches of Mon-Khmer) and that they may even reflect several distinct infixes in early Mon-Khmer.

Phonological generalizations about infixation:

Assuming that the choice between infixation of a cluster and infixation of a single consonant has to do with the structure of the underlying verb (CC-infixation after a single onset consonant, C-infixation into an onset cluster) the next question is whether there is some phonological regularity accounting for the remaining variation, i.e. on the one hand -rn- versus -mn-, and on the other hand -r- versus -n-. When considered jointly, these alternatives may be reduced to a choice between affix forms containing /r/ (i.e. -r- or -rn-) and affix forms which are purely nasal and contain no /r/ (i.e. -n- or -mn-). The conditioning factor, if any, must be sought in the relationship between infix and remainder of the wordform; there is no evidence from the data above that the quality of the stem initial consonant plays any conditioning role in contemporary Mlabri infixation.

In Mlabri infixes containing /r/ are much more frequent than the other possibilities (although *-mn- is otherwise frequent in Mon-Khmer).

This suggests that infixation involving /r/ nowadays represents the "default" choice in forming transparent derivations by infixation, i.e. that it is the occurrence of purely nasal infixes that requires special explanation (although one must of course expect a residue of old forms which cannot be explained synchronically). It seems as if the deviations from default infixation are in fact not random but reflect two different tendencies:

– (1) There seems to be a strict constraint against deriving forms in which /r/ occurs twice as a result of infixation. In the selection of ɟmnuur (rather than *ɟrnuur) the choice of infix according to this constraint may be called *dissimilatory* (since the constraint operates between occurrences of /r/ in different syllables); in cases such as chnrɛɛt (rather than *chrrɛɛt) the choice of infix implies the local form of dissimilation, i.e. *differentiation* (it eliminates the clash between two adjacent occurrences of /r/). A dissimilatory behaviour of sequences of liquids has also been observed for Kmhmu, although the allomorphy of infixes behaves somewhat differently in that language (see Svantesson 1983, p. 30 and 97).

Some examples were given above of wordforms which look like instances of infixation with -r-, although they are not really derived by infixation, or at least the source verb has not been identified. There are likewise some occurrences of nouns with internal /n/ plus consonant which look like infixal forms without being derivable from verb stems which actually occur in Mlabri: gnrɛɛ 'curry', hnrɤɤʔ 'girl (of a certain age)', ɟnraaʔ 'liquor'. If we disregard the history of these forms (which can be traced for gnrɛɛ, for example), we may note that they are all in agreement with the avoidance of */rr/, which seems to be a phonological well-formedness constraint operating in various languages of the area.

– (2) It is possible that there is a tendency toward nasal harmony in word formation: a tendency for forms which contain nasals to maximize the number of nasals when the structure is augmented by infixation. This would account for a remaining deviation from the default choices, as in bnliiŋ (rather than *brliiŋ). Although one instance is too meagre evidence, there is an additional form in α-Mlabri which would be explained by the same tendency: tmnʌɲ 'speech, words' (rather than *trnʌɲ) from tʌɲ 'to speak'.

Word internal /mn/ is strongly suggestive of infixation either in a prestage to Mlabri (which at least in some cases is Proto-Mon-Khmer) or perhaps in other cases within Mlabri itself or in a Mon-Khmer language from which the word has been borrowed. This does not mean that *all* such forms can or should be accounted for as (synchronically) infixal.

Prefixation to stems with onset /n/ is another possibility. There is in fact a residue of at least two β-Mlabri wordforms with internal /mn/ which cannot be associated with any underived stems in Mlabri; both have a velar onset: gɯmnaat 'belt', ʔɛɛw kɯmnah 'somebody else's daughter'. It is a shared characteristic of these residual forms that if they were due to infixation, the occurrence of -mn- (rather than -rn-) would not be explained by the regularities (1)-(2) suggested above. (There is an additional wordform of the same consonantal make-up, which is a variant pronunciation of the term for 'pineapple': pleʔ ganat, pleʔ gmnat; here the labial nasal is probably due to contamination with the word for 'pineapple' in the variety of Thai spoken by the Mlabri: mak nat).

The dissimilatory and harmonizing tendencies posited are probably relatively recent regularities which occur on top of an earlier, more complex pattern of infixation. For example, the occurrence of a *bilabial* nasal in the infix -mn- must be given a special explanation. As mentioned earlier, the historical origin of the present pattern of allomorphy may be complex. The essential thing about the emergence of a secondary pattern of allomorphy is that Mlabri has somehow developed a set of *morphophonemic preferences* which influences the output of the mechanism of infixation (seen as a choice among different options). The apparent existence of dissimilatory and consonant-harmonizing factors is interesting, both because these are not among the most frequent regularities in languages and because there are no similarly strict constraints on what is a possible phonological wordform.

4.1.2 Prefixation.

The Mlabri lexicon is characterized by a richness of pretonic, reduced syllables (or minor syllables), but only a few of these are prefixes. Some pretonic syllables are due to vowel epenthesis in initial consonant clusters which are "not permitted" in Mlabri, e.g. dəkat 'to be cold' (*/dk-/) and thaŋaap 'yawn' (*/thŋ-/ < */sŋ-/). Other pretonic syllables have arisen by infixation (see above) or reduplication (see below); still others are the reduced reflexes of words which occur in compounds.

Several of the bisyllabic or sesquisyllabic words in Mlabri look structurally as if they are the historical reflexes of prefixation to stems, although there is in most cases no support elsewhere in the lexicon for the existence of such prefixes in the language. In fact, even words of which no part has any obvious etymology in Mlabri may historically contain prefixes (which may in turn be the reflexes of cliticization of particles). This is true of some deictic and descriptive adverbials of space and time, e.g. təkʌh 'over there, far away' and ladooŋ 'high up'. – The expressions tak kun tak kwaan and tak kun tak naaj , both referring to phenomena of the remote past, are mostly spoken with retraction of /k+k/ into one consonant: takun and takwaan, as if they contain a prefix ta-, but I have transcribed tak everywhere.

There is only one instance of entirely transparent (overt) prefixation in Mlabri: *causative formation. This process involves the transitivization of verbs by means of the productive prefix* pa- or ba-, as in bɯl 'die' – pabɯl 'kill', kɯm 'throw' – bakɯm 'throw away; discard'. This is, on the other hand, a morphological formation which is interesting for several reasons: (i) it is a widespread, archaic feature of Mon-Khmer; (ii) its morphological transparency is preserved unusually well in Mlabri (in many other languages it is more or less fused with the following stem-initial consonant, cf. Tin pɤl 'die' – mbɤl or mpɤl 'kill'); (iii) it occurs with several verb stems across the lexicon (to the point of looking like a truly *productive* formation in Mlabri); (iv) the alternation between two allomorphs is typologically remarkable.

By inspecting the examples of words with pa- and ba- in the dictionary below one sees that the distribution of these two prefix forms is not at all random. It is regular according to a remarkable allomorphic principle: the former occurs before stem-initial voiced consonants, the latter before voiceless consonants. There is apparently *voicing dissimilation* between the initial consonant of the prefix and that of the stem. This regularity was not obvious when we wrote about α-Mlabri although we listed some entries with pa- others with ba- (Egerod and Rischel 1987). The presence of such dissimilation between syllable onsets is interesting also because there is no general constraint in Mlabri phonology against identical onsets in consecutive syllables; on the contrary, the latter pattern is a regular feature of *reduplication* (see 4.1.3 below). As a matter of fact, there are some apparent or real counter-examples to the dissimilatory principle (see below), but the overwhelming number of forms are in accordance with it, and they suggest that there is a genuine and strong tendency to dissimilate the syllable-initial consonants in causative formations, whatever the origin of this phenomenon. - The forms paʔem 'to make (somebody) sleep' (ʔem 'to sleep') and paʔɯm 'to bathe (somebody)' (ʔɯm 'to bathe'), both with causative /pa/ before the laryngeal /ʔ/, suggest that this onset does not pattern with voiceless oral stops (but rather belongs with /ʔb/ etc.) and that the generalization about dissimilation should be formulated accordingly.

Because of the particular status of the alleged dissimilation principle I wish to present and discuss all the evidence that may seem to speak against it. This is motivated also by an observation to be made below: that some apparent exceptions may not be causative formations at all but contain a different type of material although they are morphologically important in their own right.

The form baɟah 'wash' with voiced onset + voiced onset looks like an exception to the prevailing dissimation in causatives, but it may not be a morphological causative (at least from a synchronic point of view) since no verb *ɟah has been recorded in Mlabri. It is different with the form which is phonetically [pakʌlh] 'to hit and inadvertently break', i.e. with voiceless onset + voiceless onset; it contains a verb kʌlh and is thus a genuine exception to dissimilation in causatives if in fact its initial morpheme is the causative prefix. Similarly with [patɯklʌk] 'to tickle' and a few other such forms.

What is phonetically a pretonic syllable [pa-] on Mlabri verb stems does not necessarily convey a causative meaning, however. The phonetic form [paluh] 'to abuse' contains a stem luh which according to my (admittedly very limited) data denotes the activity of scolding, not the resulting state of the culprit, i.e. the augmented form does not seem to differ in transitivity from the minimum verb form. Although [paluh] is phonetically one word, its initial part may be a shortened, proclitic version of a (poorly attested) preverb paa, since I have sometimes heard a rather long vowel in this syllable in a very slow and distinct speech, e.g. in the phrase [paː luh paː phit] 'to abuse' (a parallel construction with two synonymous verbs luh and phit of which the second is a borrowed verb meaning 'to quarrel' in Northern Thai).

There are a few additional verb forms which are suggestive of such a preverb paa since I have heard them with a fairly long vowel in the first syllable: beside paa tɯklʌk 'to tickle' there is, for example, paa cɯpcaap 'to chirp, to twitter'. It is my assumption that the preverb adds the meaning of 'motion' or 'agitation' to that of the main verb (in paa cɯpcaap it may refer to the bird's movements of beak and neck, and in paa luh it may add a component of violence to the scolding). – The form paaʔ ʔbom or paa ʔbom (it is uncertain what is the adequate representation), which denotes the act of brooding or hatching, may belong here as well; the speaker who explained its use to me, imitated the characteristic movements of the sitting hen.

Both from a phonetic and a morphological point of view, however, the combinations with the assumed preverb paa almost have the status of single words. Some of the main verbs in question are known to me only in combination with the preverb, which is phonetically cliticized and has vowel shortening except in extremely distinct speech. Such cliticization of paa may be the explanation of [pakʌlh], as well; I have heard a rather long vowel in the first syllable when my Mlabri consultant spoke in dictation style to me.

It remains an open question how to interpret such forms. I cannot even rule out the possibility that the optional length of /pa(a)/ in some (all?) of these words is spurious and just reflects an over-distinct pronunciation which the particular speaker sometimes chose when I asked him to repeat words. Thus it must be admitted that my tentative distinction between paa and the causative prefix rests on quite shaky evidence. (The dictionary of this monograph contains a verb pair pablah, paa blah with different glosses: 'to push' and 'to move in different directions'; that, however, may be a spurious distinction, a flaw in my raw data.)

4.1.3 Reduplication.

Reduplication, with or without vowel alternation between the reduplicating and the reduplicated syllable, is a very frequent phenomenon in Mlabri words. It is a word formation device, but words with reduplication are in most cases *not* synchronically derivable from simple stems.

In Mon-Khmer languages it is expected that reduplication may occur as a morphological device in the so-called *Expressives*, i.e. expressive words which (i) accompany ordinary clause-type predications without being syntactically integrated into the clause structure and which moreover (ii) may have a characteristic phonetic structure giving associations about the action that is being talked about (*flop* in English is such an expressive word). Mlabri has several examples of this kind, e.g. words which express repeated involuntary action. The words butbot and thʌkthɤɤk, which express the meanings of 'trembling' and 'having palpitations', respectively, occur with an intensifying function in an elaborate expression meaning 'to be extremely frightened': klol hot butbot thʌkthɤɤk (from the basic predication klol hot 'heart fall' i.e. 'be startled'). In this example the expressive words are added after a main verb like descriptive adverbials.

In other instances there is an expressive verb before another verb. The reduplicative pjɯrpjɯɯr expresses the meaning of 'open one's eyes widely'; it combines with dɤŋ 'to look (at)' to express that somebody is gazing and staring: pjɯrpjɯɯr dɤŋ.

It is, however, for the moment unclear to me how to delimit "Expressives" as a separate word-class in Mlabri, since some of these words behave much like ordinary verbs (occurring with an immediately following verb of motion), and others seem to behave like adverbials. In any case, it is with reduplication in Mlabri as in other languages of Indochina: the phenomenon is not restricted to specifically expressive words. In Mlabri it even occurs on nouns denoting ordinary physical objects (see examples below).

It is indisputable that reduplication often has a symbolic value. The most obvious expressive function is direct sound symbolism, as in the names of objects which emit repetitive sounds, e.g. muŋmooŋ 'gong'. Reduplication also occurs in verbs which denote repeated or continued action: dumduum 'to rock a child in one's arms'. It may be meaningful to speak of the same encoding of meaning by reduplication in verbs or expressives which denote postures, e.g. those which denote a person's way of directing his gaze, cf. pjɯrpjɯɯr, dɤŋdɤŋ 'to stare', dɤwdɤw 'to look upwards'. On the other hand, it is difficult to see what is the symbolic value of reduplication in stative verbs such as klɯhkleh '(to be) shallow'. It is possible to come up with various (more or less plausible) suggestions, e.g. that reduplication serves to signal that the quality denoted by the underlying verb is present in a moderate degree or is present over a great expanse. Unless the unreduplicated verb stem exists beside the reduplicated one, so that their meanings can be directly compared, however, such interpretations are likely to remain pure guesswork.

From the point of view of morphology, reduplication is a conspicuous feature which suggests that the word is a derived form.

Most such wordforms in Mlabri seem *completely lexicalized*, however, and many of them may be *very old fossils in the language*. There is most often no corresponding non-reduplicated word stem in (modern) Mlabri, and if there is such a stem, the identification may be semantically far-fetched and perhaps spurious (cf. klɯhkleh above versus kleh 'hard, loud').

Altogether, it is often impossible to associate special semantic features with phonologically reduplicative structure. This is true in particular of wordforms in which the first syllable is phonologically reduced; only occasionally can the underlying stem be retrieved, and even when there is a convincing etymology within Mlabri, the semantic relationship may be unclear, cf. kɯtkeet 'spout (e.g. of a kettle)' versus its etymological base keet 'ear'.

To return to the question of reduplication in particular subsections of the lexicon, it is well-known that there is something special about the naming of animals or birds and that this is an area where one may expect sound-symbolism. Reduplication is in fact used in some such names in Mlabri, e.g. micmɛɛc 'ant' (which is prototypical according to the general behaviour of reduplication in Mlabri but has an etymologically remarkable vowel quality /ɛɛ/ in the main syllable instead of the expected */o/).

It cannot be excluded that reduplication has a symbolic function in more sets of nouns than is immediately understandable for an outside observer. It is conspicuous, for example, that there is reduplication in the names of several *body parts* such as: kukɔʔ 'neck' (the non-reduplicated stem occurs in Monic: *kɔɔʔ, according to Diffloth 1984, p. 95), klkiil 'knee' and mujmuj 'hair' (α-Mlabri has another derivation without reduplication). There may be a very interesting explanation, but what is it?

It is noteworthy that there is reduplication in certain terms for age-and-sex categories of persons in Mlabri: β-Mlabri burbur 'young man', α-Mlabri gutgɔɔt 'young woman'. This phenomenon has a parallel in Malay (e.g. lakilaki '(young) man', as pointed out to me by S. Egerod).

The next question is how to determine in what instances it is warranted to identify a similarity across syllables as reduplication in the strict sense: as a word-formation device. Since Mon-Khmer languages are known to reduplicate word stems to a great extent, it is interesting to consider the possibility of reduplication, or at least alliteration/assonance, whenever a pretonic syllable is partially similar to the following full syllable. This is particularly motivated in the case of words whose status and meaning invite an interpretation of their sound-shape as symbolic. Some animals' and birds' names are sound-symbolic with allitteration and assonance but with different terminations in the two syllables, cf. kuukwap '(species of) frog' and pompoo 'elephant'. The echo effect and the choice of specific vowel qualities in such names undoubtedly serves an expressive purpose: in some instances it imitates the characteristic sound of the animal; in other instances it may convey an idea about size or behaviour.

Not all instances of partial similarities between the syllables of a word are so obviously motivated, however. It must also be taken into consideration that from a purely statistical point of view, some bisyllabic wordforms must be expected to look reduplicative by chance (unless there is a constraint *against* partial similarity between consecutive syllables in non-reduplicative forms).

Moreover, it is essential whether we are speaking of reduplication from a historical-comparative point of view or from a strictly synchronic point of view. It is well-known that historical phonology may wipe out the traces of old reduplication and on the other hand create pseudo-instances of reduplication. In Danish, for example, there are plenty of wordforms such as *hunhund, bebo, forføre* with phonological structures which look vaguely reduplicative although the wordforms have nothing whatsoever to do with reduplication, and on the other hand there are preterite verb forms such as *fik, hed* which were originally reduplicative although there are no obvious traces left of their earlier bisyllabic status.

For reasons such as those mentioned above, I think it is a sensible descriptive strategy to deal first and foremost with the most transparent and general repetitive patterns. This is what I shall do in the following, although the account certainly does not exhaust all descriptively relevant phenomena associated with reduplication.

It was mentioned in the introduction to this whole section on word formation and morphology that Mlabri exhibits a tendency to regularize its word-formation mechanisms. This is true also of reduplication. The predominant patterns involve (a) repetition of the consonantal parts of two consecutive syllables (i.e. both onset and coda if the stem syllable is closed) and (b) either harmony or qualitative-quantitative "ablaut" between their vocalic parts. Whenever the two syllables form one word, the first syllable is pretonic to the second and it is often reduced to a vowelless pre-syllable (a minor syllable).

Unlike infixation, reduplication in Mlabri consistently preserves the integrity of the stem syllable; there is no adjustment of syllable boundaries or simplification of consonant clusters although reduplication may create rather awkward segment sequences.

There are three regular ways in which the first syllable of reduplicatives may be realized with syllabicity (the following examples are all from β-Mlabri; also cf. the α-Mlabri material in Egerod and Rischel 1987).

– (1) The full syllable may be reduplicated in its entirety with preservation of the same vowel quality in both syllables, with or without vowel shortening in the first syllable, e.g. dɤlhdɤɤlh 'to lean back while stretching oneself'. Several of these words clearly represent a type of compounding. This pattern may be seen as something quite different from the remaining types, in which the full syllable is copied as a preceding syllable with a short high vowel or no vowel, i.e. with a qualitative and quantitative "ablaut" between the two syllables.

– (2) If the coda is a voiced sonorant this segment may become syllabic: tŋtuuŋ 'bamboo section beaten to make it resonate', klkiil 'knee'.

Under the same conditions there is often optional insertion of /r/ before the sonorant; this is possible in both of the two words given above: trŋtuuŋ, krlkiil.

– (3) The first pretonic syllable may have a short high vowel which generally exhibits harmony with the vowel in the full syllable. Vowel harmony involves both place of articulation and rounding: /i/ occurs in harmony with the series /i, e, ɛ/, /ɯ/ with the series /ɯ, ɤ, ʌ/ and /a/, and /u/ with the series /u, o, ɔ/, cf. likliik 'to be burnt', prijhprɛjh 'crisp', kɯckaac 'to scrape' and hɲuʔhɲɔʔ 'to have a wrinkled face'.

As shown by muɲmɔɲ 'to move the lips (as when suppressing a smile)', reduplication with a harmonizing vowel may occur even in instances where reduplication with a syllabic sonorant, with or without insertion of /r/, would seem structurally possible. Many forms are lexicalized with an obligatory vowel in the first syllable, e.g. muɲmɔɲ (not *m̩ɲmɔɲ), other wordforms can be heard with two or even three optional pronunciations: tŋ̍tuuŋ = tr̩ŋtuuŋ = tuŋtuuŋ.

There is a special subtype under (3) above: the sequence /wu/ regularly occurs as the harmonic copy of syllable-initial /wa/: wulwal 'hip', and the vowel /u/ alone occurs as the harmonic copy of /wʌ/ or /wa/ after a syllable-initial consonant: kujkwʌj 'to wrap', kutkwat 'to embrace'. This is true also if the vowel of the main syllable is long: kunkwaan 'to sprawl'.

The types above are all frequent. There are also cases of (apparent) reduplication in which the vowels do *not* exhibit vowel harmony, e.g. lɯkliik as a more common pronunciation of likliik above or kɯtkeet (see above) instead of expected *kitkeet. In cases such as these, where the vowel of the first syllable only differs from the expected in the dimension of front-back, it may be a matter of assimilation, cf. that the unexpected back vowel in both of the examples above is followed or preceded by a back consonant. Minor discrepancies may also be due to a tendency to generalize one particular vowel in pretonic syllables; there clearly is such a preference for the vowel /i/ in one of the idiolects which I have consulted.

There are sometimes substantial discrepancies in vowel quality, however, cf. the nonharmonic rounded back vowel in hɲuc.hɲec 'to be lying in a heap', the nonhigh vowel in thʌkthɤɤk 'to have palpitations' or the nonharmonic high vowels in the pronunciation wulwɯɯl of the word for 'hip' (otherwise wulwal; see above). It is certainly not all reduplicatives that follow the regular patterns (1)-(3). Still, these patterns are so characteristic and widespread throughout the lexicon that it makes sense to talk of them as prototypical in Mlabri.

When a lexeme consists of two identical syllables of which one reduplicates the other (with at most a difference in vowellength, i.e. type (1) above), it is often the case that the stem is also attested without reduplication in the language (either in α-Mlabri or β-Mlabri or in both), cf. *muj 'hair', which occurs with (covert) prefixation in α-Mlabri klmuuj or kulmuuj but with reduplication in β-Mlabri mujmuj.

If the stem of a reduplicative form also occurs as a word by itself, there is often vacillation between pronouncing the reduplicative as two words, as a phonological compound or with a reduced pretonic syllable. For example, it is possible to say pjɯɯr pjɯɯr, pjɯɯrpjɯɯr or pjɯrpjɯɯr in the meaning of 'to stare'.

To round off this presentation of reduplication, I wish to mention that Mlabri also exhibits *echoing with ablaut* of stressed syllables *across intervening unstressed syllables or minor syllables*. An amusing example with a strictly reduplicative pattern is betrec betrac, which in its entirety means 'to have diarrhoea', whereas I do not know that any part of this construction means anything by itself. Partial echoing with ablaut occurs across a minor syllable in tak drnaʔ drnɤɤm 'long ago'. Echoing with vowel harmony can also occur across a separate grammatical word or prefix; if one removes the intervening material this may reduce to prototypical reduplication, as in the expression tak kun tak kwaan 'long ago', in rapid speech [takun takwaːn] (which is explained by the Mlabri as "Northern Thai təkɔɔn nii" and which has a conspicuous similarity with that very expression).

It is remarkable that when expressions are thus elaborated, *it is the second, not the first, part of this construction that is independently meaningful in Mlabri:* tak refers to something as belonging to the past, and kwaan means 'large' (I do not know that kun means anything by itself).

Such distant reduplication is, however, a very unfrequent type of word formation in Mlabri. – "Elaborate expressions" with partial phonological similarity, as exemplified by tak kun tak kwaan, seem on the whole rare (as against their proliferation in Thai), whereas one frequently encounters pairs of phonologically unrelated but synonymous verbs or nouns in ritual language.

4.1.4 Compounding

Compounding cannot be distinguished rigidly from phrase formation on the basis of present insights, at least not if the constituent single words have preserved their phonological shape and their meaning.

There are instances where two lexemes seem to have been amalgamated into one whole with phonological modification of one or the other component (or both), e.g. kɯrmɯt 'thunderstorm', which is undoubtedly derived from kɯr 'thunder' and rəmɯt 'wind'. Such forms may be historically compounds but now look superficially like instances of overt or covert prefixation.

As for synchronically transparent constructions, my main principle has been to analyse concatenated lexemes as phrases rather than compound words (unless the analysis seems awkward for one reason or another, cf. below). Apart from the overwhelming occurrence of nuclear constructions there is in Mlabri (as in other languages of the area) a coordinate noun construction: mɤʔ mɤm 'mother (and) father'. One could argue that these forms could be either compounds or phrases; in the present work such coordinate constructions are written as sequences of separate words.

On the other hand, even if a complex form consists of fully recognizable and phonologically autonomous lexemes its syntactic function or its semantics may certainly motivate treating it as one rather than two words. In light of the scarcity of information on the language, it is difficult to make decisions of this kind.

4.1.5 Inflection

Inflection as a morphological device which is used in order to express syntactic relationships is not expected in a language of this area. Mlabri can indeed be described as a language without inflection, which is the assumption in this monograph. There are, however, at least two different grammatical phenomena which might be construed to represent inflection. One is the occurrence of a perfective marker ʔa (see on Syntax below); in Egerod and Rischel (1987) this morpheme was written as a prefix on verb stems but it is here taken to be a separate word. The other inflection-like phenomenon is the occurrence of two fossilized forms: ʔot 'my' and mɛt 'thy' which are probably formed from ʔoh 'I' and mɛh 'you (sg.)' by suffixation of a dental stop (see section 5.1.1 below on di in noun phrases).

4.2 Word Semantics

From the point of view of word semantics, Mlabri exhibits striking features, some of which are clearly ascribable to the status of the language as the traditional vehicle for communication among members of a tiny hunter-gatherer tribe. Other features are due to contact with neighbouring peer languages which has led to semantic transfer or word borrowing. In section 2.1.2 above, some aspects of word semantics were mentioned in passing, from the point of view of *language contact*. The remarks below are rather concerned with immanent structure and lexical representation, although it must be emphasized that with such a language spoken in a multi-ethnic and multi-lingual community there is something artificial about studying the language in total isolation: to arrive at a deeper understanding of the use of metaphor and of idiomatic expressions in general one must also look at the data from an areal and if possible also from a diachronic perspective (although some metaphorical expressions may certainly be quite specific to this language).

The dictionary below gives ample evidence of the occurrence and extent of *variation in meaning within individual lexical items*, i.e. polysemy, including metaphorical or metonymical extensions of meanings, etc. This is found even with stative verbs.

An uncontroversial example of metaphorical use of a stative verb is the Mlabri word ɟruʔ 'deep', which is typically used about deep water but occurs at least in one collocation where it is metaphorical since it describes the intensity, 'depth', of darkness: bah ɟruʔ. I have been told that this expression refers to the unpenetrable darkness experienced if one wakes up long before sunrise (ʔa bah is the very early morning) and open both eyes widely in order to see something. – If one is looking at the black evening sky (or the darkening of the sky during a tempest), on the other hand, the comment 'it is dark' is made by using the verb kaɲit which also means 'be unable to see anything' (and which is appropriate, e.g. if one closes both eyes).

A more controversial example is wec 'far', which is about physical distance but may perhaps occasionally be used about future time as well. On a certain occasion when I was leaving the Mlabri area, I remarked that I would return in five or six months, and my companion exclaimed:

wec, which (in the situation and based on the prosodic characteristics) I interpreted, *not* as an explanatory comment *'[that's because you travel] far away', but as a responsory exclamation (of dismay) '[that's a] long time [ahead]!'. – It is worth noting that the Mlabri use a quite different semantics when talking about the past. Thus, the verb prɯm is used both about distance in backward time and about state of decay: an ancestor who lived long ago is mlaʔ prɯm just as an old and worn-out but still existing blanket is ɡncaj prɯm.

From a typological perspective such examples are anything but surprising; the most remarkable aspect of metaphors involving a transfer from one sensory or cognitive domain to another is their apparent occurrence in much the same form in widely different language communities of the world.

The use of *nouns* with "transferred meanings" as an innovative lexical device is so universal that it is trivial to mention that a Mlabri can refer, for example, to the lid of a cookie box as its ɡlɤɤʔ or kampoŋ, i.e. its *head*. Nevertheless, by way of illustration of the lexical potential, I shall mention two small sets of terminology both of which refer to *items which are secondary in relation to the traditional hunter-gatherer culture* although one of them is totally integrated in Mlabri forest life, whereas the other still stands out as an external feature of civilization. Both terminologies are loaded with metaphors:

There is a locally widespread device for air supply to the charcoal fire used when forging. This machinery, in Mlabri called rɯpthɯp, consists of a pair of vertically placed air pumps each with a piston which can be pumped up and down, and with an outlet pipe close to the bottom (each pump resembling a bicycle pump). The whole thing is made of bamboo sections and other organic material. The vertical bamboo tubes are just called ʔat diiŋ which means 'the bamboo section(s)', but the remaining parts have names of human body parts: the piston is ʔat puuj 'the stomach' (i.e. the organ inside the body), the lever used to pump it up and down is ʔat blɛɛŋ 'the arm' and the small outlet pipe at the bottom is ʔat ʔdoŋ 'the penis'.

The choice of terms is less coherent in the case of a modern artifact like the flashlight, in Mlabri gɔɔŋchooŋ, but the parts certainly have their names. The front glass is named with a loanword: ʔat pralit, since there is nothing comparable in Mlabri culture. Otherwise, the terminology is a mixture of terms from different areas of daily life: if, for example, we remove the interior parts under the front glass, these are named ʔat khɛj mat 'the eyeball' (the bulb) and ʔat thoŋgot 'the cup' (the concave mirror around the socket of the bulb); the metal plate which appears under the concave mirror and which seals off the front part from the batteries is, not surprisingly, ʔat dʌl 'the flat end'.

There is nothing extraordinary about the inventiveness which underlies such terminology. It is mentioned here only to show that a combination of loanwords and of semantic extensions of Mlabri words enables the Mlabri to speak at a certain level about implements which lie outside their traditional culture without necessarily switching to another language.

The etymological relationship between noun classifiers and ordinary nouns in Mlabri also reflects semantic extension, which may have happened under the direct or indirect influence of Thai semantics when the use of such classifiers gained ground in the language. A strange example is ɟɯn which means 'candle' and is at the same time classifier for such cutting implements as knives and axes; this is somewhat reminiscent of Thai, in which the word lêm is classifier for sharp and pointed objects and also for candles.

All of this contributes to illustrate that the Mlabri language is not as static as one might be tempted to assume.

To proceed to examples with less predictable meaning, I have recorded some but not many Mlabri idioms which consist of Noun + Noun but have a denotation quite outside the semantic field of either noun, although the semantic shift is based on a shared feature of sensory impression. This (globally extremely well-known) type of idiom may be illustrated by the following two uses of mat 'eye', which allude to different characteristics of eyes: mat rwaaj 'tiger's eye' i.e. 'button' (with shape and pattern similar to the feline iris) and mat ʔjoc 'hen's eye' i.e. 'malleolus' (protruberant like the hen's eye; on the 'eye'-metaphor as an areal feature cf. Matisoff 1983, p. 79).

Similarly, I have recorded just a few idioms in the form of lexicalizations of whole sentences which make some kind of sense on face value but actually have a quite different (figurative) meaning. I do not know how numerous such idioms are in Mlabri.

There are some amusing expressions of this kind which refer to the sun or the moon. One is mat klaj klduɯl tawɪn, which may perhaps be construed to mean 'the eyes are bashful because of the rump of the sun' (in modern syntax it should perhaps rather be *mat klaj ʔat tawɪn di klduɯl to convey that meaning) but which actually means 'to screw up one's eyes while looking in the direction of the sun' (semantically closely related to wiŋcɛɛr 'to look through narrow eye slits'). Another, which is shared by α- and β-Mlabri, is kiʔ thʌp pmpoo, which if translated literally would mean 'moon roasts elephant', although no Mlabri of either group has ever been ready to explain what notion underlies its actual meaning: '(it is) full moon'.

So much for metaphorical usage and semantic extension. Another major aspect of word semantics is *partial similarity in meaning* (and more specifically *partial synonymy/antinymy*) within sets of lexical items: "semantic fields" or "word fields".

Some dictionaries of Mon-Khmer languages are arranged in such a way that words of different word-classes are listed in different sections of the dictionary, and within each such section a further division is made into subsections defined by certain, more or less explicit semantic criteria. This has the advantage of giving the reader an easier overview of the lexical material within different semantic fields, although the definition and delimitation of such fields is often controversial. Since the dictionary below is arranged strictly alphabetically, it does not at all provide easy access to this aspect of word semantics. It seems, therefore, appropriate to give some instructive examples of sets of lexical items in Mlabri which constitute semantic fields.

Before going into this I wish to repeat a statement made in passing earlier, namely that the Mlabri lexicon very obviously reflects the traditional culture of the people by its emphasis on differentiation within certain semantic fields. This is the same kind of phenomenon that is so often illustrated in linguistic lore by the richness of terms for 'snow' in Eskimo. I do not find that very surprising linguistically, whereas it is obviously a matter of substantive importance for anthropological studies. It is much more interesting to note if there are putative conceptual categories which might be salient within the cultural setting of the Mlabri but which nevertheless seems to be absent from the lexicon. The Mlabri language characteristically lacks certain hypernyms for phenomena which one might *a priori* expect to be basic-level categories, e.g. cover terms such as 'monkey' or 'snake' (cf. Thai). This is obviously of interest for cognitive studies, but I shall not go further into the issue here. It can be studied more profitably with reference to the joint material from α-Mlabri and β-Mlabri, of which the former awaits final publication.

Turning now to the question of semantic differentiation by lexical means, there are particular subsections of the lexicon each which would off-hand invite a special approach in terms of a joint semantic treatment as a *semantic field*. Although it is impossible to go into detail with all such lexical sets here, I wish to mention some of the most interesting ones. One of these is the set of *verbs of motion, body gestures and postures*.

The semantics of such verbs is a topic which could easily fill many monographs. On the other hand, it is difficult to approach such verbs as constituting a semantic field, especially if there is every reason to believe that one's lexical coverage is incomplete and that some of the translations are probably inadequate. The verbs which I have collected (and which occur as lexical entries in the dictionary below) amount to a considerable number but they undoubtedly represent just a fraction of the complete vocabulary within this field.

Another area with striking characteristics is *deictics* in the widest sense, including personal and demonstrative pronouns (and complex expressions which function as a kind of pronoun) as well as deictic adverbials.

As one expects of a human language, this section of the lexicon poses intricate analytical problems both from a pragmatic, a semantic and a syntactic point of view. In the present monograph, the topics of Pronouns and Deixis play a considerable role in the rather sketchy presentation of Mlabri syntax (chapter 5 below), but I have refrained from any in-depth treatment of these matters.

Deixis (understood in the broad sense of this term) leads over to a conceptually intriguing semantic area: *expressions of time*. Mlabri culture is characterized by a static(-cyclic) conception of life and time and by a correspondingly low emphasis on the chronology of previous generations and the fixation of past events in relation to previous generations. But it must be emphasized that this characteristic (which is not unexpected of a typically tribal culture) certainly does not mean that the Mlabri lack vocabulary referring to time (also cf. the remarks about deixis and temporal expressions in chapter 5, subsections 5.1.1 and 5.1.2 below).

There is of course a terminology to do with *time deixis*, namely with two distinct subsets specifying (i) (backward or forward) distance in days from the reference point, i.e. terms such as nɛɛ 'yesterday', paaj 'the day after tomorrow' and (ii) subjective evaluation of (backward or forward) distance in time from the reference point, i.e. terms such as tak ʔɤ-hɤɤj 'very long ago' and rəʔʌh 'in a moment'. The reference point of the former set is tawɪn nɛh 'today'; that of the latter set is paan gʌh 'now, then' or (tak) ɲaam gʌh 'at that time, then'.

And there is (as also expected) a fairly detailed terminology to do with *cyclic events*, such as (iii) the time periods of the day (and night) according to the position of the sun and the amount and colour of light in the sky: ʔa bah 'early morning', ʔa gaɲ thwɛɲ 'late afternoon' etc. and (iv) the various parts of the month according to the behaviour, shape, and size of the moon in its various phases: kiʔ ʔa thʌp pompoo 'full moon', kiʔ ʔa rɛɛm 'vaning moon' etc. There is even a term referring to the year: hnʌm; and the term ɲaam means 'time' or 'season', which can be qualified to refer to specific seasons, e.g. ɲaam glʌŋ 'the rainy season'.

Presenting a more complete list of Mlabri terminology referring to time would be an easy task but, in my view, of limited interest without a thorough analysis, which I cannot carry out on the basis of my present data. The terminology is all contained in the dictionary below but with rather tentative translations. I shall just mention a couple of interesting lexical details:

A relatedness between expressions for 'morning' and 'tomorrow' (which amounts to homonymy in German: *morgen, Morgen*) is found also in Mlabri. To express the concept 'this (past) morning' the β-Mlabri say tak ɟruɯ, and their term for 'tomorrow' is ɟruɯ ('tomorrow morning' is ɟruɯ tak ɟruɯ). In no other instances that I know of in Mlabri, is there such a lexical relatedness between the ways in which backward and forward time is encoded, but it is easy to point to a universally available conceptualization of a shared semantic feature: both the morning and the next day represent *the arrival of a day after a night*.

I wish to mention also that the Mlabri do not count days and nights in either days or nights but in "dusks". The salient notion in this case is probably that if something takes more than one day, it will be necessary to find shelter and to see to it that people are put up for the night. Thus the dusk becomes the crucial part of the day-and-night cycle as soon as a project (such as a hunting expedition) includes a night.

As soon as one gets beyond a few nights, the Mlabri do not seem to have much need for specifying time in their traditional culture. On the other hand, pseudo-quantitative expressions are extremely common: one may speak of a certain number of months or even years, just to convey the sense of 'a very long time'.

Instead of going into further detail with any of the above-mentioned semantic fields I shall illustrate the lexical "exploitation" of certain other semantic fields which are in a sense easier to approach, although they turn out to present tricky problems in Mlabri. The first subsection below deals with *negation*, at first sight a very narrow semantic field, which nevertheless shows some lexical differentiation in Mlabri and also invites a comparison of α-Mlabri and β-Mlabri. This will be followed by subsections on verbs of consumption, colour terminology and kinship terminology.

4.2.1 Negation

Negation in β-Mlabri involves various categories of entities, which I shall tentatively distinguish as (i) *negative response predicates* (= particles of "yes-no" type), (ii) *other negative predicates, (iii) negative modal auxiliaries* and (iv) *negative preverbs*. Semantically, it is the fourth category that is most interesting, but typologically the others are noteworthy as well, and I shall begin with a brief presentation of these:

– (1) There is at least one *negative response predicate*, bah 'no', and there is a corresponding affirmative entity koo? 'yes'. In itself, the existence of such a separate set of predicative particles makes Mlabri stand out from the pattern of affirmation-negation known from Thai, for example. (As for denying or endorsing a proposition, it deserves mentioning that Mlabri has various affirmative expressions other than koo?, e.g. ʔa chɯŋ chiʔɛh and ʔa mɛɛn which both mean 'that's correct'; the latter also occurs in negated form: chak mɛɛn 'that's not correct'.)

Returning to the negative predicates of Mlabri, bah is not the only option. It is also possible to use the verb noɲ, which otherwise means something like 'there is none (left)', as a one-word response with negative meaning. The two lexemes are clearly not synonymous, but my material is too meagre to fully reveal the differences of meaning between them. It seems, however, that bah is used to deny the correctness of a proposition, whereas noɲ is a negative existential predicate. As an extension of its existential meaning, the latter can also be used as a refusal, a one-word utterance denying somebody access to something (as when saying 'No!' to a child).

– (2) The negative predicate bah can also function as a *clause-replacive* inside an utterance. Just as in (i) above it then functions to *deny an assumption made by the other party*, cf. the following complex explanation: ba thɔɔŋ tɛɛ mɔ mɤʔ mɔ mɤm, ba kham tɛɛ mɔ mɤʔ mɔ mɤm, dadrooj tɛɛ bah 'Ba Thong had one set of parents, Ba Kham had another set of parents: he was not his younger brother', where the denial occurs in the negative clause dadrooj tɛɛ bah, literally: 'younger-sibling but no'. The other clause-replacive, noɲ (also cf. (1) above), can – with its negative existential meaning – be used to express the negated alternative within a *disjunctive set of mutually contradictory alternatives*. This is clear from the following utterance which expresses a request for information: choop ni ba chak ʔi tɔp toc glaŋ chala noɲ 'ask Ba Chak if I Top has married or not!', where the crucial part of the construction is toc glaŋ chala noɲ, literally: 'take husband or not'.

– (3) As one might expect of a language in Indochina, Mlabri also has a *negative modal auxiliary*, gʌm (apparently the etymon that appears in Khmer as kom = negative command). It is mostly used to encode the meaning of negative imperative but also – with a causative-resultative verb – to encode preventive intentionality, as in bacheer di gʌm beec 'soothe it (a child) so it does not cry'.

– (4) We shall proceed now to negative preverbs occurring inside clauses with the function of *negating single verbs*. These are the most interesting negative words from the "semantic field" perspective. There are (at least) four such items: ki, kibi, met and chak. The most important negative preverbs are met and chak, of which the former seems to be used to negate factive verbs, stative verbs in general, and perception verbs (met mʌc 'not see' i.e. 'I don't know'). The latter is used to negate dynamic verbs and it also expresses various modalities (intentionality, potentiality etc.).

It is possible to encounter both negative preverbs in one complex predication: met ŋaam chak toc 'not pretty not take', i.e. 'won't have an ugly one' (it appears from such an example that predications with met may form the cognitive point of departure for predications with chak).

The two negations chak and met may sometimes combine with the same lexical item but they then encode different meanings in accordance with the generalization above, cf. ʔoh chak jɤɤm 'I am not staying' vs. met jɤɤm 'is not there'. With the modalities inherent in the meaning of chak, there is the possibility of lexicalization of special idioms containing this preverb, cf. chak bɤɤn 'do not fancy' as against the predictable, static meaning of met bɤɤn 'cannot'.

As for kibi, this preverb seems rather neutral with respect to the differences between met and chak mentioned above, but it may differ from both of these along a different dimension (although its distribution certainly overlaps with that of the other preverbs). It is my impression that kibi is often used to express a temporary negative state, as in kibi biiʔ 'not full' (i.e. 'still hungry') or to make a factual statement by denying the opposite, as in kibi chɛʔ 'not many' (i.e. 'few').

It seems from my (meagre) data that kibi can be used if the negative polarity is played down, even to the point of encoding very mild requests in negative form. The following exchange of utterances was presented to me by a Mlabri speaker as a typical piece of discourse of this kind (note the two occurrences of 'not look after', expressed as kibi dɤŋ and chak dɤŋ, respectively): kibi dɤŋ ʔot ʔɛɛw ʔot ŋwɛʔ 'Can't you look after my child (please)?' – ʔoh chak dɤŋ 'No, I can't look after it!'.

This leads over to the question what is the difference in meaning between met and kibi when these two preverbs combine with ʔɛl to form expressions meaning 'not yet'. It is my impression that met ʔɛl underlines the durational aspect: it typically implies that the discourse participants are anticipating the forthcoming fullfilment of an event which may occur once in the course of time (e.g. for a certain girl to become a married woman: met ʔɛl toc glaŋ 'she has not married yet'). In contrast, kibi ʔɛl typically implies that one is talking about a rather trivial and recurrent event which for some reason is still pending (as in kibi ʔɛl boŋ 'I have not eaten yet').

In α-Mlabri, the most common negative preverb is kibɔ or (in younger speech) kɔbɔ, which seems neutral with respect to the distinction between met and chak in β-Mlabri. The latter words also occur in α-Mlabri (as mit, chak) but are mainly used in certain fixed expressions.

The two varieties of Mlabri collide semantically with respect to the use of ki, however. In α-Mlabri, ki always has negative polarity, and that is also true in some cases in β-Mlabri. The expression ki chɛʔ, for example, means 'not many' in both varieties. The β-Mlabri question ʔa ki toc (said toward the end of a meal) likewise has a negative semantics according to its Northern Thai paraphrase: "bɔ ʔaw lɛɛw kɔ" i.e. 'you don't want any more?'. Negative polarity is also unambiguously present if there is an explicit contrast between clauses without and with ki: kan hlɯɯ ʔoh ʔa toc, kan ki hlɯɯ ʔoh chak toc 'if remain, I PERF take; if not (ki) remain, I not take', i.e. 'I'll have some if there is some left, but I can do without if there isn't any left'. In most expressions in β-Mlabri, however, the use of ki is not associated with negative polarity but implies a concession on the speaker's part, cf. ki bɤɤn 'that is also possible' (bɤɤn means 'can').

This difference may become fatal, at least for a linguistic field worker who shuttles between the two groups, when it comes to the expression ki mɛɛn. In α-Mlabri this means 'that is not correct!' (just like β-Mlabri chak mɛɛn) and may be used for example if one emphatically denies an allegation made by somebody else. On the contrary, in β-Mlabri it means 'that's also correct', or 'yes, you can also say it that way'. If, for example, a β-Mlabri speaker wants to say that two expressions such as miɲiŋ and mɯlh (male and female speech for 'woman') are both possible, he says: miɲiŋ ki mɛɛn mɯlh ki mɛɛn, i.e. 'It is OK to say "miɲiŋ" and it is also OK to say "mɯlh"'.

This strange alternation in meaning is found also with bɔ, which is the well-known word for 'not' in Northern Thai and forms part of the negative preverb kibɔ in α-Mlabri but means 'also' in β-Mlabri. (The situation underlying such shifts in polarity may perhaps have been one in which certain constructions were possible both with or without another preverb which carries the negative meaning. Ambiguity with regard to polarity is not all that strange; a similar situation is found with the Thai word jaŋ which may mean 'still' or 'not yet' depending on the context.)

These observations do not at all exhaust the topic, but they may suffice to demonstrate the intricacies of negation in Mlabri.

In the remainder of this extensive section on word semantics, I shall discuss a couple of fields in which some semantic work has already been done. The section will be rounded off by a presentation of the most complex issue: the kinship terminology of β-Mlabri.

4.2.2 Eating, Drinking and Smoking

This is one coherent semantic field in Mlabri and it exhibits some very particular features, cf. the discussion of three α-Mlabri verbs for 'to eat' in Thongkum (1983). By way of introduction it is possible to set up a number of non-trivial characteristics of this semantic field which are all shared by α-Mlabri and β-Mlabri:

– (1) a distinction between, on the one hand, terms for eating food of a type which requires much biting and/or chewing: α-Mlabri

ʔɤɤʔ, boŋ, β-Mlabri boŋ and, on the other hand, terms for eating juicy or jelly-like food, such as bananas, which involves specific use of the tongue: α-Mlabri pɤj, β-Mlabri lat 'to lick' or lat boŋ,

– (2) a sharp distinction between the above-mentioned terms for eating and a different terminology for drinking: α-Mlabri wɤɤk but β-Mlabri ɟrʌʌk,

– (3) the use of one and the same word (in α-Mlabri wɤɤk, in β-Mlabri ɟrʌʌk) both as a noun 'water' and as a verb 'to drink' in the sense of consumption of water or liquor (incidentally, 'to suck mother's milk' is expressed by the word booʔ, which is also a noun meaning 'breast'),

– (4) extension of the word for 'to drink' to also mean 'to smoke tobacco (or opium)', cf. α-Mlabri wɤɤk kɔɔk 'smoke pipe', β-Mlabri ʔjaa ɟrʌʌk 'tobacco smoke', i.e. 'tobacco for smoking'.

In all these respects we find the very same semantic pattern in the two varieties although the verbs in question are (with the exception of boŋ) totally different etyma in α-Mlabri and β-Mlabri.

Whereas the subdivision of 'eating' into types of activities under (1) above is a semantically interesting topic in itself, the information under (2)-(4) is typologically important for the characterization of Mlabri as against Thai on the one hand and the neighbouring Mon-Khmer languages on the other. One finds similar patterns in Tin, for example, but these shared characteristics *all differ completely from Central Thai*. In Thai the semantic polarization between eating on the one hand and drinking/smoking on the other hand is not a dominant one; on the contrary it is general usage to employ a cover term (kin) for eating/drinking (although there is also an availability – depending on speaking-style – of specific words such as thaan for eating and of other words such as dùɯm for drinking). Furthermore, the noun 'water' in Thai is a separate word which cannot possibly be used as a verb. Finally, Thai has a separate term for the activity 'to smoke'.

The two varieties of Mlabri differ, however, with respect to the presence or absence of a further semantic subdivision of *types of consumption of solid food*. There is a consistent lexical distinction in α-Mlabri depending on whether one eats (boŋ) meat or eats (ʔɤɤʔ) vegetables such as edible tubers or rice. In β-Mlabri the word boŋ is used indiscriminately about all such food consumption (the corresponding cover term is pɔŋ in Tin). It is even possible in β-Mlabri to extend this verb to be used about the consumption of liquor: boŋ ɟnraaʔ, which looks like a calque from Thai kin lâw.

4.2.3 Colour Terminology

Colour terminology constitutes another particularly interesting semantic field. Theraphan L. Thongkum (1985) reports on a study using colour charts in which she has established what range of colours can be labelled with each of four major colour terms in α-Mlabri. She finds that "any colours will be classified by the Mla bri' into one of four categories": the term balak (in our current notation bəlaak) is used for white, ivory, pink, pale blue, pale green, silver grey, lavender, beige etc.; the term thuk wɛk (thukʔwɛk) is used for black, brown, navy blue, dark green, grey, purple etc.; the term bɨnliŋ (bnliiŋ) is used for green, blue, turquoise etc.; finally the term lɛŋ is used for yellow, gold, orange, red, maroon etc.

No similar study has been performed for the colour terms in β-Mlabri. My comments below are based on my own impressions of the meanings of certain colour terms but are meant to be suggestive with respect to the possibility of somehow *explaining* the use of these terms. What is said here refers exclusively to β-Mlabri terminology, which is rather different from that of α-Mlabri.

In the paragraph below, colour terms will be referred to only as descriptive verbs (adjectives). It is, however, frequently the case that a colour is referred to by a noun phrase consisting of the noun ɟuk plus the colour verb as a modifier (as in Thai), cf. the β-Mlabri expression ɟuk thwɛɲ '(of) red colour'.

There are some immediately conspicuous characteristics of colour terms in β-Mlabri. One is that they seem to be for the most part semantically derived. Another is that except possibly for the word(s) for 'deep red' there seem to be no colour terms which refer specifically to salient colours of the rainbow. This is surprising since the rainbow is an important concept in Mlabri culture. Altogether, the indigenous colour terminology of Mlabri seems to comprise very few terms, and it is worth noting that it is typologically close to the basic colour terminology of certain Austronesian languages (cf. Conklin 1955).

The colour terms used in both α-Mlabri and β-Mlabri are in part descriptive Thai terms for cloth of different colours and in part terms referring to natural phenomena of practical importance. In addition to the words which have become standardized as the basic colour terms, it is possible to make up other colour terms, e.g. by using the name of an object with a characteristic colour (e.g. 'wax', ʔjak ʔjek) as the name of that colour.

I elaborate on this (perhaps trivial, perhaps marginal) phenomenon because the description of the peculiar colour "system" below, or the statements about colour terms in α-Mlabri by Thongkum (1985), might otherwise convey the impression that Mlabri speakers are totally constrained by traditional terminology if they are faced with the task of making less usual colour discriminations in their own language.

To take up another issue: it is widely assumed (on the basis of contentions made by Berlin and Kay a quarter of a century ago) that colour names should be defined with reference to *focal*, prototypical colours rather than with reference to boundaries between colours. The remarks below on Mlabri colour terminology are neutral in this respect, since there is nothing in my data which permits me to define either focal colours or colour boundaries with sufficient precision.

The question of focal colours has a diachronic dimension as well. As for the β-Mlabri word thwɛɲ, which denotes a deep red colour, as in the evening sky, there is a suspiciously similar word in Katuic which means 'black'. If these words are at all related, the Katuic evidence might suggest that the focus used to be on the darkness of the colour, whereas it is now clearly the redness that is most salient.

It seems possible to sort out a couple of binary distinctions in β-Mlabri colour terminology (without at all exhausting the possibility of naming specific colours in this language):

In one dimension (of hue) there is a word thwɛɲ meaning both 'ripe' and '(deep) red' (used about ripe fruits or sugar cane, for example). Another word bnliiŋ (related to a word for 'alive') means on the contrary 'unripe' and also 'green'. In α-Mlabri, the latter word stands for a wide range of colours: "green, blue, turquoise, etc." (Thongkum 1985, p. 68); in β-Mlabri bnliiŋ and a related form braliiŋ are both used about fresh green colours which are significant in nature (braliiŋ refers specifically to pale bluish green), although I have also heard bnliiŋ used about the metallic grey colour of a plastic raincoat.

Assuming that bnliiŋ is basically 'green', what then about the other characteristic light colour: 'yellow'? There is a β-Mlabri word hlɯɯŋ which, according to its etymology, would be expected to refer specifically to that colour, and indeed, a Mlabri explained its meaning by giving the Thai word for 'yellow' (which is the etymological source of hlɯɯŋ). It is, however, my impression that this is the extensive colour term of β-Mlabri (much like bnliiŋ in α-Mlabri): I have heard it used about a whole range of more or less insipid colours from slightly pink over yellow and greenish all the way to blue, though yellow may well be the focal colour. It is strange, anyhow, that the language has a loanword for such an essential, natural colour as yellow; why not derive it from an association with the bright sun, for example? In α-Mlabri it is obvious that the colour 'yellow' used to be associated with coloured items from the outside world: α-Mlabri always uses the complex loanword phahlɯɯŋ, i.e. 'yellow cloth' in Thai, in the meaning of 'yellow colour'.

The term thwɛɲ (considered to be "male language") and its equivalent lɛɛŋ (considered to be "female language") occur in expressions for 'evening glow'. The former term can be recognized in Bernatzik's (correct or spurious) word for 'rainbow' in "Yumbri" (Bernatzik 1938). It is interesting to compare this with the observation above that the β-Mlabri word hlɯɯŋ covers not just one salient colour but a broad section of the spectrum which can perhaps be characterized as *very far from deep red* (a distinction involving both hue and saturation). Thus thwɛɲ and lɛɛŋ may have obtained their fixed meaning of '(deep) red' via involvement in two closely related colour distinctions: one associated with the properties 'ripe'-'unripe'; the other with colours and colour spectra in the sky.

In another dimension, having to do with intrinsic brightness versus darkness, there is a word bəlaak meaning 'white' (in a broad sense covering 'silver grey' etc.), and a word chɛɛŋ referring to the other end of the scale: 'black', 'dark grey', 'dark blue', perhaps also 'of dirty colour'.

It is possible also to discriminate between darker and lighter shades of a specific colour. For 'blue' there is a word kamiin referring to a very light blue shade, and then there is the already mentioned word hlɯɯŋ which may be used for a shade that is lighter than chɛɛŋ but darker than kamiin. The use of the three different names for 'blue' seems to be *relative* rather than absolute, however.

When I once checked the terminology for blue colours on a blouse with sections in a darker and a lighter blue colour, I found that different sections adjacent to each other were consistently given different colour names. But if I pointed to different parts of the blouse while it was worn by its owner he sometimes named the same dye differently depending on the amount of daylight to which each area happened to be exposed at the moment. Thus, although there were only two dyes, the speaker employed three different colour names. It did not seem relevant to his use of colour terms to normalize with respect to brightness (e.g. by considering the overall composition of the blouse or by moving the garment to vary the exposure to light).

4.2.4 Kinship Terminology

The study of kinship systems has a long tradition as a favourite topic for semantic field study within linguistics and anthropology. Since kinship terms reflect several basic properties of the social organization and of mutual relations of loyalty, obligation and respect within family networks, this semantic field is of paramount importance for the study of the culture. It is, however, also one of the most interesting semantic fields from a purely linguistic point of view. Mlabri kinship terminology deserves study from both of these views, although the present exposition is for the most part limited to purely linguistic considerations.

Although comparison of the kinship nomenclatures of α-Mlabri and β-Mlabri shows interesting and surprisingly great differences, which call for sociolinguistic explanations, the discussion of this topic – as of other topics in the present monograph – focusses narrowly on β-Mlabri (the α-Mlabri kinship system has been treated in a different format and in rather less detail in Suebsaeng 1992). The overall picture of the linguistic usage is complex enough even with this limitation.

The exposition below is based on limited data (mainly from two male speakers); because of the few persons surviving in the β-Mlabri group the posibilities of checking and rechecking information by referring to the family relationships between existing persons are soon exhausted.

As might be expected, the kinship terminology of Mlabri shows some influence from Thai languages. It exhibits various autonomous features, however, which make the study of this field particularly challenging.

The kinship nomenclature of Mlabri, as of many other languages, overlaps with nomenclature used to label persons in terms of age, sex or prestige (e.g. taaʔ is a kinship term but also occurs in the meaning of 'senior male'; ʔuuj may mean both 'mother' and 'female'). Some kinship terms also function as pronoun-like terms of address. An exhaustive account of Mlabri kinship terminology is thus a complicated venture.

In practical fieldwork I have been most confused by the standard terms for (elder and younger) siblings, since these are also used to refer to one's friends, as in Thai. Mlabri people use the expression rooj diŋ, 'younger-sibling elder-sibling' when they talk about those who belong to the same ethnic group and the same generation as the speaker, but who are in most cases not the speaker's real siblings. This has been a source of confusion to me whenever I concerned myself with family pedigrees.

If, however, a Mlabri is urged to account for exact family relationships it is possible to specify – also within the bonds of the Mlabri language proper – that a certain person is a *real* sibling. When talking *about* a sibling this can be done by adding explanatory comments such as dəmɔ mɤʔ dəmɔ mɤm '(we are of) one mother, one father'; when speaking *to* a person it may be done by using a different nomenclature (borrowed directly or indirectly from Northern Thai) which refers specifically to true siblings: ʔaaj for 'brother' and ʔɯɯj for 'sister'.

The expressions mɤʔ mɤm 'mother father' i.e. 'parents', ʔuj jooŋ 'woman and man' or 'mother and father', hma(a)j glaŋ 'wife and husband' and rooj diŋ 'younger-sibling elder-sibling' i.e. 'siblings' (or 'friends') show a characteristic absence in Mlabri of *single lexemes* used as collective terms for dyadic sets of relatives. This is in agreement with Thai, the peer language of much of Indochina (although there is a reversal of the ordering in these dyadic sets in Mlabri as in some other Mon-Khmer languages).

Otherwise, collective expressions which refer to a local Mlabri group or to subsets (e.g. children) of such a group are abundant in Mlabri (though perhaps more so in α-Mlabri than in β-Mlabri). Such terms very often have a kinship flavour.

Although it is customary to set up lineage charts and to fit the kinship terms of a given language into such charts in order to explain their meaning, I have chosen a different approach, both because it would take a very profound knowledge of the language and culture to be able to present *the* kinship system of Mlabri as a close-knit system and because it is not the system as such but the *salient semantic dimensions* in Mlabri kinship nomenclature that constitute the topic I wish to deal with here.

The anchoring point in the analysis below is that a "relative" is necessarily understood and defined as *somebody's* relative. I shall call this "somebody" the *reference person*.

A major problem when one performs a structural analysis of a semantic field is to decide whether the set of lexical items under analysis form a closed or an open set. In Mlabri (as in other languages) there is both a core terminology of single lexemes and a set of elaborated terms formed by adding some modifying lexeme (thus yielding a distinction like English *brother* vs. *younger brother*). I am primarily concerned with the former terms, which I shall refer to as *unmodified*, whereas the latter are occasionally brought in as *modified* kinship terms.

The most basic dimension is one of *lineage* or more precisely: *relative generation*. One might a priori set up a dimension of lineage with four or five (or more) terms which correspond to generations: grandparents, parents, self, children, grandchildren etc. It does not seem to me, however, that Mlabri kinship terminology motivates such a single, multi-valued dimension of lineage, as I do not know of social patterns spanning more than two generations. Rather, I assume that there is, from the perspective of the reference person, a basic distinction between three kinds of genealogical family relations, namely such that involve ascending lineage ("+1"), such that involve "same" generation ("0") and such that involve descending lineage ("-1").

I shall here speak of such a dimension of relative generation with three terms: 'previous' (which comprises both one's parents, uncles and aunts, one's spouse's parents, one's grandparents etc.), 'same-as' (e.g. oneself, one's spouse, one's siblings, cousins etc.), and 'subsequent' (children and their spouses, nephews and nieces, grandchildren). Further subdivisions are then to be taken care of by additional semantic dimensions (see below).

Another very basic dimension in kinship systems is that of *lineal* versus *collateral* relationship. In Mlabri this seems to intersect very much with other dimensions (see on proximity of relatedness below), and I am not sure about its status. The reference person (or ego) is obviously a term in two orthogonal sets of relationships: with parents and children on the one hand and with siblings (brothers and sisters) on the other, but the latter may be defined simply as first-order blood relatives who are on the same level of lineage as the reference person.

The third dimension is that of *relative age*. Siblings are specified as 'younger' or 'elder' relative to the reference person; as mentioned already, there is no cover term for 'siblings' but there are terms for 'younger sibling', rooj or dadrooj or kumɔɔm, and for 'elder sibling', diŋ. When one speaks about somebody's children as a set, the dimension of relative age looks different since neither of the children is likely to be a "reference child". The dimension here comprises two or three terms expressed in terms of modifiers after ʔɛɛw 'child': ʔat ʔɛɛw kldɯl 'the first (i.e. eldest) child', ʔat ʔɛɛw tuul 'the last (i.e. youngest) child' and (if there are more children:) ʔat ʔɛɛw grɤɤŋ 'the child in the middle'.

Digression on the concepts of 'first' and 'last':

The use of the modifiers kldɯl 'rump' and tuul 'tip' to rank certain relatives according to age calls for a digression. To me this usage is highly counter-intuitive; one might expect exactly the opposite: the tip is what comes first, and the rump what comes last. As mentioned in section 2.1.2 above the terminology seems to represent a rearrangement of word meanings relative to neighbouring languages. The translations which I have given are *not* unfounded; the very same use of the modifying terms appears in terms for wives (which have been checked repeatedly with Mlabri speakers): hma(a)j kldɯl definitely means 'first wife' whereas hma(a)j tuul is 'second wife' (I greatly prefer the latter translation to *minor wife*, which implies something like 'mistress', whereas to my knowledge a Mlabri's hma(a)j tuul is just the wife who succeeds a former, e.g. a deceased, wife). Clearly, the Mlabri terminology for ordered sets of wives or children is *not* based on a ranking principle which reflects each person's status in a static sense. Rather, the terminology makes sense if it is considered as being based on a conceptualization of life as *a chronological succession of events facing us*. According to this metaphor, time may be said to disappear behind us, while wives and children appear successively on the scene, and thus the elder ones may be visualized as being "behind" the younger ones in time. This attempt at a metaphorical explanation – for what it is worth – should however also be considered in relation to the use (in both varieties of Mlabri) of the same 'rump'-terminology when referring to the last person of a group, which is walking in single file.

For some reason, the use of kldɯl vs. tuul does not extend to one's own siblings, nor to previous generations. A special case of nomenclature worth considering is that of a child who refers to its mother or stepmother if the father has more than one wife in the course of his life. I have not come across any term for stepmother (although such a term may well exist), but it is possible to distinguish between two mothers, one being the speaker's father's first wife, and the other his second wife. This is done with a terminology which recalls a different metaphor than that of kldɯl – tuul, namely the well-known metaphor of "major" versus "minor" wife: the father's first wife is the speaker's mɤʔ ʔdiŋ 'big mother', and his second wife is the speaker's mɤʔ chet 'little mother'.

Returning to the basic dimensions of Mlabri kinship terminology, there is next the dimension of *sex* (or, as some prefer to say, *gender*). In kinship systems this feature may operate on more than one level in complex semantic structures, as when one is referring to the 'father's sister' or the 'mother's brother'. In the analysis of the basic kinship terms of Mlabri, however, it probably suffices to operate with a "flat" semantic structure with regard to the utilization of this feature and just state that some terms are semantically specified for 'male' or 'female' sex of the person referred to, whereas others are unspecified.

It is known from several languages that if the sex differentiation is not fully covered in kinship terminology, there is likely to be a language-specific "parameter setting" specifying a point on the lineage scale (relative to the reference person) such that family-members belonging to generations above this point are specified for sex whereas family-members belonging to generations below the point may not be thus specified.

In some languages, a *grandparent* or *parent* who is referred to as a single individual must be specified for sex, whereas a *sibling* or a *child* is not specified by a single kinship term (cf. Thai). In other languages, the dividing line is a generation lower: the specification of sex is also obligatory if a *sibling* is referred to as an individual (cf. English daily usage), whereas it is possible to use a sex-neutral term when referring to a *child*.

In Mlabri (as also in Thai) the basic, unmodified kinship terms reflect an intermediate "parameter setting" such that only relatives whose generations are 'previous' relative to the reference person (grandparents, parents, uncles and aunts) are regularly specified for sex whereas close relatives whose generation is 'same-as': siblings, or 'subsequent': children and nephews/nieces, may not be thus specified (the setting is, however, pushed one step with the use of the address terms ʔaaj 'Elder Brother' and ʔɯɯj 'Elder Sister', which are recent loanwords.

The terms rooj 'younger sibling' and diŋ 'elder sibling' are not really technical terms for true siblings. They are exact correspondences to Thai nɔ́ɔŋ and phîi and are thus also used about younger and elder kinsmen or friends in general.

As soon as there is a need for sex specification in ordinary kinship nomenclature beyond what is permitted by the "parameter setting" of this language, the Mlabri must switch to modified expressions. One may then use one of the modifiers məɲiŋ, muɯlh, and kmɲah for 'female', and one of the modifiers ləmeet and laŋ for 'male'. Thus one can say, for instance, 'elder sister': diŋ kmɲah or diŋ muɯlh, 'younger sister': rooj kmɲah or rooj muɯlh, 'son': ʔɛɛw laŋ or ʔɛɛw ləmeet, 'daughter': ʔɛɛw kmɲah or ʔɛɛw məɲiŋ or ʔɛɛw muɯlh, 'younger sibling's daughter': rooj di ʔɛɛw muɯlh etc. (the choice among the alternatives listed above is determined by other semantic features; see later).

The dimensions set up so far specify a number of theoretically possible kinship categories. These possible categories do not, however, provide an adequate model of the basic kinship terminology of Mlabri. One may add a fifth dimension, represented (in Radcliffe-Brown's descriptive framework) by *proximity of relatedness* labels: one's parents and siblings and children being 'first order relatives', the others within the range of family relationships considered here being related through a shared relative and thus 'second order relatives' (grandparents, uncles and aunts, nephews and nieces).

The linguistic rationale for distinguishing *proximity of relatedness* from *relative generation* as two separate dimensions in the analysis of Mlabri kinship terms is that this makes it simpler to account for the way in which meanings are encoded in Mlabri lexicon, namely with a *common* term meaning both 'grandfather' and 'uncle' taaʔ, a *common* term meaning both 'grandmother' and 'aunt' jaaʔ, and (like in Thai:) a *common* term meaning both 'grandchild' and 'nephew/niece' nɔɔʔ. This suggests a cognitive categorization of all such relatives – elder or younger – as kinsmen who are close relatives but *not* next-of-kin (the validity of this assumption must ultimately be tested by a functional analysis of the kinship system). The feature 'second order relatedness' combines with lineage features: 'previous' (= descending generation) or 'next' (= ascending generation) and in part with an additional sex feature: 'male' or 'female' to make up the componential meanings of the terms above. Note that the sex distinction is neutralized in nɔɔʔ, in accordance with the "parameter setting" stated earlier.

The terms taaʔ and jaaʔ (or its variant ɲaaʔ) are, like diŋ and rooj, cover terms for genuine family members as well as kinsmen. They may be used vaguely about kinsmen who are at least one generation younger than the speaker; thus, I was told that the husband of a certain married female Mlabri would use the terms taaʔ and jaaʔ to refer to his spouse's uncle and aunt. What was more interesting, however, was that she herself would not be expected to use these terms, according to my source. I guess that this was because of a constellation of two factors: (1) she would be obliged to use more precise kinship terminology about her blood-relatives than her husband and, (2) the uncle in question is her father's *younger* brother and thus not really a senior from her perspective (see later on ʔaaj and diŋ).

The dimensions so far are intended only to take care of the kinship system of blood relatives. To this one must somehow add a sixth dimension specifying the difference between that kind of relatedness and *relatedness through marriage*, i.e., between *consanguineal* and *affinal* relatedness. Obviously, the most important terms of the latter category are the two terms for 'spouse': glaŋ for 'husband' and hmaaj for 'wife' (with subdivision into hma(a)j kɨdɯl and hma(a)j tuul if there is a succession of wives). There is no sex-neutral cover term for 'spouse' in Mlabri.

As for in-laws, I wish to mention first that separate terms exist for parents-in-law, mɤʔ thaw 'mother-in-law' and mɤm thaw 'father-in-law', i.e. modified terms for 'mother' and 'father'.

The word thaw is Thai/Lao and conveys the meaning of 'grey' or 'elderly'. According to the evidence available to me, combinations of the terms for 'mother' and 'father' with thaw do not appear to be used in the sense of 'mother-in-law' and 'father-in-law' in either Tin or Kmhmu, but this particular usage is documented for the Katuic language Kui spoken southeast of the present Mlabri area (Sriwises 1978, p. 57 and 75).

As for one's brother-in-law or sister-in-law, the general terms for siblings of one's own generation can be used. The question then arises what is the criterion or combination of criteria which determines how to deal with relative age: whether the use of rooj, for example, implies that one's in-law is one's junior or that one's married sibling is one's junior, and similarly whether the relative age expressed by using diŋ refers to one's in-law or to one's married sibling. One of the male β-Mlabri speakers told me that he used to call his elder (half-)brother's first wife diŋ; he had not had much opportunity to talk to his brother's second (now also deceased) wife and was very much in doubt as to what he would call her, but he thought that he would say rooj 'younger sibling' (although to judge from her appearance she must have been considerably older than the speaker).

There are more specific "in-law" terms, however. Before dealing with the terms which seem to have relatively well-defined meanings, I wish to mention an apparent kinship term of this category: roh. One speaker said that he would address his elder half-brother's daughter's husband by using this term, but it is impossible to make any generalization from my data about the meaning of roh in β-Mlabri. The remaining terms are also rather intriguing, however, in that they involve, or may combine with, the numeral bɛɛr 'two':

As for children and their spouses, one of the speakers claimed that one's son-in-law is referred to simply as one's "child"; thus, ʔɛɛw bɛɛr may be used either about one's two children or about one's child and the child's spouse. In some cases it is appropriate to make explicit the kinship status of the in-law, and this can be done, according to one speaker, by using the term jooʔ or ʔɛɛw jooʔ about that person alone and joʔ bɛɛr about the couple, whereas another speaker claims that he uses the expression ʔat bɛɛr (literally 'the second one'??) about his daughter's husband, as in the phrase met ɲaŋ ʔat bɛɛr 'her husband is not present'. – Alternatively, it would always be possible to make an explanatory statement something like ʔot ʔɛɛw di glaŋ 'my child's husband', I was told.

This leads over to a somewhat different issue: how to refer to a married couple as such. The standard term for two persons forming a procreating couple is ʔuuj jooŋ 'woman man'; if it is essential to focus on their having a marriage, it is also possible to say hma(a)j laŋ or hma(a)j glaŋ 'wife husband' (note the constant ordering of female before male, or junior before senior, in Mlabri constituent ordering). There is, however, a special term for 'married couple', namely chɔŋ prdaw (formally the Thai numeral 'two' plus a noun which I know only from this fixed expression). Thus, one can refer to a daughter and her husband as ʔɛɛw chɔŋ prdaw.

Another term for couple, which occurs much more frequently, is a combination of a kinship term with bɛɛr, the Mlabri numeral 'two' (cf. the expression ʔat bɛɛr mentioned above). Thus, instead of ʔot ʔɛɛw chɔŋ prdaw one may say ʔot ʔɛɛw bɛɛr 'my child and my child's spouse', and similarly one can refer to a young couple of one's own generation as dadrooj bɛɛr and to a couple of one's children's generation as kumɔm bɛɛr. Similarly, rooj bɛɛr and diŋ bɛɛr are the proper expressions when referring to, respectively, one's younger sibling and his/her spouse, and one's elder sibling and his/her spouse.

The construction N + bɛɛr is not reserved for married couples, however; it is a neutral term referring to any two persons of the same generation who form a very close-knit family group, be it a married couple or two persons who are siblings. Thus, a girl can address her two brothers as ʔaaj bɛɛr if at least one of them is older than she, and a boy can address his two sisters as ʔɯɯj bɛɛr if at least one of them is older than he. The terms dadrooj bɛɛr and rooj bɛɛr, which can refer to married couples, are also used when talking to or about one's two younger siblings, and even – more vaguely – about any couple of young close relatives. A further term referring to a couple of young relatives, is nɔʔ bɛɛr; this expression is probably only used about much younger people (nɔʔ means 'grandchild' or 'nephew/niece').

The question how to refer unambiguously to children and to children-in-law, calls for a remark of a more general nature: the Mlabri are of course not constrained by terminology; they can easily express and specify quite complex types of family relationship in spite of the limited kinship nomenclature dealt with here. It is perfectly possible for the semantic structure to become quite complex, as when one is talking about somebody's grandparent or somebody's parent's sibling, and specifying the exact nature of the relationship for all links in the chain between the reference person and his/her relative. In such cases the Mlabri speaker can, without difficulty, bypass all terminology involving the feature of 'second order relative' and instead spell out the complex relationship in detail by expressing it as a *hierarchical configuration of first order relationships*, by means of noun phrases whose syntactic complexity directly mirrors the semantic complexity. Thus, it is perfectly possible to express 'my paternal grandmother' as ʔot ɟooŋ di mɤʔ or ʔot mɤm di mɤʔ 'my father's mother', and to express a concept such as 'younger sibling's child' by saying rooj di ʔɛɛw instead of the ambiguous term nɔɔʔ.

There is, however, certainly a difference in usage. Elaborate kinship expressions which spell out the exact nature of a complex type of relatedness, seem to be used only by the Mlabri if being explicit is crucial (e.g. because a fieldworker puts persistent questions about genealogical relationships). At one point I was told about the speaker's father's uncle, and he then said ʔot mɤm di luŋ - taaʔ using first the Thai word luŋ 'uncle' to be precise but immediately making a self-correction to the more natural Mlabri term taaʔ 'second order elder male relative'.

The framework used so far was made up of six, more or less basic, dimensions: *relative generation*, *lineal* versus *collateral* relatedness, *relative age*, *proximity* of relatedness, *sex* (of the relative), and *consanguineal* versus *affinal* relatedness. The whole presentation was a compromise between two approaches: one being to pinpoint *on a language-specific basis* what are the salient semantic features of the core terms, the other being a characterization of this kinship system within *a more or less standardized framework* for the typology of such systems. Much of what was stated for Mlabri above makes sense also for other languages of the area (several properties are shared by the Thai kinship system, for example, although I have accounted for "skewed relations" by applying the notion "proximity of relatedness", unlike Paul Benedict's classic analysis of the Thai kinship system).

The semantic dimensions presented above do not provide an exhaustive analysis of Mlabri kinship terminology, however. It seems necessary to add at least four more dimensions. These are of a more peripheral and more specific (but perhaps more interesting) kind, and they are in part encoded by modifications (elaborations) of primary kinship terms.

First, as mentioned above, there is often an ambiguity in kinship terminology in that the same term may be used about persons related by blood and also about one's kinsmen or friends. It is possible to use special terms or modified terms to make explicit that one is talking about *blood relatives*. This is true on three different levels of lineage: parents, siblings, and children.

As for parents, mɤʔ 'mother' and mɤm 'father' are standard terms for genuine (biological) parents but at least the former can also be used if one wants to address a person as one's peer or benefactor or, more directly, as one's father-in-care (this is an old tradition; as seen from Bernatzik's account of 1938 he was addressed in this way; and from my very first encounter with the β-Mlabri I have likewise always been addressed as mɤm).

To return to the kinship concepts of 'father' and 'mother', there are special terms for the parents of a new-born infant (an "ʔii choo", see later): its mother is mɛɛ choo, and its father is ta bɔ choo.

The words ʔuuj and jooŋ, which otherwise mean 'woman' and 'man', respectively, can also be used to mean 'mother' and 'father'; these terms seem to be semantically more marked than mɤʔ mɤm in that they are then always understood in the sense of genuine (biological) parents. (Often the term ɟooŋ is used instead of jooŋ; this seems to introduce an additional semantic dimension: specification of the speaker's point of reference, see below).

As for children, ʔɛɛw (which is ambiguous in that it also means 'something small') is the standard term for 'child, offspring'; a son-in-law may, according to one elderly male speaker, also counts as the ʔɛɛw of the father-in-law. The term ŋwɛʔ is sometimes used instead of ʔɛɛw to emphasize that one is referring to a person as somebody's (typically: one's own) *child in the strict sense*. The two terms can be combined into an elaborate expression ʔot ʔɛɛw ʔot ŋwɛʔ 'my child' or mɛt ʔɛɛw mɛt ŋwɛʔ 'your child'. – On the other hand, the term ʔɛɛw bɛɛr, which one would a priori expect to imply a duality of persons whenever it is used, may be neutral in this respect and refer instead to a person or persons as being "child(ren)" in some indirect way (cf. the use of ʔat bɛɛr about an in-law, as mentioned above). Thus, if one is taking socially care of somebody else, it is appropriate to use the term ʔɛɛw bɛɛr about the person(s) in one's care (one's "luuk liaŋ") no matter whether it is a matter of one person or several persons. If a whole family is supported by somebody outside the group, they are collectively his or her ʔɛɛw bɛɛr nɛŋ hmuu (using the term nɛŋ hmuu which unambiguously denotes 'the whole group').

It seems that some of the remaining doublets in Mlabri kinship terminology reflect a specification which is slightly different from that for "genuineness of relatedness", namely a specification for the speaker's *point of reference*, i.e. whether a relative is specified in relation to the speaker himself ('ego') or to some other person ('alter') whose relative is spoken of. Thus, whereas the term mɤm can be used quite generally in the meaning of 'father' (also as a term of adress), there are two other terms jooŋ and ɟooŋ (which are hardly used as terms of address) of which the former is often used about somebody else's father, the latter typically about one's own father: ʔat jooŋ 'the father' vs. ʔot ɟooŋ 'my father'.

The terms ʔɛɛw laŋ 'son' and ʔɛɛw kmɲah 'daughter' are used about somebody else's children (the modifier laŋ, which as a separate term means 'husband', occurs also in the expression rooj laŋ "younger brother", i.e. 'younger male relative' or 'younger kinsman'). In contrast, ʔot ʔɛɛw ləmbuuŋ makes precise that one is speaking about one's *own* child. It can be specified also whether this is a son or a daughter: ʔot ʔɛɛw məɲiŋ/lameet 'my child female/male'. Most often, however, one would just say ʔot ʔɛɛw.

In addition to these more idiosyncratic lexicalizations encoding something about the speaker's point of reference, it is possible to use expressions involving the lexeme chak in the meaning of 'with reference to self'. The expression ʔat chak, with preposed definite article, means 'the person himself/herself' (cf. the expression ʔat bɛɛr 'the other one', i.e. the person's spouse, which was mentioned above). This lexeme chak is used as an epithet, for example in distinguishing between reference to the person's own child, ʔɛɛw chak (note: a child-in-law is also an ʔɛɛw chak), and reference to somebody else's child, kumɔɔm chak (namely: not-genuine-child relative to self). The expression kumɔɔm chak is also used as an address term when talking to younger relatives.

This leads over to a further distinction, which I know too little about, namely the difference between terms used when *speaking about* relatives, and kinship terms used as *address terms*. Very often these are the same, but at least in some cases there is a difference of usage.

By "kinship terms used as address terms" I do not just refer to the use of such terms as speaker-dependent proper nouns used to address the appropriate persons (as in *Please help me, Mother*) but also to their use as the functional equivalent of a second person pronoun (as when a speaker chooses to appeal to his/her mother by saying *Can Mother help me, please?*). A less sloppy terminology might be called for, but in view of the scarcity of information on this whole issue which can be extracted from the Mlabri data, the terminological vagueness does not do much harm.

As for siblings or kinsmen of the same generation, the most unmarked address terms are rooj and diŋ. As stated earlier, these are totally ambiguous: the former may just mean something like 'junior of same generation', and the latter 'senior of same generation', although they are very often used about true siblings. In contrast, there are two (borrowed) terms ʔɯɯj 'Elder Sister' and ʔaaj 'Elder Brother' which seem to be used only when a Mlabri addresses close blood relatives, more specifically *true siblings*.

This raises the question who counts as a "true sibling". One of the speakers claimed that he himself would be addressed by his elder brother's daughter as ʔaaj, whereas his wife would be addressed by her as diŋ. This is consistent with the above generalization if we assume that he, as her uncle, would count as an elder sibling in the strict sense because he is *a close blood-relative who is older than she but younger than her father*, whereas his wife does not exhibit such close blood-relatedness and can only qualify as elder "sibling" in the vague sense.

To round off this listing of dimensions in Mlabri kinship terminology, there is sometimes a distinction of *spheres of usage:* some terms are used specifically by *female speakers* ("female language"), others by *male speakers* ("male language"). This differentiation occurs at least with the modified terms ʔɛɛw mɯlh 'daughter' (female language) versus ʔɛɛw məɲɩŋ with the same meaning (male language). At one point it was also explained to me that kumɔɔm 'younger relative' is female language whereas **dadrooj** with the same meaning is male language, but there is very conflicting evidence on this.

To sum up, it seems possible to account componentially for the kinship terminology in Mlabri by distinguishing *five primary dimensions:* relative generation, relative age, proximity of relatedness, sex, and relatedness by marriage, and *three secondary dimensions* which mostly specify something about the nature of the relatedness from the speaker's point of view. The latter set of dimensions are in many cases not utilized, or one may say that there is an unmarked "default" choice for each of these dimensions.

Such a componential analysis is in itself only a very coarse account of kinship nomenclature, but I hope it has served to demonstrate two things: (i) The Mlabri kinship nomenclature reflects a strong cultural emphasis on *relationships of the first order* (true siblings, parents and their children), and on the *exact nature of the relatedness* within such first order relationships. (ii) The Mlabri conception of relatedness is such that *certain in-laws count as blood relatives* (this might suggest that "blood relatedness" is not really the proper term to use when one discusses Mlabri kinship institutions).

The analysis would become more interesting if compared with a careful study of *the functional status of various family relationships within the culture.* Unfortunately, it has not been possible within the limitations of my fieldwork to systematically address such anthropological issues as the institutions of marriage, descent and standardized social relations. As a result, the lexical entries for kinship terms in the dictionary below do not tell the whole story.

Mlabri kinship terminology refers in many instances to the *age* of a person. As mentioned in chapter 2 above, titles used with personal names include the etyma taaʔ, jaaʔ used to mean senior male and senior female. There are also a variety of lexical items which specifically refer to age categories when used as full nouns. I shall illustrate the relative richness of terminology in this field by listing some terms for *children and young people.*

In β-Mlabri, a newborn infant (which has not yet been given a name) is ʔii choo, and a small baby is ʔɛɛw thwɛɲ. A child old enough to be able to walk is rɛɛm chet, and if somewhat older, dik theeŋ. A young girl is luŋguh; a girl old enough to marry but not yet married is hnrɤɤʔ ; if she has married one can refer to her status as miɲiŋ ʔa bɤɤn laŋ. A young, and specifically an unmarried man is hnum or baaw (both loanwords); when fully adult he is tareeŋ, and if married he may be referred to as ləmeet ʔa bɤɤn hmaaj. Interestingly enough, the terminology found in α-Mlabri is almost totally different (the only shared term I know of is luŋguh meaning 'woman' in α-Mlabri).

It seems appropriate here to comment briefly on a related and difficult area: the use of *titles* with personal names. α-Mlabri and β-Mlabri both use the Thai words taaʔ, jaaʔ (which also have the general meanings of 'grandfather, uncle' and 'grandmother, aunt') when they refer to senior males and females but in α-Mlabri these words are also the regular titles with names of seniors: if a man is ta mʌc, his wife is ja mʌc. In β-Mlabri, taaʔ and jaaʔ as titles before names, exist but seem obsolete; I have heard them used only with the names of ancestors who died long ago and whose names have an altogether archaic flavour: ta hlew, ta luaam, ta runcun (or ta rɯncɯn), jaa klup and ja chiheen.

Nowadays, the β-Mlabri use another set of titles (also of Thai origin): bɔ(ɔ) (senior male), mɛ(ɛ) (senior female), ba(a) (junior male) and ʔi(i) (junior female or, in the case of very small children, neutral).

As mentioned already in the preface the biologically based classification of people into 'female' and 'male' pervades Mlabri linguistic usage. It is interesting that there is nevertheless neutralization in the naming of small children. Especially among the α-Mlabri, the otherwise female title ʔii is used with the names of boys up to puberty. This might suggest that children are categorized conceptually as forming one category, which is aligned with the category of (adult) females. That makes sense socially, but it is at variance with the ways in which the Mlabri otherwise speak about their children.

In this context it should be taken into consideration that titles such as ʔii reflect a very recent influence from Lao and Northern Thai and are thus not indicative of traditional Mlabri conceptualization. In fact, the only male β-Mlabri whom I know to have a very young son prefers to refer to him as ba woŋ with a *male* title, although I have heard others call the boy ʔi woŋ.

The choice between a junior or senior title is not primarily dependent on marital status, but rather on the absence or presence of offspring. Both the title and the personal name itself may change with major events during a lifetime. A person may have at least three different names through his or her life. These changes occur with marriage and childbirth.

Items from the two sets of titles above may be combined. I have often heard the male senior of one of the households referred to as ta bɔ chuʌŋ. This seems to be the only usage in which the old titles are not obsolete. On the other hand, family-members within a household often refer to or address each other simply by name, without using any title. This may seem to cause potential ambiguities, as when the father bɔ khit and his son ba khit may both be called khit in very informal speech within the family. It is my impression, however, that this use of a name without title never extends to the senior woman of a household; she is always mentioned or addressed with the title mɛɛ (Thai for 'mother') preposed to the name.

This leads over to the question of *Name-Sharing* among husband and wife and child. Such name-sharing is the rule in α-Mlabri but it may not have been the prevailing usage among the β-Mlabri in former time when the senior titles ta and ja were used as in α-Mlabri (I have never heard ta hlew's wife referred to as *ja hlew, for example). Name-sharing is, however, found along with the titles bɔ(ɔ), mɛ(ɛ) etc., so that there is one name in the family which is shared by the senior man and woman and also by one of their children, whereas the other children are given quite different names (thus it is not quite appropriate just to call the shared name a "family name"). I was told by bɔ khit that it would be proper to address his wife as mɛɛ khit, and he did that himself all the time; her maiden name was mentioned to me only when I asked specifically about it.

With these issues we have switched from a semantic to a social perspective. The conventions for the naming of persons call for a *functional* explanation. Suebsaeng (1992, p. 89-90) points out that name-sharing combined with the changes of name after each marriage limits the depth of descent tracking to three generations and that it offers possibilities for the Mlabri "to select spouses under the pressure of limited population and incest prohibition". I agree on this as a general hypothesis (some of the α-Mlabri data in Suebsaeng 1992 deviate from my own data, however); it falls in line with the apparent scarcity of kinship terms for distant relatives although it does not fully explain the care with which types of close relatives are specified (see above).

Finally a word about the *Personal Names* themselves. There does not seem to be much left of the traditional repertory of proper names among the β-Mlabri, so there is no way to study what semantic fields used to be exploited in the use of nouns as names: the oldest names are not etymologically transparent, and the present names look, on the whole, like quite recent borrowings (mostly words of Thai-type).

The α-Mlabri for the most part have *two different names* at the same time: a Thai-based name (which is referred to as a *nickname* by Suebsaeng 1992, but which is always the name used in external relations) and a name of Mlabri origin. I have not observed anything similar to that in the case of the β-Mlabri.

Chapter 5
Syntax

Except for the section on "Clause and sentence" in α-Mlabri in Tongkum (1992, p. 53-57) there seems to be no previous information about Mlabri syntax available. This is not very surprising; what is more remarkable is that, with the exception of Kmhmu, the grammars of the Mon-Khmer languages closest to Mlabri have not been described in much detail either.

What has been written earlier on minority languages of Indochina has been using a variety of approaches, e.g. Transformational Grammar, Tagmemics or Lexicase Grammar. This easily creates a situation in which readers of such work, if they (like myself) belong to other traditions, tend to focus on the understanding of the formalization itself without necessarily obtaining easy access to an understanding of the linguistic phenomena.

I have here chosen the opposite extreme: to present and discuss the findings in an informal way within the framework of a rather traditional overall arrangement of the presentation. Up to now the all-encompassing problem in linguistic work on Mlabri has been just to *understand* the words, phrases and sentences that are available as raw material. It has been my main ambition to characterize β-Mlabri grammar in a way which is both general and explicit enough to serve as easily accessible input to genetic and typological studies.

One of the major problems is how to define word-classes. That problem, however, is essentially the same for all languages of the area. In this presentation, no attempt has been made to offer rigorous definitions of categories such as Noun, Verb Adverb, and so on. For purely practical reasons, I operate with a pooled category of words of "minor" lexical categories which are here referred to as Grammatical Words (some would say Function Words, as distinct from Semantic Words or Lexical Words).

It is possible, and perhaps useful, to subdivide grammatical words into three main categories: (1) "Adverbs & Minor Verbs" (i.e. Preverbs, Coverbs, Directional Verbs, etc.), (2) "Connectives" or "Connectors" (i.e. Conjunctions, Relativizers, Possessive Marker, etc.), and (3) "Inflection-like Markers" (Article, Aspect Marker).

This somewhat arbitrary subdivision creates a problem with Prepositions, however, since these are from one point of view Transitive Adverbs, from another point of view Connectives taking nouns (rather than verbs or clauses) as complements.

Since much of what is stated below will sound almost trivial for readers familiar with Mon-Khmer languages, I wish to point out that Mlabri also has its characteristic and in some instances rather unique features, which are treated along with more well-known phenomena. These features include the use of grammatical devices to encode such meanings as 'perfective', 'definite' and 'possessive' and they also include the order of sentence constituents in Mlabri.

5.1 Phrasal Syntax

For ease of exposition, the present outline of β-Mlabri syntax is divided into two parts. I shall deal first with "phrasal syntax", understood as *the internal structure of the major constituents of clauses*: noun phrases, adverbial phrases and verb phrases. Afterwards (in section 5.2 below), the structure of whole sentences will be described.

5.1.1 Noun Phrases and Pronominal Constructions

In Mlabri syntax there is one type of syntagm which is fairly easy to recognize: the Noun Phrase. It is, however, a different matter to define what is meant by "Noun Phrase". Depending on one's theoretical orientation the definition may be based on external or internal criteria. On the one hand one may define noun phrases with reference to a basic property of their phrase-internal structure: that they (typically) contain a noun (noun phrases considered as maximal projections of nouns). On the other hand one may consider noun phrases from the point of view of their *function*, as arguments of verbs (sentence subjects, objects, etc.) or as complements to prepositions. The other extreme, then, is to call a syntactic constituent a "noun phrase", whenever it fulfills such syntactic functions, irrespective of whether the phrase actually contains a noun or whether it consists of other material (e.g. a clause or even a verb).

I shall here tacitly assume that external and internal criteria such as those above converge on a type of nominal constituent in Mlabri which is a *Noun Phrase* in the strict sense, and I shall base the exposition (which makes no claims as to exhaustiveness) on the prototypical noun phrase.

It makes sense to narrow the scope in this way since sentence arguments in Mlabri are always coded by syntactic constructions which contain either a substantive or a personal pronoun (unless the argument in question is pragmatically predictable and therefore happens to have a *null* representation in the syntactic string). More specifically, the arguments are encoded as noun phrases not as clauses.

This is indisputably true of sentence subjects (I have not come across Mlabri sentences which invite an analysis with a clausal subject, as in English *that he is ill worries me*). Whether or not it is found to be true of sentence objects depends on one's analytical framework. According to one analysis a sentence such as dɤŋ mɤm ɟrʌʌk 'look father drink' i.e. 'observe that Father drinks' contains a clausal object. According to another analysis it consists of two consecutive clauses linked together by a shared (in Y.R. Chao's terminology: "pivotal") constituent; in this case the noun mɤm 'father' is the object of the first clause and the subject in the second. I greatly prefer the second type of analysis, which in my view makes more sense with such constructions. Accordingly, there are no sentences in my data which force an analysis with a clausal object.

In Mlabri there exists a noun phrase type similar to complex noun phrases in Thai, i.e. with a *bipartite structure* comprising a central and a peripheral (optional) constituent.

I shall here refer to the central constituent of the noun phrase as "definitional and descriptive". It contains as its nucleus a noun, and it may contain additional modifying material.

I shall refer to the peripheral (i.e. initial and/or final) part of the noun phrase as "specificational and quantifying". It consists of, on the one hand, demonstrative and article-like material and, on the other hand, numerals and (sometimes) classifiers serving as carriers of numerals. There may even be adverbial material present in this constituent of the noun phrase, which encodes quantitative, qualitative and deictic information.

Before going further into the structure of noun phrases I wish to make a few comments on *referentiality* and on nouns versus pronouns.

As in other languages, noun phrases encode information which may (depending on the context) be higher or lower on a scale of referentiality. It is mostly noun phrases which consist of a single noun that are used in a generic sense: mlaʔ krʌw biɯk, literally 'person fear bear' i.e. 'the Mlabri are afraid of bears'. A single noun may, however, also be semantically incorporated in a verb phrase so that the degree of referentiality is nil: boŋ juuk 'eat rice' (often used to mean just 'eat' like the Thai equivalent kin khâaw). Contrariwise, a single noun may have a very high degree of referentiality in a discourse situation: it may function like a second or third person pronoun. A very frequent example is mɤm 'father' which is used respectfully to mean 'you' or 'he', but in appropriate contexts other nouns which denote persons or animals may have a similar referential status. It must be emphasized that although Mlabri has a set of first and second person pronouns (which are used extremely frequently), there seems to be no specific third person pronoun so that anaphoric or deictic reference to third person must be encoded by means of more or less conventionalized noun phrases.

After this digression we shall consider the more or less complex internal structure of the "definitional and descriptive" part of noun phrases.

The simplest noun phrase consists of a substantive or pronoun: ʔɛɛw 'child' (or 'children'), ʔoh 'I'. The noun may be preceded by the definite article: at ʔɛɛw 'the child' (or 'the children').

The material preceded by the article sometimes raises questions of word-class membership. This is true of certain directional and locational expressions functioning as noun phrases such as ʔat ti nɛj 'the inner, the inside' (of which ti and nɛj are borrowings from Thai). This expression may, for example, refer to the inner set of wings of an insect but only if this set is contrasted with ʔat luɤt 'the outer (part), the outside', i.e. the outer set of wings. In themselves the expressions ti nɛj and luɤt have no denotations other than 'inner' vs. 'outer'. If wings are semantically contrasted with other body-parts, then both sets of wings of an insect are indiscriminately referred to as ʔat hnʌr 'the wing(s)'.

And now to more complex constructions. Leaving aside for the moment the existence of a language-specific *possessive construction* with di (which will be dealt with separately below because of its typological importance) the two main types of complex constructions are Noun + Noun and Noun + Verb:

(i) The nuclear construction contains a succession of two nouns. In the majority of cases the first noun is the semantic and syntactic head, while the second noun contributes to the referential and descriptive meaning of the noun phrase e.g. by defining *location or possessor*, as when mlaa 'person' and briiʔ 'forest' combine to form mlaʔ briiʔ 'forest people', 'people of the forest', i.e. 'Mlabri'. The second noun may also define a *specific status or function* in relation to some (explicit or implicit) referent; the meaning of the attribute is then often metaphorical (or seemingly metaphorical), as when tuul 'tip, point' combines with ʔɛɛw 'child' into ʔɛɛw tuul 'youngest child'. In still other cases the modifying noun has an appositional status: the semantic relation of the head noun to the modifying noun is a more or less *symmetrical, characterizational relation* which corresponds to that between subject and predicate noun in a clause, as when ʔɛɛw 'child' and ləmeet 'man' combine to form ʔɛɛw ləmeet 'son'.

There is furthermore a semantically and syntactically interesting construction in which a noun denoting size is followed by a noun denoting the object referred to. This occurs very frequently with ʔɛɛw 'small' (also meaning 'child, offspring'): ʔɛɛw chindɛh 'small cup', etc. It also occurs with blaaj 'big' (which has a very limited distribution), e.g. blaaj pompoo 'big elephant' or blaaj trlɔh 'big pot', and (only sporadically?) with kwʌŋ (a word which otherwise occurs as a classifier for pots and the like): kwʌŋ kiiʔ, which seems to mean 'many months'. At first sight one may speculate that the qualitative modifier comes before the head in such expressions, but maybe the size-word is to be understood as an abstract noun which functions as the syntactic head of the construction, whereas the noun having material denotation is its modifier: 'a smallness of cup', 'a bigness of elephant', etc.

This construction may even involve a succession of three nouns beginning with the size-noun and ending with the noun which in itself denotes the gross category of things referred to. Whereas a pointed knife is tɔʔ tuul 'knife (with) tip' (which a modifying second noun), I have been told that big and small knives of this type are called blaaj tuul tɔʔ and ʔɛɛw tuul tɔʔ, respectively. This invites an analysis according to which blaj tuul 'big tip' or ʔɛɛw tuul 'small tip' forms one constituent of a left-branching noun phrase, and tɔʔ the other constituent, since the meaning of the third word is qualified by the combined meaning of the first two words (the lexicalization blaaj tuul tɔʔ is a hyponym of tɔʔ, not of tuul). I would otherwise have guessed that such expressions should be analyzed quite differently, namely as right-branching with a second constituent tuul tɔʔ 'tip (of) knife', in which case they should specify the size of the *tip* rather than the size and shape of the *knife*. (I am indebted to Søren Egerod for suggestive commentaries on the various constructions with blaaj and ʔɛɛw.)

Another conspicuous construction is phakhaaw girwɛj 'white ball-shaped' i.e. 'round white object', e.g. a white rubber or plastic ball with which children play. Semantically it is interesting that whiteness rather than ball-shape here seems to be encoded as the basic property of the thing denoted (needless to say, this contention only makes sense if the construction is to be understood as head + modifier like most noun phrases). Also from a strictly syntactic point of view the construction is strange since phakhaaw is otherwise a stative verb (adjective), which frequently occurs as a modifier after a noun. It is hardly relevant to the analysis that colour names such as phakhaaw are originally noun phrases in Thai (denoting cloth of specific colours); it is more relevant that girwɛj is probably a nominalization (from a putative verb *gwɛj). The material does not permit any generalizations, however.

Finally, two nouns which enter a *coordinate* construction may be semantically on a par with each other in that they denote complementary parts of a pair: mɤʔ mɤm 'mother father', i.e. 'mother and father'; ʔuuj jooŋ 'female male', i.e. 'woman and man'; and rooj diŋ 'younger sibling (and) elder sibling'. The construction is well-known from the grammar of Thai etc., so there is no reason to comment specifically on it here except by pointing out that such coordinate constructions behave as *phrasal constructions not compounds* with respect to referentiality: a term such as mɤʔ mɤm refers to the two members separately, not jointly. I have never heard a sentence in which a coordinate construction was headed by one determiner, although the concept of 'one set of parents' is important: it is used when a Mlabri wants to explain whether two persons are true siblings, i.e. have the same parents. In such cases it is hardly possible to say *dəmɔ mɤʔ mɤm; it is necessary to specify each term separately with the same determiner: dəmɔ mɤʔ dəmɔ mɤm 'one(-and-the-same) mother, one(-and-the-same) father'.

Such constructions are actually used when necessary. For example, once when I was told about two Mlabri men that they were rooj diŋ 'younger and older sibling' I became confused because they were not supposed to have the same parents according to the predigree which I was working on. I was then told that I had misunderstood the speaker: the two were just "brothers" in the sense of kinsmen of the same generation (cf. Thai phîi nɔ́ɔŋ). The speaker used a long explanation to clear this up in which the determiner mɔ 'one' occurred four times: ba thɔɔŋ tɛɛ mɔ mɤʔ mɔ mɤm, ba kham tɛɛ mɔ mɤʔ mɔ mɤm, dadrooj tɛɛ bah; i.e. 'Ba Thong had one set of parents, Ba Kham had another set of parents, he wasn't a younger sibling'.

Mlabri also exhibits complex noun phrases containing *nouns or noun phrases conjoined by a connective*: nɛŋ, nɯŋ, lɯŋ, which is similar in function to Thai kàp and thus sometimes translatable as a conjunction 'and': mɤm nɛŋ ʔoh 'Father and I'. However, other occurrences of these connectives clearly show that they are prepositions rather than conjunctions, i.e. that they form adverbial complements together with the syntactic material governed by them: jɤɤm nɛŋ ʔɛɛw 'stay with (the) children', krɔɔ nɛŋ mɛh 'request (something) from you'. There is no connective in coordinate noun phrase constructions such as ʔmɛh ʔoh bɛɛr mlaaʔ 'you I two person' i.e. 'the two of us'.

It is not clear to me to what extent it is possible (or at all fruitful) to subclassify nuclear constructions of the various kinds above as either phrasal constructions or compounds.

Possessive constructions represent by far the most striking feature of Mlabri syntax. Typologically, what one expects to find in this geographical area is a construction with *Possessum (as Head) followed by Possessor (as Modifier)*. In Mlabri there is an extremely frequent Noun Phrase type N+N which consists of Head plus Modifier (cf. above) but it is not a strictly possessive construction: its domain of use is with a modifier which is *non-referential* and is understood as qualifying the meaning of the head, as in mlaʔ briiʔ 'man forest', i.e. 'forest people'; ʔɛɛw ləmeet 'child male', i.e. 'son'; and ʔɛɛw braɲ 'child/young dog', i.e. 'whelp'. (The more elaborate possessive construction N+N+N, as in Thai, with an intervening word which denotes that the referent of the first noun is the 'possessed thing' of the referent of the last noun, does not seem to exist in Mlabri.)

If possession in the strict sense is intended, and if the possessor is high on the scale of referentiality, the regular Mlabri construction is *Possessor plus Connective plus Possessum*, which is very unusual for a Mon-Khmer language (there is nothing like it in Tin or Kmhmu). The connective used in this construction is di. Thus braɲ di ʔɛɛw means 'the young of the dog', 'the dog's whelp(s)'.

The word di is not limited to functioning as a connective in possessive noun phrases. A homophonous word di occurs also in complex predicate constructions: ɟak di thɛh chɤm 'go IMPERATIVE well just', i.e. 'take care on the journey!' (the construction V + di + V is taken up in section 5.1.3 below). Even if di in this case is considered a different function word for the purpose of grammatical description, the question remains how to classify the connective di in possessive constructions, e.g. as a resumptive possessive pronoun or a postposition. (The dual role of di, as a connective in possessive constructions and as a complementizer, is strangely reminiscent of Modern Chinese də.)

A construction consisting only of *Connective plus Possessum* occurs if the Possessor is already established in the discourse so that the reference relations are clear, e.g. in constructions such as ʔat mɤm guɯt hɔɔt di ʔɛɛw 'the father misses his child' (in this case the word di superficially translates as a reflexive possessive pronoun). In such cases constructions with the definite article ʔat (which expresses that the referents belong together, cf. below) may also occur.

These findings show that di is not a postposition which marks the preceding nouns as possessor but a determiner occurring in front of the possessum. Semantically it resembles possessive pronouns.

There are two indisputable possessive pronouns in Mlabri: first and second person singular: ʔot, mɛt, as in ʔot gɛɛŋ 'my house' and mɛt ʔɛɛw 'your child(ren)'. These forms occur in environments where (generalizing from the construction N+di+N) one might expect combinations of ʔoh 'I' and mɛh 'you' with di (the latter constructions are also heard, at least in α-Mlabri). – See futher the paragraph on Deixis and Anaphoric Reference below.

Clearly, *referentiality* is a crucial aspect of possessive (as against Head-Modifier) constructions in Mlabri. This aspect may, however, escape the analyst's attention if Thai is used as the medium of communication in data elicitation: one then easily supposes that a construction such as braɲ di ʔɛɛw is largely synonymous with ʔɛɛw braɲ.

Another main type of construction within the definitional and descriptive part of Mlabri noun phrases involves *a verb (or verb phrase) in second position as a descriptive modifier*. Such constructions are frequent, an example being pleeʔ 'fruit' and chat 'be sour' which can combine to form pleʔ chat 'orange (fruit)'. The very same type of construction may occur as a clause and may even form a complete sentence by itself: mlaʔ chɛʔ 'people be numerous', i.e. 'there are many people'.

As in many other languages of Indochina it often seems obscure whether a verb is to be understood as a noun phrase modifier or as a clause predicate. From a cognitive-semantic point of view there is obviously a distinction between elaborating a nominal argument and making a proposition or question, but if one determines that there should be two types of predication in the syntax of a language of Mlabri type, there may be a risk that the resulting categories reflect the descriptive framework rather than being genuine properties of the language.

The interpretation is normally unambiguous with regard to parsing if the verb(-adjective) in question follows a postverbal sentence object: glɤh cəboh chuuŋ definitely means 'climb a high mountain' (one might perhaps construe situations in which a combinations of two propositions 'climb the mountain, it is high' is a possible interpretation, but I presume that prosody would disambiguate such an utterance). There is, however, a possibility of genuine ambiguity of meaning if the noun in question stands in utterance-initial position. Although the syntax may be neutral in relation to different interpretations, such ambiguity is nevertheless a cognitive reality. It is often *referentiality* that is the crucial issue.

A string such as juuk kibliiŋ boŋ met bɤɤn, literally 'rice raw/unripe eat not can', may be understood as a sequential combination of (i) a predication which reports an observation about a portion of rice to which the utterance makes unique reference and (ii) the corollary of this observation, i.e. two coupled clauses: 'the rice is raw (or: unripe), one cannot eat it'. There is, however, another possible interpretation according to which juuk kibliiŋ is a topicalized argument to boŋ so that there is a single proposition, namely a didactic statement about rice as a generic category: 'one cannot eat raw (or unripe) rice'.

Such ambiguities of parsing may well be resolved by prosodic means (I would speculate that it might perhaps be signalled by a pronounced break after kibliiŋ in the former case versus a lesser break or no break in the latter case) but I have no empirical data which make it possible to settle such issues. Moreover, it is often difficult to make speakers of the language provide Northern Thai paraphrases of Mlabri sentences, and vice versa, that are so exact that they give a decisive clue to the interpretation, especially since Thai shares some of the structural and semantic ambiguity of predication. The translation of examples in the dictionary below as either phrasal or sentential is often somewhat arbitrary; in many cases two alternative readings are both technically possible if the string is considered in isolation.

Several of the speech tokens constituting the data employed here were gathered in purely monolingual settings so that the understanding of each utterance was not just disambiguated by the context but entirely dependent upon a successful understanding of the discourse. This means that the translations given may at times represent a certain amount of guesswork also with regard to the interpretation of predication as "adjective-like" or "verb-like". Such difficulties are certainly not unique to Mlabri studies but they are enhanced by the difficulties associated with field work on this language.

That concludes my presentation of constructions within the definitional and descriptive part of noun phrases in Mlabri. If we proceed now to the "peripheral", the *specifying and quantifying parts of the noun phrase*, we find that most grammatical words of determiner and quantifier status *precede* the nucleus of the noun phrase. This is true, for example, of interrogative ʔitɯ 'which', as in ʔitɯ mlaaʔ 'what person?, who?' (here α-Mlabri differs in having a two-place determiner: tɯʔ mlaʔ ɲʌʌ).

Deictics, on the other hand, occur after the nucleus of the noun phrase, e.g. nɛh 'here' in tawɪn nɛh 'day here' i.e. 'this day' = 'today'. Formally this is a noun phrase but in expressions of time it may function as an adverbial phrase. Material of this kind, such as ɲaam gʌh 'time this' = 'now(adays)', which otherwise occurs in clause-final position as sentence adverbial, may also occur as a postnominal adjunct within a noun phrase of argument status (i.e. functioning as sentence subject or object): dɔ mlaʔ ɲaam gʌh met mʌc cɯɯ 'people nowadays have no experience of them' (referring to certain mythological giant ants)'.

Numerals mostly occur before *Classifiers* (see below). There is, however, also a construction with just one noun preceded by a numeral: mɤm toc bɛɛr hmaaj 'father had two wives'.

In noun phrases which are of a bipartite structure, the second (specifying and quantifying) part has as its nucleus a classifier, to which determiners, quantifiers and deictics are allocated (as in Thai): mlaʔ ləboʔ ɲʌʔ 'person piece that-one' i.e. 'that person'. The word ləbooʔ is a general classifier; there are also more specific classifiers selected by the meaning of the noun (see the entry "Noun Classifier" in the English-Mlabri Index). β-Mlabri has a fair number of classifiers, more than we have recorded for α-Mlabri though apparently fewer than Tin.

Classifiers are used particularly if *number* is specified (and if the items are considered as a set rather than as individual referents). The numeral then occurs before the classifier: chɯɹɛɛ bɛɛr ləboʔ 'shirt two piece(s)' i.e. 'two shirts'. In combination with numerals *measure terms* may also occur in the syntactic slot occupied by classifiers (as in Thai), cf. lam dəmɔ wec 'wood one length' in mɛh ɟak pɤjh lam dəmɔ wec 'you shall cut off one length of wood'.

The use of classifiers is tricky in the case of nouns which refer to human beings. If the classifier has a demonstrative modifier such as gʌh 'this', there are several options. One is to use the word mlaaʔ, which means 'human being' (or more specifically: 'ethnic Mlabri'), as a classifier: mlaʔ gʌh. Another option is to use the all-purpose classifier: ləboʔ gʌh. A third is to use as classifier the Thai word for 'body': too gʌh (Central Thai tua).

These classifiers, however, cannot always be used indiscriminately when referring to human beings; if the classifier is modified by a numeral, it seems inappropriate to use too (perhaps because it has certain connotations due to its origin as a word for 'body': it is not appropriate to speak of a multitude of girls as a series of human bodies). Thus, although it is perfectly in order to say miɲiŋ too gʌh 'this girl', one must say miɲiŋ bɛɛr ləboʔ or miɲiŋ bɛɛr mlaaʔ in order to convey the meaning of 'two girls'.

If the meaning of the nuclear noun is understood from the context, it can be left out so that the classifier with its determiner(s) fills the subject or object slot alone: too gʌh, too ɲʌʔ, too ʔa noɲ 'this person, that person, all of them'. Since the classifiers are in themselves nouns, and since demonstratives such as gʌh function both as pronominal determiners and as adverbials, one might claim that a sentence constituent such as too gʌh, which lacks a preceding nucleus, allows for two syntactic analyses: as classifier plus determiner (literally: 'person this') or as nuclear noun plus adverbial (literally 'body here'). The solution must be based, in each single case, on the evidence for one or the other analysis which *the context* provides.

Determiner function is a difficult issue in the analysis of Mlabri. Mlabri differs from Thai and several other languages of the area by having (in addition to postnominal determiners such as gʌh and ɲʌʔ) a Prenominal Determiner ʔat which may be classified as a kind of *Definite Article*. It identifies the referent of the noun phrase as an integral part of the situation that is being talked about (rather than referring back to an antecedent in the discourse, see further the paragraph on Deixis and Anaphoric Reference below). This article has the phonological form ʔat in β-Mlabri (in α-Mlabri the form ʔat occurs only in conservative speech; it has been replaced by ʔak in younger speech). There is nothing similar to this prenominal determiner ʔat (or ʔak) in either Tin or Kmhmu.

Downgrading of referentiality, on the other hand, occurs when a noun is governed by the word dɔ in a construction which denotes an indefinite quantity, or an indefinite number of items from an open set, as in the following passage (from a mythological narrative): dɔɔk dɔ ʔuj jooŋ, dɔɔk dɔ ʔuj jooŋ 'put dɔ woman man, put dɔ woman man', i.e. 'place people there in couples, one couple after the other'.

With negative met, dɔ encodes the meaning of 'there not being any X who', cf. the sentence (cited for a different purpose above): dɔ mlaʔ ɲaam gʌh met mʌc cɯɯ 'of person time this not experience' i.e. 'nobody nowadays has any experience of them', 'people nowadays have no experience of them'.

The dɔ-construction in object position is reminiscent of the "partitive genitive" which is used in some languages to encode 'indefinite quantity' (superficially it resembles such phenomena as the French use of *de* + Definite Article + Noun; in Mlabri, however, there is a significant absence of the Definite Article ʔat after dɔ). Its position before a noun and the indefiniteness which it encodes may suggest that dɔ is a kind of pronoun. It also occurs in quite different syntactic positions, however, e.g. in verb phrases such as ʔa dɔ thɛh (in α-Mlabri ʔa dɔ ʔdii) 'PERF dɔ be-good', i.e. something like 'that is all right', 'that is fine with me', and clause-initially in a statement about a natural cause: kuup (tɛɛ) dɔ mɛʔ hot '(but) there are clouds dɔ rain falls', i.e. 'there are clouds because it rains' (or perhaps more exactly translated 'clouds stem from the fall of rain'). All these uses of dɔ may perhaps be assigned to one lexical item if that word is a generalized connective (also see section 5.2.2 below), perhaps basically a preposition meaning something like 'of, from'.

Both semantically and pragmatically, the construction V + dɔ + N differs in complex ways from the construction V + N (with N as a straightforward sentence object). The latter is referentially ambiguous: it may encode the object as non-referential (incorporating it semantically with the verb) but on the contrary it may also may encode the object as having specific reference. The construction with dɔ, on the other hand, always seems to encode indefiniteness ('some N'): it may be said to imply a covert existential proposition or question which underlies this indefiniteness ('there is some N such that...', 'is there some N such that...?') but no referential identification.

Moreover, the dɔ + N construction also occurs in subject position, at least with a following negation, which changes the overall semantics of the construction (cf. the example above; this is the only example of a subject noun phrase with dɔ which I have recorded so far).

These remarks are very tentative, indeed; the semantics of dɔ-constructions cannot be analysed satisfactorily on the basis of the meagre data at my disposal.

The use of dɔ with mass nouns is illustrated by the following bit of discourse, which I happened to overhear. A small boy was throwing up, and his father asked the boy's mother: gɯm dɔ hmiʌŋ 'Has he been chewing "miang" (fermented tea)?', to which the latter answered: boŋ dɔ khanom dɔ gɛjh, dɔ miʌŋ met gɯm 'He has eaten biscuits (khanom) and crab's meat (gɛjh), but he hasn't chewed any "miang"' (the two renderings of the word "miang" reflect variation).

Numerical quantification is another strange phenomenon in Mlabri syntax, though the particular features are distributional and configurational rather than semantic. Quantification may be implemented as *modification on a classifier* placed after the semantic head of a complex noun phrase: kwʌr bɛɛr mlaaʔ 'outsider two person' i.e. 'two outsiders (non-Mlabri)'. It may also be implemented as modification on a noun which occurs alone, provided that the noun in question is one that occurs as a classifier: dəmɔ mlaaʔ 'one person' or 'one and the same person' (such constructions might be described as consisting, on a more abstract level, of a *latent* noun followed by Numeral plus Classifier).

Numerical quantification by means of such simple or complex constructions is strictly limited to numbers that can be counted on one hand, and there are severe constraints even on the use of the lowest five numerals.

The first five Mlabri numerals are mɔɔj bɛɛr pɛʔ pon thɤɤŋ, but only the numerals '2' and '4' occur as quantifiers on noun phrases, and the former is often replaced by the Thai numeral sɔɔŋ (chɔɔŋ). Precise numbers higher than '2' or '3' are seldom expressed when speaking Mlabri. Mlabri linguistic usage does not even include a simple expression for 'three items': the speakers do not ever say *pɛʔ mlaaʔ in the meaning of 'three persons', and although it is quite usual to say pon mlaaʔ, that expression will mostly be understood as meaning 'several people' rather than exactly 'four people'. If a Mlabri needs to express the exact number '3', then the point of departure is the salient number '2'; after that an adverb hlooj, which apparently means 'odd' or 'and an extra one', is added at the very end of the noun phrase: bɛɛr ləboʔ hlooj 'three pieces (e.g. three fruits)'.

Traditional Mlabri culture hardly uses numerical concepts such as 'ten days from now', and on the whole they seem to prefer to use a Thai phrase in order to express numbers higher than three or four. I have, however, occasionally heard such expressions as gajh gal tawɪn 'nine (or) ten days', which is probably a linguistic calque.

There is another, interesting option: it is possible for speakers who know how to count to ten in Mlabri to count upwards while looking at or mentally visualizing a set of items, and to use this series of numerals as one complex noun modifier. On one occasion a Mlabri speaker talked to me about a large group of spear-carrying Mlabri persons (i.e. α-Mlabri) whom his parents had once met: they were mɔɔj bɛɛr pɛʔ pon thɤɤŋ thaal gul tiʔ gajh gal mlaaʔ, i.e. 'one, two, three, four, five, six, seven, eight, nine, ten people'.

These remarks on numerals may be rounded off with some remarks on the lexeme bɛɛr 'two' which is used as a noun. In kinship terminology the salient notion of 'pair' is associated with bɛɛr, e.g. in expressions referring to groups of two (or even three) relatives all of the same age relative to the speaker. Thus rooj bɛɛr or dadrooj bɛɛr, literally 'younger-sibling two', may be used when addressing two younger cousins. The lexeme bɛɛr is, however, also used to refer to *a single person* as somebody who belongs to a pair, in particular when referring to the mate of the person one is talking about: mɛt ɲaŋ ʔat bɛɛr 'his/her mate is missing', i.e. 'he has no wife' or 'she has no husband' (it is tempting to assume that ʔat bɛɛr basically means 'the second one', but I have no other evidence for ordinal numerals in Mlabri being formed by means of ʔat followed by a cardinal numeral).

Deixis and anaphoric reference: Deixis is a complex topic, also in the case of Mlabri. There is fairly little literature on this topic with regard to the languages to which Mlabri shows the most affinity (Filbeck 1991 discusses in some detail the use of pronouns and other determiners in a Mal dialect of Tin).

Before looking at the various sets of words which involve deictic or anaphoric reference, it is necessary to point to a structural complication with deictic words in Mlabri: their word-class membership and precise syntactic function is often obscure, as far as my limited material goes. Some may be claimed to have a pronominal status, others an adverbial status, and still others a status which seems to be sometimes adverbial and sometimes adnominal. An example of such an unclear status is nɛh, which off-hand may be taken to be either an adverb ('here') or perhaps a noun ('this place') in expressions such as jɤɤm nɛh 'sit here' (the verb jɤɤm often takes nouns as object complements: jɤɤm briiʔ 'live forest' i.e. 'live in the forest; lead a forest life', jɤɤm gɛɛŋ 'live house', i.e. 'be at home' or 'live in a house'). The same word nɛh may be considered either as a loosely connected locative complement ('here') or as a pronominal determiner ('this') when it modifies tawɪn 'day' in tawɪn nɛh 'today'. – I have not yet arrived at any useful taxonomy of deictics; hence the unsystematic presentation below.

If we look first at adverbial (or even adnominal) lexical material which denotes *proximity or distance in space or time*, some forms are clearly referential in a deictic sense; others seem just to code spatial or temporal location, cf. the contrastive pair təkʌh 'up there far away', lakʌh 'up above', 'up in the sky'.

Personal pronouns as a category seems weakly represented in Mlabri; I am not sure whether there is a single "original" pronoun surviving in the language. There are first and second person pronouns in singular and dual: ʔoh 'I', ʔah 'we (dual)', mɛh 'you (singular)', bah 'you (dual)'. The dual forms may be elaborated by the addition of jum or ɟum to convey the meaning of plurality. There is no corresponding simple third person pronoun, except that hnɛʔ is occasionally used as a highly respectful anaphoric term, e.g. in myths when referring to The Creator (in α-Mlabri bnhnɛʔ occurs as a respectful second person pronominal form).

This pattern with only singular and dual first and second person pronouns as generally used "primitives" is remarkable. The four forms cited above look suspiciously "Khmuic": some have very similar correspondences in Tin, others in Kmhmu. The word ʔoh 'I' has its closest cognate in Kmhmu, although that language has a final glottal stop where Mlabri has /h/ (Tin has reflexes of a different, very widespread Mon-Khmer pronoun).

The four monosyllabic personal pronouns are hardly very recent loans from a Khmuic language, but they clearly represent the Khmuic component in Mlabri. They are conspicuous in that unlike Tin and Kmhmu, Mlabri has made a phonologically symmetrical system out of them in which all four forms end in /h/. This symmetry, which is further enhanced by the possessive forms which end in /t/ instead of /h/ (see below), suggests that they form a close-knit system in Mlabri.

Nevertheless, I hesitate to consider Mlabri to have an old 2x2 pronominal system (let alone to reflect on "primitive conceptualization" on the basis of this pronominal system). One must keep open the possibility that the present system of four terms arose out of Khmuic-based pidgin which the Mlabri may have used in the past in their intermittent contact with villagers speaking Kmhmu or Tin. If one or two Mlabri approached a village for the purpose of barter trade there would hardly be a need for other pronouns than first and second person singular and perhaps dual/plural.

The doublets jum and ɟum are enigmatic. One might speculate that such a doublet of forms for the first person plural might encode a difference of *inclusive versus exclusive*, but I have found no clear corroboration of this. It is, however, my impression that

ʔah jum refers to an occasional cluster of people (*meyum* "group" in Bernatzik 1938 may be mɛh jum 'you folks' and thus contain the same jum), whereas ʔah ɟum is the appropriate designation of a close-knit group of kinsmen to which the speaker belongs. There may perhaps be a symbolic value associated with the difference between /j/ and /ɟ/: there are likewise doublet forms which denote the important concept of 'father': jooŋ, ɟooŋ, of which the latter refers specifically to one's *own* father. These doublets, however, may have arisen simply by borrowing (jooŋ may be a borrowing from Kmhmu).

The noun phrase ʔat tiiʔ takes the place as a third person pronoun. It is used indiscriminately to refer to *one or several persons*, except that ʔat bɛɛr 'the two' may be used instead if one is referring explicitly to a duality of persons: ʔat bɛɛr ɟak tipiaaʔ 'the two go what', i.e. 'why did they go?'. Instead of the "default" expression ʔat tiiʔ one may also use a more specific noun phrase deictically, and then refer anaphorically by the default term, as in the following bit of a dialogue, where dik theeŋ 'little baby' means 'our baby': dik theeŋ ɟak ginɛŋ 'Where has our baby gone?' – ʔat tiʔ jɤɤm nɛh 'He is here!'.

I do not know what concept underlies the expression ʔat tiiʔ. Since tiiʔ means either 'hand' or 'eight', and ʔat is a kind of definite article (somehow related in meaning to the possessive pronouns, see below), there are two possible interpretations. An expression 'the eight ones' makes sense in the meaning of 'the several ones; the group', but then the use of the same expression to refer to *one* person seems strange unless one assumes that it was earlier a honorific term. One should, however, not discard this interpretation offhandedly, since numerals are used in other similar expressions. The expression ʔat bɛɛr (which seems entirely parallel to ʔat tiiʔ) was mentioned above; cf. also that ʔah thɤɤŋ, literally 'we five', is the standard pronominal expression which means 'we (plural)' in α-Mlabri.

The other possibility is to view ʔat tii as a *pars pro toto* expression, i.e. to take tiiʔ in the sense of 'hand' or 'hands'. When it is used figuratively, such an expression can easily refer indiscriminately to a single person ('the hand' or 'his hand') or to several persons ('the hands' or 'their hands'). This interpretation may be said to receive support from the existence of another expression of the same kind which can also be used to encode the meaning of third person, ʔat chak, literally 'the chest' or 'the body'. It is possible to say ʔat chak ɟak ginɛŋ more or less with the same meaning as mlaʔ ɟak ginɛŋ 'where did the person go?', but I suppose that the subject phrase of the former sentence is semantically more empty and thus closer in meaning to a third person pronoun. It is also possible that the use of chak conveys the meaning of 'self', but my material is too limited to show this clearly.

Possessive pronouns constitute a very important typological feature of Mlabri. There are two such pronouns, both with singular meaning only: ʔot 'my' and mɛt 'your'. These are obviously formed on ʔoh 'I' and mɛh 'you' by the addition of suffixal (formerly enclitic) material, which now appears as -t. The existence of such morphologically derived forms is very surprising since nothing similar occurs in either Kmhmu or Tin, although the personal pronouns themselves bear all the marks of being Khmuic. The addition of possessive -t is perhaps a fairly recent feature in Mlabri (this is not unlikely considering the transparency of the underlying pronouns in these formations).

These two possessive pronouns can be used only as Determiners on Nouns, as in ʔot gɛɛŋ 'my house' and mɛt hmaaj 'your wife'. To form a noun phrase meaning 'belonging to X' the β-Mlabri must use constructions with a specific lexical item bʌr (br-), which specifies the concept of 'belonging' when followed by a nominal expression. It often covers the concept of ownership (of alienable items), e.g. in the following question and answer: bʌr ʔitɯ mlaʔ gʌh 'of which man this', i.e. 'whom does this belong to?' – bʌr ʔat tiiʔ 'it is his/hers'.

Constructions with bʌr (br-) may, however, also encode the meaning of 'belonging functionally in a certain environment', as in the following explanation about a domesticated herb: ɲaŋ brgɛɛŋ, brbriiʔ met ɲaŋ 'it occurs domesticated, in the forest it does not occur'.

The various examples above seem difficult to put on a common syntactic denominator unless bʌr is classified as a preposition (bʌr X which means something like 'of X', with the sub-meanings 'having X as habitat', 'belonging permanently to X'). As the last two examples above show, bʌr may attach proclitically to its regimen and it then reduces to a minor syllable br-. This happens regularly if it is followed by one of the light personal pronouns ʔoh, mɛh, as in the following question and answer: brmɛh (with question intonation) 'is it yours?' – brʔoh 'yes, it is mine'.

In fact I have too meagre data to determine the word-class membership of this entity bʌr, br-. It clearly has predicate properties in that constructions which are headed by bʌr are not just noun phrases but function as complete sentences, cf. bʌr bah ɟum 'it is yours (pl.)!', as against bah ɟum di gruɤɤ 'your (pl.) belongings'. On the other hand it is conspicuous that there exists a noun brʔiiʔ (with an obsolete synonym brʔɔɔŋ) which means 'name' in α-Mlabri: ʔoh choop mɛt brʔiiʔ 'I request your name', i.e. 'what is your name?'. The prefix-like material br- in α-Mlabri brʔiiʔ, brʔɔɔŋ may perhaps originally reflect the concept of 'belonging-to-referent', but the syntax clearly shows that brʔiiʔ is a noun and not a prepositional phrase.

The definite article: The word ʔat, which I have called a "definite article" above, constitutes another typologically striking feature associated with referentiality.

It is my impression is that the use of ʔat is normally dependent on the theme of the discourse. It is used to identify the specific item talked about as an integral or inalienable part (or possession) of the person, thing or situation that functions as theme. Thus the determiner ʔat is used regularly when *parts of a complex structure or organism* are named, e.g. body parts or the different parts of a tree or plant: gʌh ʔat lam 'this is the stem', gʌh ʔat ləbooʔ 'this is the leaf' etc. The definite article is regularly used when talking hypothetically or didactively about the functionally determined components of something, e.g. the ingredients of a meal.

The usage is sensitive to functionality in this sense. Once a Mlabri first apologized for the blandness of the soup which we were eating: chapaʔ ʔat prɛʔ '[it] lacks *the* spice' and then began to explain to me what chapat prɛʔ means *without* using the article on prɛʔ in the latter, metalinguistic context.

One can, on the other hand, use the definite article even when referring to a nonexistent but potentially meaningful and inalienable part of something, as when a Mlabri explained about "the fruits" of the "goh" tree, which has edible leaves but *no* fruits: mɛt ɲaŋ ʔat pleeʔ, bɔŋ tɛɛ ʔat lmbʌr, literally 'not exist the fruit, eat however the leaf' i.e. 'it does not have fruit, but we eat the leaves'.

Such examples contrast with other, more or less analogous examples in which the definite article is *not* used. I was told, for example, that one would say tɔʔ gɯnwak mɛt ɲaŋ thrɛɛŋ 'knife be-chipped not exist edge' in the meaning of 'the knife is chipped, it is blunt'. The reason for not saying *mɛt ɲaŋ ʔat thrɛɛŋ in such a case may be that that would have the wrong implication that the speaker is referring to a type of knife which has no cutting edge. I assume that mɛt ɲaŋ thrɛɛŋ has been lexicalized in the meaning of 'be blunt', implying that the item referred to has indeed an edge which is supposed to be sharp.

An example such as kinʔdeep ʔat tiʔ ʔat ɟɤɤŋ chɛʔ 'centipede the hands the feet are-abundant' i.e. 'the centipede has many legs' (which is unfortunately rather unique in my material) shows that the definite article may *not* be used generically when introducing a theme (see 5.2.1 below about extra-clausal themes), whereas it occurs on a following sentence-subject which refers to functional parts of the entity referred to by the theme. This is the opposite of the use of the definite article in the English paraphrase 'the centipede has many legs'.

As suggested by these random examples, the definite article of Mlabri invites a closer study from the point of view of referentiality.

It is also common to use ʔat to refer to the status of a referent as *"belonging" via family relationship* to the referent presented as sentence topic. Thus one may say, for instance, mlaʔ gɯt hɔɔt ʔat ʔɛɛw laŋ 'the man misses his son'. Alternatively, the possessive marker di may be used to express such a semantic link of "possession" between family members: mlaʔ pajɤʔ di hmaaj 'the man calls his wife'.

On the other hand, the determiner ʔat may be dispensed with as a marker of referentiality if there is *direct deictic or anaphoric reference* (without the intermediate step of a "possessor"). Thus it is perfectly possible to say mlaʔ dɤŋ kwʌr, kwʌr dɤŋ mlaaʔ 'Mlabri look-at outsider, outsider look-at Mlabri' with unique reference of both mlaaʔ and kwʌr, as a comment to a situation in which two persons present during the discourse are staring at each other (this kind of comment was made on an occasion where the speaker's small child was staring at me with much curiosity and caught my attention). Similarly, in a discourse in which a certain Hmong person is already established as a theme, it is perfectly possible to use the noun mɛɛw 'Hmong' anaphorically and to say, for example, maʔ mɛɛw 'give Hmong' in the sense of 'give it to the Hmong (the one we have been talking about)'.

My present conclusion is that the determiner ʔat may well be called a "definite article" but that it typically codes referentiality in a specific way: via anaphoric reference to an explicit or implicit "possessor". In that sense ʔat may be categorized together with the possessive marker di, which often has a clearly *reflexive* meaning (like Latin *suus*, Danish *sin*).

As mentioned earlier the form ʔat is etymologically enigmatic. There is a phonological detail which may be of significance: ʔat ends in -t just like the possessive pronouns ʔot and mɛt discussed above. This may be a coincidence, but it is worth speculating whether ʔat might perhaps have arisen along with ʔot and mɛt as a possessive pronoun (possibly by addition of the possessive marker di to *ʔa-; Tin has a third person plural pronoun ʔah). The finding that ʔat tends to encode a very specialized type of referentiality (unlike the definite article of many other languages) could well reflect such an origin.

5.1.2 Adverbial Phrases

Before proceeding from Noun Phrases to Verb Phrases, we shall take a look at Adverbs and other material which make up more or less complex Adverbial Phrases (see further section 5.1.3 on Verb Phrases and section 5.2.1 on Constituent Order).

Although adverbials are discussed in some detail both in this section and elsewhere in the monograph, it has not yet been possible to perform a rigid analysis of constructions which function adverbially, nor to perform a rigid classification of lexical material into adverbs and words from other classes. "Adverb" is here understood as a broad category including both Prepositions (since these may be regarded as transitive adverbs) and the subclass which I prefer to call Preverbs, i.e. a particular type of adverb- or auxiliary-like grammatical words ("Adverb-

Auxiliaries" in the terminology of Mary Haas' Thai-English dictionary) such as mɛt 'not', ʔdɛj 'indeed' (from Thai). The latter subclass comprises several single words in Mlabri which unmistakably have the characteristics found with adverbs in Indo-European languages, and which may express polarity, modality or temporality, e.g. chak 'not', ki 'also' or 'not' (cf. 4.2.1 above on negation), gɔɔj 'carefully' (etc.) and chɛɛm 'again'.

It has been difficult and not seldom impossible for me to identify the exact meaning of individual adverbs or more precisely: to identify how the presence or absence of a certain adverb influences the meanings of the sentences in which it has been observed. As for the neighbouring languages, some of which have influenced Mlabri, there is an unfortunate but understandable scarcity of available information on the syntax and semantics of adverbials. The generalizations about adverbials in this monograph are based on very limited observations and may not all be adequate.

Temporal expressions (cf. the introductory remarks in chapter 4, section 4.2 above) may consist of single words, which in some cases have the status of verbs but in other cases are more noun-like. Both may be true of terms for times of the day. The term for 'late afternoon' is a special type of verb phrase containing a clause: ʔa gaɲ thwɛɲ ('PERFECTIVE sunshine red'; this expression is "male language"); whereas, the term for 'dusk', ɟjʌl, may be classified as a noun since it can be quantified by a numeral, bɛɛr ɟjʌl 'two dusks' (i.e. 'for two nights'). If we look at the term for 'morning' tak ɟrɯw, however, it contains an element tak which can be preposed to adverbs to encode the meaning of 'past', as in tak ʔa hɤɤj or tak ʔɤh hɤɤj 'long ago'. The word ɟrɯw may be tentatively classified as an adverb on this basis, unless it can be shown that tak has the function of turning nouns into adverbials (also cf. the remarks about tak ɲaam gʌh below).

Looking further at ɟrɯw one observes that this is a word which also means 'tomorrow'; it thus belongs to a different set of terms together with tawɪn nɛh 'today', nɛɛ 'yesterday' and paaj 'the day after tomorrow'. Among these, the term for 'today' is structurally aberrant since it is a Noun Phrase: 'day this'. There are several adverbial phrases of a temporal meaning which are structurally noun phrases which consist either of Noun + Demonstrative, as illustrated by tawɪn nɛh, or Numeral + Noun, as illustrated by bɛɛr ɟjʌl above. Expressions of the latter type do not only denote duration of time as an abstract concept, but they may also in some cases involve temporal deixis (time relative to the present), as in mɔ hnʌm mɛh ʔa pruk 'one year you PERF come', i.e. 'you will be back in a year from now?'.

In narrative discourse, when relating myths of the past, the expression tak ɲaam gʌh occurs extremely frequently, as an extra-clausal filler which means something like 'that happened then, long ago'. It consists of the element tak mentioned above plus ɲaam gʌh, which in itself is an unmistakable noun phrase meaning 'time this', although it here functions adverbially as seen also by the occurrence of tak as a modifier. The same word ɲaam occurs in expressions for the seasons of the year, e.g. ɲaam juuk hndoom 'time rice ripe': the early hot season.

The expression paan gʌh (in rapid speech pan gʌh), if taken verbatim, means 'time this'; it may either refer deictically to actual time (i.e. 'now') or refer to the time of narrated event (i.e. 'then'), and in these senses it belongs to the above subclass of adverbials. In monologue-like discourse, however, pan gʌh or the repetitive pan gʌh pan gʌh may also be an extra-clausal filler which signals text coherence (much like English 'and then ... and then') or simply a hesitation device.

The following utterance, said by a Mlabri just before he went downhill to slaughter a pig, illustrates the apparent ambiguity in the use of the expression pan gʌh pan gʌh (as time adverbial or filler); it was was said rapidly without any pauses signalling its internal structure: ʔoh ɟak ɟuur pan gʌh pan gʌh ʔoh ɟak pabɯl chiiŋ, literally 'I go descend time this time this I go kill pig'.

After these remarks on temporal expressions which may be considered to have an adverbial status, we shall proceed to a third, different subclass of adverbs, which is well represented in Mlabri, namely those that *encode spatial relationships*. This subclass comprises on the one hand Locational Adverbs, such as ladooŋ 'up there', and on the other hand Directional Adverbs. The most interesting adverb of the latter kind is tih, which may convey the notion of 'out' or of 'in' (e.g. out of or into a house) depending on the locus chosen by the speaker.

Prepositions: Mlabri possesses an (apparently small) fourth sub-class: that of true Prepositions. These can be regarded as *Connectives having the syntactic status of Transitive Adverbs*. Prepositions take nouns or noun-like entities as complements, as in ti trlɔh 'into the pot', ti grɤɤŋ 'in the middle'; the complement may also be a deictic: ti nɛh 'in here'.

In addition to ti 'in, into' (which may have some connection with the adverb tih but looks as if it reflects an influence from Thai) there are a few other true prepositions within the same semantic field such as kɛj 'out of', ni 'in', and tu 'from'. By far the most widely used word of this category is lɔŋ, which is related in meaning to ti and ni but covers a rather different and much broader semantic range.

In some contexts lɔŋ conveys the notion of entering a specified area, as in ɟak lɔŋ briiʔ 'go into the forest' or ɟak lɔŋ luɤt ('go into the exterior' i.e.) 'go out'. In other cases, however, lɔŋ has a purely directional meaning, as in ɟak lɔŋ kldɯl ('go towards the back' i.e.) 'move backwards'. This even occurs with a sentential complement: ɟak lɔŋ tawɯn pruk ('go towards the sun rises' i.e.) 'go east'. Finally, lɔŋ seems to have a more locational meaning in some cases, e.g. keeŋ lɔŋ ʔdɯt 'carry on back' (there is some lexical affiliation between lɔŋ and the word lɯŋ exemplified above).

Locational meanings are often encoded by a Verb + Noun construction without any preposition: ʔem gɛɛŋ 'sleep house', i.e. 'sleep at home'. However, constructions with Prepositions such as ni 'in' also occur: ʔem ni gɛɛŋ 'sleep in (one's) house'. Similarly, the Conjunction-like word lɯŋ 'with, and' occurs in constructions such as toc lɯŋ ʔoh 'get (something) from me', in which lɯŋ (which certainly does not have any directional, "ablative" meaning) introduces the location of the beneficiary.

Directional meanings may be encoded by Verb + Noun if the basic notion is that of passing a boundary, e.g. blʌk gɛɛŋ 'enter house', i.e. 'enter the house, go inside', pak blɛɛŋ 'penetrate arm' i.e. '(for a thorn to) prick through the skin of one's arm'. Otherwise, directionality may be encoded via a Directional Verb such as glɤh 'to rise, upwards' or via a Directional Adverb such as tih. Finally, the construction may involve Preposition + Complement.

It is a question how fruitful it is to attempt to make *a rigid distinction between Prepositions and Coverbs*, e.g. to classify tɔ in maʔ tɔ mlaaʔ 'give to a Mlabri' as one or the other (also cf. tɔw 'until' in tɔw ɟjʌl 'until dusk'). We are clearly in the realm of Coverbs with such constructions as ʔbɔɔk maʔ mɛh 'tell (to) you' since maaʔ is indisputably a Mlabri verb which as a full verb means 'to give' (also see discussion under "Serialization" in the final part of section 5.1.3 below).

To round off this section, it should be mentioned that also certain Determiner-like words have a rather strong affinity to Prepositions. This is true of Possessive di and of the Indefinite Quantifier dɔ (cf. 5.1.1 above).

5.1.3 Verb Phrases

We shall now take a look at Verb Phrases (or "Maximal Projections of Verbs") to the extent that such an entity can be recognized as a syntactic constituent in Mlabri.

I here assume that the Verb Phrase consists of the sentence verb and other material which is closely connected to the verb, whereas I have not so far found it to be descriptively advantageous always to include sentence objects within a larger "Predicate Phrase" (and thus to make the sentence essentially bipartite: Subject – Predicate, as is done in much syntactic work, e.g. within the tradition of transformational grammar). This, in my view, may be warranted in case the noun phrases in question are *obligatory* complements within the lexical frame of the verb in question, but otherwise, I here treat the nominal arguments encoded as subject and (direct and indirect) object as being on the same level with respect to their syntactic relations to the sentence verb.

We shall first consider various kinds of grammatical material which occurs in verb phrases.

Perfective versus Non-Perfective is expressed by an inflection-like modification of verbs. Mlabri has a perfective marker ʔa which comes close to being an inflectional prefix. Like the determiner ʔat (see above), the perfective marker ʔa is typologically and genetically remarkable; it has no counterpart in either Tin or Kmhmu. It is a highly integral part of Mlabri grammar, both in α-Mlabri and in β-Mlabri, so it must be of some considerable age in the language.

In a string of verbs forming a complex predication (concatenated verbs, see on Serialization below) the perfective marker generally occurs before the last part of the complex predication: boŋ ʔa laac 'have finished the meal' (literally: 'eat PERF finish'). When sentences are translated between Mlabri and Northern Thai, it functions as the equivalent of Northern Thai lɛ̂ɛw (although the latter is an adverb occurring in final position): Mlabri ʔa bii? = N. Thai ʔim lɛ̂ɛw 'be satisfied, have eaten enough'.

The aspect marker ʔa is used also to express *promised (future or hypothetical) action*: ɟruɯ ʔa wʌl 'tomorrow PERF be-back' I.e. 'I shall be back tomorrow', mɛh maʔ ʔoh chɯrɛɛ ʔoh ʔa toc 'you give me shirt I PERF take' i.e. 'if you give me a shirt, I will certainly accept it'. The last example consists of a conditional clause followed by clause expressing the promise. A similar construction with ʔa on the second predicate occurs also in *conditional commands*: mɤm, chi ɟrʌʌk ʔa ɟrʌʌk 'Father, if you are thirsty then drink!'.

The difference between statements and requests or commands is sometimes expressed by the use of di as second person imperative marker or ʔa di as first person plural (inclusive) imperative marker. This use of di may be a regular feature of the encoding of "imperative" meaning when a verb is followed by another verb in a resultative construction; di then occurs between the two verbs as a connective: boŋ di bii? 'eat till you are full!' (also cf. the example ɟak di thɛh chɤm mentioned in section 5.1.1 above). There is another form ta, which seems to have a resultative meaning. For some reason it hardly occurs in my material except for one example, which on the other hand is reliable as it was checked carefully with the speaker: toc lam keh ta hŋ.kah 'take stick break so-that break' i.e. 'to break a stick' (it is possible that some occurrences of ta in my data have been erroneously identified as tɛ, i.e. the connective tɛɛ with vowel shortening).

Such resultative constructions pose problems of syntactic analysis: should they be viewed formally as complex verb phrases *or* as sequences of close-knit clauses without any overt subject in the second clause?

Should the two examples above be treated differently in this respect? This type of problem is anything but unique to Mlabri, and the solution is of course highly dependent on one's descriptive framework. I shall not go further into this issue here.

With single verbs the status of an utterance or part of an utterance (e.g. as telic or non-telic) is most often not overtly marked in β-Mlabri. Syntax itself may not tell whether an utterance is to be understood as a request or a command, for example. Moreover, as with other languages of this area and of this linguistic type, it is often unclear whether predications which involve stative ("adjectival") verbs are to be identified as descriptive epithets (syntactically noun adjuncts) or as separate clauses. The string gɛɛŋ chrɔɔɲ may mean either 'the house is dry' or 'a dry house' (as a noun phrase or an elliptic clause), and even in a specific context a reasonable analysis is not always self-evident. The lack of obligatory marking seems to make many utterances formally, and sometimes even semantically, ambiguous.

The analytical problems may be quite subtle, cf. the following example in which the controversial string jɤɤm gɛɛŋ chrɔɔɲ is embedded in a complex utterance: jɤɤm gɛɛŋ chrɔɔɲ, ɟak lɔŋ luɤt chɯkkɔʔ, *verbatim* : 'stay house dry, go into exterior wet'. The lexical parallelism between the two halves suggests a corresponding syntactic and semantic parallelism, and I guess that without any situational context the whole meaning would be construed as two disjunctive "if-so" statements forming *a piece of commonplace reasoning* : 'If you stay inside you'll be dry; if you go out you'll be wet'.

The utterance above was said to me by a Mlabri when we were sitting together under a roof, and I was contemplating going out into the pouring rain. It was obviously meant to apply to my actions on this specific occasion. This does not rule out the possibility of its being a piece of good advice structured as a philosophical statement, but I suppose it could just as well be understood as *an imperative clause* jɤɤm gɛɛŋ chrɔɔɲ followed by an explanatory statement ɟak lɔŋ luɤt chɯkkɔʔ, i.e. 'do stay in the dry house (or: in the house, it's dry), for if you go into the forest you'll be wet!'.

Off-hand the utterance I heard seems to me two-way ambiguous: both with regard to modality and with regard to the "adjectival" or "verbal" understanding of the verb chrɔɔɲ. As said before it is very likely that prosody helps to disambiguate such complex utterances, but so far I have not been able to integrate such criteria to a satisfactory degree in my analyses.

Explicative verb complements: One of the more difficult issues in Mlabri syntax (as in many other languages) is the parsing and categorization of verb complements.

Adverbs which express location or direction occur as verb complements: leh tih 'come out!'. As stated earlier, some adverbs occur as prepositions, so that we have nouns (noun phrases) embedded in post-verbal prepositional phrases: lʌp tih trlɔh 'pour into pot' (tih may mean 'into' or 'out of' depending on the viewers orientation and the inherent semantics of the verb).

There is a variety of descriptive complements which occur after the verb which they belong to. The grammatical classification of these complements is not always obvious. One of the most important ones is jʌk 'thus, like this', e.g. in ʔɤh jʌk 'do like this'.

This word has a very specific syntax, in part with noun-like characteristics: it can be governed by a connective (e.g. də or chɯŋ in də jʌk, chɯŋ jʌk 'like this') and in its reduplicated form jʌkjʌk it can occur in constructions such as ʔoh ɟak ʔbɔɔk maʔ mɛh jʌkjʌk 'I go tell give you thus-thus', i.e. 'I shall tell you how' or 'I shall tell you what to do'.

A specific type of verb complement is found with *verbs of posture or motion* which take an immediately following complement which qualifies the verb, as in ʔem rakɤɲ 'sleep on one's side'. Other complements, in a similar construction with the verb, may specify the singularity of a referent, the reciprocity or joint action or presence of referents. Examples are: jɤɤm dəmɔj 'live alone', glaʔ trdɯŋ 'talk together'; also full-fledged noun phrases occur in a similar function, cf. bɛɛr mlaaʔ hlooj 'two person(s) extra', i.e. 'three persons' in ʔat tiʔ ɟak bɛɛr mlaʔ hlooj 'they were three persons leaving'.

In this realm of syntax I see no sharp category division between material which one might prefer to call "adverbial complements to the verb" and material which one might like to refer to as "subject predicatives".

Unlike expressions of reciprocity, Mlabri does not seem to possess a *distributive*, monoclausal construction with a postverbal complement meaning 'each' or 'each separately', nor does it seem to have a monoclausal construction in which the predicate expresses referential identity of something shared by two or more subject referents. Such relationships seem always to be coded by a combination of two or more parallel clauses.

The word hak may occur in each of two successive clauses to indicate that the predicates following hak are referentially mutually exclusive, as in the following statement (from the text sample in section 3.5 below) about the family relationship between the speaker and his half-brother: ba phet hak mɔ mɤʔ, ʔoh hak mɔ mɤʔ 'Ba Phet and I have *different* mothers' (hak mɔ mɤʔ), literally: 'Ba Phet on-the-one-hand one mother, I on-the-other-hand one mother' (from α-Mlabri we have examples such as ʔoh hak di pol, ʔot mjɤɤ hak di pol 'I have one blanket, my wife another blanket'). In contrast, a construction with parallel clauses but without hak is possible if the predicates are referentially identical: ba phet dəmɔ mɤm, ʔoh dəmɔ mɤm 'Ba Phet and I have *the same* father (dəmɔ mɤm 'one-and-the-same father').

Although the examples above illustrate the use of hak, they also differ in the use of the word forms mɔ and dəmɔ. It is my assumption that there is a crucial difference in β-Mlabri between the use of these forms in such constructions, namely so that dəmɔ is (mostly?) used in cases of referential identity, and mɔ in cases of referential non-identity.

It is interesting to look at the morphological composition of dəmɔ from this perspective: the word form appears in Mlabri as a transparent formation consisting of mɔ with a preposed connective də which may be viewed as establishing a referential link to an antecedent. One can observe the same relationship between mɔj 'one' (as a member of the number series: mɔj bɛɛr pɛʔ, etc.) and dəmɔj 'alone', as in ʔoh jɤɤm dəmɔj 'I live alone' (also cf. jʌk and də jʌk above).

The distributive meaning of a statement may also appear from the pairing of subjects and predicates in itself, *without* involving the word hak. For example, a configuration of paired indefinite expressions each headed by mɔ ("one X one Y, one X one Y") is a normal way of expressing such relationships in β-Mlabri.

Unlike the abstract explanations exemplified above I have experienced the latter usage in very concrete situations, as when I was once giving away some bags I had brought along, and it became important to convey the meaning 'There is one bag for each person!'. When this became clear to the oldest person in the household (via an explanation in simplified Thai: "khon la baj"), he took over and shouted: mɔ mlaʔ toc mɔ kwʌŋ, mɔ mlaʔ toc mɔ kwʌŋ, i.e. 'one person take one container, one person take one container' (kwʌŋ is the classifier for bags and other containers). Neither on this nor on other occasions did I ever come across any way of explaining such an arrangement by packing all the information within a single clause.

It is relevant to the question how to express distributive relationships in Mlabri that there may not be any single word which functions as a universal quantifier. Although it is perfectly possible in β-Mlabri to say ʔa noɲ nɛŋ hmuu 'PERF be-complete with group' in the meaning of 'everybody, all members of the group', that expression is a descriptive phrase with a strictly collective meaning (the α-Mlabri often say thuk khon under similar conditions, using a Thai phrase).

I have tried in vain to elicit a way of saying, for example, 'we eat every day'. A β-Mlabri speaker told me that one would just say boŋ chɛʔ 'eat much' (stating that the situation is the opposite of one of starvation); if, however, one really wants to be explicit it is possible to spell out some of the events and say: boŋ tawɪn nɛh, boŋ ɟrɯw, boŋ chɛʔ 'eat today, eat tomorrow, eat much'.

As a conclusion to the various pieces of anecdotal evidence above, there is an apparent absence in indigenous Mlabri of specific linguistic devices for referring jointly to distributive and/or repetitive phenomena with retention of the distributive or repetitive aspect of the information to be encoded. It is my feeling that this is not just an arbitrary result of the interplay between syntax and lexicon. I am inclined to think that it reflects a deep-rooted characteristic of the way in which the Mlabri traditionally organize their apprehension of such phenomena in daily life.

Postverbal complements of various kinds can be followed by *appositional material which occurs in extraposition* to elaborate the (explicit or implicit) clause subject. Both types of constituents are present in ʔem bɛɛr mlaʔ ʔuj jooŋ 'sleep together, woman and man', the complement being bɛɛr mlaaʔ 'two person(s)', and the appositional material ʔuj jooŋ 'female male'. There is no formal cue, however, as to whether it is one or the other constituent that is present in sentences such as ɟak ʔem hmaj laŋ 'go sleep wife husband', which is conceivably ambiguous between (i) 'we, wife and husband, are going to sleep' and (ii) 'we are going to sleep as wife and husband' (I do not know whether prosody and rhythm may disambiguate).

Serialization: There is a major issue remaining: the linear and strict arrangement of verbs which follow after each other within one sentence, the so-called serial construction. Serialization of verbs is characteristic of a vast area of Southeast Asian languages, including the Khmuic ones (cf. data on Tin in Filbeck 1975). Mlabri as well uses this syntactical device to a large degree.

This is not the place to go into the general theoretical issue how to define and formally represent serial constructions. From a strictly syntactic point of view certain apparently serial constructions may be *complex verb phrases*, whereas others may be more adequately handled as *sequences of clauses which all share the same subject*. With respect to serialization, Mlabri does not immediately present itself as markedly different from other languages of the area. Thus, just to give an impression of this phenomenon in Mlabri it may suffice to exemplify it in a traditional descriptive format. It would require more penetrating analysis than I have made so far to determine to what extent Mlabri exhibits typological features which are at variance with areal-linguistic expectations.

I have found it convenient to present the phenomenon of serial constructions *before* looking at the overall order of sentence constituents which is treated in section 5.2.1 below, but I wish to leave open the question of how to define the syntactic domain of serialization.

The remarks below are confined to some general observations relating two two topics: how serial verb arrangements encode information structure in this language, and to what extent serial constructions, or constructions which are more or less similar to serialization in the strict sense, involve grammaticalization (there is a rich, recent literature on these topics with reference to Southeast Asian languages, e.g. Bisang 1992; in accordance with the overall format of this monograph I do not here deal with the question of theory-specific formalization).

As in Thai (and languages influenced by Thai) the local or translocational aspect of the completion of a complex action is often spelled out by verb chains such as 'take – go' or 'take – come' (Thai ʔaw paj, ʔaw maa). Although the non-initial verbs may be reduced to *directional* modifications and thus grammaticalized to a greater or lesser extent, they may also express steps in a series of actions. We seem to have an intermediate situation with the following explanation about a wild plant which is used when manufacturing brooms: chak tɤl, ɟak pɤjh toc pruk, *literally* 'not cultivate, go cut take come' (the point of the second part of the statement being that one can just go out and fetch the material). A string such as ɟak loh krɛc boŋ 'go look-for gnaw eat' exhibits a clear-cut succession of independent full verbs which spell out distinct steps in a happening; it occurred in the utterance hwɤk pruk ɟak kɛj hntor, ɟak loh krɛc boŋ, which means 'the mouse comes out of its hole and looks for something to eat'.

In both the serial examples above, there is an *iconic* relationship between the succession of verbs and the sequence of elementary actions or events. This I would call semantically *prototypical* serialization (well-known e.g. from Thai). The opposite is a non-serial utterance such as the following (a true, spontaneous remark): ʔoh chak ɟak, ʔoh chi thapuul, ʔoh jɤɤm 'I am not going, I have a stomach-ache, (so) I stay here', where the relationship between consecutive verbs is not one of progression (but of contrasting and explaining a cause); here, the chain is effectively broken by resumption of the subject pronoun.

There are many instances of verb sequences which do not at all encode a complex action in progressive steps, but in which *the first verb encodes a very specific meaning and the second verb a much broader meaning within the same sphere*, cf. pruk ɟak 'come move' and pjɯr-pjɯɯr dɤŋ 'stare look' in mlaʔ pruk ɟak kɛj gɛɛŋ, ʔat tiʔ pjɯr-pjɯɯr dɤŋ mlaaʔ 'the man comes out of the house and the others stare at him' (this type of construction, in which it often makes sense to speak of a main verb followed by a semantically related "secondary" verb, i.e. a relationship similar to that between noun and classifier in a complex noun phrase, is also well-known e.g. from Thai). In the examples above there is an almost hyponymical relationship between the two successive verbs.

Such constructions are not prototypically serial in the above sense since they do not spell out distinct steps in a series of interrelated events. Instead, the second verb *qualifies the meaning conveyed by the first verb*, for example by adding the semantic aspect of initiated or continuous action.

There is another category of verb concatenations: grammaticalized serial constructions in which the second verb serves to specify the *valency relationships* of the first rather than to add a separate predication. This is the construction Main Verb plus Coverb, as in ʔbɔɔk maʔ + N 'to tell (to) N' (maaʔ, which otherwise means 'to give', is here grammaticalized as a Coverb in conspicuous accordance with the dual role of Thai hâj, cf. discussion at the end of 2.1.2 and at the end of 5.1.2 above).

In still other instances, which also represent grammaticalized serial constructions, the second verb is semantically unrelated to the main verb and just functions as a *temporal or aspectual marker*. This is true of *inchoative* constructions with ɟak, cf. kan ʔoh bɔ glaʔ ɟak, mɛh di tɔɔ 'if I also speak go, you IMPER answer', i.e. 'answer me if I speak to you!'. It is likewise true of constructions in which jɤɤm is grammaticalized with a purely *stative* meaning, as in pɯh jɤɤm 'to be up (after the night's sleep)'; also cf. the following remarkable statement about an old portable wireless set which, to the Mlabri's dismay, did not light up when switched on though the radio could still play: grooʔ tɛɛ grooʔ jɤɤm, ʔat chɯɯk ʔuulh tac, literally 'make-sound though make-sound STATE, the string fire break', i.e. 'although it goes on making sounds, the electrical wire is broken'.

Beside their semantically reduced auxiliary function in the constructions above, the words ɟak, jɤɤm also occur as main verbs: 'to go', 'to sit, to be in a state', whereas a marker such as chɤm, which conveys the sense of continued action (as in bɔŋ chɤm 'you just go on eating!'), may occur only in adverbial function.

After these examples of complex verb constructions which do *not* exhibit iconic serialization, I shall round off by pointing out that sequences of semantically related verbs may pose questions of semantico-syntactic analysis even though the word meanings are not ambiguous at all, namely if the second verb can be construed to be either a Main Verb or a grammatical word of the category Directional Verb. For instance, the expression kɯm glɤh, literally 'throw rise', was used by a speaker explaining how a mythical hero (after a collapse of the World) took a crossbow and fixed the stars on the firmament by shooting upwards. The words are easily understood (as describing an action with a different direction than kɯm hot 'throw fall' = 'to throw something on the ground') but the question is whether to interpret them as a monoclausal construction of main verb plus directional verb which describes one action: 'threw (it) in upward direction' or as a biclausal sequence which describes first what the person does and then what the object does (i.e. with different implied subjects): 'he threw (it) and then it moved upwards'.

There is often a high degree of similarity with more well-known languages such as Thai in the idiosyncratic behaviour of individual verbs or verb-like material. Verb concatenation in Mlabri bears all the marks of a Southeast Asian areal feature.

5.2 Sentence Syntax

Most Mlabri sentences include a verb unless they are elliptical. The statements below mostly refer to such prototypical sentences. Genuine *nominal sentences*, however, occur as well; not surprisingly, an important subset of these are definitional or identificational sentences which contain a demonstrative or personal pronoun and a nominal predicate: ʔoh mlaʔ briiʔ 'I Mla Bri' i.e. 'I am a Mlabri', gʌh tipiaaʔ 'that what-thing' i.e. 'what's that?'.

In addition, Mlabri, like many other languages, permits commentary or exclamatory utterances which are syntactically non-elliptical but which nevertheless contain only one nominal argument and no overt predicate. One speaker suggested the following situation in which such an utterance might occur: a person sees some people arguing and asks ʔɤɤ, glaʔ tipiaaʔ 'Oh, what are they saying?' and obtains the answer ʔii ʔoj, dadrooj bɛɛr dadrooj tiiʔ 'Oh my, those kinsmen!' (which in the context may mean something like 'they are quarrelling, as usual!'). The answer in this case consists of two interjections ʔii and ʔoj followed by a complex nominal expression which literally means 'brother two brother eight' (referring to a plurality of kinsmen). In my more spontaneous speech data, however, I have not come across any such examples.

Sentence-types: Before going into the linear arrangement of sentence constituents, it is convenient to make a few remarks on the encoding of *sentence-types* (as understood from a functional perspective). The data which I have been able to analyse so far do not suffice to determine to what extent sentence types such as neutral statements, assertions, affirmative or negative answers, questions, commands and exclamatory sentences are formally distinguished in this language. As mentioned earlier, *intonation* certainly plays an important role, but that awaits further study (cf. section 3.3 above). As for *segmental* marking, however, a few statements can be made:

Questions have no obligatory segmental properties which set them off from statements or commands except for the type of question which involves the presence of an *interrogative noun modifier*, such as ʔitɯ 'which' or dʌlh ʔdɤɤ 'how many'.

Negative questions which imply a positive expectation from a politeness perspective occur in Mlabri: ʔa ki toc 'PERF not take' means something like 'aren't you going to have any more?' if said at the end of a meal. (The negation used in this case is the semantically ambiguous lexeme ki, but I gather both from the communicative situation in which this expression was used, and from a paraphrasing explanation which I received afterwards, that the question is to be understood as having *negative* polarity.)

The identification of an utterance as a "yes-no" question is mainly a matter of intonation (and voice quality and mimicry), unless the question is explicitly marked as such by means of the final interrogative particle lɛh. I do not know under what conditions this particle is used; it is my impression that questions without segmental marking are more frequent. It is possible instead to start a question by calling the addressee's intention. This involves the use of an exclamatory particle such as ʔɯh which gives the question the status of an appeal: ʔɯh brmɛh 'are you taking this?' (brmɛh in itself is understood as 'it is yours', but on my inquiry the question above was unambiguously paraphrased as suggested by the translation).

The structure of *answers to questions* may be sensitive to the degree of expectation or the presuppositions underlying the question. Thus, one Mlabri speaker told me that the question ʔɯh brmɛh (said while holding an item in a way suggesting that one is willing to hand it over to the addressee) might be answered in the affirmative by saying ʔa toc 'PERF take', i.e. 'yes, I'll take that!'. The alternative strategy of formulating a presupposition-neutral "yes-no" question mɛh toc 'you take?' (said with high-pitched intonation, cf. 3.3 above), on the other hand, triggers an *echo* answer: ʔoh toc 'I take'.

Commands have a characteristic intonation (see 3.3 above); segmentally, they are only obligatorily marked if they have *negative polarity*: as in Thai and other Southeast Asian languages there is an auxiliary meaning 'don't!', in Mlabri gʌm. It is used regularly both in α- and β-Mlabri: gʌm beet 'don't cry!'.

As for positive polarity the connective di seems to be used regularly in α-Mlabri to signal imperative meaning of a verb. It is, however, *not* obligatory as an imperative marker in β-Mlabri. In β-Mlabri the use of di in a command serves rather to mollify the speech-act into a polite wish or admonition or warning. In that use, the connective di occurs also after a conditional sentence, as in kan ʔoh glaʔ, mɛh di tɔɔ 'if I speak (glaʔ), you must answer (tɔɔ)'.

Ordinary commands or requests are mostly unmarked: boŋ 'eat' will in appropriate situational contexts be understood in the imperative sense (boŋ can also be the echo answer to a question and means 'yes, I eat (it)'; such affirmative answers have rising intonation on the verb). Still, it is possible also in β-Mlabri to introduce a sentence with di followed by a verb; an utterance of that type will necessarily be understood as a very explicit command: di boŋ 'eat!'.

Constituency at the clause or sentence level: The preceding sections commented on various characteristics of noun and verb phrases in Mlabri. In the remainder of this chapter such phrasal constituents, and their interconnection with or without connectives, will be considered at the clause or sentence level. I wish to emphasize once again that this is not a full nor a formally explicit Mlabri Grammar (the term "clause" will be used rather loosely about any kind of nexus construction with or without an explicit subject noun phrase; I sometimes speak of "verb phrase" and even of "predication" instead without having arrived at any terminological consistency, the perspective being sometimes structural and at other times functional).

The size of sentences in Mlabri varies considerably. In a dialogue they are often short but nevertheless loaded with information. A characteristic example is the reaction which I elicited from an elderly man when I asked him whether he would remember to give some meat from me as a gift to his daughter's household (she and her husband were absent that day). He looked at me reproachfully and said: ʔot ʔɛɛw 'my child', which under the circumstances – and with its paralinguistic accompaniment – unambiguously meant: 'of course I will, she is my child, you know!'. – Except for answers to questions, however, the utterances in my data typically exhibit a more complex syntactic structure.

Before going into syntactical configurations it is useful to make the general observation that there is no constancy in the degree of morphosyntactic redundancy across languages: the isolating languages of Southeast Asia do not necessarily make up for the lack of inflection by syntactic elaboration. One might expect rigid explicitness in terms of specification of syntactic arguments, but on the contrary in these very languages, sentence-material which can be inferred from the linguistic or situational context, is often left out, and Mlabri is no exception. This may lead to a high degree of structural and semantic ambiguity of utterances if they are considered in isolation when subjected to linguistic analysis (cf. the discussion of modifier versus predicate above).

In dealing with sentence syntax I must necessarily touch on various *sentence-semantic and pragmatic* issues but not in any systematic way; Mlabri connected speech has not at all been studied to such a degree as to permit generalized statements about these topics.

5.2.1 The Status and Order of Sentence Constitutents

Mlabri is, not surprisingly, an SVO-language: ʔat ʔuuj krɔkkrɔk ʔat ʔɛɛw "the hen clucks at the chicken" (with the signalling from the hen to its chicken being encoded as a transitive verb) represents the unmarked word order in sentences which contain both subject, verb and object. Intransitive sentences have the unmarked order SV: ʔoh jɤɤm 'I stay'.

The unmarked order SV(O) is found in sentences in which the nominal arguments are spelled out and appear as sentence constituents. Under appropriate pragmatic conditions, however, the verb may occur without overt arguments. Especially the *subject* of a verb (transitive as well as intransitive) is very often missing and must be inferred from the context. This is also often true of the object of a transitive verb.

Such ommission of arguments may sometimes be viewed as deletion under coreferentiality with an antecedent noun phrase, but in fact the conditions are situational rather than linguistic. If, for example, a person is handing another person a gift, the former may ask mɛh toc lɛh 'you take QUESTION' and the latter may choose just to answer toc 'take'. The only argument that is made explicit, then, is the very first mɛh 'you' (so as to establish the addresse as the intended destination of the thing that is handed over). Once this is done, all the relevant arguments have unique referentiality in the discourse situation because of deixis. Consequently, there is no need for explicit reference to the object of toc in either question or answer, or to the subject of toc in the answer.

This is all as one might expect from a language spoken within the Southeast Asian linguistic area. Still, it deserves to be mentioned as an interesting feature of syntactic typology that languages such as Mlabri seem grammatically rather unconstrained with respect to the possibility of leaving out arguments in the encoding of such sentences (compared to languages which spell out the identity of referents all the time), whereas on the contrary the anchoring point of the sentence, the verb, is retained and used as an echo when answering in the affirmative (also cf. the brief survey of sentence-types in the beginning of 5.2 above).

If there are two actants in each of two connected clauses, and these are pairwise coreferential, one actant may be presented in the first clause; the other in the second clause: kan mʌc mɛh, kha hɔɔk pabɯl 'If see you tribe spear kill' i.e. 'the "Spear Tribe" people will kill you if they see you'. The order of constituents unambiguously indicates what is subject and what is object: NP+V is Subject+Verb, V+NP is Verb+Object. It seems that, whatever the number of constituents present in a sentence, their *unmarked* order (on clause or sentence level) is in accordance with the overall scheme (S)V(O), the constant feature of this ordering being that the subject is *the noun phrase immediately preceding the verb*.

Subjecthood: Before considering the behaviour of sentence objects it may be useful to discuss the concept of subjecthood in Mlabri from a semantic and a syntactic point of view.

It may be that subjects are in the majority of cases *animate* and even *human* (in accordance with universal expectations), but this is not so obvious if one considers only sentences which do not have *personal pronouns* as subjects. Altogether I do not think it is a feature of the design of the Mlabri language (cf. below). – Forces of nature behave like animate subjects: one says kɯr groo?, *lit.* 'thunder make-sound', using the verb groo? which does not express a particular sound or sound impression but rather the production of species-specific cries (of birds, etc.).

There is a close affinity between syntactic and semantic subjecthood. With transitive verbs there is of course often an animate argument as subject, be it an active agent as in tom?oo? krʌp mlaa?, *lit.* 'cobra bite man', or an experiencer as in mla? krʌw biɯk, literally 'man fear bear'. If there is no animate actor, however, it may just as well be an inanimate argument that is treated as agent and thus encoded as subject: lam tɯjh glɤɤ? *lit.* 'tree hit head' or cembeelh pak ɟɤɤŋ, *lit.* 'thorn penetrate foot' (I do not like to claim that this is a special semantic case: "Instrument" raised to the status of subject; I presume that the perspective is just as in the transitive sentences above, i.e. the speaker presents the information that the tree and the thorn perform unpleasant actions).

Similar forms occur with stative verbs which have optional object complements. The subject may be animate or inanimate and it is likely to have very specific reference or a generic meaning. Once, after I had almost broken a tooth while chewing rice and finally produced a small stone from between my teeth, a Mlabri commented: kɛp jɤɤm juuk, *lit.* 'stone stay rice' which probably meant 'the stone was in the rice!'. The existential meaning 'there was a stone in the rice!' would be equally appropriate in the situation, but I suppose that the verb ɲaŋ must be used instead of jɤɤm in order for kɛp *not* to be understood deictically.

The types above cover the typical constructions with two-place predicates. I have not come across anything which I would suggest as a *passive* construction with downgrading of the agent to a secondary (optional) status.

When a statement has an *existential* meaning, verbs which mean 'to appear' have no preceding subject but a following argument in object position, e.g. pruk mɛɛm 'come blood' i.e. 'there is blood coming out or leh muɯr or pruk muɯr 'come snot' i.e. 'mucous comes out of the nose'. This is a straightforward way to convey the idea that there is an emergence of matter of a specified kind but *with no specific reference*.

It is a different question how to understand the semantics and the syntax of sentences such as ruʌŋ ɲaŋ wɔk 'creek be/have spirit', i.e. whether ɲaŋ in this case is to be understood as transitive: 'the creek has a spirit', or whether ruʌŋ is to be understood as locational, and ɲaŋ wɔk as an existential statement: 'in the creek there is a spirit'. This is a well-known analytical problem, which is posed in a quite similar fashion by other languages of the area.

Returning to the existential construction exemplified by pruk mɛɛm, one might expect this very type of verb-noun construction to be used to express natural phenomena such as 'it rains'. Other languages of the area do exactly that: the literal translation of the expressions used in Tin and Kmhmu is 'comes rain' or 'appears rain'. Mlabri, however, sides here with Thai in using a different conceptualization, the idiomatic expressions for these natural phenomena in Mlabri being mɛʔ hot 'rain falls', kɯr grooʔ 'thunder sounds' etc., with SV syntax.

The just-mentioned SV configuration, when used with existential verbs, may also express that some familiar phenomenon (which is then encoded as the subject) affects a person: ʔot cheʔ ɲaŋ, *lit.* 'my lice exist', i.e. 'I have lice'. Here both the syntactic analysis and the semantic interpretation become more tricky. The form ʔot is well documented as a possessive pronoun, and in the vast majority of cases in which such pronouns occur as a constituent of a noun phrase in Mlabri, the noun phrase in question has *unique reference*. The existential meaning of the sentence ʔot cheʔ ɲaŋ, however, certainly speaks against such referentiality.

The problem with the referentiality above might suggests that the expression ʔot cheʔ ɲaŋ is not in line with productive modern Mlabri syntax but is a relic from an older state of the language in which possessives did not yet encode referentiality of the possessed object, or in which the forms simply meant something else. One possibility is that ʔot, mɛt were originally locative forms (I owe this suggestion to Søren Egerod).

Constituent order, topicalization and focus: As stated earlier, the unmarked constituent order in Mlabri clauses is SVO. When a statement implies the speaker as *experiencer or witness* of an event, it is common to use an ordinary sentence of SVO-type with a "naked" (determiner-less) subject (rather than a construction which explicitly encodes an existential meaning or a construction which focusses on the experience). This is current usage even when the subject of the transitive construction is inanimate: cembeelh pak ɟɤɤŋ 'thorn penetrate foot', i.e. '(somebody) had a thorn in his foot'.

It is, on the other hand, perfectly possible to put *semantic focus* on the object or to make the object into topic or theme, by placing it initially before the verb. If the subject is expressed as well, then the word order is OSV: chɯrɛɛ ʔoh ʔa bɯk, *lit.* 'shirt I PERF put-on', i.e. *'the shirt* I'll put on!' or 'as for the shirt, I'll put it on!'.

Viewed in isolation, a sentence example such as chɯrɛɛ ʔoh ʔa bɯk is open to two different analyses, I think: (1) a close-knit clause structure with a marked constituent order because of semantic focus on chɯrɛɛ, (2) a presentation of a theme chɯrɛɛ plus a clause in which the referent of the theme is the latent object: ʔoh ʔa bɯk [chɯrɛɛ]. Such ambiguity is likely to disappear when the sentence is spoken as a real utterance (occurring in a context and interpreted on a pragmatic basis).

If the object noun phrase is fronted in a more complex sentence, e.g. involving verb seriality to spell out the various steps in a process, it is likely to be a matter of topicality rather than focus. The following was an explanation which I obtained about the procedure to be followed if the head of an axe is loose: ʔat hlek mlaʔ chɛɛm pal ɟuur - ɲʌn boc 'the iron person insert beat descend – because be-loose', which means 'one sticks the iron spike in [i.e. into the upper end of the wooden shaft] and one beats so that it sinks [into the shaft] – because it [i.e. the axe-head] is loose' (the last two words were added afterwards, as an afterthought).

In this case, the reason for having the constituent order OSV, with ʔat hlek 'the iron' as O and mlaʔ 'person' as S, is obviously that the iron spike is the most salient ingredient in the process (cf. the use of the definite article to show that it is a necessary part of the setting): the thing to be explained about and hence the referent to be established first. Incidentally, the axe-head and the shaft are not referred to explicitly since that would be redundant in the particular situation where the participants were looking at an axe with a loose head. I suppose the encoding of agent could be dispensed with as well, without making the sentence sound odd.

There are some instances in which the distinction between focus and extra-clausal theme is *syntactically* quite transparent so as to show that this is a structural difference in the Mlabri language:

– (1) The object noun phrase of the second of two semantically contrasting clauses may be fronted because there is a polarization between the referents of the two objects: ʔoh mak too gʌh, too ɲʌʔ met mak 'I like CLASSIFIER this, CLASSIFIER that not like', i.e. 'I like this person; that person I don't like'. This is obviously a matter of focus since it involves two contrasted referents.

– (2) On the other hand, there are explicit cases where a theme is introduced pre-clausally, its referent being immediately resumed within the clause: ʔoh ʔot juuk ʔa noɲ, *lit.* 'me my rice PERF gone', i.e. 'as for me, I have no more rice'. There are also instances in which the coreferentiality between pre-clausal theme and sentence-subject is not overtly encoded but can be inferred: kinʔdeep ʔat tiʔ at ɟɤɤŋ chɛʔ, *verbatim* 'centipede the hands the legs are-abundant' i.e. 'the centipede has many legs'. Here, the centipede is theme ("as for the centipede...") but the expression "the hands and feet" constitutes the subject of the verb.

Indirect and direct object: We have not yet considered what happens in sentences with *two object noun phrases*, that is, when one grammatical object is the semantic object, and the other is the beneficiary or addressee (I shall here follow traditional usage and refer to the former as the "Direct Object" and to the latter as the "Indirect Object").

Unlike Tin, which seems to have a rather variable word order, and unlike Thai, which regularly places the direct object before the indirect object, in Mlabri *the indirect object is placed before the direct object*. This is seen in complex sentences which contain maaʔ 'give': mɛh maʔ ʔoh chɯrɛɛ 'you give me shirt'. The same analysis can be extended to sentences which contain krɔɔ 'ask for': ʔoh krɔɔ mɛh thʌc 'I ask-for you meat' i.e.'I request some meat from you' or 'please give me some meat'.

The above observation is at variance with the statement of Tongkum (1992, p. 54) about α-Mlabri: "In clauses or sentences that have both a direct and an indirect object, the direct object comes before the indirect object". Tongkum gives two examples as substantiation of her statement, but one of these is a (semantically very marginal) sentence containing a causative form of a transitive verb and hence three nominal arguments (structure: X *make-smell* Y Z = 'X makes Y smell Z'). The structural arrangement which accompanies causative verbs in pa- or ba- is an interesting issue, but in my view it is *not* compelling evidence for the order of direct and indirect object after other, non-causative verbs.

The other example given by Tongkum is a sentence construction which contains (possessive or otherwise connective) di: ʔoh maʔ pol di ʔɛu 'I gave the blanket to my child', where pol is 'blanket' and ʔɛu (in my notation ʔɛɛw) is 'child'. This is indeed a crucial example. In recent α-Mlabri data I have observed the opposite constituent order: *indirect object before direct object* (just as in β-Mlabri) in constructions containing the verbs 'ask for' (α-Mlabri choop) and 'give' (maaʔ), but the examples which I have recorded differ from the one given by Tongkum in an important respect: there is in these examples *no connective* di *before the constituent referring to the addressee or beneficiary*. I guess that there is a superficial regularity such that the constituent order is sensitive to the presence or absence of di on one of the constituents: a constituent headed by di probably always comes last, e.g. ʔoh choop mɛɛw di charɛɛ 'I request a shirt (charɛɛ) from the Hmong (mɛɛw), ʔoh maʔ pol di ʔɛɛw 'I give a shirt to my child', not *ʔoh choop di charɛɛ mɛɛw, *oh maʔ di ʔɛɛw pol. The syntax (and semantics) of such constructions is, however, still poorly understood. – Altogether, there seems to be a strong tendency in both varieties of Mlabri to reduce the valency of transitive constructions. Although there may be conflicting organizational principles which operate in Mlabri syntax with regard to this feature of constituent order, the evidence is still too meagre.

Sentences with an indirect object seem infrequent in actual discourse (the above statement about constituent order was based on elicited rather than spontaneous data). It is, however, not always easy to determine whether a sentence verb has one or two noun phrases as objects. There are borderline cases which contain the possessive marker di. This grammatical word has multiple functions and combines both with verbs and nouns. When it is associated with a noun phrase it is always a marker of possession but it occurs in two types of syntactic construction: it may connect Possessor and Possessum within one phrase, as in mɤʔ di diŋ 'mother POSS older-sibling' i.e. 'mother's older sibling', or it may have anaphoric reference across the sentence verb, as in ʔoh lom di mɤʔ 'I love POSS mother' i.e. 'I love my mother'. Now, how should we analyse sentences such as keeŋ mɛɛw di ʔuulh 'carry Hmong POSS firewood'? It is obviously a possible solution to regard it as containing just one object noun phrase: 'the Hmong people's firewood'. It was actually uttered in a context in which it clearly referred to hired labour, however. This suggests a semantic interpretation which involves both an object ('firewood') and a beneficiary ('the Hmong'), the proper paraphrase being 'carry firewood for the Hmong'.

The question, then, is whether a sentence such as the one above is structurally ambiguous and if so what kind of cognitive "reality" can one associate with such ambiguity. Is it equally possible both to take mɛɛw di ʔuulh as one constituent (the syntactically well-supported analysis) and to take mɛɛw and di ʔuulh as separate syntactic constituents at clause level? The latter solution seems more in line with the meaning of the sentence as uttered on a given occasion, but it would involve a use of di to mark coreferentiality with an "indirect object" which is at variance with the general pattern found in my (admittedly very limited) material: when functioning as a determiner, di otherwise *has the sentence subject as its antecedent*.

If it is possible to view mɛɛw and di ʔuulh as two separate constituents one might even contemplate the possibility of such an analysis for sentences such as ʔɛɛw boʔ ʔat ʔuuj di booʔ 'child suck the mother POSS breast'. It may not be beyond question that the proper analysis is in terms of just one constituent ʔat ʔuuj di booʔ 'its mother's breast'; perhaps it makes sense to view this sentence as involving, in addition to the acting child, both an experiencer 'its mother' and an object 'her breast'.

Such questions of analytical ambiguity may be viewed as strictly syntactic issues. Sentences such as those above pose, however, no less of a challenge from the point of view of semantic interpretation. What is the proper paraphrasing of such sentences? If the former is both syntactically and semantically ambiguous, what then about the latter? Does it make sense to claim that it is syntactically ambiguous although its meaning is absolutely unambiguous?

Clearly, the question of indirect objects in Mlabri cannot be properly addressed without access to much more extensive data than the surprisingly few examples in my material that may qualify as "Sentences with Indirect Objects".

It would be interesting to study to what extent the scarcity of indirect objects is suggestive of a strategy by which the arguments which potentially form indirect and direct objects are integrated into one complex noun phrase, or to what extent it is suggestive of a strategy such that the latter argument is encoded within an adverbial phrase, possibly even as part of a separate clause.

The observation that *indirect objects are infrequent in discourse* reflects a more general regularity of Mlabri: that there is such a strong exploitation of the serial principle that arguments of verbs are seldom encoded as anything but Subject or Direct Object. One manifestation of this tendency in Mlabri is that the semantic role *Instrument* is generally encoded via a separate Coverb which takes the noun phrase in question as Direct Object. The verb used in β-Mlabri is toc 'take, fetch', and the equivalent in α-Mlabri is ʔek (toc in α-Mlabri means specifically 'grasp with the hand'). The semantic content of the word as a full verb may be more or less preserved when it is used as an instrumental Coverb, as seen from the two examples below.

The combination of toc plus Object roughly means 'take X and...' or 'use X to...'. The following sentence deserves to be presented both in α-Mlabri and in β-Mlabri since it represents an institutionalized action in Mlabri culture (i.e. hitting dogs in order to keep them off the food or the blankets): α-Mlabri ʔek kol tɛk braɲ = β-Mlabri toc lam tɛk chɔɔʔ 'take stick hit dog'. The exact translation would be 'take a stick and hit the dog'; the sentence can also be given the less elaborate but functionally rather equivalent paraphrase 'hit the dog with a stick', with an instrumental complement instead of a two-step predication.

The meaning of 'take' must, on the other hand, be assumed to be completely faded out in favour of the instrumental meaning in the next example: toc tiʔ jɔh pruk 'take finger pull come' i.e. 'use one's fingers to pull it (e.g. a thorn) out' or 'pull it out with one's fingers'.

An interesting question, which has already been raised earlier, is to what extent phrasal constructions in Mlabri are calques from other languages. As for the construction with toc above, this is deep-rooted in Mlabri although the extension of toc or ʔek to function as Coverbs bears some resemblance to the use of the verbs ʔaw and cháj in Thai.

The examples above might convey the impression that Mlabri always spells out all steps in a complex action. Stepwise predication is, however, not the only way to handle complex propositions. If, for example, translocation (rather than use of an instrument) is involved, the Patient of the first predication may instead be topicalized and appear sentence initially. The steps in the complex action are then viewed as one action and expressed by one verb. Thus, instead of the expected toc ʔat mɯj chaj takiʌŋ 'take the oil put lamp' I have heard ʔat mɯj chaj takiʌŋ in the meaning of 'fill oil on the lamp', with topicalization of the argument 'oil' which moreover carries the definiteness marker and thus signals that the substance spoken of is the "belonging" one: the one used with lamps (rather than some other substance such as animal's fat, which is also mɯj).

The position of adverbial phrases: The presentation of word-order phenomena has so far concentrated on constituents of noun and verb status (S, V and O). The placement of adverbial constituents of various kinds is, however, a complex issue and apparently a semantically crucial one. The subclass which I refer to as Preverbs (mɛt 'not', etc.) is here included among adverbials, as understood in a broad sense.

Adverbials may occupy at least three different positions relative to S, V and O. The arrangement is sensitive to the semantics of the adverbial, e.g. whether it has negative polarity:

Negative preverbs have their unmarked placement between the subject (*if* there is an explicit subject) and the verb: ʔoh mɛt ʔɛl bon, literally 'I not yet eat'. If the construction involves a modal auxiliary, the order of constituents (disregarding the subject which is often latent) is

(Verb (+ Object)) + (Negation) + Auxiliary,

i.e. a word order which matches that of Thai. This overall order may be illustrated by the following model examples: bon bɤɤn 'eat can', mɛt bɤɤn 'not can', bon mɛt bɤɤn 'eat not can' and bon juuk mɛt bɤɤn 'eat rice not can'.

Directional and Locational Adverbials are placed in final position after the verb and the object (if there is an object): dɔɔk ladoon 'store (it) high up (on a shelf)'. This holds true also in questions: mɛh ɟak ginɛn, literally 'you go where'. Directional and locational adverbials which encode a nominal argument occur clause-finally as well, e.g. toc chɯrɛɛ lɯn mɛh 'receive a shirt from you' and jɤɤm nɛn mɛh 'be together with you'.

Under appropriate conditions such directional, locational, or modal adverbials may form utterances by themselves (since the rest of the proposition can be inferred from the context).

The topology of Temporal Adverbials is more complex. Adverbials which involve some kind of *temporal deixis* occur sentence-initially and thus *separated from the sentence verb*, e.g. rəʔʌh thahaan ʔa pruk 'soon soldier PERFECTIVE come', 'the soldiers will be here in a moment' and mɔ hnʌm mɛh ʔa pruk 'you will come in a year?'.

The same may be true of complements containing a verb (complements of clause status) which express a temporal connection between events without involving deixis: ɟʌt jɤɤm nam ɲaaw bɯl 'when stay Nam Jaaw die', i.e. '[she] died when [we] were at Nam Jaaw'.

It is, however, no simple matter to define the structural position occupied by such a clausal complement if the predicates have no overt subject(s). I suppose the sentence above, if taken out of context, is ambiguous as to whether jɤɤm 'stay' and buɯl 'die' have the same subject referent or not. It is conceivable that overt subject noun phrases can occur in different positions relative to such a complement and can thereby reduce referential ambiguity, but my data do not permit any statement of this kind.

In contrast, the light, non-deictic adverbial hɛh (which encodes relative not absolute time: 'first, before doing something else') always occurs in clause-final position: boŋ juuk hɛh '(we'll) eat first (and then...)'.

I suppose there is a special explanation whenever an adverbial which might seem to involve temporal deixis, occurs *after the verb*, e.g. mɛh ʔa boŋ juuk tak ɟruɯw 'you PERF eat rice time-of morning'. At first sight this sentence (which is intended, though not syntactically so marked, as a question) would seem to mean 'Have you had a meal this morning?', and one would then be forced to consider whether there is a difference of topicalization or of semantic focus between initial and final placement of the adverbial tak ɟruɯw. It turns out, however, that boŋ juuk tak ɟruɯw has been lexicalized in β-Mlabri in the meaning 'eat breakfast' and thus does *not* involve temporal deixis at all. I suppose that the unmarked (and perhaps the only possible) "reading" of the sentence above is 'Have you had your breakfast?'.

In other instances the choice between initial and final placement of a temporal adverbial may have other semantic implications but still involve presence or absence of deixis:

The expression dʌlh ʔdɤɤ ʔat tawɩn, *lit.* 'amount what the day(s)' occurs in my data with *initial* placement in the meaning of 'when', i.e. when temporal deixis is involved: dʌlh ʔdɤɤ ʔat tawɩn mɛh wʌl jɤɤm nɛh 'amount what the day(s) you be-back stay here' = 'when will you be back?'. It occurs, however, with *final* placement in the meaning of 'how long', i.e. without temporal deixis: choʔ thapuul dʌlh ʔdɤɤ ʔat tawɩn 'ache stomach amount what the day(s)' i.e. (according to the situation in which it was said) 'how many days has she been having a stomach-ache?'. I cannot decide on the basis of my data whether this difference of constituent order is an obligatory distinction in the coding of the two meanings.

The utterances above exhibit a syntactic phenomenon which is known from other languages of the area: a quantifying expression which is immediately followed by a noun phrase without any copula verb: 'how many [are] the days' (the presence of the definite article ʔat on the noun makes it entirely explicit that the quantifying expression is *not* part of the noun phrase but stands in a predicative relationship to it). The information structure of the first utterance may perhaps be paraphrased as 'how many are the days until you come back?' and that of the latter as 'with her having a stomach-ache how many are the days?'. Under such interpretations the specification of time is the basic part of each utterance; the predication about action or state is an expletive complement to the temporal predication.

It may be preferable to call the position of adverbials such as hɛh *clause-final* rather than *sentence-final* (although it is sentence-final as well if nothing follows). There is the possibility of adding an adverbial which indicates the speaker's attitude (politeness, down-playing, benevolence), such as chɤm 'just, at one's convenience', at the very end of an utterance in which case it occurs clause-externally, after all other final adverbials: ʔoh ɟak ɟrʌʌk hɛh chɤm 'I go drink first just' i.e. 'I will just drink some water'.

The initial or final placement of the temporal adverbials discussed above contrasts with the syntactic behaviour of chɛɛm, which has an iterative meaning. The latter forms part of the verb phrase proper and seems to occur as a preverb (according to my terminology), cf. the different placements of rəʔʌh and chɛɛm in rəʔʌh ʔoh chɛɛm boŋ 'soon I again eat', 'I'll eat again in a little while' (note that chɛɛm occupies the same syntactic position as the negative chak in ʔoh chak boŋ 'I am not eating').

This ends the remarks on constituent order. The following paragraphs deal with the occurrence of clauses as constituents of more complex utterances.

For practical reasons I have divided the survey below into a subsection which deals with the use of grammatical words (here called Connectives) which tie clauses together, and a following subsection which deals with clauses which occur in a syntactic arrangement without such connecting words.

The information given below is very tentative and incomplete. It is based on my impressions from a variety of communicative situations, but I have not performed any systematic study of this phenomenon so as to match the important study of interclausal relations in Kmhmu by Premsrirat (1991). It is worth mentioning, however, that the mechanisms of connecting clauses to each other differ very much from one language to another within this linguistic area (the grammatical material which I am dealing with looks extremely different from the Kmhmu material in Suwilai Premsrirat's paper).

5.2.2 Clause-Mates With Connectives

Although clauses and sentences in β-Mlabri often contain no overt connectives (see 5.2.3 below) they may well be conjoined by conjunction-like connectives which make explicit what kind of relationship there is between the parts. I find the behaviour of these connectives so interesting that it must be dealt with in some detail, although I do not yet possess anything like a complete repertory of these grammatical words.

There are some *Coordinating Conjunctions* in Mlabri. In β-Mlabri the closest equivalent to Thai kàp 'with, and' is nɛŋ. As mentioned in section 5.1, however, this is really a preposition, and there is no evidence in my data for nɛŋ being ever used to conjoin clauses. There is another frequent connective which is of interest in this context: chala, which means 'or' in the strictly disjunctive sense. It implies a choice between two mutually exclusive possibilities, as when asking which of two options is the valid alternative. This connective can conjoin clauses; it occurs either before the second clause or before each of two consecutive clauses: (chala) ɟak lɔŋ gʌh chala ɟak lɔŋ gʌh '(either) go this way or go that way?'.

There is a third connective glɤɤʔ which seems intermediate in meaning between nɛŋ and chala. I suppose it can be used equally well to conjoin nouns, adverbials and clauses. Whereas the conjunction glɤɤʔ is very frequent in α-Mlabri speech, it occurs much less often than chala in my β-Mlabri data. The few examples of glɤɤʔ in β-Mlabri which I have collected suggest that it is a conjunctive rather than disjunctive operator, and I suppose one might posit 'and/or' as a rough common denominator of its meanings. It may be used by a speaker if he enumerates things that should ideally both/all be done (ɟak joh run glɤʔ ɟak ʔɤh ʔuulh 'to tear up weeds and also to cut some firewood') or if he posits equally good alternatives (ɟak tih glɤʔ tih 'go through there or through there', referring to two routes of equal length).

In narrative discourse there is a frequently occurring particle ʔan, which may in some cases resemble a conjunction or complementizer in its distribution. The latter interpretation would seem possible in the following case (from an explanation about a burning hot liquid which existed in the remote past according to an old myth): pen ɟrʌʌk pluŋ ʔan likliik bɛʔ '[it] is hot water "ʔan" scorches the ground'. But most occurrences of ʔan that I have heard, occur before independent and fully structured clauses, in which case it makes more sense to suggest that its connective function (if it has a connective function at all) is associated with a higher level of text structure (there are some occurrences of this kind in the text samples in section 5.3).

Often, however, it is impossible to construe any connective function for ʔan. It may even disrupt an otherwise close-knit constituent structure and then it most of all resembles a hesitation phenomenon, as in the following example recorded from a free rendering of a narrative about a hero who had a wife living in the sky: glɤh toc ʔan - hmaaj '[he] ascended and took "ʔan" – [a] wife' (ʔan was here spoken with a lengthening of the nasal and a slight pause before the next word).

From this syntactically strange distribution I conclude (very tentatively) that ʔan is not really a clause-level connective but rather a "filler" associated with the discourse situation as such, a discoursive comment on the part of the speaker, although it probably also serves to signal text coherence and is used as a hesitation device. I guess its range of functions in discourse can be roughly indicated by English paraphrases such as 'well', 'now, let me see', 'you see', 'and' or 'but'. (In this discussion I have deliberately avoided any reference to the existence of a word ʔan in Thai; I think the meaning or meanings of the Mlabri word must be established first, independently of the possibility of external influence on the language.)

Comparison: This is one of the grammatical phenomena which play a prominent role in syntactic typology. In Mlabri, comparison as parametric calibration against a standard ("X is bigger than Y") is a very unusual phenomenon, and I doubt that it belongs to genuine Mlabri syntax. The normal construction seems to be simple juxtaposition of two contrasting statements.

It does, however, seem possible to express this meaning also by using a Mlabri sentence corresponding in structure to the Thai comparative construction, namely with the conjunction lɯ(ɯ), which undoubtedly reflects the Thai etymon *hlɯa with an entirely regular correspondence Mlabri /ɯɯ/ = Thai /ɯa/, although this must be a very recent borrowing (the same etymon occurs in Mlabri in the expected conservative form hlɯɯ and then means 'be left, be extra'). In an elicitation session the speaker first rendered 'my husband is taller than I' as ʔot glaŋ chuuŋ, ʔoh chibɛʔ ('my husband is tall, I am short', cf. 5.2.3 below), but later she suggested ʔot glaŋ chuuŋ lɯ ʔoh, literally 'my husband tall than I', as an alternative way to express the same, and she gave some additional sentences of similar structure. I have never come across such sentences in natural conversation, however, and it is my suspicion that they are quite marginal and might not be judged by more conservative speakers as belonging to Mlabri proper.

The speaker in question is unusually fluent in the other languages which are spoken in her immediate environment. This of course creates a situation which is favourable to language mixing. Moreover, on this particular occasion I deviated from my general practice of avoiding direct translation from Thai to Mlabri. Translating obviously provokes syntactic transfer.

As for the equality relation ("X is as big as Y"), there is a conspicuous absence in my data of sentences in which this is encoded by means of a static verb plus a conjunction. I have noted just one instance in which the postverbal adverb jʌk 'thus, like this' functions in this particular way. It occurs in a sentence, which was said in a bilingual context by one of the younger Mlabri speakers. A Hmong lady came up to me and asked for medicine (in Hmong) because she had a sore foot, and the young Mlabri translated her characterization of the intense pain as choʔ jʌk purdur ʔuulh 'hurt thus burn (N) fire', i.e. 'it hurts like a burn'.

I do not know whether the above is a current or a marginal construction in Mlabri. In other cases, when something is judged to be equal or equivalent, the Mlabri may state two propositions in parallel and add a comment such as dəmɔ ŋɔɔr or gɯɯn drchɤʔ 'in the same way', 'it is the same thing'.

Although the young Mlabri who produced the sentence with jʌk above is fluent in his native language, his speech sometimes shows strange aberrations from that of elder speakers. He is fluent in Northern Thai and Hmong as well, and considering the bilingual setting there is every reason to suspect that his linguistic performance on this occasion was not all genuine Mlabri syntax.

Other connectives: The remainder of this subsection will deal with connectives and connective-like material which encodes some kind of asymmetric relationship between clauses or between predicative constructions (or between an explicit clause and an implicit context).

Although there are several connectives which are in general use in contemporary β-Mlabri, two of these, ʔi and ɲʌn, occur far more frequently than the rest.

The all-purpose connective is ʔi. In some instances it functions in a way which may be best described by talking about a kind of relative clause formation, although the meaning seems rather to involve cause or intent, or the like. An example is mlaʔ ʔi pabɯl chiiŋ ɟak ginɛŋ ʔat chak 'man so kill pig go where the body', which I understand as 'the man, in order to slaughter the pig, where did he go, he himself?' = 'where did he go to slaughter the pig?'.

By using ʔi as a predicate-connective one may also link an explanatory clause to the preceding string. It often occurs in commands which are warnings; the clause headed by ʔi spells out the consequences of doing otherwise: gʌm ɟak ʔi hot 'don't go or (you'll) fall!'. This use of ʔi may occur in two steps e.g. in proverb-like warnings: gʌm ʔɤh ʔi chrɛʔ, kɯr ʔi poh 'don't work so-that there-is-fuss, thunder so-that strike', i.e. 'don't be such a pest, or the lightning will strike!' (a possible remark to a child who causes too much disturbance).

To make things more complicated, there are also elliptical utterances which consist only of a verb phrase headed by ʔi; these may be understood as explanations of or answers to an implicit proposition or question. A special case is ʔi ʔɛl, which in young persons' speech seems to have replaced mɛt ʔɛl 'not yet', i.e. with the connective ʔi replacing the negative preverb. It is said all the time in the utterance ʔi ʔɛl bɔŋ 'for eat yet', which functions illocutionally to express one's interest in having a meal, by explaining the cause: 'I have not eaten yet, you see'.

The (also frequently used) clause-connective ɲʌn conveys a meaning of causal connection. It regularly occurs on the second of two clauses to introduce the reason for, or explanation of, the preceding proposition. The implicit subject of the last clause may then be coreferential with either the subject or the object of the preceding clause: (ʔot mɤm ʔbɔɔk maʔ ʔoh,) ʔoh mɛt mʌc cɯɯ ɲʌn ki chɛt '(my father told me,) I have no recollection myself because I was very small'; ɟak toc kr.waac ɲʌʔ kwac gɛɛŋ ɲʌn rɤʔ (a command) 'fetch that broom and sweep the house (i.e. the floor), it is dusty!'; mlaʔ krʌw biɯk ɲʌn krɛc 'man fears the bear because it bites'.

The two connectives ʔi and ɲʌn may seem to be related in meaning in some instances, but in other cases they function differently. I have no example of ɲʌn implying potential consequences (like ʔi does in some cases); in my data it always seems to define an already existing situation as the reason for experiencing or doing something.

The words ɲʌn and ʔi may even occur in immediate succession in the meaning of 'so that not -': ɟak ʔbuʔ ɲʌn ʔi ɟram 'walk slowly so you don't get exhausted!'. This is understandable if ɲʌn encodes the meaning of 'because', and ʔi encodes the meaning of '(if not) then -' (like in gʌm ɟak ʔi hot above).

There are at least two more grammatical words, jʌw and biaʔ, which can function more or less like ɲʌn: ʔɛɛw beec jʌw ŋaʔ = ʔɛɛw beec biaʔ ŋaʔ 'the child cries because it itches'. The former of these two words occurs several times in my recordings of narrative prose, but I have practically no data on the meaning and use of the latter word.

In addition to these four connectives which are related in function, there are various connectives and other grammatical words which have some affinity to the above but behave differently, namely kan, jʌw, ɟʌt, dɔ, tɛɛ, hak and kɔ. It is difficult to systematize the presentation of these (the material available to me is very meagre):

If two clauses stand in an implicational relationship, the first clause may be introduced by a function word which encodes this information. The only such word that I have heard frequently is kan, which gives the clause a *conditional* status ('if, when').

Utterances with kan may (1) refer to a hypothetical situation, as in the earlier cited example kan mʌc mɛh, kha hɔɔk pabɯl 'if see you tribe spear kill' i.e. 'the "Spear Tribe" people will kill you if they see you'. They may also (2) be didactic statements about habitual consecutive events: kan pap ʔa hn.doom, biip toc boŋ ʔat ti nɛj 'when the "pap" fruit is ripe, you press it so that it breaks, and you take what is inside and eat it'. Finally (3), the clause with kan may refer to an anticipated future event; the following clause is then of course a statement or command about the corollary of this expected event: kan mɛh wʌl gɛɛŋ gɔɔj wʌl gɔɔj dɤŋ chɤm 'when you be-back home gradually be-back gradually look just' i.e. 'on your way home take it easy and look where you are going!'.

The complementizer jʌw (see above) can also present the first clause as *causal* : jʌw chi glɤʔ chi gɯm hmiʌŋ 'because ache head wish chew fermented-tea', i.e. 'as I have a headache I wish to chew fermented tea'. The complementizer ɟʌt, on the other hand, seems to convey a purely contemporal meaning 'at the time when': ɟʌt jɤɤm nam ɲaaw bɯl 'when stay Nam Jaaw die'. i.e. '[she] died when [we] were at Nam Jaaw'. In my data ɟʌt is infrequent and is used only to refer to the time of past events.

Explanations of how something comes into existence or happens may be expressed by connecting the explanatory clause to a thematic entity by means of dɔ, as in the following bit of conversation about the formation of clouds (which was already cited in section 5.1.1): kuup (tɛɛ) dɔ mɛʔ hot '(but) there are clouds because it rains (the full statement is given and commented in section 5.3 below). It is likely that dɔ is a generalized connective (perhaps basically a preposition, as suggested in section 5.1.1 above?).

It would be interesting to know whether dɔ could be replaced by ɲʌn without a change of meaning. Whereas the sentence above, with clauses connected by means of dɔ, encodes general knowledge about a natural phenomenon, it seems that ɲʌn typically involves an appraisal of a certain behaviour (which is described in the clause preceding ɲʌn) as a meaningful and appropriate reaction to a situation (which is described in the following clause).

If clauses are somehow contrastive in meaning, this is not (at least in my data) indicated by a connective which occurs at the transition from one clause to the other. If it is marked at all, the clauses, and particularly the second clause, may contain a particle such as tɛɛ 'but, you see' which occurs in a syntactic slot *between the first noun phrase of the clause and the verb* : mlaʔ ki chɛʔ ..., kwʌr tɛɛ chɛʔ 'there were few Mlabri ..., but there were many outsiders'.

A somewhat similar function may be performed by the word hak, which apparently encodes the meaning 'separately', and occurs in the same slot as tɛɛ above: mɛh gʌm pajok maaʔ, ʔoh hak pajok ɟrʌʌk 'don't you lift it (the long bamboo tube used as a cup), I (can) lift it and drink myself!'.

If the first of two successive clauses specifies the temporal setting for the content of the second, and the whole sentence is a purely factive (not conditional) statement there seems to be no complementizer which corresponds to kan above. Instead, the second clause may contain kɔ 'and then, also' occurring in the same slot as tɛɛ, hak above jɤɤm rɤɤʔ ʔoh kɔ mʌc 'stay maiden I also see', i.e. 'I saw her when she was a young girl'.

In the just-mentioned example kɔ 'and then, also' of the second clause serves to tie the two clauses together. Often, however, conjoined clauses just follow after each other without overt features except for prosody to mark that they are interrelated. This will be discussed in the following section.

5.2.3 Clause-Mates Without Connectives

Like other languages of the area Mlabri makes much use of complex utterances which consist of successive clauses conjoined *without* any use of clause-connectives (also cf. the discussion of seriality in section 5.1.3 above).

With my limited data and limited understanding of this language I often cannot decide whether the presence or absence of connectives in otherwise similar constructions encodes an essential difference in sentence-meaning, or whether it rather reflects a difference in speaking-style. There might be a difference in explicitness or degree of casualness or even a difference between addressing more fluent and less fluent Mlabri speakers. – In dealing with these issues one must take into consideration that some of the Mlabri connectives are identifiable as recent loanwords.

It is difficult to make generalized statements about the syntax and semantics of complex utterances in which there are no connectives relating their constituent clauses to each other (or other formal clues to the proper analysis). Nevertheless, I shall attempt to illustrate some ways in which complex cognitive structures may be encoded without clause-connectives.

It should be stated first that Mlabri possesses the device of *relativizing without a complementizer*, a genuine example being kheep mɤm maʔ ʔoh ʔa noɲ, ʔa tac 'the slippers Father gave me are used up, they broke', literally 'slipper(s) father give I/me PERF finish PERF break'. This example is transparent because the relativized argument is the object of the relative clause, and because there is a separate, overt subject argument in the relative clause.

The analysis is less obvious if the crucial arguments are not overtly expressed. It is then a problem to decide whether we are faced with a relative clause without complementizer or a relativizing/complementizing verb phrase. An example is met ɲaŋ ɟiʔdɤɤ ʔbɔɔk maʔ mɛh 'not exist anything tell give you', i.e. 'there is nothing (more) that I can tell you'. One analytic problem with this string is that it is not clear whether ʔbɔɔk maʔ mɛh 'tell give you' is to be understood with an implicit first person subject.

Complex sentences which contain verbs in the sphere of mental or linguistic processing (e.g. perception, imagination, knowledge, information transfer or command) exhibit the syntactic construction mentioned in section 5.1.1 above, in which a noun or noun phrase serves as the link ("pivot") between two verbs with different subjects. The example given earlier may be repeated here: dɤŋ mɤm ɟrʌʌk 'see father drink', where mɤm 'father' qualifies both as object of dɤŋ and as subject of ɟrʌʌk.

The word mɛh 'you' may not have the same dual role in the string ʔbɔɔk mɛh ɟak joh run 'tell you go tear weeds', a string which occurs embedded in the following complex message (presented to me as an illustration of the use of the verb ʔbɔɔk): mɛɛw ʔbɔɔk ʔoh, ʔoh wʌl ʔbɔɔk mɛh ɟak joh run, glɤʔ ɟak ʔɤh ʔuulh, ɟak geet ʔuulh ɟak maʔ mɛɛw. This is all about the work to be done that day, as ordered by the Hmong person for whom the Mlabri is working, and it is supposed to mean: 'the Hmong (Meo) told me, and I come to tell you (as well) to tear up weeds, and also to work on firewood, to cut some firewood and to bring it to the Hmong'. The tricky thing about this example is that according to the explanation given me, it did not specifically mean that *the other* person should do the work but rather that 'I was told, and I tell you, that *we* must do so-and-so'.

When one is analyzing Mlabri grammar it is not always so simple to specify the meaning with reference to hierarchical constituent structure (with or without "empty nodes" and "traces"); it easily becomes a stright-jacket forcing the analyst to posit structure which is not really there.

The piece of discourse above can also be used to illustrate a different feature of Mlabri syntax: the *sequential arrangement of structurally parallel clauses*. In the example above each of the clauses is headed by ɟak 'go (and)' in order for the totality of clauses to convey the meaning of consecutive actions.

There are other sequences of clauses of parallel structure which exhibit a polarization of meaning so that a contrastive effect is obtained: ʔot glaŋ chuuŋ, ʔoh chibɛʔ 'my husband is tall, I am short'. This is the general way to express *comparison* in Mlabri, and it is also used as the equivalent of Thai constructions with kwàa when translating between languages. If I ask, for example, how one would say "my husband is taller than I" the immediate response is the sentence above (although constructions with luɯ exist, see section 5.2.2 above).

There are still other complex utterances without clause-connectives which consist of successive clauses which are more or less exact semantic parallels. The duplication of meaning has a stilistic value and may serve to elaborate a point (an example is the comment on life in the forest cited at the end of the introduction to this monograph).

In narrative or didactic style the same clause may be repeated over and over in invariant form in order to express that something happens several times, possibly in a regenerative/cyclic fashion. This is exemplified by the repeated string ʔem bɛɛr mlaʔ ʔuuj jooŋ, literally 'sleep two person(s) female male' in a mythological narrative which explains how one couple became the ancestors of all the Mlabri in the remote past: ʔem bɛɛr mlaʔ ʔuj jooŋ, ʔem bɛɛr mlaʔ ʔuj jooŋ, ʔem bɛɛr mlaʔ ʔuj jooŋ (...), ʔa ɲaŋ ʔɛɛw 'woman and man slept together, woman and man slept together, woman and man slept together, (...) – and they had children'.

Often, however, two consecutive predications exhibit some kind of dependency relationship, i.e. possibly a syntactic *subordination*, although there may not be a connective which makes that explicit. In the discussion about modifiers versus predicates in section 5.1.3 above, the following example was cited: jɤɤm gɛɛŋ chrɔɔɲ, ɟak lɔŋ luɤt chɯkkɔʔ. It was pointed out then that the first part can probably be understood in two different ways: 'if you stay inside you are dry' or 'do stay in the dry house!'. If we look at the second part, however, the only pragmatically meaningful interpretation is one in which ɟak lɔŋ luɤt chɯkkɔʔ 'go into exterior wet' contains a conditional clause and can be translated as an *"if – so"* construction: 'if you go... then you'll be wet'.

The degree and type of subordination between such clauses varies. In the same strip of conversation in which the utterance above occurred the Mlabri speaker made a similar remark once again, but this time he used the negative imperative verb gʌm 'don't!' so that the whole string up to (but not including) the last word was an explicit command: wʌl jɤɤm chrɔɔɲ, gʌm ɟak lɔŋ luɤt 'come and stay inside where it is dry, don't go out in the forest!'. This utterance was rounded off by an additional predicate phrase chɯkkɔʔ 'wet' as in the example above, though this time it had the status of an explanatory comment: 'for it is wet' (or 'or you will be wet'). The added phrase might formally also be an epithet to luɤt, i.e. 'the wet outside', but *prosody* probably disambiguates since one would expect no break before chɯkkɔʔ in the latter case.

There is a further type of utterance in which there is a conditional or resultative relationship (*"if – so"* or *"and – then"*) between two consecutive clauses even though there are no connectives to signal this coupling between the clauses. One subtype is didactic statements such as ʔat mujmuj chat mlaaʔ, buŋbɔŋ 'if the hairs (of a poisonous caterpillar) touch one's skin it swells'. Another important subtype is commands such as kibi biiʔ, boŋ di chɛʔ 'not satisfied, eat for-it-to-be much', i.e. 'if you are not satisfied (you must) eat a lot!'.

The last type of construction to be illustrated here is one in which the first of two coupled clauses clearly expresses a state of affairs or a motivated expectation, *not* a hypothetical situation, and the second clause expresses the consequences of this real or assumed state of affairs:

A sentence such as jʏʏm dəmɔj ʔoh ŋɔɔm 'live alone I be-lonely' consists of two coupled predications; it was clear from the context in which it was uttered that the first clause was not to be understood as conditional but as causal (the whole thing states a factual background plus an unfortunate situation which arises from it). Syntactically, the first part (jʏʏm dəmɔj 'live one') has the form of a verb phrase which is appositional to the subject of the following clause, the whole thing meaning '(as I am) living alone I feel lonely'.

The sentence mɛh maʔ ʔoh chɯrɛɛ, ʔoh ʔa toc, 'you give me shirt, I PERF take' (which has been presented earlier for other reasons), occurred in a discourse context in which the speaker could not possibly fail to understand that I was presenting a gift to him and he expressed his positive reaction to this: 'since you give the shirt to me (or: if you really give the shirt to me), I certainly accept it!'.

It is my feeling that the absence of a conjunction in the first clause is pragmatically highly significant (my material also contains otherwise similar sentences which are headed by kan 'if'; I suppose the speaker would have said kan mɛh maʔ ʔoh ... if he just wanted to discuss the implications of a hypothetical situation).

Concluding remarks about clause concatenation: In the examples above, the condition or cause is mentioned before the derived effect or action. Altogether, there is often a temporal or causal progression thoughout an utterance, i.e., meaning is reflexted by syntax in an essentially iconic fashion. The progression of events encoded by serial verb constructions is another manifestation of this tendency. Such implementation of complex utterances with predominantly "natural" order of their meaningful elements and without redundant clause connectives and morphology, is a well-known feature of languages of Southeast Asia.

5.3 Samples of Connected Speech

In the preceding sections on sentence syntax, some of the syntactic examples consisted of several interconnected clauses, but on the whole the phenomena were observed within a narrow scope. The scope is even narrower in the dictionary below, since each illustrative phrase has been reduced to a minimum, i.e., to the material that is necessary in order to illustrate the meaning and use of the entry in which it occurs.

Although the study of discourse structure as such is outside the scope of this monograph, I shall round off the present section by presenting some additional speech samples to illustrate the composition of spoken Mlabri, as I have recorded it on tapes of connected speech. The samples below are admittedly rather short (they have been cut out of longer conversations or narrations) but they may suffice to illustrate some different styles and types of discourse. (In these speech samples and their translations, commas and semicolons are used to make the overall text structure more transparent; in several cases these marks also reflect audible breaks or even pauses, but this is not always the case).

In the first speech sample the Mlabri speaker, the oldest surviving member of the group, explains about sickness and ritual cure: 'if your personal spirit falls off you get a fever and you are aching; you then kill a chicken, you tie around your arm, and you get well and strong' (the magic rite outlined here is not at all specific to the Mlabri but is well-known all over the area):

> loon hot, mlaʔ dakat, choʔ; pabɯl ʔjoc, chuʌk blɛɛŋ; ʔa thɛh, ʔa reew.

Structurally this utterance starts with two clauses of identical structure although the first is to be understood as a hypothetical proposition (loon, the personal spirit, falls off the body) and the second – together with its elaboration by the extra predicate choʔ 'ache' – as the explanation of the effect of the hypothetical event (you get sick and your body aches). Then two parallel clauses follow both of which describe the measures to be taken (you make your personal spirit return to your body by sacrificing a chicken *and* tying a string around your wrist). Finally there are two entirely parallel and almost synonymous clauses which state the promised effect of the magic rites (to recover).

Note that (i) all clauses of the utterance above occur serially without clause-connectives, (ii) only the first and the second clause have explicit subjects because there is no switch of (implied) subject after the second clause, (iii) the clauses which state the expected and promised effects of the rites are distinct from all preceding clauses by containing the perfective marker ʔa.

In the next speech sample to be presented here there is an overall organization of sequential chunks on two different levels. On the lower level pairs of predications occur in close succession to express a temporal/causal connection; on the higher level the whole utterance exhibits a succession of several such complexes (realized as chunks of speech with more or less audible breaks in between), the totality of which expresses a temporal/causal progression. In this case a Mlabri was explaining about the Sun, the Moon, the Stars, etc. – all being up there thanks to the abovementioned mythical hero – and I then asked him about the clouds in the sky, whether they had been put there in the same way. No, he said, the elders told nothing about that. Then came a very adequate explanation of a cyclic natural phenomenon: '(but) there are clouds because it rains; when it rains then afterwards it is wet; when it is no longer wet it will be sunshine; it becomes gradually hot here so the steam rises':

> kuup tɛɛ dɔ mɛʔ hot; mɛʔ hot lac, chukkɔʔ; chukkɔʔ ʔa lac, ʔa gaɲ; pluŋ ʔɔɔk ʔɔɔk nii, ʔat cuŋ glɤh .

The Mlabri version of this utterance has the same gross structure as my preceding translation. The first five words stand in a (non-iconic) causal construction with dɔ as a connective; this is an introductory statement which defines the theme to be explicated. Then comes a strictly iconic succession of clause pairs without clause-connectives. For reasons which I cannot explain the turning point consisting of drying-up plus breakthrough of the sunshine is expressed as a sequence of punctual events by means of the perfective marker ʔa which occurs twice, first to express Futurum Exactum ('when it is no longer wet') and then to express Future ('it will be sunshine'); whereas, the other events in the total process are not marked in this way.

Unlike the first utterance, which was absolutely unmixed Mlabri, this second utterance happens to exhibit a couple of grammatical words borrowed from Thai but fully integrated into β-Mlabri, tɛɛ dɔ, and even an instance of code mixing or intersentential code switching: the words ʔɔɔk ʔɔɔk nii 'appear, appear here' are plain Thai.

The next speech sample is a passage from a spontaneous conversation in which the speaker explains about his relatives, in this case his half-brother Ba Phet. It is interesting because it shows how the Mlabri use parallel syntactic constructions to explain about coreferentiality and non-identity of referents (the material was exploited to some extent in sections 4.2.4 and 5.2.2 above):

> ba phet ʔot rooj (...) ʔot rooj - dəmɔ mɤm; ba phet dəmɔ mɤm, ʔoh dəmɔ mɤm, bɛɛr mɤʔ; ba phet hak mɔ mɤʔ, ʔoh hak mɔ mɤʔ; mɤm toc bɛɛr hmaaj

In literal translation:

> Ba Phet my younger-sibling (...) my younger-sibling – one father; Ba Phet one-and-the-same father, I one-and-the-same father, two mother; Ba Phet on-the-one-hand one mother, I on-the-other-hand one mother; father take two wife. The overall meaning can be paraphrased thus: 'Ba Phet is my younger brother; Ba Phet and I have the same father but different mothers: our father had two wives'.

The last speech-sample consists of a passage from the Great Flood Myth. It represents an extremely informal type of narration, with performance phenomena which make the syntax look less organized in comparison with the much more rigid style of the preceding two samples. The passage runs as follows, as far as I can sort out from my recording of the narrator's rapid and often rather indistinct rendering of it (the kommas and semicolons reflect my understanding of the compositional structure, which may not be entirely correct):

> (1) --- ʔɤɤ – ʔa glɤh bɛɛ, glɤh dɔ ʔuj jooŋ ʔuj jooŋ ʔuj jooŋ pan gʌh pan gʌh; (2) ʔan, ɟrʌʌk ʔa brɤɤl glɤh ʔa ɟak kadɯp klɯɯr; (3) ʔan - ʔi ʔa pajok glɤh, ʔa pajok glɤh ʔa ɟak hɔɔt ʔa ɟak klɯɯr-klɯɯr; (4) ʔan bɛɛ ʔa wʌl glɤh ʔa laac *(hesitation)* ʔa tit ladɯŋ; (5) laac ʔa *(hesitation)* hrlooj ɟak hrlooj ɟak; (6) ʔa laac nii ʔa ɟak hot, ɟak hot, ɟrʌʌk nii ʔa ɟak ɟuur, tit chi bɛɛʔ; (7) kwʌr mlaaʔ put-tut-tut-tut ʔuj jooŋ ʔuj jooŋ ʔuj jo-o-oŋ.

A verbatim translation runs approximately as follows:

> (1) --- erh – PERF ascend raft, ascend some-of woman man woman man woman man time this time this; (2) and – water PERF flood rise PERF go push-at heaven; (3) and – as PERF lift rise, as PERF lift rise PERF go reach PERF go sky-sky; (4) and raft PERF come rise PERF finish *(hesitation)* PERF touch up-above; (5) finish PERF *(hesitation)* float go float go; (6) PERF finish this PERF go fall, go fall, water this PERF go fall, touch close-to earth; (7) Outsider Mlabri "put-tut-tut-tut" woman man woman man woman man!

This word-per-word translation makes the meaning and composition of the text disintegrate, in part because of the small-talk character of the rendering, in part because it ignores important linguistic, paralinguistic and extralinguistic cues. In the oral rendering there is both the prosody (which for example signals that ʔuj jooŋ is to be understood as one whole 'man-woman', i.e. 'couple') and the very lively gestures and mimicry of the speaker, which compensate for the preponderance of elliptical constructions and redundant repetitions. As I understand the passage from my total impression of it (integrating speech and visual performance), it means approximately the following:

> (1) --- they climbed the raft(s), several couples, you see, (2) and the flooding water rose so high as to touch the sky, (3) and as it lifted them up *(hesitation)* they collided with what was up above. (5) When that was over *(hesitation)* they

floated along, (6) and then the water sank until they touched the ground, (7) and they trotted out: ousiders (i.e. the various other human tribes) as well as Mlabri, several couples!

The words of the narrative above were spoken very rapidly and extremely informally, as it was the speaker's intention to inform me about the contents of the old story, not to present a codified version of a greater or lesser part of the great flood myth. At my request the speaker elaborated on one particular episode in this narrative, which forms part of a very loosely knit pattern of traditional Mlabri knowledge. I have heard about such matters several times from the same speaker and found that he varies both his coverage of subject-matter and his formulations considerably from one occasion to the next. In most cases he has just made a few sweeping remarks about the flood itself since he is much more interested in telling what happened after it: the restitution of the earth and the regeneration of mankind.

As for vocabulary there is one word laduɯŋ 'up above' which I only know from this text, and a strange, expressive string of syllables put-tut-tut-tut, said in falsetto voice, which the speaker probably uses to symbolize the trotting of a multitude of persons; the remaining words in this text also occur in other data.

The word bɛɛ in (1) and (4) above is the same etymon as Thai phɛɛ 'raft'; as I understand the myth there were several rafts which were surrounded by water and eventually squeezed together when the water rose, but there is no cue to this in the passage cited here. The words glɤh bɛɛ in (1) might, if viewed in isolation, seem to mean '(then) rose the raft(s)', but in fact the verb has an implicit preceding subject 'they' (which is explicated by dɔ ʔuj jooŋ etc.), and glɤh is transitive: 'ascend'. This is unambiguous in another rendering of the myth in which the same speaker said ʔat tiʔ glɤh bɛɛ with ʔat tiiʔ 'they' as the explicit subject.

Finally a comment on the particle ʔan occurring in (2), (3) and (4) is needed: this word is frequent in narrative style and probably has a variety of discoursive functions (see the discussion in 5.2.2 above); I have here chosen simply to render it as 'and'.

Part II
Lexicon

Chapter 6

The Selection of Lexical Information

The list of linguistic material with translations (referred to as the "Mlabri-English Dictionary") which forms the bulk of the remainder of this monograph contains a sample of lexical items which could be retrieved without too much difficulty during very limited periods of encounter with the speakers of β-Mlabri. Thus the vocabulary presented here cannot be expected to be in any sense exhaustive nor statistically representative of the total Mlabri vocabulary. Whenever I have checked up on words which I had recorded already, the Mlabri speaker would suggest additional, new vocabulary to me. Also in ordinary conversation new words have constantly turned up. Obviously, there is much more everyday vocabulary which I have not recorded so far. Still, I hope the list below will convey a certain impression of the language.

The coverage of vocabulary associated with religious life, with the manufacturing of artifacts, with work in the forest and with wild nature is much poorer than the rest. I must emphasize in particular that I have not considered it an essential task for me as a general linguist to record the wealth of zoological and botanical terminology. Although this terminology is certainly interesting and should be recorded before it is forgotten, a serious treatment of such specialized vocabulary would require both the collection of specimens and the assistance of experts in order for me to be sure that the species had been correctly identified. As it is, animals, birds, insects, trees and herbs often appear in the word list with no identification beyond a vague description or mention of a category to which the item seems to belong: "insect species", "species of edible tuber" and the like.

The Mlabri-English dictionary and the English-Mlabri index presented below were originally developed from the same base.

The two word lists are, however, not equivalent in coverage. Although the English-Mlabri list can be consulted in itself, it was designed as an *index* to the much more elaborate Mlabri-English dictionary, and thus it is greatly lacking in information about semantic detail, spheres of usage etc.

I regret that new data have forced me to make a great many last-minute additions and amendments. This was done at the risk of introducing inconsistencies between the spellings or translations of similar material in different parts of the dictionary and particularly inconsistencies between the dictionary and the English-Mlabri index. Hopefully, the discrepancies are of minor consequence.

6.1 Simple and Complex Lexical Entries

In the Mlabri-English dictionary most entries consist of one word only. More complex (also lexicalized) material is, if possible, arranged under single-word entries. Separate entries which consist of two words are used only if there is no way of assigning them to a single lexical entry.

As mentioned in 4.1.4 above, there are some concatenated words which might be regarded alternatively as compounds or as phrases. In the dictionary below the latter solution has generally been preferred. – Aside from morphosyntactic and semantic arguments for or against one or the other solution, there is etymological information to be gained by separating forms into words as much as possible: it reduces the work of searching for cognates across the vocabulary. There are, however, not many candidates for an analysis of forms as compounds anyway.

Within each entry, a distinction is made between *phrasal lexical items* and *illustrative phrases*.

Phrasal lexical items (idioms, collocations etc.) are arranged in alphabetical order under single-word main entries.

Illustrative phrases are examples picked in order to illustrate the ordinary, productive use of a lexeme or a collocation. Such material is listed in alphabetic order in the section of each entry where it belongs, i.e. either directly under the main entry word or under one of the phrasal sub-entries. Illustrative phrases which have been extracted from a real discourse have been cut down to the material that is necessary to illustrate the lexical usage under consideration. This applies specifically to phrases which illustrate the use of verbs. Specific material which functions as Subject or Object in an extracted sample has been cut off if it does not contribute independently to the understanding of the lexical entry (I elaborate on this point in order to make explicit that the lexical material cannot be used for syntactic analyses, e.g. with regard to the pattern of occurrence of clauses without a Subject Noun Phrase). In some instances, however, it seemed more informative to enter a rather complex sentence preserving the characteristics of a sample from real discourse. Such examples often contain major internal boundaries marked phonetically by pausal and intonational breaks, these boundaries are indicated by *commas* or by *space plus hyphen plus space* in the transcriptions.

6.2 Phonemic Notation and Alphabetic Ordering

The notation used here is largely congruent with the one used for the α-Mlabri vocabulary in Egerod and Rischel (1987). The only major notational difference is the symbolization of the following four phonemes: the high and half-high unrounded back vowels ɯ ɤ (in E&R: ï, ë), the voiced palatal stop (or affricate) ɟ, and the syllable-final aspirated lateral lh (in E&R: hl).

There is, however, a difference in the analysis with regard to *quantity*. Vowel length, which is phonemic (but in a state of instability both in α- and β-Mlabri), was left unmarked in Egerod and Rischel (1987) whereas all forms in the present vocabulary are marked for vowel length. Since the actual length of vowels in individual word forms varies very much, from speaker to speaker and as a function of phrasal context, the information about vowel length in the present publication must be taken with reserve.

Alphabetization: Entries are arranged strictly in accordance with standard alphabetic order, except when special rules apply for phonetic symbols (see below). Entries which consist of two words are alphabetized according to the first word. Other rules for alphabetization are given below.

The alphabet of vowels is as follows: a, ʌ, e, ə, ɤ, ɛ, i, ɪ, ɯ, o, ɔ, u. Words are never entered with an initial vowel; if there is no other consonant initially the word has a (predictable) glottal stop and is transcribed accordingly (with initital ʔ).

Long and short vowels/diphthongs are treated as equivalent in the alphabetization of words.

As for consonants the alphabet is as follows: b, c, ch, d, g, h, j, ɟ, k, kh, l, m, n, ɲ, ŋ, r, (s), t, th, w, ʔ. Except for the aspirated stops, letter combinations such as hn, ʔj follow this strict alphabetization.

Pretonic syllables: Mlabri is characterized by the occurrence of pretonic "minor syllables", which contain no vowel or a reduced vowel, syllabicity being carried instead by a sonorant consonant. It is a problem for the phonemic analysis that minor syllables are somehow intermediate between consonant clusters and syllables. The relationship of minor syllables to the process of infixation (see 4.1 on Morphology above) is a little tricky. It is rather clear that a minor syllable plus a main-syllable onset appears if infixation results in a non-permitted initial cluster (such as /bnl/), but it is unclear what happens with regard to syllabicity if infixation results in a permitted word-initial cluster (/grw-/ in the word grwɛɛc 'finger' vacillates between being a cluster and being a minor syllable /gr/ plus onset /w/). Altogether it may be difficult to decide whether a form which begins in three consonant segments is bisyllabic ("sesquisyllabic") or simply contains an initial cluster (the entry forms given here may in some cases reflect erroneous analyses).

One the other hand one can hardly make a consistent distinction between minor syllables and other pretonic syllables, i.e. syllables with a clearly articulated vowel. There is much variation particularly in the pronunciation of pretonic syllables with a final sonorant, e.g. [gɯn-] or [gən-] both vary with [gn-] (realized with a syllabic nasal). For expedience such variation has been kept to a minimum in the entries. Notations *without pretonic vowels* are here favoured over notations with a vowel if both notations seem appropriate, and the quality of the (optional) vowel seems predictable. This applies especially to forms of the structure C(V)(C)C.C(C)V(C), where the structure before the syllable boundary (marked by the period mark) is a minor syllable C(V)(C)C which ends in a sonorant (/l, r/ or a nasal).

Syllabification: The conventions for syllabification of *sequences of minor syllable and main syllable* are for the most part self-explanatory, but for clarity and ease of reading the syllable boundary after a vowelless minor syllable is always indicated by means of a period mark, e.g. gn.rɛɛ. As for *intervocalic consonants or consonant sequences* the "default" rule is for VCV to be syllabified with the syllable boundary before the consonant, and for sequences of two or three intervocalic consonants to be syllabified with the syllable boundary after the first consonant.

There are important exceptions, however. Above all, there is an ambiguity with respect to intervocalic representations which consist of /h/ plus consonant symbol or consonant symbol plus /h/ because of the use of notations such as /hl hr hm hn hɲ hŋ ch kh ph th/ to represent special consonant types which occur syllable-initially (cf. chapter 3, section 3.1 above). I have chosen to disambiguate such complex symbols, whenever they occur intervocalically in lexical entries; that is, in such cases there is always a syllable boundary mark somewhere, no matter whether it occurs after the first vowel or between two consonants. In order to facilitate the reading of entries I have also (somewhat redundantly) indicated syllable boundaries, whenever the symbol /ʔ/ is involved.

As a matter of fact, the syllable boundary is not always easy to determine. The word rip.hɛp (insect species), for example, was first transcribed as "r.phɛp" (also in our α-Mlabri data), but I later found this to be wrong, at least for β-Mlabri. The word tɯk.lɤk 'to tickle' used to occur in my data as "tə.klɤk", but I have found that when said distinctly it is tɯk.lɤk. Altogether, syllable division remains an unsolved problem; I do not even know in which environments there is a possibility of contrast between different syllabifications.

These conventions for marking syllable boundaries have been

observed only in the Mlabri-English dictionary and the index, not in the descriptive chapters above.

Rhythm: The syntactically complex examples within the dictionary entries below might have been marked for certain features of rhythm and intonation, at least in cases where they are on record as whole, natural utterances. I have preferred not to add such features to the transcription, however, since it could not at all be done consistently.

The absence of prosodic marking makes two comments necessary:

(i) Pauses and intonation breaks tend to occur at clause boundaries, of course. It should be noted, however, that the commas interspersed in the transcriptions are primarily there for the purpose of making the structural organization of meaning more transparent; they do not consistently reflect observed prosodic characteristics.

(ii) Although a phonetic stretch is organized in stress-groups typically consisting of one, two or three words (of a varying number of syllables) and with final stress, this organization is not reflected in the transcriptions (except indirectly by vowel shortening, which is a frequent but not obligatory accompaniment of stress reduction in non-final position). In the absence of any marking of stress-groups it is sometimes obscure how stretches should be parsed, an example being tun wʌt wʌt gɛɛŋ, which at first glance looks as if it contains a reduplicative constituent wʌt wʌt but which can only be parsed meaningfully as a construction with of two constituents: tun wʌt and wʌt gɛɛŋ. This is what is signalled by the actual pronunciation, with stress on the second and the fourth word.

6.3 Phonological Variation

Both in α- Mlabri and β-Mlabri there is considerable variation in the pronunciation of individual words. This is in itself a very interesting feature of the language. It is, however, not yet possible to reflect this variation adequately in a dictionary, because it is too poorly understood.

The data collected so far are too heterogeneous (also in the degree to which they are phonetically reliable) and at the same time too limited. It would have taken much more study in order for the analyst to be able to handle the various *parameters of linguistic variation* and be successful in distinguishing genuine linguistic variation from simple *errors* in his own transcriptions. This is no simple task, especially if one is working with Mlabri: as stated already in the Preface above, it is a challenge to do reliable field work on this language.

There is a considerable amount of *variation* in the phonetics of Mlabri word forms. One the one hand there is very much variation due to *speaking style* in a broad sense (variations in tempo, distinctness level etc.). The speakers whom I have consulted certainly speak differently depending on whether they are engaged in small-talk, whether they are using narrative style or whether they are passing information about their language to the outside observer. They have been adjusting their speaking style to a greater or lesser extent, when I was supposed to understand or even be the sole addressee. The extreme situation, which occurred very frequently, was one in which a speaker slowly and distinctly dictated a word form or phrase to me after I had first tried to take it down from more natural speech. This obviously creates a considerable amount of heterogeneity in the data presented here. In particular, there is a formidable and to a large extent unsystematic variation in my notation of vowel length even in analogous environments.

On the other hand, the pronunciation of Mlabri words shows a certain *variation across speakers*, both in the form of idiosyncracies in the pronunciation of individual word forms and in the form of general pronunciation habits. In the present monograph I have treated data from all speakers as one set in spite of some such individual variation (the existence of individual variation is frequently stated, however).

But then there is variation in the field data which seems entirely fortuitous and not clearly correlated with either speaker or style. For example, there are a few words which I have heard with a glottalized initial consonant in some cases but with a plain consonant in other cases: ʔjoc or joc, ʔwec or wec. There is also often variation in the notation of vowel quality, or in the notation of voiced or voiceless initials in unstressed syllables. Some of this variation seems to reflect that the language is in a state of flux with respect to the pronunciation of certain word forms, but of course deviant forms may also be simple errors. I have included such occasional variant forms (with referencing to one main form) only if this seemed warranted by the data.

This leads over to the other main source of variation in field work data: undetected errors. In the case of Minor Mlabri (β-Mlabri) this is a particularly unpleasant problem since the use of this vernacular may soon be discontinued, so that it will be increasingly difficult or eventually impossible to check the greater or lesser validity of the data presented here (as for my own work, I shall of course make generally available whatever corrections and amendments I find it necessary to make when working on Mlabri data in the future).

There are several word forms in the raw data which later (when I was consulting the same speaker) turned out to have been transcribed erroneously and which could thus be corrected before editing. This is not, however, just a matter of regarding earlier data as more faulty and more recent data as necessarily more correct. Even the most recent raw transcriptions from the field may contain grave errors. This, I think, is mainly due to *shift of attention* during the course of my field work, a phenomenon which must be familiar to anybody doing field work. With increasing knowledge of the language one tends to focus more and more on grammar and discourse structure, and the language also became a means of accessing information about the culture. During my field work on Minor Mlabri I also often experienced that the data had to be taken down in a hurry, while the speaker was still concentrating on the issue. In such cases it may become the main issue just to pick up what is said and to understand what it is all about.

One's linguistic attentiveness certainly also varies with greater or lesser familiarity with the lexical material itself. The field worker may (deliberately or even without being conscious of it) use a simplified, normalized notation of well-known words and phrases but at the same time be attentive to fine phonetic detail in the transcription of unfamiliar expressions. This means that the resulting notes are sometimes quite "hybrid": mixing broad and fine transcriptions even within the same phrasal example. When one works with Mlabri speakers who are not prepared to take a metalinguistic attitude to their own speech and to repeat linguistic data several times without getting off the track, such hybrid material may stand as *the* raw data without further qualification.

In the editing phase one normalizes, of course, if the purpose is to give a broad transcription. It is obviously helpful to check the raw data from the field by listening to tapes afterwards. I have not found it practically possible or even appropriate to have several days or weeks of communication on tape, however. Moreover, with variable phenomena (such as the greater or lesser shortening of non-final vowels in Mlabri) there is no simple way to standardize the presentation, unless one chooses a very radical solution and discards transcriptions made in the field in favour of data which exist on tape. This would be an entirely unacceptable solution. As for my Mlabri material, several word forms exist only in the original field notes, and I consider these to be the most basic form of lexical data. They may even be more representative as dictionary entries than later transcripts from tape exactly because the field notes most often represent the integrated impression of several tokens of each word form (repetitions or occurrences in a variety of phrases). I have, therefore, edited the dictionary entries *on the basis of all kinds of data* in spite of inherent inconsistencies.

In the dictionary below, variant forms are to some extent given with cross-referencing, but much of the variation found in the raw data has been eliminated in favor of a certain standardization of entries. There are six major types of difficulties which have to do with variation or phonological indeterminacy. A survey of these types of variation is given below (the dictionary can be consulted without constant reference to this survey, however).

– (I) Minor syllables exhibit enormous variation in vowel quality and variation between presence and absence of a vowel. If there is no audible vowel, the most sonorant consonant of the minor syllable takes over syllabicity. Sometimes a parasitic r is heard, and there may even be variation in minor syllables between the types CVrC, CVC, CrC and CC (with the second C being syllabic). In the entries such variation has been kept to a minimum. The main principle has been to consider the vowel to be optional and non-phonemic and thus to use notations without a vowel (i.e. with "minor syllables"), provided that the quality of the optional vowel seems entirely predictable. This reduces the risk of giving exaggerated, over-distinct pronunciations as entry forms (although the Mlabri generally pronounce grammatical words and minor syllables very indistinctly, the persistent elicitation of word forms may provoke even a Mlabri to produce spurious dictation forms).

It was often impossible to decide what form to prefer, and to be consistent in the choice of entry forms. Thus, one (good) speaker insists on the vowel /i/ in the pretonic (pre-stress) syllables of several words where all other speakers pronounce minor syllables without any clear vowel. Moreover, there are probably several entries with /ɯ/ in the pretonic syllable which might just as well have been entered with a vowelless presyllable (a minor syllable). Cross-referencing has to some extent served to remedy such situations.

– (II) There is much variation in the duration of phonemically long vowels. Moreover, although length is phonemic, the distinction is not always clear even when words are said in isolation, and speakers do not always agree on vowel quantity. Entry forms are of course given with the assumed phonemic vowel quantity; sometimes the length mark is put in parentheses, which may either indicate a genuine vacillation in vowel quantity or uncertainty on my part. Phrase internal vowel shortening is indicated impressionistically in phrasal examples. Unfortunately, this could not be done very consistently, partly because the prosodic rules have not been established, and partly because vowel shortening is not only regulated by structural features but is also to a very high degree a function of the speech tempo and distinctness level chosen by the speaker (or requested by me) on each particular occasion.

– (III) Several word forms exhibit variation between two different vowel phonemes or some indeterminate vowel quality which is inconsistently assigned to one phoneme or another in the raw data. Such variation or indeterminacy is found in some words with /ɔ/ - /ʌ/ and /ɛ/ - /a/ before palatals; moreover, a preceding r sometimes causes problems in vowel assignment. In cases where there is genuine doubt about the quality of the vowel, or where speakers differ on the pronunciation of a word form, the dictionary contains both (all) variant forms, but one of these is used as head entry to which the others are just cross-referenced.

– (IV) There is sometimes variant pronounciations of sequences which contain a high vowel or glide between a consonant and a lower vowel, e.g. so that one informant says kwʌŋ, another kuʌŋ. In clear-cut cases of doublet pronunciations there are sometimes two separate entries in the dictionary (though with cross-referencing to one head entry).

– (V) There is some lexical variation between final /c/ and /k/ and sometimes between final /c/ and /t/. Such variant forms are always given separately, but with cross-referencing to one head entry.

– (VI) In some words with a minor syllable plus a main syllable there is variation between presence and absence of a stop which splits up a sequence of homorganic sonorants: hn.drɤɤʔ or hn.rɤɤʔ. It might seem preferable to use an entry form *without* the stop consonant in such cases, but I am not sure that the variation is fully predictable, and very often the form with an audible stop seems to represent the predominant pronunciation. Some cross-referencing has been used.

It should finally be mentioned again that one obvious use of Mlabri word lists in scholarly work is the inclusion of Mlabri material in *etymological comparisons* within Austroasiatic. From that point of view I have judged it as preferable to enter reference forms which represent *distinct pronunciation*.

6.4 Morphology and Alphabetization

The many grammatical markers or affixes of Mlabri present a problem for alphabetization. The main principle is strict alphabetization of single word forms, i.e. even of phonologically complex word forms which are related to other lexical entries by prefixation or infixation, provided that the complex forms in question are indisputably single words. This applies also to word forms which contain the highly frequent causative prefix pa- or ba-: such word forms are entered strictly alphabetically but (generally) cross-referenced with the underived verb.

Word forms containing interrogative ti-, tə- or -tɯ are also entered as whole words: tipiaaʔ or təpiaaʔ 'what', ʔitɯ 'which', although both piaaʔ and ʔi occur as separate words (and although there is an interrogative morpheme tɯʔ of word status in α-Mlabri). With more hesitation I have entered the negative preverbs kibɔ and kɔki as single entries although they can be analyzed into ki, kɔ and bɔ, all of which occur as separate entries. Occasionally it seems warranted to have a grammatical morpheme both as a lexical entry and as a clitic integrated into separate lexical entries, for example the morpheme bʌr or br- 'belonging to'.

Other grammatical morphemes which occur in pretonic position (e.g. ʔa, di and ʔi before verbs, ʔat, di and dɔ before nouns) are here separated off and treated as separate words, whenever this latter analysis is possible.

Names with a pretonic marker such as bɔ(ɔ) for 'senior male' are treated as noun phrases (bɔ + khit, not bɔkhit); these markers appear as separate entries in the dictionary although they do not have the status of fully independent words.

As a rule, complex forms which contain more than one noun or verb base are treated as phrasal expressions rather than compounds (such expressions are listed under the appropriate single-word entries), except if this analysis is unsupportable for semantical or phonological reasons. Word bases are thus on the whole given as entries only in their "naked" form and/or with causative prefix.

6.5 Word-class Membership

Word-classes in Mlabri, as in many other Southeast Asian languages, pose severe problems of definition and delimitation. The solution of these problems would seem to be a necessary prerequisite to serious work on Mlabri lexicon and grammar. This is, however, equally true of several other languages of the area, and I have preferred not to treat it as an issue specific to β-Mlabri.

Both in the introduction to chapter 4, in chapter 5 and in the dictionary and index below I have assumed a "natural" classification of lexical material into noun-like and verb-like words plus a residue of "grammatical words" (which may be more noun-like or more verb-like).

The grammatical tags N = NOUNS and V = VERBS, which are used for disambiguation in some lexical entries below, are reasonably well-founded semantically and syntactically (e.g. verbs can be negated, nouns cannot).

Words which denote non-tangible phenomena such as physical sensations, however, are in some cases word-class hybrids, e.g. ŋaʔ which occurs as a verb 'to itch, it itches' and even takes an object: ŋaʔ cheeʔ 'it itches because of lice', but which also occurs in noun-like function as sentence object: gehgeh ʔot ŋaʔ '(I) scratch my itch', i.e. 'I scratch myself because it itches'.

As in other languages of the area the word-class *Verbs* includes static verbs which (at least from the perspective of languages distinguishing between verbs and adjectives) may be said to have a dual role: as sentence verbs and as adjectival modifiers to nouns. The string ɟrʌʌk thɛh is a predication which may be translated as 'good water' or 'the water is good' depending on the context.

The real problems of word-class assignment occur with the residue of lexical material. The first problem is the occurrence of verb-like grammatical words, which one may choose to call "Minor Verbs", "Auxiliaries", "Coverbs", "Secondary Verbs",

"Adverbs", "Preverbs" (my term as used above for a certain subclass), "Particles" or "Markers", depending on the intended coverage of each such category and the syntax and semantics of the particular words. As stated several times above, I have made no particular effort in this monograph to work within a consistent and fully adequate terminology, but in the dictionary section I put considerable emphasis on giving informative translations and providing transparent examples of usage so as to illustrate the basic semantic and syntactic properties of the lexical items. I have, in addition, specified for most minor verbs or adverbs whether they occur before or after verbs: in *preverbal* position or in *postverbal* position.

The second problem is the classification of those grammatical words which serve to glue words, phrases or clauses together, i.e. complementizers, conjunctions etc. This is a problem area because these grammatical words are so evasive, as they are often optional. Whenever I heard some utterance and wanted to check up on its lexical make-up and its meaning, the Mlabri tended to repeat the string (or paraphrase it) with less use of complementizers and conjunctions than in their spontaneous wording. For this and other reasons it is often unclear to me what is the total semantic range and/or the total range of syntactic possibilities of such words. Throughout the present monograph I have preferred to use just one term: CONNECTIVE to refer to this kind of function word.

6.6 Homonymy and Polysemy

Polysemy within entries in the Mlabri-English dictionary is not accounted for in a quite consistent way. The general principle has been to mark polysemy by using *Arabic* numerals, and to list homophonous lexical entries with *Roman* capital numerals. The homophony solution was, however, chosen whenever there were good reasons for doing so (often irrespective of etymology). Thus, information that really refers to a single lexeme is often distributed over two or more consecutively numbered lexical entries if that was found convenient for the arrangement of lexical information or for the semantic and syntactic alignment of the Mlabri-

English dictionary with similar lists for α-Mlabri or other languages or dialects.

The semantic or syntactic range of a shared word often differs between α- and β-Mlabri, in some cases because of influence from Thai word semantics on one or the other variety. Letting this purely technical principle override both intuition and etymological considerations is consistent with the general conception of the Dictionary as an organized presentation of raw data.

6.7 Spheres of Usage and Reliability of Information

The present work is strictly limited to the presentation of material which belongs to β-Mlabri (Minor Mlabri) proper; on the other hand I have striven to give a detailed and careful documentation within this framework.

As said in the Preface, all cross-referencing between different languages and even between α- and β-Mlabri had to be postponed because the extended and revised material now available on α-Mlabri is still in the process of being edited for publication by Søren Egerod and myself. Ideally, all words recorded from α-Mlabri speakers should have been checked with β-Mlabri speakers, and vice versa. Although this has been done to some extent (both in a joint session with Dr. Egerod and in my own field work) the words thus checked cover only fractions of the vocabularies of α-Mlabri and of β-Mlabri.

These spot checks show that systematic comparative field work of this kind is a desideratum both from a sociolinguistic and a comparative point of view. It would, on the one hand, increase the documented vocabulary for each variety and, on the other hand, yield very interesting information about the absence, limited use or undesirability of a number of words in one variety of Mlabri, words which are current in the other variety of Mlabri. Most of our work on α-Mlabri was, however, done before this became an issue, and moreover, it has turned out to be a psychological strain on Mlabri speakers to be consulted about words which are blacklisted in their own variety. The information which we have retrieved so far is too fragmentary and unsystematic, and I have preferred not to include any of this in the lexical entries below.

As mentioned in the Preface and in chapter 1 above, there is an independent and very important source which has presented a small sample of β-Mlabri vocabulary: Michel Ferlus' 1964-list. Dr. Ferlus put his data at my disposal soon after I had begun recording β-Mlabri, so I have had the advantage of having access to this sample all along. There is, however, both a timespan of a quarter of a century between his data and my own and a difference in the circumstances under which the field work was done. To ensure homogeneity, the vocabulary published here includes only material that I have gathered myself, but it is indicated whether a lexical item occurs – with a more or less equivalent translation – in Dr. Ferlus' list.

Dr. Ferlus' forms are often identical or at least notationally equivalent to mine (which is encouraging, of course), but there are several differences of detail. Occasionally, i.e. if there are discrepancies which I find to be strongly suggestive of a genuine and interesting difference in phonological form, I quote Ferlus' phonetic notation. Most of the aberrations, however, just seem to reflect different transcription conventions, although there are also instances in which the form Ferlus has taken down somehow seems incomplete.

Dr. Ferlus collected his raw-data during one brief encounter (without being able to recheck later); not surprisingly they reflect some of the same difficulties of phonological discrimination and identification and some of the same types of phonetic variation which I can observe in my own data (such as the very slight and often almost imperceptible aspiration which distinguishes /-lh/ from /-l/ or the sometimes unstable glottalization which distinguishes /ʔj-/ from /j-/). I have not considered it useful to go into such detail here; the essential thing for me has been to state to what extent the same lexical items were recorded in Laos back in 1964.

Restricted use of vocabulary – sex-specific language: It is a very essential aspect of Mlabri words whether they are used indiscriminately by all speakers or are somehow restricted. I have sometimes indicated that a word seems to be used rarely but it is more interesting to note that there is a lexical polarization not only between α-Mlabri and β-Mlabri but also to some extent within β-Mlabri.

Sex-specific language is the most interesting issue of this kind. The occasional labelling of forms as "female language" or "male language" in the lexical entries below refers to the informants' own intuition about the forms. I have judged it interesting as information about attitudes toward linguistic usages, although it is not always corroborated by my observations of the actual usage of male and female speakers (hence the quotation marks around "female lg." and "male lg."). This information about sex-differences in linguistic habits is fragmentary; it occurs only with forms which I happened to discuss with Mlabri speakers from that particular point of view. Very often such discussion disclosed the existence of synonyms or near-synonyms which I did not know of before. It is possible that several more words could be categorized as "female" or "male"; in principle all words deserve being checked for such a categorization.

Unfortunately the information I have obtained about the speakers' assessment of words (as female or male language) is skewed: it was mostly supplied by male speakers and often lacks corroboration (or dismissal) from female speakers. Obviously, the two sexes may not have the same judgments about sex-specific language. My data on this topic is still too meagre to do more than just point to the existence of the phenomenon.

Adequacy and degree of coverage of the β-Mlabri lexicon below: Because of the difficulties associated with the type of field work which I have performed, and the limited time available for field sessions with β-Mlabri speakers, it is likely that there are occasional mistakes in the lexical entries. Question marks sometimes occur in the entries to express strong uncertainty about a form or a gloss, but there are in fact numerous weakly attested or otherwise problematic lexical entries beyond the ones which have been marked specifically below.

Except for the question how to choose suitable entry forms in cases of variation, I would now consider the transcription of the entry forms themselves as a minor problem. There are more serious problems associated with the meaning and use of the less frequent lexical items. In spite of several years of checking and rechecking my β-Mlabri material still comprises poorly attested (sometimes perhaps spurious) words which deserve further scrutiny.

Some translations of words or phrases may seem unconvincing because the words in question look like well-known Mon-Khmer words or loanwords from Thai and thus should have easily predictable meanings. I have tried to determine the meanings of words without much emphasis on the existence of real or apparent cognates in neighbouring languages. In fact, I have *not* systematically checked lexical items against Northern Thai and other languages of the area. That should ideally have been done, of course, but even with words which look suspiciously alike across languages it may be advisable not to jump to conclusions about borrowing or genetic relatedness and hence about shared word meanings. It should also be taken into consideration that because of the cultural situation of the Mlabri, loanwords may not always have been adopted with the same meanings as in the lending languages (the word gnrɛɛ 'curry' mentioned in section 2.1.2 above is a case in point).

Still, whenever there is a striking mismatch between a gloss in the dictionary and the meaning of an apparently related word in some well-documented language, there may be reason to take the information which I have obtained with some reserve, unless the lexical entry in question contains illustrative examples which together define the meaning of the Mlabri word beyond any reasonable doubt. I hope that with these warnings Mon-Khmer scholars will nevertheless find it possible to make use of the dictionary.

On the other hand I have sometimes with regrets had to dismiss material which I could not (yet) handle although I knew it to be genuine Mlabri.

There are several words which I have heard used in conversation or in narratives but which I have not yet retrieved in formalized field sessions. Such words often seem semantically transparent because of the context in which they occur and/or the gestures and mimicry which I observed during the conversation or narration. This may be deceptive, however, if the word only occurs in one specific context so that there is *no independent evidence* for its semantics. Such material has been left out unless I have had the opportunity of rechecking the meaning of the particular phrases, which has sometimes proved very difficult.

It must be emphasized once more that the lexical material which is presented below covers only a fraction of the total β-Mlabri lexicon. This is not only a matter of specialized (and sometimes more or less forgotten) zoological and botanical nomenclature; some of the lexical items which I know to exist although I have not been able to include them, are important verbs or grammatical words.

With the diminishing use of the mother-tongue among the β-Mlabri and with the ongoing change of lifestyle it is hardly practically possible to retrieve additional lexical items to such an extent that one ever approaches a "complete" lexicon. I do not even expect that there will ever exist a complete and exact identification of the many vaguely translated animal and plant names which occur on my list, although it would have been interesting to have a thorough documentation of such nomenclature from a hunter-gatherer language in Northern Indochina.

At the completion of this volume I strongly feel the need for additional documentation of the language itself (not to mention aspects of spiritual culture such as traditions and beliefs), the most basic research objectives being (i) to record natural speech material and (ii) to work more intensively with Mlabri speakers in order to arrive at a thorough understanding of conversational and narrative Mlabri. The lexicon below is of course a key to such work. There is no doubt, however, that more extensive study of discourse material will yield both supplementary linguistic forms and substantial corrections to the specimens of grammar and lexicon contained in this monograph and thus contribute to a more adequate coverage of the vanishing vernacular of the β-Mlabri.

Chapter 7
Mlabri-English Dictionary

b-

ba- *Causative Marker (cf.* pa-*), see entries beginning in* ba-

baa : junior *(used as title before the name of an unmarried male person)*

bac *in:*
- ʔjek bac : the bees are active visiting the flowers

ba.cheer : hush a child soothingly
- ba.cheer di gʌm beec : soothe it (a child) so it does not cry

ba.choolh : put up rafters (for a roof)

bah I : darkness before sunrise
- bah ɟruʔ : it is pitch dark (at night)
- ʔa bah : it is very early morning and still dark
- ʔa ɟjʌl ʔa ʔem ... ʔa bah ʔa ɟak : at dusk we go to sleep, ... in the early morning we leave
- ʔa loh bah : while it is still dark (at night)
- ʔjoc ʔa drɤh ʔa loh bah : the rooster crowed while it was still dark

bah II : no; that's not correct; that's not the case
- dadrooj tɛɛ bah : (he) was not (the other's) younger brother, you see
- ʔoh bah : it is not mine
- chinaat ʔoh tɛɛ bah : it is in fact not my own gun

bah III : you two; you (plural)
- bah bɛr mlaaʔ : you two
- bah di pruk : come, both of you!
- bah gʌm ɟak : don't go out, you two!
- bah ta bɔ chuʌŋ : you and Mr Bo Chuang
- bah ɟum : all of you here; you folks (also used when addressing two persons who belong to a group)
- bah ɟum gʌm ɟak : don't go out, you folks!
- ʔoh wʌl pa.rwaʔ bah ɟum ɟak boŋ juuk : I have come to invite all of you to a meal
- bah thɤɤŋ : you (pl.) over there
- bah tiiʔ : you (pl.) over there
- bah tiʔ bah thɤɤŋ : all of you

bahaaʔ *in:*
- pijh bahaaʔ : landslide

bahot : throw down; let fall
- paat bahot ʔat ʔjak : cut off the wax (of the beehive) and let it fall to the ground

- prak bahot : open the hand and let something fall

baɟah : wash *(V)* (specifically about hair)
- baɟah glɤɤʔ : wash one's hair *("female lg.")*
- baɟah kampoŋ : wash one's hair *("male lg.")*

bakɯm : discard; throw away; give up on something; divorce somebody
- chak chi bɤɤn hmaaj, bakɯm : he did not like his wife and left her
- ʔa prɪm chak toc, bakɯm : it is old, so I don't want it, throw it away!
- ʔat grɯɤɤ ʔa prɪm, bakɯm chak toc : my things are old and useless, I won't have them any more

bakkah : (1) flower

— : (2) the outmost part of a broom
- thɯp ɲuul bakkah chooc : broom made of thin "chooc" stalks

bakoot : have something sticking in one's throat; have a dry sensation in the throat

bakuh : tip something over (so that it falls on one side) *(V)*

ban I *(the Thai word for 'thousand'; in a fixed expression also containing the Thai word for 'hundred':)*
• ban hnʌm rɔɔj hnʌm : many, many years ago

baan II : town; village *(preposed to Thai names of villages or towns)*

baruul : animal species (reported to be black, smelly but edible)

baat : baht (Thai money)
- mɔɔj baat : one 10-Baht note *(sic accord. to one informant!)*

batac : break something

batit : close together
- jɤɤm batit : stay/rest close together
• batit bɛʔ : placed on the ground
• batit tr.dɯŋ : close together

batoʔ : use something as firewood; make a fire
- kaɲit, toc darɔʔ batoʔ di tawɯn : it is dark, take a split bamboo stick and make a fire to light up!
- lam bɯlbɯl wʌl toc batoʔ : bring some dry branches and use them to make a fire
- toc ʔuulh batoʔ, rəmɯɯt reew : let's take some firewood and light it; it is stormy weather!
- tr.leet ɟɯn batoʔ ɟjʌl : roll a wax candle and light it at dusk

ba.thuul : have something (meat, vegetables) with the staple food
- ʔoh chak boŋ juuk, met ɲaŋ ɟi.ʔdɤɤ ba.thuul : I don't feel like eating, there is nothing to eat with the rice
• ba.thuul juuk : have something (meat, vegetables) with the

rice

ba.ʔaaʔ : polluted
- ɟrʌʌk ba.ʔaaʔ : water which is not fresh any more; rotten water

bʌr I *(often proclitically and reduced to* br-*)* : of; belonging to
• bʌr bah ɟum : is it yours (pl.)?
• bʌr mɛh : is it yours (sg.)?
• bʌr ʔah ɟum : it belongs to us
• bʌr ʔitɯ mlaʔ gʌh : whose is this?; whom does this belong to?

bʌr II *in:*
• kiʔ ʔa bʌr : it is full moon

bʌt : scoop up
• bʌt ɟrʌʌk : drink out of one's hands

beec *(some say:* beet*)* : cry (weep)
- ʔat ɟum beec : our baby is crying

bel.wet : swing (back and forth)

beet : = beec

bet.rec bet.rac : have an attack of diarrhoea

bə.chih *(the first vowel very variable)* : be torn; split lengthwise; crack (also about desiccated soil)
- ʔee, diiŋ juuk bə.chih : look, the bamboo tube we are boiling the rice in is cracking!
• ʔa bə.chih : it (e.g. a shirt) is torn

bəlaak : white (*"female lg."*)

(+Ferlus)

bə.ʔɔɔt *see* bɔ.ʔɔɔt

bɤɤn : (1) can; knows how to; is physically able to
• chak bɤɤn : cannot; does not have the opportunity of
- ʔoh ʔa chak bɤɤn boŋ, chaw ʔeeʔ : I have not had a chance of eating, so I'm hungry
• ɟi.ʔdɤɤ ʔa dɔ bɤɤn : anything whatsoever (will do)
- boŋ ɟi.ʔdɤɤ ʔa dɔ bɤɤn : eats anything whatsoever
• met bɤɤn : cannot; is not able to
- leh met bɤɤn : I cannot come
- ʔɤh met bɤɤn : be exhausted
• ʔa dɔ bɤɤn : be OK (to do or to use)
— : (2) *in:*
• chak bɤɤn : doesn't like; cannot stand it/him
— : (3) acquire
• chi bɤɤn : want to have
- met chi bɤɤn glaŋ : I don't want any husband
• ʔa bɤɤn : have; have obtained
- ʔoo, ʔa bɤɤn tawlii : that's great, now we have lamps!
• ʔa bɤɤn hmaaj : married (said of a man)
- ləmeet ʔa bɤɤn hmaaj : a married man
• ʔa bɤɤn laŋ : married (said of a woman)
- miɲiŋ ʔa bɤɤn laŋ : a married woman

bɤttɤɤʔ : smoke from the fire-

place; smoke-laden air ("female lg.")
- bʏttʏʔ ʔuulh : smoke from the firewood

bɛɛ I : raft; floating vessel made of logs
- glʏh bɛɛ climb a raft

bɛɛ II : goat

bɛɛ III see kibɛɛ

bɛɛk : bear (N) ("female lg.") (Ferlus has final -t)

bɛɛr : (1) two (+Ferlus)
- bɛɛr pɛʔ pon hnʌm : a few years ago
- bɛɛr tawɩn : in two days
- bɛɛr tawɩn tak bn.nʌʔ : the day before yesterday
- bɛr thɯɯ : twice

— : (2) in:
• bɛɛr - hlooj : three (+Ferlus in the meaning of 'three to four')
• bɛɛr mlaʔ hlooj : three persons
- ʔat tiʔ ɟak bɛɛr mlaʔ hlooj : they were three persons leaving
• bɛɛr too hlooj : three "bodies" (e.g. three fish)

— : (2) a group of two (or more) kinsmen
• hna bɛɛr hna ɟum : our kinsmen over there
• ʔaaj bɛɛr : (speaker's) two brothers
- ʔaaj bɛɛr ɟak ginɛŋ : where are you going? (said to one's brothers)
• ʔat bɛɛr : they (two); both of them
- ʔat bɛɛr ɟak tipiaaʔ : what are those two going out to do?

• ʔɯɯj bɛɛr : (speaker's) two sisters
- ʔɯɯj bɛɛr ɟak ginɛŋ : where are you going? (said to one's sisters)

— : (3) (postnominal epithet to kinship terms:) married relative; married couple; in-law(s)
- met ɲaŋ ʔat bɛɛr : has no spouse; is single
• dadrooj bɛɛr : married younger sibling and/or his/her spouse (?)
• diŋ bɛɛr : married elder sibling and/or his/her spouse (?)
• kumɔm bɛɛr : married relative(s) of next generation
• rooj bɛɛr : married younger sibling and/or his/her spouse
• ʔɛɛw bɛɛr : married son or daughter and/or his/her spouse

bɛʔ : earth; ground; soil (N) (+Ferlus)
- cuʌk tɯp bɛʔ : bury
• bɛʔ thaluh : plains (flat land)
• bɛʔ licpɛɛc : muddy soil
• chibɛʔ see chibɛʔ

bi see kibi

bia (cf. biaʔ) in:
• chal.ʔbuut bia min : it (the meat) stinks of maggots

biaʔ : because
- ʔɛɛw beec biaʔ ŋaʔ : the child cries because it itches

biʌʌc : (1) soft; sufficiently boiled, in:
• ʔa biʌʌc : it is sufficiently boiled

(also cf. tom*)*
- biʌc klol : feel sad; sad

— : (2) young
- tak kun tak bɛʔ biʌʌc : "long ago when the earth was young" *i.e.* in the remote past

bibɛɛp : have quavering lips

bi.chih *see* bə.chih

biɯk : bear *(N)*
- biɯk krɛc : the bear bites

bin.hnɛʔ *idiolectal variant of* bn.hnɛʔ

biip : (1) squeeze
- biip pʌp : squeeze it so that it breaks

— : (2) suck
- ʔjiŋ-ʔjɛɛŋ krɛc kr.lʏʏt biip mɛɛm : the mongoose bites the throat and sucks blood

bip-bɛɛp : speak in a soft voice, almost whispering

bir.wɛɛc : stripes going crosswise (e.g. on garment or on an animal's fur)

biiʔ : be full (as regards hunger)
- boŋ gɔɔj di biʔ chɯm : you just go on eating till you're full!

biʔ-bɛʔ : the mouth parts of a crab

biŋ *in:*
- kiʔ biŋ : full moon
- kiʔ ʔa biŋ : the moon is full
- ʔoo, kiʔ ʔa biŋ ʔa thʌp pompoo : see, the moon is full! *(old expression)*

bɯk : put on (covering the upper part of the body)
- bɯk chɯrɛɛ ruʌŋ pliin : put the shirt on inside out
- chɯrɛɛ ʔoh ʔa bɯk : I'll put on the shirt
- gɯncaj bɯk dəkat : cover oneself with a blanket because one is cold

bɯl : (1) die; dead (+*Ferlus*)
- bɯl ʔa prɪm : died long ago
- bɯl dəmɔ tawɪn : died yesterday
- kɯr poh bɯl : the thunder strikes out and causes one to die
- lam bɯlbɯl : dead wood; dry wood
- lam bɯlbɯl lɯk.liik thɯʔ.thaʔ : the charred stump of a burned tree
- ʔa bɯl : is dead
- ʔa bɯl ɟak : is long since dead

— : (2) *(Preverbal)* terribly; very much
- bɯl (ʔa) chaw ʔee? : be very hungry

bɯlbɯl : dead; dry (said of logs and branches)
- lam bɯlbɯl wʌl toc batoʔ : bring some dry branches and use them to make a fire

bɯlh.ralh *see* bɯrh.ralh

bɯl.joom.jeem : twilight
- pan gʌh ʔa bɯl.joon.jeem, rə.ʔʌh ʔa thm.rɯm : now it is twilight, it will soon be dark

bɯnnʌʔ *see* bn.nʌʔ

bɯnnɔʔ *see* bn.nʌʔ

bɯnrajh : withered twig; firewood *("male lg.")*

bɯp : sharp (said of the sharpened edge of a knife)
- met bɯp : blunt

bɯr- *see* br-

bɯrh.ralh *(also heard as* bɯlh.ralh*)* : light (of weight) *("female lg.")*

bɯw *see* rɯw

bjaalh : the span of one's outstretched arms; fathom
- mɔ bjaalh : one fathom
- bɛɛr bjaalh pirpiip laaʔ : two fathoms and one yard

blah *in:*
- pa(a) blah : move in different directions

blaaj : (1) *(Prenominal)* big
- bla(a)j chəmɔɲ : a big star
- blaaj gr.nɯh : big flames
- gɯh-gɯh-gɯh, pen blaaj gr.nɯh : there are increasingly big flames

— : (2) *(in expressions of largeness or intensity:)*
- bla(a)j gʌw : big *(i.e. tall?)*
- ɟr̴ɴ bla(a)j gʌw : big frog
- bla(a)j guul : heavy (rainfall)
- bla(a)j guul mɛɛʔ : cloudburst
- ʔɤhɤɤj, mɛʔ bɔ bla(a)j guul : oh my, what a rain!
- bla(a)j kwaan : big; full-grown
- joc bla(a)j kwaan : hen
- bla(a)j pɯɯn : tall; high
- bla(a)j riiŋ *in:*
- mɛʔ bla(a)j riiŋ : it rains in large amounts

- bla(a)j wec : long (of visible length)

blʌk : (1) enter
- gʌm blʌk : don't enter!
- kaʔ blʌk hntor : the fish swims into the cavity
- thʌc blʌk thrɛɛŋ : I have a shred of meat between my teeth
- toc bɛɛ blʌk gɛɛɲ : go into the house with a goat; put a goat into the house (e.g. for slaughtering)
- wɔk blʌk jɤɤm mlaʔ di chak : spirits enter people's bodies

— : (2) *(after action verb:)* in(to)
- ʔbit blʌk : screw (something) in

blɤp *see* moʔ

blɛɛŋ : (1) arm; stalk of a plant; side branch of a tree; piston arm

— : (2) medulla; pith

blɛt : split rattan or the like for weaving utensils
- toc ʔat blɛt wʌl ɟwiin tirwiil : take some split rattan and decorate a weaved plate with the material

bliiŋ : (1) raw *(+Ferlus)*
- bon bliiŋ : it (the food) is raw
- ki bliiŋ : raw
- kɔ bliiŋ : raw
- met ʔɛl tɯŋ kɔ bliiŋ : it is raw, it hasn't been boiled yet

— : (2) unripe (of fruit)
- ki bliiŋ : unripe

— : (3) green
- druʔ bliiŋ : green banana leaf

— : (4) (be) alive

- ki bliiŋ : (be) alive
- ɲaŋ bliiŋ : be still alive

blɯkdɯk : have palpitations (of the heart)

blɯt : become invisible; vanish; be extinguished *(Ferlus has a similar word but with the opposite meaning)*
- ɟrʌk blɯt : the stream (creek or river) dries completely out
- ʔuulh ʔa blɯt : the fire is extinguished
- kiʔ blɯt : the moon is becoming "extinguished" (end of the last quarter)
- kiʔ rɛɛm blɯt : the waning moon shrinks so that it becomes invisible
- kiʔ ʔa blɯt : the phase when the moon is "extinguished"
- kiʔ ʔa noɲ ʔa blɯt : the (waning) moon has shrunk and has become invisible

bloom : lick; suck
- bloom tiiʔ : lick one's fingers

blot : growl (of tiger)

blɔn : opening (at top of basket)

bluuʔ : thigh *(+Ferlus)*

bn.hnɛʔ : you (polite form of address, neutral as to sex of addressee)
- bn.hnɛʔ tiiʔ : *id.*

bn.liiŋ *(or* binliiŋ*)* : (1) green; grey; light blue

— : (2) raw

bn.nah : past *in:*
- mɔ hnʌm bn.nah : last year
- mɔ hnʌm tak bn.nah : last year

bn.nʌʔ *(or* bɯnnʌʔ, bɯnnɔʔ, bn.nɔʔ*)* : the day before yesterday; some time ago
- bn.nʌʔ nɛɛ : three days ago
- tak bn.nʌʔ : some time ago; in the past

boc : be loose
- kwɛk boc : the axe has a loose head

boh I *in:*
- lə boh : this size

boh II *see* ʔboh

-boh *see* chiboh, chohboh

bohboh : boil something; be boiling
- tom gʌm bohboh, tom pluŋ ʔɔn ʔɔk : don't let it boil, just heat the food!
- ɟrʌʌk bohboh : boiling water
- ɟrʌʌk ʔa bohboh : the water is boiling
- lɔj bohboh : be boiling; let something boil
- di gʌm lɔj bohboh : don't let it boil!

boom : bottle
- ɟn.raaʔ boŋ bɛr boom : drink two bottles of liquor

bontuʔ : grave *(N)*
- cuʌk tɯp ʔat bontuʔ : bury in a grave

boŋ : eat; consume (all kinds of food, even liquids)
- boŋ gwaj mlaaʔ : eat together (the whole group)
- boŋ chɛʔ thɯɯ : eat several times

- bɔŋ gɔj pleʔ lak : eat the "soup" in which a sweet gourd has been boiled
- bɔŋ het : eat mushrooms
- bɔŋ kwaaj : eat taro
- bɔŋ mɔ tuptoop : eat one package (i.e. of medicine)
- bɔŋ ɟn.raaʔ thaŋɔɔt : drink liquor and get drunk
- bɔŋ pleʔ chat : eat oranges
- bɔŋ pleʔ ʔjaa : take pills
• bɔŋ dok bɔŋ jen : eat poor food
• bɔŋ gɯntak : chomp one's food while eating
• bɔŋ juuk : eat rice; eat village-type food (+Ferlus)
- bɔŋ juuk gn.rɛɛ lm.bah : I eat rice with cabbage curry
- bɔŋ juuk ɟjʌl : have supper
- bɔŋ juuk tak ɟrɯw : eat breakfast
- ɟak bɔŋ juuk ginɛŋ : where are you going to eat?
- ʔɤh chuʌn bɔŋ juuk : live as a villager
• bɔŋ thɛh bɔŋ mɤk : eat good food
• bɔŋ tipiaaʔ : what have you eaten?
• bɔŋ ʔa chaw eeʔ : I am hungry still after eating
• bɔŋ ʔi biiʔ : eat until you are full!
• gr.wah bɔŋ : eat something which has been distributed within the group
• lat bɔŋ : eat something soft and juicy (e.g. a fruit)

borthor (*also heard with initial m- or with final -l*) : hair; quill (*"female lg."*)
• borthor glɤɤʔ : hair on one's head (+Ferlus)

botbot *see* **butbot**

booʔ : (1) breast; nipple (+Ferlus)
- ʔat ʔuuj di booʔ : the mother's breast
— : (2) suck (milk, said of babies) *cf.* **pabooʔ**
 ʔɛɛw chi booʔ : the baby is thirsty
• ki boʔ jɤɤm : being a baby; in one's infant years
— : (3) *in:*
• pleʔ booʔ : papaya

bɔ (*Particle of unclear but affirmative meaning*) : indeed; being rather -
- keeŋ ɟak bɔ nikniit : carry something with a bent back
- ʔɤhɤɤj, kɯr bɔ ruŋ.mruŋ : oh my, what a thunder!
• bɔ gɯɯn dr.chɤʔ : the two expressions mean the same; it is the same thing
• bɔ tak
 in expressions of past time, such as:
- bɔ tak jʌk wʌl jʌk : quite some years ago
- bɔ tak ɟrɯw : this morning
- bɔ tak ʔa hɤɤj : long ago
- bɔ tak ʔa hɤɤj bɔ tak kun : long, long ago
• bɔ tɔw : until
- mɛʔ hot tak ɟrɯw bɔ tɔw ɟjʌl : it rains constantly from dawn to dusk

bɔɔ I : title of senior man; Mr.

bɔɔ : II) *in:*
- bɔɔ ʔboh : this size *(often reduced to* baboh*)*

bɔɔ III *in:*
- bɔɔ chuʌk : Bo Kluea ("Salt Well", a locality)

bɔh : ashes *(+Ferlus)*
- bɔh ʔuulh : (ashes of) fireplace; kitchen
- kibi ɲaŋ gɛɛŋ ɲaŋ bɔh : "does not live with house and ashes": has no home
- ʔjak bɔh : ashes

bɔɔn : dance *(V)*

bɔ.ʔɔɔŋ *in:*
- ɲaam bɔ.ʔɔɔŋ : the dry and hot season

bɔ.ʔɔɔt *(or* bə.ʔɔɔt*)* : smoke from the fireplace; smoke-laden air *("male lg.")*
- ʔɣhɤɤj bɔ.ʔɔɔt : phew, what a smoke!
- bɔ.ʔɔɔt ʔuulh : smoke spreading from the firewood

braliiŋ : (pale bluish) green
- ʔa leh ta braliiŋ : the green sprouts are just coming up

bralit *in:*
- bralit ɟak : collect one's belongings and move to another place

braŋ : horse

brarulh *in:*
- brarulh chibɛʔ recede; sink (about flooding water)

braaw *see* pleeʔ

brɤɤl *in:*
- ɟrʌʌk brɤɤl : the water is flooding
- ɟrʌʌk brɤɤl glɤh : the flooding water is rising

brɛŋ : cut an edge into shape
- brɛŋ thoŋgot : cut the edge of a bamboo cup into shape

briin *see* tiin briin

briiʔ : forest (the whole world of the Mlabri)
- glaʔ briiʔ : speak "forest (language)", i.e. speak Mlabri
- jɤɤm briiʔ : live in the forest (not in the villages)
- lɔŋ briiʔ : in the (deep) forest

br.kiiŋ : on top; up above
- dɔɔk br.kiiŋ : put (it) on top of something *(V)*

br.mɛh : yours
- br.mɛh ɲʌʔ : that thing of yours; *(with question intonation:)* is that yours?
- toc br.mɛh ɲʌʔ *(marked prosodically as a command:)* hand me that thing of yours!

br.nah I *in:*
- lɔŋ br.nah : thunder *(old word)*

br.nah II *see* pr.nah

broʔ : cut oneself *("male lg.")*

br.pooŋ : underneath
- dɔɔk br.pooŋ : put (it) under something *(V)*

brulh *in:*
- brulh chibɛʔ recede; sink (about flooding water)

brwatbrwat *in:*

- lʌʌr brwatbrwat : swallow

br.wɛɛc *(or* bɯɯr.wɛɛc, bir.wɛɛc*)* : school
- blʌk br.wɛɛc : enter the school; go to school
- ɟak ʔɤh br.wɛɛc : attend school

br.ʔoh : my property; mine; yes, it's mine!

bukbuk *in:*
- ʔa bukbuk : be delapidated
- gɛɛŋ prɪm ʔa bukbuk, kan dʌm ɟɤɤm ʔɤh hmɛʔ : our house is old and delapidated, if we are to stay on we must build a new one

buuk : face *(N)*
- rɯp.paʔ buuk : wash one's face
- lɔŋ hna buuk : in forward direction
- ɟak lɔŋ hna buuk : go straight ahead

buntuʔ *see* bontuʔ

buŋ : pool of water on a surface (transl. uncertain)
- buŋ ruʌŋ : pool of water
- kum buŋ : hold some water in the hollow of one's hands

buŋbɔɔŋ : swell (inflammation of tissue); be swollen

bur- *also cf.* br-

burbur : young man

burɔrɛɛl *in:*
- ʔa burɔrɛɛl : the time just after sunset

burthor *see* borthor

but-bot *(expressive)* : shaking; trembling

buʔ.bɔʔ : loose fibres on the stem of a plant (e.g. fibres on the medulla of a "thoom" stem)

c-

calamaaʔ *reportedly the same vegetable as* pleʔ hlak.hlek, *i.e. a melon-like gourd species ("female lg.")*

cam : hit; knock in
- cam hlek : hit a nail

caŋ cɯʔ : posture with bent knees and spread legs
- ɟɤɤm caŋ cɯʔ : sit with spread legs

caaw *in:*
- caaw naaj : officials

cʌlh *in:*
- ɟak cʌlh dɤŋ hmaaj : pay visits to a prospective wife

cʌr *in:*
- pleʔ cʌr : fruit species (resembles but is smaller than lychee)

cʌt *in:*
- cʌt ɟɤɤm : rest *(V)*
- glɤh cʌt ɟɤɤm : find a more elevated place to rest
- com dok cʌt kl.kiil : squat while resting one's elbows on one's knees

cej-dej *in:*
- mʌʌr cejdej : crawl with the head bent, looking back between the legs
- rɛɛm chet mʌʌr cejdej : the little child crawls with its head

bent etc.

ceet : touch something with the tongue-tip
- ceet lɛɛl : taste something with the tongue-tip

cembeelh *see* cɪmbeelh

cewcew *in:*
- hn.taʔ cewcew : short-tailed

cəkoo : pointed mountain peak

cʏh : just; a moment ago
- ʔituɯ mlaʔ pruk cʏh : who came a moment ago?

cɛɛʔ : vulva
- ɟwɛj cɛɛʔ : engage in intercourse
- toc cɛɛʔ : have sex with a girl
- ʔʏh cɛɛʔ : copulate; have sexual intercourse

ciaak : deer (probably: sambar deer) (*"female lg."*) (*Ferlus has initial ʂ*)

ciaŋ : mynah (bird species)

cіʌc : the skeleton or body of a person (?, translation uncertain)
- cɔɔ cіʌc : stretch oneself (while lying down)

ciʏʏk : grasp (seize)

cinbriin : cricket

ciɔr : pull

cip-cɛp : wink (with the eyelids)

cɪmbeelh (*or* cembeelh) : (1) thorn (*"male lg."*)
- cɪmbeelh pak ɟʏʏŋ : I have a thorn in my foot
- toc tɔʔ paat cɪmbeelh : remove a thorn from the skin with a knife
— : (2) thorn-like sections of the red layer (ʔat thwɛɲ) of a "thoom" stem
— : (3) needle
- toc cɪmbeelh ɟeŋ : sew with a needle
- toc paaj chaj cɪmbeelh : thread a needle

cɯɯ (*cf.* ɟɯɯ) *in the verb complex:* mʌc cɯɯ, *see* mʌc

cɯj : be here

cɯn : blade of a knife or spade

cɯŋ-rʌŋ *in:*
- cɯŋ-rʌŋ gɛɛŋ : house pole (in village house)

cɯpcaap : chirp; twitter
- ʔjoc pa(a) cɯpcaap : the bird twitters

cɯʔ *see* caŋ

cɯʔ-caʔ : the involucre of a corncob

cn.rak : comb (*Ferlus:* ʂndrɛk)

cŋ.gɯɯɯ *see* ɟŋ.gɯɯɯ

cok I : hoe (N)
- toc cok klukklɔk joh run : use a hoe to remove weeds

cok II *in:*
- cok toc : take something out; produce something
- cok toc ni dɛj chɯrɛɛ : take something from the breast pocket
- cok toc ti cot : take something from the bag

com **I** : liver

com *in:*
- com dok : stoop *(V)*
  - jɤɤm com dok : sit squatting and stooping

cot : bag
- cok toc ti cot : take something from the bag
- lʌʌp ti cot : put (something) into one's bag

cɔɔ *in:*
- cɔɔ ciʌc : stretch oneself (while lying down)

cɔk : bite (with a jerk of the head, said of poisonous snakes)
- tom.ʔooʔ cɔk : the snake bites

cɔʔ **I** : few
- mlaʔ cɔʔ : few people

cɔʔ **II** : (homemade) cigarette
- cɔʔ ɟrʌʌk : cigarette
- cɔ ʔjaa : cigarette

cɤɤw : shout; call (somebody)

crɔɔl : pull *(V)*

cuʌk : dig shallowly; grub
- toc chooʔ ɟak cuʌk ʔeeʔ : take a digging stick and dig for edible roots
- cuʌk boŋ : dig up (tubers) in order to eat (them)
- cuʌk tɯp *see* tɯp

cuɤl *in:*
- gʌm wʌl kwɤn wʌl cuɤl : sit properly or play somewhere else!

cuŋ : visible air moving upwards (*e.g.* a pillar of smoke rising from a fire, or mist rising after a rainfall)
- ʔat cuŋ glɤh : the smoke/mist rises
- cuŋ chimbɛp : air exhaled from a person (if visible in cold weather)
- cuŋ ʔuulh : smoke rising from the fireplace

ch-

chabaaj : carry (a bag) with a shoulder strap
- chabaaj laaʔ : carry on the shoulder

chaj *(perhaps also* chɛj*)* **I** : put; give; place; fix; fill something into/onto -; insert (*"male lg."*)
- chaj di ŋaam : insert it (an ear ornament) so it looks beautiful
- chaj ʔat chɯɯk glɤɤʔ : put strap(s) around one's forehead (to carry a bag)
- chaj ʔat chɯɯk laaʔ : put strap(s) around one's shoulders (to carry a bag)
- ʔat mɯj chaj takiʌŋ : fill (the) oil on the lamp
- chaj ti thoŋgot : fill it into a cup
- chaj mʌʌlh : give a name
- ʔoh chaj ʔɛɛw di mʌʌlh : I give a name to my child

chaaj **II** : string (*"female lg."*)

chajh : monkey species (small)

chak **I** : not; do not; will not (*Preverbal, apparently most-*

ly about mental disposition, cf. met)
- chak bɯl : not to die
- ʔoh chak dɤŋ : I cannot look after him/her!
- ʔoh chak ɟak ʔoh jɤɤm : I stay at home
- ʔoh chak leh : I'm not coming
- ʔoh chak ʔem, chi kampoŋ : I could not fall asleep because of a headache
- ʔoh chak ʔem, ʔoh pɯh jɤɤm : I am not asleep, I am up already!
• chak bɤɤn : (1) do not like; cannot stand it/him; (2) cannot *(Postverbal)*
• chak chi bɤɤn : do not like
• chak chi toc : do not want to have/obtain
• chak grɤj : have not yet managed to *(Preverbal)*
- chak grɤj ʔem : cannot fall asleep
• chak mɛɛn : that's not correct; you cannot say that (in Mlabri)
• chak toc : won't have it; don't want it
- ʔa chak toc : I don't want that; I can't use that
- ʔat gruɤɤ ʔa prim, bakɯm chak toc : the things are old and useless, throw them away, I won't have them
• kibi chak *see* ʔdaaj
• ʔa chak : don't! *(Preverbal)*

chak II : (1) body
- thɯt chak : wipe one's body
• mlaʔ di chak : a person's body
- mlaʔ di chak ʔa noɲ : the whole body
• wʌl jɤɤm kap chak kap chrʌnt : come and stay inside me! (invoking a spirit)
— : (2) the core or most substantial component of something, e.g. solid pieces of food in a soup, the body inside a snail's shell, or the pith (medulla) of a plant stem
- ʔat chak ʔi kwɛl jɤɤm : the snail's body is rolled up in a spiral
— : (3) chest; torso
• pluŋ chak : I have a chestburn
- ʔoh met thɛh, pluŋ chak : I feel miserable, I have a chestburn
— : (4) person
• chak kom.ruujh *see* chak-kom.ruujh
• ʔat chak : he (himself)
- mlaʔ pabɯl chiiŋ ɟak ginɛŋ ʔat chak : where did he go, the one who killed the pig?
- ʔat chak ɟak ginɛŋ : where did he go?
— : (5) oneself; one's own
- gɛɛŋ chak : one's own house
• kumɔɔm chak : address term to younger relative
• ʔɛɛw chak : one's "own" children (including in-laws)

chak-kom.ruujh *(or* chak-km.ruujh*)* : be old; be aging
• hɲuʔ-hɲɔʔ chak-kom.ruujh : old, wrinkled person

- ʔa chak-kom.ruujh : has reached old age

chala : or
- chala ɟak lɔŋ gʌh chala ɟak lɔŋ gʌh : shall we go this way or that way?
- ɟak lɔŋ gʌh chala ɟak lɔŋ gʌh : shall we go this way or that way?
- ɟak rih chala rih : shall we go this way or that way?
- ɟak tih chala tih : shall we go this way or that way?
- toc glaŋ chala noɲ : has married (already) or not (yet)

chalii : corn; maize (*"female lg."*)
- chalii thwɛɲ : ripe corn(cob)

chaloo : corn; maize (*"male lg."*)
- chaloo thwɛɲ : ripe corn(cob)
- thʌp chaloo : roast corncobs

chalɔɔʔ : leaf (big size species) (*in Ferlus' list it means 'roof'*)
• kɛɛ chalɔɔʔ : palm tree species

chal.ʔbuut : stink
- chal.ʔbuut bia min : it (the meat) stinks and is full of maggots

chaŋ I *in:*
• pleʔ chaŋ : bitter, nut-like fruit species ("mak khom")

chaaŋ II : elephant (*"female lg."*) (+Ferlus)

chapat : (1) beat; smash; hit
- chapat pleeʔ : hit a ball
- chapat ʔot chiʌɲ : swat that mosquito on my skin!
• chapat tiiʔ : clasp one's hands
— : (2) wash clothes by beating them against something in water
- chapat chooŋ : wash trousers
- chapat ʔa toc ʔa wʌl bɔŋ : wash it (the raw food) and take it home and eat it
- chɛɛŋ, ɟak chapat ni ruʌŋ : it's dirty so we must wash it in the stream
• chapat ɲoɲ-ɲeɲ : wash (clothes) by rubbing
— : (3) hit oneself; hurt oneself
- ʔoh chapat reew ʔi cho? : I hit myself badly and it hurts!

chapaʔ : be bland of taste
• chapaʔ chuʌk : there is too little salt in it
• chapaʔ prɛʔ : lack spices; be bland
- chapaʔ ʔat prɛʔ : it (the food) lacks the appropriate spices

chat I : astringent; sour
• pleʔ chat : orange (fruit)

chat II : (of something pointed:) hit; stab (*V*)
- ʔat mujmuj chat mlaaʔ, buŋbɔŋ : if the hairs (of the poisonous caterpillar) touch one's skin it swells
- ʔɛɛɛ, ʔoh pagrɛɛt chat hwɤk : hey!, I managed to decoy and stab a rat!

chaat : mat (on floor)
- thampɯɯl chaat : lay out the mat

chaw ʔeeʔ : be hungry

chawoj : husk (*V*); rinse rice

grains by shaking

chaaʔ : dig with the snout (said of pigs)
- chaʔ bɛʔ : dig the soil with the snout

cha.ʔɯɯl : stink

chʌm : stumble; fall
- ɹak ɹak ʔa chʌm : I fall all the time while walking
- ŋɔr hlɛŋ, chʌm : the path is slippery so you fall
• phalaat chʌm : slip and fall
- teen ŋɔr hlɛŋ phalaat chʌm : slip and fall on a slippery path

chʌɲ *see:* chiʌɲ

chʌr : stand upright *(V)*
- ʔa jɤɤm ʔa chi kl.dɯl, chʌr : my behind aches from sitting, I'll stand up
• chʌr jɤɤm : be standing upright
• chʌr ʔa jɤɤm : sit down (after standing)
• jɤɤm ʔa chʌr : rise (after sitting); stand up

cheh : dig something out (e.g. remove a thorn from the skin with one's nail or a knife)
- cheh cımbeelh : dig a thorn out

chen.ʔdeh *see* chın.ʔdeh

cheŋ- *see* chŋ-

chet : minor, *in:*
• ki chet : who is still a child
- ʔoh met mʌc cɯɯ ɲʌn ki chet : I don't know because I was still a child (when it happened)
• mɤʔ chet : mother who is/was the father's second wife *(acc. to one informant)*
• rɛɛm chet : small child (below puberty)
- mɤʔ ɲaŋ rɛɛm chet : Mother has a small child
• rumgum chet : finger, particularly little finger (pinkie)

cheeʔ : lice
- mɛt che(e)ʔ ɲaŋ : you have lice
- ŋaʔ cheeʔ : it itches because of lice

chəboh *see:* chiboh, choh.boh

chəkɯʔ *in:*
• chəkɯʔ mat : have something in one's eye
- dɤŋ, ʔoh chəkɯʔ mat : please look at my eye, I have something in it

chəmɔɲ : star *(+Ferlus)*

chərɛɛ *see* chɯrɛɛ

chə.ʔɛh *see* chi.ʔɛh

chə.ʔuʌk : bamboo species (rather slim but tall)
• hwɤk chəʔuʌk : bamboo rat

chɤm *(also* chɯm; *posttonic, clause final Particle)* : just; continue to -
- bon gɔɔj di biʔ chɤm : you just go on eating till you're full!
- glaʔ ba.khit di pruk chɤm : tell Ba Khit to come!
- gɔɔj bon chɤm : go on eating; you just go on with your meal!
- gɔɔj wʌl gɔɔj dɤŋ chɤm : on your way home take it easy and look where you are go-

ing!
- ɟak di thɛh chɤm : be careful on your journey!
- mɛh bɔŋ chɤm : please go on eating! (said by a person leaving the meal)
- wʌl di dɤŋ chɤm : take care on your way home!
- ʔa dɤŋ chɯm : take care!
- ʔa gɯɯn wʌl chɤm : hopefully (you) will be back!
- ʔoh ʔa ɟak chɤm : I'll leave you for now
- ʔoh ʔa wʌl chɤm, ɟrɯw ʔa leh : I'll go home and come again tomorrow
• hɛɛ chɤm : first; just
- ʔoh ɟak ɟrʌʌk hɛɛ chɤm : I'll just drink some water

chɛɛ I : soak *(V)*
- toc juuk chɛɛ : soak the rice (the day before steaming it)

chɛɛ II : the side of the chest
• ɟi.ʔɛɛŋ chɛɛ : ribs

chɛɛ III *in:*
• wɔk paŋ chɛɛ : the dragon spirit ("wɔk paŋ")
- wɔk paŋ chɛɛ ɟɤɤm ruʌŋ : the "wɔk paŋ" lives in the stream (the water)

chɛɛm I : raise; feed up
- chɛɛm ʔjoc : raise chicken
- chɛɛm chiiŋ : raise pigs

chɛɛm II : again; some more *(Preverbal)*
- chɛɛm bɔŋ mɔ thɯɯ : eat once more
- chɛm ɟak toc juuk hɛh : do you want more food first?
- ɟrɯw paaj chɛm wʌl ʔɛɛw : will come back home to the children in a couple of days
- rə.ʔʌh ʔoh chɛm bɔŋ : I eat again in a little while
- tawɯn nɛh glaʔ ʔa nɔŋ ɟrɯw chɛɛm glaʔ : talking is over for today, we'll talk again tomorrow
- ʔoh chɛm ɟak toc : I'll take some more

chɛɛŋ : black; dark blue; greyish black; dirty colour *(Ferlus: 'black')*
- chɛɛŋ ɟak chapat : it's smudged so we must wash it
• ɟuuk chɛɛŋ : dark or dark blue colour

chɛw : wait; wait for
• chɛw mlaaʔ : wait for somebody
• chɛw rə.ʔʌh a toc : I'll fetch it for you in a moment!
• chɛw hɛh : wait for something or somebody before acting
- chɛw dɤŋ hɛh : let's wait and see!
- chɛw hɛh ʔɛl biʌc : we must wait because the food is not yet ready ("soft")
- chɛw rɯm hluak bɔŋ hɛh : you (the children) must let the adults eat first!
- ʔoh kibi ʔɛl bɔŋ juuk, ʔoh chɛw hɛh : I haven't eaten, I am waiting

chɛʔ I : (1) *(Full Verb)* abound; be numerous; there is much of it
- bɔŋ di chɛʔ : eat much!

- gr.laʔ chɛʔ : there are many words (in the language)
- jɤɤm chɛʔ : be many people together
- ruʌŋ chɛʔ, ɟak met bɤɤn : there is much water, we cannot advance here
• ɟak chɛʔ : be(come) plentiful; abound
• ki chɛʔ : just a little
- juuk ki chɛʔ : just a little rice
• kibi chɛʔ : only a few; only a little
- mlaʔ kibi chɛʔ : a few people
• met chɛʔ : only a few; only a little
- mlaʔ met chɛʔ : a few people
• ʔa chɛʔ : there are many of them
— : (2) (*Prenominal Modifier*) many
- boŋ chɛʔ thɯɯ : eat several times
- dəmɔj chɛʔ ɟɯɯ : a single person who changes his/her name several times
• chɛʔ hnʌm : "many years"; for a very long time; very long ago
• chɛʔ mlaaʔ : all of us; everybody; many people
• chɛʔ tawɪn : several days; for a while; a while ago
- ʔa bɯl chɛʔ tawɪn : died a while ago
— : (2) (*Postverbal Modifier*) very much
- dəkat chɛʔ : be very cold
- gɯt chɛʔ : be worried
- glaʔ chɛʔ : speak a lot

• met chɛʔ : not much; (only) a little

chɛʔ **II** : ferocious

chi **I** : want to
• chi bɤɤn : want to have; would like to receive; desire
- chak chi bɤɤn hmaaj, bakɯɯŋ : he did not like his wife and left her
• chi boŋ : desire to eat something
- chi boŋ thʌc : I desire to eat some meat
- kibi ʔɛl chi boŋ : I'm not hungry yet
- ʔa chi boŋ juuk : need something to eat
• chi booʔ : (the baby) is thirsty
• chi gɯm : want to chew something
- jʌw chi glɤʔ chi gɯm hmiʌŋ : as I have a headache I wish to chew miang
• chi gɯr : want to
- chi gɯr ʔem : want to go to sleep
• chi ɟrʌʌk : be thirsty
• chi piaaʔ : want something nice to eat
- chi piaaʔ ʔa noɲ : there is no good food left
- chi piaaʔ thʌc boŋ ʔa noɲ : I would like some meat but there is none left
• chi ʔem : be sleepy
- ʔoh ʔa chi ʔem : I am sleepy

chi **II** : feel pain
• chi glɤʔ : have a headache
- jʌw chi glɤʔ chi gɯm hmiʌŋ : as I have a headache I wish to

chew miang
- chi gomgoʔ : have a stitch in one's side
- chi ɟɤɤŋ : have pain in the leg
- chi kampoŋ : have a headache
- chi kl.dɯl : have a sore behind
- chi klol : feel pain after eating
- chi kukɔʔ : have a sore neck; have pain in the neck
- chi liŋeew : have a stitch in one's side
- ʔoh hmujthɔj ɟur-ɟur, ʔoh chi liŋeew : I ran too heavily, I have a stitch
- chi thapuul : have a stomach-ache
- chi ʔdɯt : feel pain in the back

chi **III** *in:*
- chi jʌk : such a one; something of this kind
- chi jʌk kɔ chi bɤɤn : I also want one like that

chi **IV** *see* chibɛʔ

chi **V** *see* chi.ʔih

chiʌɲ *(or* chjʌɲ*)* : mosquito (+*Ferlus*)
- chiʌɲ krɛc : the mosquito bites
- chiʌɲ krɛc, chapat chiʌɲ : the mosquito bites, and one smashes it

chibɛʔ : (1) close to the ground *(cf.* bɛʔ 'soil; ground'*)*
- brarulh chibɛʔ : sink down to the ground (about flooding water)
- ɟrʌʌk ʔa ɟuur, brarulh chibɛʔ : the water has receded and sinks down to the ground
- brulh chibɛʔ : sink down to the ground (about flooding water)
- gɛɛŋ chibɛʔ : house with a dirt floor

— : (2) low; short *(referring to body-size)*
- ʔoh chibɛʔ, ʔot glaŋ chuuŋ : I am short, my husband is tall; I am shorter than my husband

chiboh *(also pronounced* chəboh, *also cf.* choh-boh*)* : steep mountain
- glɤh chiboh : walk up a mountain
- chiboh tuul : mountain with a pointed peak

chilaɲ *in:*
- ʔɛɛw chilaɲ : baby
- dumduum ʔɛɛw chilaɲ : hold a baby soothingly in one's arms

chim- *see* chm-; ɟm-

chimbɛp *(also* chm.bɛp*)* : lips; mouth (+*Ferlus*)
- cuŋ chimbɛp : air exhaled from a person (if visible in cold weather)
- ʔat ʔaaj chimbɛp : one's breath
- ʔɯŋ-ʔaŋ chimbɛp : sleep with an open mouth

chin : women's skirt (*"male lg."*)

chinaat : gun (+*Ferlus*)
- chinaat ʔoh tɛɛ bah : it is in fact not my own gun

chin.ʔdeh *see* chɪn.ʔdeh

chindɛh *see* chn.dɛh

chiŋ I *see* chɯɯŋ

chiiŋ II : pig (+*Ferlus*)
- plɯɯŋ chiiŋ : pigs' trough
• chiŋ brii? : boar
• chiŋ gɛɛŋ : domesticated pig

chiit : inject
• chiit ?jaa : have an injection

chiw *in:*
• chiw glɤɤ? : carry in a strap across the head

chi.?ɛh *or* chə.?ɛh *in:*
• chɯŋ chi.?ɛh : be correct
- ?a chɯŋ chi.?ɛh : that's right; that's correct

chi.?ih : be talkative
• gʌm chi.?ih : be silent!

chi(-)?jʌj : bowels (*apparently obsolete word*)

chɪn.?deh (*variable vowel; also heard as* chn.?deh) : how; what (is it)?
- ɟak chɪn.?deh : how shall I go?; what way shall I take?
- mɛh peŋ chɪn.?deh : what are you doing with the gun?; is that a way to aim!
- ?ɤh chɪn.?deh : how shall I do it?
- ?oh choop dɯŋ mɛh chɪn.?deh : I ask you how to do this
- mɛt mʌʌlh chɪn.?deh : what is your name?

chɯɯ I : buy (*V*)

chɯɯ II : straight (not bent)

chɯ.chɯɯ : just; simply; only
- cho? bɯl chɯ.chɯɯ : they (people in old days) became ill and just died
- met ɲaŋ ɟi.?dɤɤ ba.thuul, boŋ dɔ juuk chɯ.chɯɯ : we have nothing but rice to eat
- ?oh chak boŋ juuk tipiaa?, boŋ juuk chɯ.chɯɯ : I ate only plain rice (*i.e.* with no meat)
- ?oh chak ?em ?oh ɟak jɤɤm chɯ.chɯɯ ?a dɔ thɛh : I'm not going to sleep, I can just relax

chɯh : go away! (said to scare off an animal)

chɯɯk : (1) string; rope; strap (e.g. of a bag)
• chɯɯk glɤɤ? : a strap around the forehead
• chɯɯk kɤɤp : shoe-laces
• chɯɯk khɛɛp : the rubber string on a sandal
• chɯɯk laa? : a strap around the shoulder
• chɯɯk paneŋ dɔɔk grɯɤɤ : clothesline
• chɯɯk thɯh.prah : rope of bast; fibres of bast

— : (2) an object resembling a string or rope
• chɯɯk thit ɲu? : the antenna of a wireless set
• chɯɯk ?uulh : electrical wire

— : (3) string-like body-part
• chɯɯk chɔɔt : oesophagus (uppermost part)
• chɯɯk kindiiŋ : the umbilical cord; the navel string
• chɯɯk kr.lɤɤt : oesophagus (uppermost part)
• chɯɯk puj : oesophagus (low-

est part); gullet

chɯkɯh : shovel up; dig for roots
- chɯkɯh ʔeeʔ : dig for taro

chɯkkɔʔ : wet (V)
- gʌm ɟak lɔŋ luɤt, chɯkkɔʔ : don't go out or you will become wet!
- nɔɔm chɯkkɔʔ bɛʔ : the ground is wet of urine

chɯm see chɤm

chɯn.ʔdeh see chɪn.ʔdeh

chɯŋ- also see chŋ-

chɯŋ in statements about identity or correctness:
• chɯŋ chi.ʔɛh : be correct
- ʔa chɯŋ chi.ʔɛh : that's correct; that's right
• chɯŋ jʌk : in this way
• dooj chɯŋ ɲʌʔ : thus; so
• lə jʌk ... chɯŋ ɲʌʔ : it is like this it should be done
- ɟak lə jʌk mɛh chɯŋ ɲʌʔ : go this way!

chɯŋ-gaɲ (also chiŋgaɲ) : embers; glowing firewood
- chɯŋgaɲ ʔa blɯt : be extinguished (fireplace)
- chɯŋgaɲ ʔuulh : embers; glowing firewood

chɯr- also see chr-

chɯrɛɛ (or chərɛɛ) : shirt (+Ferlus)
• chɯrɛɛ bɯk : shirt
• dɛj chɯrɛɛ : breast pocket
- cok toc ni dɛj chɯrɛɛ : take something from the breast pocket

chɯrh.kalh : quill, e.g. of porcupine ("male lg.")

chɯrkaan : creeper species (wild, with a spicy pith used in cooking)

chɯrmɯɯl : soul
• mlaʔ di chɯrmɯɯl : a person's soul (which leaves the body at death)

chɯr.ʔbat (or chr.ʔbat) : trousers
• chɯr.ʔbat hnep : trousers Northern Thai or Hmong style (fastened by folding and tightening)
• chɯr.ʔbat kl.reel : shorts; short trousers
• ʔat ɟɤɤŋ chɯr.ʔbat : the legs of a pair of trousers

chɯt in:
- toc lam chɯt chɯt : lean on a stick while walking
- toc lam chɯt ɟak : walk with a stick

chjʌɲ see chiʌɲ

chm.bɛp see chimbɛp

chm- also see ɟm-

chn.deh see chɪndeh

chn.dɛh : pottery; cup
- ʔɛɛw chn.dɛh : small cup

chn.rɛɛt : comb (N)
- toc chn.rɛɛt chrɛɛt prwɯcprwʌc glɤɤʔ : comb and set the hair orderly

chŋ- also see chiŋ-

chŋ.ker : lying on one's side
- ʔem chŋ.ker : sleep on one's side

- bɯl chŋker : die lying on one's side

chŋ.kɛr : nail (on finger or toe) (*Ferlus has -tɛl/-tɛr*)
- chŋ.kɛr ɟɤɤŋ : toe nail
- chŋ.kɛr tiiʔ : finger nail

chŋ.tɯŋ : winnowed wall made of split bamboo (*Ferlus: ʂŋtəŋ in the meaning of 'wall'*)

chɔɔ *in*:
- mɛɛ chɔɔ : woman who has recently given birth to a baby
- ʔii chɔɔ : newborn baby

chooc : plant species, the fine sticks of which are used for making brooms
- bakkah chooc : flower of "chooc"
- thɯp ɲuul bakkah chooc : (standard type of) broom made of "chooc" fibres

choh.boh : mountain; big hill
- glɤh choh.boh : walk uphill

choolh : oblique or vertical rafters

chooŋ I : trousers
- chooŋ mujmuj : trousers of shaggy fabric

chooŋ II *in*:
- gɔɔŋ chooŋ : flashlight

choop : ask; ask about
- ʔoh choop mɛh, mɛh tɔɔp : I ask you, and you answer
- ʔoh choop mɛt mʌʌlh chin.ʔdeh : what is your name?
- choop dɯŋ - : ask (somebody)
- ʔoh choop dɯŋ mɛh chin.ʔdeh : I ask you how to do this
- choop ni - : ask (somebody)
- choop ni ba chak : ask Ba Chak

chot : sip; eat liquid food with a leaf cup or a spoon
- chot gɔj : eat soup

chooʔ : (blade of) digging stick or spade (*+Ferlus*)
- cho ʔeeʔ : (1) digging stick for digging taro
- gɯr chooʔ : (handle of) digging stick; (handle of) spade

choʔ : (1) be ill; fall ill
- choʔ bɯl chɯ.chɯɯ : they (people in old days) became ill and just died

— : (2) have a sore -; feel pain in - (*+Ferlus*)
- choʔ glɤʔ choʔ klol : have pain in head and chest
- choʔ ɟɤɤŋ : have pain in the leg
- choʔ kampoŋ : have a headache
- choʔ kr.lɤɤt : have a sore throat
- choʔ kukɔʔ : have a sore neck
- choʔ thapuul : have a stomachache
- choʔ ʔdɯt : feel pain in the kidney region
- choʔ ʔjen : have a stitch in one's side

— : (3) be aching; it hurts
- thapuul choʔ : my stomach hurts
- ʔoh chapat reew ʔi choʔ : I hit myself badly and it hurts!
- choʔ ʔa noɲ : it hurts all over
- gʌm ki choʔ ki greet : in order not to feel pain (ritual formula)

cho.ʔuum : smell good *(V)* *(considered to be Lua' by one informant)*

chɔj : necklace

chɔkchɔɔr : stripes going lengthwise (e.g. on garment)
- chɯree chɔkchɔɔr : striped shirt

chɔɔŋ : two
• chɔɔŋ pr.daw : a married couple

chɔɔt *in:*
• chɯɯk chɔɔt : oesophagus (uppermost part)

chɔɔʔ : dog
- chɔɔʔ bla(a)j kwaan : a big dog

chraɲ : scrape food off (e.g. meat off a bone our out of a shell) with one's teeth
- chraɲ bon : eat scraping the food off with one's teeth

chreelh *see* pleeʔ

chrɤl : palm tree species

chrɛɲ *see* chraɲ

chrɛɛt : comb *(V)*
• chrɛɛt glɤɤʔ : comb one's hair
• toc chn.rɛɛt chrɛɛt prwɯcprwʌc glɤɤʔ : comb and set the hair orderly

chrɛʔ *in:*
• ʔɤh chrɛʔ : make mischief (said of fussy children)
- rɛɛm chet ʔɤh chrɛʔ : that child is a pest!

chriilh : scrape dirt away from the ground
- chriilh bɔh ʔuulh : scrape ashes away

chr.kʌl : muddy (of water) *("female lg.")*
- ruʌŋ chr.kʌl : muddy flooding water

chr.leeŋ : alang-alang leaves (used as thatching on village houses)

chrɔɔɲ : be dry
- kr.lɤt chrɔɔɲ : my throat feels dry (e.g. after drinking liquor)
- wʌl jɤɤm chrɔɔɲ : come and stay where it is dry (i.e. take shelter)!
• ʔa chrɔɔɲ : is dry
• ʔi di chrɔɔɲ : to dry it; to let it dry
- bit ʔi di chrɔɔɲ : wring something (the washing) out in order for it to dry
- pjaŋ kraŋ ʔi di chrɔɔɲ : unfold and expose (the laundry) to air in order for it to dry

chruʌt : lower part of the chest; solar plexus
• wʌl jɤɤm kap chak kap chruʌt : come and stay inside me! (invoking a spirit)

chuʌk I : salt *(N) (+Ferlus)*
• bɔɔ chuʌk : Bo Kluea ("Salt Well", a locality)
• pleʔ chuʌk : the glands under the lower jaw

chuʌk II : tie *(V)*
• chuʌk blɛɛŋ : tie a string around wrist
- chuʌk blɛɛŋ chuʌk loon : tie a string around the wrist for

protection
- toc paaj chuʌk blɛɛŋ : take a string and tie it around the wrist
• guɯp chuʌk : arrest and tie the hands (of somebody)
• chuʌk hnɛl : tie a string around one's ankle (ritual formula)

chuʌn : dry field
• chuʌn juuk : dry field for growing rice (+Ferlus)
• pak chuʌn : cut down weeds and shrub in the orchard ("female lg.")
• pɤjh chuʌn : cut down weeds and shrub in the orchard ("male lg.")
• ruɯh chuʌn dɛl chuʌn : remove weeds in an orchard
• ʔɤh chuʌn : work in the dry field
• ʔɤh chuʌn boŋ juuk : live as a villager

chugwʌʌʔ : down there (near by)
- ɟak ʔem chugwʌʌʔ : will stay overnight down there
- ʔat bɛɛr ɟak chugwʌʌʔ : they (both) went down there

chuh : low down; down below
- ɟɤɤm chuh : be down below

chumdɔɔj in:
• chumdɔɔj ɟrʌʌk : aqueduct; open pipe for conducting water

chuuŋ : (1) high; tall
- lam chuuŋ : a very high tree
- ʔoh chibɛʔ, ʔot glaŋ chuuŋ : I am short, my husband is tall; my husband is taller than I
— : (2) high up
- ʔac pɤr ɟak chuuŋ : the bird flies high up
• ʔa chuuŋ : be high up

chur(-)bok : hoof
- churbok ɟɤɤŋ : hoof of foreleg
- churbok tiiʔ : hoof of hind leg

chuuʔ : ginger

chwal : heavy (*apparently a stigmatized word*)

d-

dadrooj : younger sibling; you
- dadrooj ɟak ginɛŋ : where are you going? (said to one's sibling)
• dadrooj bɛɛr : (speaker's) two younger siblings; married younger sibling and/or his/her spouse; a couple of younger relatives

dalɛʔ : bamboo (a species)

daŋ : anvil

dap : hit against something; collide with something
- dap ɟuur : fall into something
- kluɯɯr wʌl dap bɛʔ : the sky came (down) and hit the earth (a mythological event)

darɔʔ : thin split bamboo strips
- kaɲit, toc darɔʔ batoʔ di tawɪn : it is dark, take a split bamboo stick and make a fire to light up!
• darɔʔ batoʔ : spill of split bam-

boo; burning split bamboo stick
- putpuʌt darɔɔʔ : spill made of split bamboo (used to singe a pig)

dʌl : the front end of something (perhaps particularly of something cylindrical)

dʌlh **I** *in:*
- dʌlh ʔdɤɤ : how many?
- gʌh prɛʔ dʌlh ʔdɤɤ : how many (grains of) spices are there here?
- dʌlh ʔdɤɤ ʔat mlaaʔ : how many people?
- dʌlh ʔdɤɤ ʔat mlaaʔ wʌl ʔɤh gɛɛŋ ɲʌʔ : how many people participated in building this house?
- dʌlh ʔdɤɤ ʔat tawɩn : for how many days?; in how many days?
- choʔ thapuul dʌlh ʔdɤɤ ʔat tawɩn : how long has he/she had a stomach-ache?
- dʌlh ʔdɤɤ ʔat tawɩn mɛh wʌl jɤɤm nɛh : when will you be back?

dʌlh **II** : (of nuts and fruits) have grown big

dʌm **I** *(Preverbal)* : onwards (in time)
- dʌm jɤɤm : stay on
- gɛɛŋ prɩm ʔa bukbuk, kan dʌm jɤɤm ʔɤh hmɛʔ : our house is old and delapidated, if we are to stay on we must build a new one
- ʔoh chak rɛɛʔ ʔoh dʌm jɤɤm : I'am not disappearing, I stay on

dʌm *(or* dɔm*)* **II** : brain

delh : deer, very small species (description fits chevrotain, mouse deer)

də *(cf.* di*)* : (1) *Benefactive Marker*
- maʔ də - : give (to) -
- maʔ də mlaʔ briiʔ : give to the Mlabri
- maʔ də tɔɔ mlaaʔ : give to the people (*i.e.* to the Mlabri)
— : (2) *(in certain expressions, cf.* di*) about; concerning; like*
- də jʌk : thus; in this manner
- ʔɤh də jʌk : do like this
- glaʔ də - : speak about -; use the term -
— : (3) *(in certain expressions:)* in; on
- jɤɤm də bɛɛr gɛɛŋ : stay in two (different) houses
- ɟak dɤŋ də ŋɔr thɛh : see to it that you stay on a trail!

dəkah : very far away; distantly

dəkat : be cold (of body)

dəkʌlh *see* dɯkʌlh

dəlaaw : bamboo species ("male lg.")

dəm.hnat : cold weather (?), *in:*
- ɲaam dəm.hnat : the cold season

dəmɔ(ɔ) *(Numeral functioning as*

Determiner) : one
- boŋ dəmɔ ʔboj : drink one glass
- dəmɔ ʔuuj (də)mɔ jooŋ : have the same parents (i.e. be true siblings)
• dəmɔ ŋɔɔr : it means the same thing; it is in the same fashion
• dəmɔ tawɪn : one day; for one day
- bɯl dəmɔ tawɪn : died yesterday
• dəmɔ thɯɯ : once

dəmɔj : alone; a single one
- mlaʔ kɔ dəmɔj bɛɛr pɛʔ pon : we were just a few people
- ʔoh dəmɔj : I, alone; I, myself

dəmpʌl : soldier

dʏl *in:*
• ʔʏh kr.nap dʏl jʏʏl : sing in the traditional Mlabri way

dʏlh.dʏʏlh : lean back while stretching oneself

dʏŋ *(also* dɯɯŋ*)* : (1) see; look; watch
- dʏŋ mʏm ɟrʌʌk : he watches father drinking
- dʏŋ, ʔoh chəkɯʔ mat : please look at my eye, I have something in it
• chew dʏŋ hɛh : let's wait and see!
• dʏŋ met plɛɛn : cannot see anything

— : (2) look out; be careful
- dʏŋ də ŋɔr thɛh : take care to follow a passable trail
- dʏŋ ɟak ŋɔr di thɛh : be careful to stay on the trail so as to be safe
- dʏŋ ʔi hot : look out, you are about to fall!
• gɔj dʏŋ : look out!; take care!

— : (3) look after (somebody)
- dʏŋ mɛt rooj laŋ : look after your little brother!
- kibi dʏŋ ʔot ʔɛɛw ʔot ŋwɛʔ : can't you look after my child (please)?
- ʔoh chak dʏŋ : I cannot look after him/her!
- ʔoh dʏŋ mɛt ʔɛɛw : I'll look after your child

— : (4) see each other; meet
• ɟak cʌlh dʏŋ hmaaj : pay visits to a prospective wife
• wʌl dʏŋ : we'll see each other again!

dʏŋdʏŋ : stare (V)
• dʏŋdʏŋ wiŋcɛɛr : stare through narrow eye slits

dʏwdʏw : look upwards

dɛɛ *see* tɛɛ, ʔdɛɛ

dɛj **I** : bag (made of fabric)
- ʔɛɛw dɛj : small bag
• dɛj chɯrɛɛ : breast pocket
• dɛj chooŋ : trouser pocket

dɛl : cut; cut down; fell
• dɛl lam : cut down a tree
• rɯh chuʌn dɛl chuʌn : remove weeds in an orchard

dɛɛn : (1) way = direction
- gʌm mʏn ɟak dɛɛn ʔdʏʏ : don't go anywhere yet!
• dɛɛn ʔdʏʏ ʔa dɔ thɛh : any place will do
- ʔʏh ɟak dɛɛn ʔdʏʏ ʔa dɔ thɛh :

you can do it wherever you want
— : (2) way = fashion
• dɛɛn ʔdɤɤ ʔa dɔ bɤɤn : it is OK in either fashion
- glaʔ dɛɛn ʔdɤɤ ʔa dɔ bɤɤn : you can say it either way

di *(cf. də)* : (1) *inter-phrasal Possessive Connective*
- mɤʔ di diŋ : mother's older sibling
- mlaʔ di chɔɔʔ : the man's dog
— : (2) *anaphoric (always reflexive?) Possessive Determiner*
- pajɤʔ di hmaaj : call one's wife
- ʔoh glaʔ di ʔɛɛw : I speak to my children
- ʔoh lom di mɤʔ : I love my mother
— : (3) in order to; in order that; so that
- ba.cheer di gʌm beec : soothe it (a child) so it does not cry
- boŋ di biiʔ : eat until one is full
- chaj di ŋaam : insert it (an ear ornament) so it looks beautiful
- dɤŋ ɟak ŋɔr di thɛh : be careful to stay on the trail so as to be safe
- dɤŋ di thɛh : be careful!; look out!
- dɔɔk juuk di ʔjen : put the (boiled) rice somewhere in order for it to cool
- glaʔ ba.khit di pruk chɤm : tell Ba Khit to come!
- ʔa pruk di jɤɤm nɛh : has come in order to stay here
- gɯt hɔɔt ʔat ʔɛɛw di wʌl toc : wants for the child to come back
• ʔi di : in order to -; in order for something to -
- bit ʔi di chrɔɔɲ : wring something (the washing) out in order for it to dry
— : (4) *(particularly in imperative constructions)* as; like; in a - way; for it to be - *(cf. də; ɟa)*
- boŋ di chɛʔ : just eat much!
• di jʌk : like this
- jɤɤm di jʌk : sit like this
• di reew : forcefully
- glaʔ di reew : speak loudly
- hmujthɔj di reew : run as fast as one's legs can carry one
• di thɛh : comfortably; carefully; well
• ɟak di thɛh chɤm : be careful on your journey!
• ʔem di thɛh : sleep well!
— : (5) *optional Preverbal Imperative Marker*
- bah di pruk : come, both of you!
- di glaʔ di glaʔ : say something!
- di ɟak : go!
- ɟjʌl di wʌl : come back tonight!
- leh di leh nɛŋ hmuu : come, all of you!
• di gʌm : do avoid that -!
- di gʌm lɔj bohboh : don't let it boil!
• ʔa di *(Reciprocal Imperative Marker)* : let's
- ʔa di boŋ, ʔa biʌʌc : let's eat, the food is ready!
- ʔa di ɟak boŋ, ʔa chaw ʔeeʔ :

let's start eating, I'm hungry!
— : (6) *in:*
* kan di : when (in future); if (in future)
- kan di bla(a)j kwaan : when one is grown up

dik *(in expressions for infants; Ferlus has:* tik *in the meaning of* 'small'*):*
* dik theeŋ : child; small child (possibly about children up to the age of puberty)
- dik theeŋ ɟak gwaa kwɤn : the child is playing at somebody else's place

dil-dɛl : cicada species

dim-rɛɛŋ *see* dɯŋ.mrɛɛŋ

diŋ : elder sibling; elder in-law (of same generation) or friend
- mɤm di diŋ : elder paternal uncle or aunt
- mɤʔ di diŋ : elder maternal uncle or aunt
- ʔot diŋ tɛɛ taaŋ mlaaʔ : my "big brother" was not my real brother
* diŋ bɛɛr : married elder sibling and his/her spouse
* diŋ km.ɲah : elder sister
* diŋ mɯlh : elder sister
* diŋ rooj : siblings; relatives or friends of same generation

diiŋ : (1) bamboo section; bamboo cylinder with a bottom (e.g. the cylinder of the air pump used with a forge) (+*Ferlus*)
* diiŋ dəlaaw : bamboo section ("*male lg.*")
* diiŋ juuk : bamboo section in which rice is boiled
* diiŋ ɟrʌʌk : bamboo section with drinking water
— : (2) a round box, e.g. a biscuit tin

diŋ.rʌŋ *in:*
* diŋ.rʌŋ gɛɛŋ : house pole

dɯgʌʔ (*or* tɯgʌʔ) : over there (on the other side)
- ɟak toc bɛɛ dɯgʌʔ : I'll fetch a goat over there

dɯk : stretch oneself (in standing position), raise oneself on tiptoe; rise (vertically)
* dɯk glɤh : stretch upwards
* dɯk ɟuur : rise and then collapse (this once happened to the earth according to mythology)

dɯkʌlh : sneeze

dɯlkul *in:*
* lam dɯlkul : log used for chopping off firewood

dɯmpʌl : tree species (with poisonous blades causing skin irritation)

dɯɯn : pull at something
* dɯɯn glɤh : pull something out
* toc dɯɯn : pull

dɯŋ **I** (*Preposition*) *in:*
* choop dɯŋ - : ask (somebody)
- ʔoh choop dɯŋ mɛh chɪn.ʔdeh : I ask you how to do this

dɯŋ **II** *see* dɤŋ

dɯŋ.mrɛɛŋ (*also* dimrɛɛŋ) : split bamboo sheet (flat piece used as floor) (*Ferlus:* ɟmrɛŋ gɛŋ)
- dɯŋ.mrɛɛŋ dɯr : (Hmong) plank bed made of split bamboo
- dɯŋ.mrɛŋ gɛɛŋ : mat of split bamboo (on plank bed in Hmong house)

dɯr : (1) bamboo species (used as material for mats)

— : (2) Northern Thai pipe (bamboo tube containing water)

dɯw : tuber (an edible species)

dm- *see* dəm-

dŋ- *see* dɯŋ-

dooj *in:*
• dooj chɯŋ ɲʌʔ : thus; so

dok : poor; miserable
• boŋ dok boŋ jen : eat poor food
• jɤɤm dok jɤɤm jen : live a miserable life
• mlaʔ dok mlaʔ jen : very poor people

dooŋ *in:*
• lɛŋ dooŋ : evening glow (*"female lg."*)
- thwɛɲ dooŋ : evening glow (*"male lg."*)

dop : the folded edge of the ear lobe

dor : throw away (*less used, "awkward" word*)

dɔ I (*or* dɔw) : (1) by the effect of; as a consequence of
- dɔ mɛʔ hot : because of the rain; when it rains

— : (2) (*immediately before nouns:*) some; whatever
- bɤɤn kɔ bɤɤn dɔ chiiŋ : we have a pig now!
- dɔ mlaʔ ɲaam gʌh : people nowadays

— : (3) (*in constructions with ʔa dɔ + a verb:*) indeed; certainly
• ʔa dɔ bɤɤn : that can be used; it is all right to do that
• ʔa dɔ ɲaŋ - : there is/are - everywhere
- jɤɤm lɔŋ briiʔ ʔa dɔ ɲaŋ ʔaŋ praŋ : in the forest you see the "ʔaŋ praŋ"-bamboo everywhere
• ʔa dɔ thɛh : whatever; whatever will do; that's all right; never mind!; it's fine with me
- ɟi.ʔdɤɤ ʔa dɔ thɛh : anything will do
- ki hnʌm ʔa dɔ thɛh : any number of years
- ʔem jʌk ʔa dɔ thɛh ʔem jʌk ʔa dɔ thɛh : I can sleep in this position or in that position
- ʔoh chak ʔem ʔoh ɟak jɤɤm chɯɯ.chɯɯ ʔa dɔ thɛh : I'm not going to sleep, I can just relax

dɔɔ II : together
- ɟak dɔɔ tih : let's go this way together!
• dɔ ʔdɔlh : together (*e.g.:* talk together) (*Postverbal*)

dɔɔ III (*Postsentential Particle*) :

certainly; right?

dɔɔk : put away; place; store (*V, also Postverbal*)
- dɔɔk juuk di ʔjen : put the (boiled) rice somewhere in order for it to cool
- dɔɔk maʔ ʔɛɛw : I keep it for my children
- paruʔ dɔɔk thʌc : hang meat up to be smoked
- toc dɔɔk ladooŋ : put it up on the shelf

dɔm *see* dʌm

dɔw *see:* dɔ

dr.chɤʔ *in:*
• gɯɯn dr.chɤʔ : mean the same thing; be identical

drɤh : crow *(V)*
- ʔjoc ʔa drɤh : the rooster crowed

dr.mɔʔ : wild animal species

dr.naʔ *see* tak

dr.nɤɤm *see* tak

droojh (*also heard as* druujh) : press something through a hole; pierce

druuʔ : big banana leaf
- təptop druuʔ : wrap (something) into a banana leaf
- toc ʔjaa lʌʌp druuʔ lɔɔm trleet : put tobacco into a leaf and fold and roll it
• druuʔ ʔjaa : leaf for rolling tobacco into a cigarette
• druʔ ʔjɯɯk : banana leaves used for thatching a traditional lean-to

dr.wiil : sieve *(N)* (used for rinsing rice grains by shaking the sieve up and down)

dumduum : hold soothingly in one's arms
- dumduum ʔɛɛw chilaɲ : hold a baby soothingtly in one's arms

dur.dɔr : slanting (pole or tree) (*"male lg."*)

g-

ga.chah : battery (for portable equipment, flashlight, etc.)
- ga.chah ʔa noɲ : the battery is low

ga.chooŋ *see* gəchooŋ

gajh : nine

gal : ten

gaŋ *see* kan

ganat : cultivated pineapple

ganɛŋ : where (*"female lg."*)

gaɲ : glow; light in the sky (*cf.* chiŋgaɲ)
• gaɲ lɛŋ : early evening (*"female lg."*)
- ʔa gaɲ lɛŋ ʔa ɟjʌl : it is already evening
• gaɲ thwɛɲ : early evening (*"male lg."*)
- ʔa gaɲ thwɛɲ : (it is) early evening (*mostly "male lg."?*)

ga.theer : blow one's nose (using the fingers) *(V)*
- ga.ther mɯɯr : blow one's nose if one is snotty *(V)*

gatooŋ *see* katooŋ

gʌh *(idiolectally also* gɔh*)* : (1) this is -
- gʌh gr.wɛɛn thɛh : this is the right hand
- gʌh la chɯrɛɛ : this is a shirt
- tipiaaʔ gʌh : what's that?
— : (2) this place; this side; here
- ɟak gʌh ɟak ɲʌʔ : ("go here go there":) to stray
- lɔŋ gʌh : over here; this way
— : (3) *(Postnominal Determiner)* this
• hnʌm gʌh : this year
gʌm *(Preverbal Auxiliary)* : (1) don't!
- gʌm blʌk : don't enter (that house)!
- gʌm chiʔih : be silent!
- gʌm hr.liiŋ : don't forget it!
- gʌm kɛl : don't stand in the way!; move away, you're in the way!
- gʌm teen : don't step there!
- mɛh gʌm wʌl kwɤn ʔot gruɤɤ : don't you start playing with my things! (said to child)
— : (2) so that not -; not to -
- ɟuʌj ʔoh gʌm choʔ ki greet : help me not to be in pain!
- tom gʌm bohboh : heat it up without letting it boil!
• di gʌm : in order (for somebody/something) not to -
- ba.cheer di gʌm beec : soothe it (a child) so it does not cry
- di gʌm lɔj bohboh : don't let it boil!
• gʌm ki : please let it not -!
- gʌm ki choʔ ki greet : let me not be in pain (ritual formula)
gʌw : (1) *in:*
• bla(a)j gʌw : big
— : (2) being an ancestor
- mlaʔ gʌw : somebody living in the past
- ʔuuj gʌw : female ancestor
-gʌʔ *see* -gɔʔ
gehgeh : scratch oneself with the nails *("female lg.")*
- gehgeh ʔot ŋaʔ : I scratch myself because it itches
geet : cut; chop
• geet ʔuulh : cut firewood
gə.chooŋ : turtle
gəmpʌk *in:*
• gəmpʌk lon : thin string around wrist for protection
gəmpɤɤlh : slip; be thrown aside (e.g. a piece of wood which is stepped upon)
gəmtɤɤm : chew
gəncaj *see* gɯncaj
gɤɤj *in:*
• met gɤɤj : not so far; never before
gɛjh **I** : freshwater crab
gɛjh **II** *see* tɔ.pruʔ
gɛɛŋ : (1) lean-to (shelter); house *(+Ferlus)*
• gɛɛŋ chibɛʔ : house with a dirt floor
• gɛɛŋ ɟuuŋ : a deserted house
• gɛɛŋ rooŋ : house with an elevated floor or plank bed
• gɛɛŋ ruu bɯɯw : a spacious house

- grɔɔk gɛɛŋ : household
- kwac gɛɛŋ : sweep the floor
- peelh gɛɛŋ : sweep the floor
- peelh gɛɛŋ ɲʌn rɤʔ : sweep the floor because it is dusty
- ʔem gɛɛŋ : sleep at home
— : (2) locality; place of residence
- gɛŋ nɔɔm : bladder

gi.chɛŋ : plant species with edible pith

gilmɛʔ : sugar cane

gimheep : suck in air (between narrowed lips)

ginɛŋ : where *("male lg.", but also recorded from a female)*
- ɟak ginɛŋ : where are you going?
- meh jɤɤm ginɛŋ : where do you live?
- mɤm ɟak boŋ juuk ginɛŋ : where are you ("Father") going to eat?
- ʔat bɛɛr ɟak ginɛŋ : where did they (two) go?

ginrɛɛ *idiolectal variant of* gn.rɛɛ

gip-wɛɛc : touch or scratch softly with a finger (*e.g.* on another person's arm to catch his attention)

gir- *also see* gr-
- gir.wɛj (*expected main form:* gr.wɛj) something round; something spherical

gɪm : spicy (*α-Mlabri has* gem)

gɯh : be ablaze
- gɯh-gɯh-gɯh, pen blaaj gr.nɯh : there are increasingly big flames
- grawɯlh ʔuulh, kibi gɯh : fan at the fire, it does not blaze!

gɯlh.galh : scrape something smooth

gɯm- *also see* gm-

gɯm : chew (or rather suck on) fermented tea, or the like
- hnɛɛp hmiʌŋ gɯm : make a lump of fermented tea and chew it
- chi gɯm hmiʌŋ : I wish to chew fermented tea
- mɛh met gɤɤj gɯm (*with question intonation*) : have you never chewed that?

gɯm-naat : belt

gɯm-pʌk : perform a ritual ceremony (for somebody's spirit)
- ɟak gɯm-pʌk taʔ jaʔ di loon : perform a ritual ceremony for the grandparents' spirits
- ɟak gɯm-pʌk ʔat ʔɛɛw km.ɲah di loon : perform a ritual ceremony for the (sick) daughter's spirit
- ɟak gɯm-pʌk ʔat ʔɛɛw laŋ di loon : perform a ritual ceremony for the (sick) son's spirit

gɯɯn : (1) return; come again
- gɯɯn leh : return back
- ɟak gɯɯn leh : go out and come back
- gɯɯn pruk : return back
- ʔoh met mʌc ŋɔr ʔa gɯɯn pruk : I don't know the way back
- ʔa gɯɯn : be back

- ʔa gɯɯn wʌl : is back; will be back here
- mɤm ʔa ɟak, mɤm ʔa gɯɯn wʌl chɤm : you're leaving, Father, but hopefully you'll be back
- r.ʌh ʔa gɯɯn wʌl : I'm back in a moment

— : (2) together
• gɯn bɔŋ : eat together; keep company while eating
• gɯɯn dr.chɤʔ : both doing the same thing; corresponding to each other; being identical; it means the same thing
• gɯn ɟak tr.dɯŋ : keep company on the way

gɯn-caj (one male speaker says: kɯncaj, perhaps also: -cɛj) : blanket
- gɯncaj bɯk dəkat : cover oneself with a blanket because one is cold
- gɯncaj prɪm : an old blanket
- gɯncaj trɯp : a blanket to cover oneself with
• gɯncaj bɪʎʎc : "fine, white cloth"
• gɯncaj hmɯrlaŋ : soft cloth (used as a loincloth or a towel)
• gɯncaj hm.pooj : mosquito net
• gɯncaj mujmuj : fur blanket

gɯn(d)rɛɛ see gn.rɛɛ

gɯntak : chomp one's food noisily
- bɔŋ gɯntak : chomp one's food while eating

gɯn-wak : chipped

- tɔʔ gɯnwak : a chipped knife

gɯp : catch; arrest (a person)
- thahaan gɯp mlaʔ kheet : the Mlabri were afraid because the soldiers caught them
• gɯp chuʌk : arrest and tie the hands (of somebody)

gɯpgɯp : grope (in the dark)
- gɯpgɯp toctoc ɟak : grope and clutch at something while walking

gɯr I : dig deeply; dig for (deep roots)

gɯr II : handle (N); haft (e.g. of knife)
- gɯr dalɛʔ : wooden handle (of knife)
- gɯr kwɛk : axe handle
- gɯr lam : wooden handle
• gɯr chooʔ : (handle of) digging stick; (handle of) spade

gɯr III see chi

gɯr- also see gr-

gɯt : think (V)
- gɯt chɛʔ : think all the time; be worried
• gɯt hɔɔt : miss (somebody); have (somebody) in one's thoughts
- ʔat ɟɟooŋ gɯt hɔɔt ʔat ʔɛɛw laŋ : the father misses his son

glaŋ : husband (= laŋ) (+Ferlus)
- toc glaŋ : find a husband; (for a woman) to marry

glaʔ : (1) speak; use a certain kind of language
- glaʔ mɤʔ mɤm : speak one's

parents' language
- glaʔ mɛɛw met bɤɤn : cannot speak Hmong
- glaʔ mlaʔ briiʔ : speak Mlabri
- pleʔ kook glaʔ : the larynx speaks, i.e. you speak with the larynx
- ʔɛɛw met glaʔ : children do not say such things
• glaʔ də - : use the term -
• glaʔ di reew : speak loudly
• glaʔ ɟa reew : speak loudly
• glaʔ kleh : speak loudly
• glaʔ km.riiʔ : speak in a very loud voice
- glaʔ di km.riiʔ : speak up so I can hear you!
• glaʔ kwɤn : say something for fun; say obscene things
• glaʔ met bɤɤn : (deaf-and-)dumb
• glaʔ prijh.prɛjh : speak in a shrill/hoarse voice
• glaʔ thɛh : say the truth
• gɔɔj glaʔ : speak in a soft voice
— : (2) speak to (somebody); talk (together); tell (something to somebody)
- glaʔ ʔɛɛw mɛɛw ʔoh glaʔ : that's what I said to the Hmong child
- ɟruw chɛm glaʔ : tomorrow we speak again
- mɛɛw glaʔ mlaaʔ : the Hmong speaks to the Mlabri
- pa(a) luh pa(a) phit glaʔ mlaʔ di glɤɤʔ : he abuses the Mlabri
- ʔoh ɟak glaʔ ʔot mɤʔ ʔot mɤm : I'll tell my parents
• glaʔ də - : speak about -

• glaʔ dɔʔ dɔlh : talk together
• glaʔ gr.laʔ : converse; talk
• glaʔ maaʔ - : speak to -
- glaʔ maʔ ʔoh : speak to me
• glaʔ tipiaaʔ : (1) what shall we talk about?; (2) what are they talking about?
• glaʔ tɔ tr.dɯŋ : talk together
• glaʔ tr.dɯŋ : talk together
• glaʔ ʔa ɟreen : have finished talking
- glaʔ ʔa ɟreen ʔa tɯk : that's all I have to say; no more talking!
• glaʔ ʔa lɛn : have finished talking
- glaʔ ʔa lɛn ʔa noɲ ʔa tɯk : no more talking!
• glaʔ ʔa noɲ : talking is over; we are not going to talk any more
• glaʔ ʔa tɯk : have finished talking
• ʔa glaʔ noɲ : we have ended our conversation
• ʔat tiiʔ glaʔ : that's what they (the old story-tellers) said
- mʌc ʔat tiiʔ glaʔ : I remember that they (the old story-tellers) said
— : (3) in:
• glaʔ di - : tell (somebody) to -
- glaʔ ba.khit di pruk chɤm : tell Ba Khit to come!

glʌŋ in:
• ɲaam glʌŋ : the rainy season

glɤh : (1) ascend; rise
- glɤh bɛɛ : climb a raft
- glɤh chiboh : walk up a mountain slope (+Ferlus)
- glɤh choh.boh : walk uphill

- glʳh lam : climb a tree (+Ferlus)
— : (2) (Postverbal) up; upwards
- hnep glʳh : roll up the legs of one's trousers
- ɟak glʳh : come up here!
- ɟrʌʌk brʳʳl glʳh : the flooding water is rising
- kwaan glʳh kwaan glʳh : grow up
- pajok glʳh : lift up
- ʔjaɲ glʳh : move into upright position
— : (3) (Postverbal) through to the outside
• dɯɯn glʳh : pull something out
• glɔlh glʳh : stick something through so that it appears on the other side

glʳʔ : or (implying that the alternatives are both possible)
- ɟak tih glʳʔ ɟak tih : did you go this way or that way?; shall we go this way or that way?

glʳʳʔ (sometimes claimed to be "female lg.") : (1) head
• chiw glʳʳʔ : carry in a strap across the head
• chrɛɛt glʳʳʔ : comb one's hair
— : (2) in expressions about abusing ("scolding somebody's head"):
• mɛɛw leew mlaʔ di glʳʳʔ : the Hmong abuses the Mlabri
• mɛɛw pa(a) luh pa(a) phit glaʔ mlaʔ di glʳʳʔ : the Hmong abuses the Mlabri

— : (3) something of onion-shape
• glʳʔ ɟweel : the edible core of a lemon-grass plant
— : (4) detachable cover; the lid of a box (cf. kampoŋ, kralit)

glɛj : shape something with repeated cuts; carve; chop up
- glɛj diiŋ : cut a bamboo section into shape
- glɛj ʔuulh : chop firewood
• glɛj pak : cut and carve something
- glɛj pak krareel : cut and carve a board into shape

glɛw : chew
- glɛw haat : chew betel

gliŋ in:
• nɔr gliŋ : highway; road

glɯn jʳʳm : sit leaning one's back to a wall or a tree

glɯŋglʳʳŋ in:
• glɯŋglʳʳŋ ɟak : walk where there is no path

glɔɔc : whistle (V) (with the lips)

glɔlh : stick something through
• glɔlh glʳh : stick something through so that it appears on the other side
- toc gʌh, glɔlh glʳh : you hold this (pin) and stick it through (said when explaining how to use the buckle of a belt)

glɔɔŋ : piece of wood; log;

trunk (of a fallen tree)
- glɔɔŋ ʔuulh : firewood

gluh : rinse the interior of something
- gluh keet, ŋaʔ : rinse the ear (the auditory duct) because it itches
- toc lam gluh gwicgwɛɛc kɯm : remove it (the earwax) by scratching with a stick

gm.hɤɤjh : gasp for breath
- gm.hɤɤjh ʔi ɟram : be out of breath

gm.nat see pleeʔ

gm.naat common variant pronunciation of gɯmnaat

gm.puur see gumpuur

gm.tɤɤm (cf. gɯm) : chew

gm.tɯl : (big) thorn

gn.caj see gɯncaj

gn.rɛɛ (variable pronunciation: gɯn-, gin-, -drɛɛ) : curry ("Chinese curry")
• gn.rɛɛ lm.bah : cabbage curry
- boŋ juuk gn.rɛɛ lm.bah : eat rice with cabbage curry
• gn.rɛɛ thʌc : meat curry; thick soup with lumps of meat in it
- boŋ juuk gn.rɛɛ thʌc : eat rice with meat curry
• gn.rɛɛ ʔdɔɔʔ : a curry containing banana sprouts

goh I : break; smash; break and fall down (said of falling trees)

goh II : tree species with fragrant edible leaves (but no fruits)
• lam goh : id.

gooj in:
• kalɯp gooj toc : fetch (a ball)

gook jeek : edible creeper species (vine)

gomgoʔ : loins; the small of the back
- chi gomgoʔ : have pains across the loins

gompuur (or gumpuur) : chalk; the white substance in mixed betel

gom-ʔwak : make a rasping sound to clear one's pharynx
• gom.ʔwak ʔjɔh : collect saliva in the mouth and spit

gɔh idiolectal variant of gʌh

gɔj I : something liquid; soup
- chot ʔat gɔj, boŋ ʔat thʌc : sip the soup and eat the meat
• gɔj mat : tears
- gɔj mat talʌr : tears are running down the cheeks
• gɔj thɯwɛŋ : a burning hot liquid (in Mlabri cosmogony)

gɔɔj II (Preverbal) : at ease; at one's convenience; moderately
• gɔɔj boŋ : eat at one's convenience
- mɛh gɔɔj boŋ di biiʔ : just eat until you are full!
- gɔj boŋ chɤm : you just go on eating!
- gɔɔj boŋ juuk : eat; eat a suitable

amount of rice (+*Ferlus*)
• gɔɔj gla? : speak softly

gɔɔj **III** (*Preverbal*) : taking care; being watchful
- gɔj ɟak dɤŋ : look where you are going!
- gɔɔj wʌl gɔɔj dɤŋ chɤm : take it easy and look where you are going on your way back!

gɔɔj **IV** *see* gwɤɤj

gɔɔk *in*:
• gɔɔk chiiŋ : pigpen

gɔɔŋ chooŋ : flashlight

-gɔ? (*in expressions of proximal location*), *see* lagɔ?, dɯgʌ?

grawɯlh : (1) fan (*N*); leaf used as a fan
• grawɯlh ʔuulh : a leaf used as a fan to supply air to the fire
— : (2) fan (*V*)
- grawɯlh ʔuulh, kibi gɯh : fan at the fire, it does not blaze!
- ʔaa, ʔuulh blɯt, grawɯlh ʔuulh : oh, the fire has died out, fan at it!

greet : it aches; it hurts; be in pain (*little used, cf.* cho?)
- gʌm ki cho? ki greet : let me not be in pain (ritual formula)

grɤɤj *in*:
• met grɤɤj : not yet
- met grɤɤj ʔem : have not slept yet

grɤŋ **I** : sieve (shaken so that the items to be sifted slide back and forth across the bottom); screen

grɤŋ **II** : middle
• mla? grɤŋ : ordinary people
• rumgum grɤŋ : the "middle fingers" (i.e. neither thumb nor pinkie)
• ti grɤŋ : in the middle (of a group, a row, or a file)
- ɟak ti grɤŋ : walk in the middle of the file

grɛh : Lua' (Tin) people

grɛɛt : scratch; rasp
• grɛɛt bon : rasp (meat on a bone, the flesh of a mussel) off with the teeth and eat it

grɯkgrak *in*:
• tɔ? grɯkgrak : saw (*N*)

grɯɯŋ : things; items
- grɯɯŋ chɛ? : there are many things; you have certainly many things!
- ɟak chɯɯ grɯɯŋ : I'm going to buy some things

grɯ? : utter a sound; speak

gr.la? : words; speech
- gr.la? chɛ? : there are many words (in our language)

gr.lɤɤŋ : rest on one's back (with the arms above the head)
- ʔem gr.lɤɤŋ : sleep on one's back

gr.lɛj : joint; wrist

grl.griil : scratch oneself with the nails ("*male lg.*")
• grl.griil glɤɤ? : scratch one's head
• grl.griil ŋa? : scratch oneself because it itches

gr.lijh *in:*
- gr.lijh ʔjen : have a stitch in one's side

gr.najh : split bamboo (bamboo stick attached crosswise on a dɯŋ.mrɛɛŋ)

gr.nɤl : supporting horizontal pole (*"female lg."*)

gr.niil : horizontal pole in the wall of a village house

gr.nɯh : flames
- gɯh-gɯh-gɯh, pen blaaj gr.nɯh : there are increasingly big flames
- gr.nɯh ʔuulh : flames from the firewood
- ʔɤhɤɤj, gr.nɯh ʔuulh : see, the firewood is ablaze!

grooʔ : utter the characteristic sound of the species (i.e. to chirp, growl, grunt, etc.)
- ʔac grooʔ : the bird chirps; the bird sings
- ʔee, ʔa groʔ kabook : listen!, the kabok bird is singing
- kɯr grooʔ : it is thundering

grɔɔk : family group; household
- mlaʔ di grɔɔk : our household
- grɔɔk gɛɛŋ : household

gr.pɯr *in:*
- gr.pɯr hn.taaʔ : coloured (hanging-down) band on Hmong female dress

gr.tʌl : elbow

gruɤɤ : things; belongings; the basic items which belong to a household

- gruɤɤ chɛʔ : there is much property
- toc pruk la gruɤɤ, pruk wʌl maʔ tɔ mlaaʔ : bring things along and give them to the Mlabri
- ʔat gruɤɤ ʔa prɪm, bakɯm chak toc : the things are old and useless, throw them away, I won't have them
- bah ɟum di gruɤɤ : your belongings
- ʔah ɟum di gruɤɤ : our belongings
- ʔot gruɤɤ : my personal belongings
- mɛh gʌm wʌl kwɤn ʔot gruɤɤ : don't you start playing with my things! (said to child)

grul *see* khawnom

grum : shade

gr.wah : distribute something (e.g. food) within the group
- gr.wah tɔ tr.dɯŋ : divide something between the members of the group
- gr.wah bɔŋ : eat something which has been distributed within the group

gr.wɛɛc (*or* gɯr.wɛɛc, gir.wɛɛc, gr.wɛɛt) : the tip (not including the nail) of a finger or toe
- gr.wɛc tiiʔ : finger tip
- gr.wɛc ʔjoc : cockspur

gr.wɛɛn (*or* gir.wɛɛn) *in:*
- gr.wɛɛn hɔɔ : left side; left hand
- gr.wɛɛn thɛh : right side; right hand

- ɟak gr.wɛn thɛh : to go to the right
gr.wɤŋ : mounting (*e.g.* the reflector mounting at the front end of a flashlight)
guh.gɔh *in:*
• guh.gɔh kɯm ʔjak keet : remove wax from the ear
gujh : hide *(V)*
- mlaʔ gujh thɛɛk : the person disappears in the shrub
gul **I** : seven
guul **II** : molar (tooth)
gumgoʔ : hip region (towards the back)
gumpuur *(also heard as* gm.puur*)* : insect species which sucks blood at night
guuŋ : pus
guur : scratch (with the nails)
gurmɔr : lower leg
gurtɔr *in:*
• gurtɔr lɔt : the cricoid cartilage; the area just below the Adam's apple
gur.ʔuur : something which has turned yellow (because it is withered)
- gurʔuur bɯlbɯl : withered (leaves)
gwaa *in:*
• ɟak gwaa : stroll; go for a visit; go out (e.g. hunting) *(Ferlus has:* ɟak gual*)*
- dik theeŋ ɟak gwaa kwɤn : the children go over to the neighbours to play
- ɟak gwaa talaat : go shopping
- ɟak gwaa ʔa wʌl : will go for a visit first and then be back
- ɟak lɔŋ ɲʌʔ ɟak gwaa rə.ʔʌh ʔa wʌl : she went down there on a visit, she'll be back soon
- mɛt mɤʔ mɛt mɤm ɟak ginɛŋ ɟak gwaa : where did your parents go?
• ɟak gwaa loh : be out looking for somebody or something
- ɟak gwaa loh hmaaj : be looking for a suitable wife
- ɟak gwaa loh ʔot ʔɛɛw : go and look for my child
gwaj *in:*
• gwaj mlaaʔ : the whole group together
- bon gwaj mlaaʔ : share a meal (the whole group together)
gwɤɤj *(also heard as* gɔɔj*)* afterwards; and then
- bon juuk hɛh gwɤj glaʔ : eat first and then talk
• ʔa gwɤɤj : afterwards; and then
- ʔaar ɟak ʔɤh chuɤn ʔa gwɤɤj wʌl bon juuk : we first go to work in the field and then we'll be back home to eat
gwɛɛc *(cf.* gwɛɛt*)* : scratch or poke with one's nail
gwɛɛt *(probably same word as* gwɛɛc*)* : hollow out ("female lg.")
- gwɛɛt : scrape in a piece of wood
gwicgwɛɛc : (1) scratch; scratch oneself

— : (2) *in:*
- hurlooj gwitgwɛɛc ɟak : swim by moving one's arms

h-

hak : (1) be separate; be different
- ba phet hak mɔ mɤʔ, ʔoh hak mɔ mɤʔ : Ba Phet and I have different mothers
- hak micmɛc, hak rɯmram, hak mot : "micmɛc", "rɯmram", and "mot" are different things (*i.e.* three different species of ants)

— : (2) oneself; on one's own
- mɛh gʌm pajok maaʔ, ʔoh hak pajok ɟrʌʌk : don't you lift (the water container) for me, I lift it and drink myself!

haat : a lump (mouthful) of betel
- glɛw haat : chew betel
- thup pruʔ haat : a lump of betel

het : mushroom (*+Ferlus*)

heer : sift (rice grains by moving sieve from side to side)

hɤɤ-hɤɤj *in:*
- ʔa hɤɤhɤɤj : long ago
- mlaʔ prɪm mlaʔ ʔa hɤɤhɤɤj : somebody who lived long ago

hɤɤj *in:*
- bɔ tak ʔɤh hɤɤj : very long ago
- tak ʔa hɤɤj; tak ʔɤh hɤɤj (*speakers differ*) : very long ago
- ʔbɔ tak ʔɤh hɤɤj : very long ago
- bɯl ʔa prɪm bɔ tak ʔɤh hɤɤj : died very, very long ago

hɛh (*often with elision of final h*) : first (*clause-final or perhaps extra-clausal Adverb*)
- boŋ juuk hɛh gwɤɤj glaʔ : eat first and then talk
- chɛm ɟak toc juuk hɛh : do you want more food first
- gʌm mɤn ɟak, ɟɤɤm hɛh : don't go yet, wait a moment!
- ɟak boŋ juuk hɛh, rəʔʌh ʔa pruk : I go and eat first, I'll be back soon
- ʔoh ɟak ɟrʌʌk hɛh chɤm : I'll just drink some water
- chɛw hɛh : wait for something or somebody before acting
- chɛw dɤŋ hɛh : let's wait and see!
- chɛw hɛh ʔɛl biʌc : we must wait because the food is not yet ready ("soft")
- chɛw rɯm hluak boŋ hɛh : you (the children) must let the adults eat first!
- rə.ʔʌh hɛh : for a moment

hɯʌ *in:*
- hɯʌ ʔbin (*sic!*) aeroplane

hɯl.hal : put out the tongue in order to cool off
- chɔʔ hɯl.hal thu.ʔuur : the dog puts out its tongue because it is hot

hlah : love (*V*)

hlaguur : corncob

hlak.hlek *in:*
- pleʔ hlak.hlek : melon-like

gourd species *("male lg.")*

hlawaac : fat in the abdominal region

hlek : iron; iron nail
- cam hlek : hit a nail
• hlek cam : iron nail
• hlek pal : iron nail
- tɔc hlek pal, pal lam : drive a nail into wood

hlɤŋ : bracelet *(+Ferlus)*

hlɛɛm : the side of something
• hlɛɛm tɔʔ : blade of a knife

hlɛŋ : muddy
- hlɛŋ ŋɔr : it is slippery on the path
- mɛʔ hot ŋɔr hlɛŋ : it rains so the path is slippery

hlin *in:*
• gʌm wʌl hlin : don't disturb me!

hlɯɯ : there is some left; there are some extra
- kan hlɯɯ ʔoh tɔc : if there is any left, I'll take it

hlɯŋ : cough *(V) (+Ferlus)*

hlɯɯŋ : any colour from blue over greenish and yellow to light rose colour

hlooj *see* bɛɛr

hlɔɔp *(final cons. sic!) in:*
• wʌl hlɔɔp : haunt
- ʔi wʌl hlɔɔp met thɛh : he/she was a bad person and now haunts the place

hluak *in expressions of adulthood:*
• rɛɛm hluak : grown-up person; adult
• rɯm hluak : grown-up person; adult
• ʔa hluak : (be) grown up *(Ferlus has:* hluak big*)*

hluut *in:*
• keet hluut : deaf

hmaaj : wife *(sic; in other languages this etymon means 'widow'; Ferlus has:* maj*)*
• hma(a)j glaŋ/laŋ : married couple
• hma(a)j hmɛʔ : new wife; present wife (if husband formerly married)
• hma(a)j kɯldɯl : first wife
• hma(a)j prɪm : former wife
• hma(a)j tuul : second wife
• ləmeet ʔa bɤɤn hmaaj : married man
• tɔc bɛɛr hmaaj : have two wives; marry twice

hmaal : spirit *(word used in rituals addressed to a protective spirit)*
• kuuk hmaal : oh Spirit! *(also see* kuuk*)*
- kuuk hmal ɟuʌj ʔoh gʌm chɔʔ ki greet : oh Spirit, help me not to be in pain!
- kuuk hmal mɯɯ : return, oh Spirit!

hmaap *in:*
• ʔem hmaap : lie on one elbow

hmaaʔ *(also heard as* maaʔ*)* : tuber species (highly edible)

hmɛʔ : (1) new
• grɯɯŋ hmɛʔ : new things *("male lg.")*
• hma(a)j hmɛʔ : one's new wife

- kiʔ hmɛʔ : new moon
- mɤʔ hmɛʔ : stepmother
- ʔɤh hmɛʔ : make a new one
- gɛɛŋ prɪm ʔa bukbuk, kan dʌm jɤɤm ʔɤh hmɛʔ : our house is old and delapidated, if we are to stay on we must build a new one

— : (2) *(clause finally:)* anew

hmiʌŋ *(also miʌŋ)* : "miang"; fermented tea leaves
- gɯm hmiʌŋ : chew fermented tea leaves
- jʌw chi glɤʔ chi gɯm hmiʌŋ : as I have a headache I wish to chew fermented tea leaves

hmitbeec *in:*
- mɛʔ hmitbeec : it rains all day

hmitgoc : insect species (which emits an itching liquid)
- hmitgoc nɔɔm mat : the "hmitgoc" "pisses" into peoples' eyes

hmɯl *in:*
- hmɯl pak : hang the washing up (on a string or a pole)

hmɯɯl *in:*
- ʔɤh loon ʔɤh hmɯɯl : perform ceremony for personal spirit

hmɯlbaaŋ : mythological spirit which lives in trees

hmɯɯn : become acquainted
- dɤŋ ʔa nak hmɯɯn : look something carefully over
- ʔa hmɯɯn : know; know already
- ʔoh met ʔɛl hmɯɯn : I do not know yet

hmɯndɯɯr *in:*
- tawɪn ʔa hmɯndɯɯr : noon

hmɯr-laŋ *in:*
- gɯncaj hmɯrlaŋ : soft cloth (used as a loincloth or a towel)

hmɯʔ.rɯʔ : itch
- glɤɤʔ hmɯʔ.rɯʔ : the scalp is itching (because of lice)
- hmɯʔ.rɯʔ glɤɤʔ : have an itching scalp (because of lice)

hm.pooj : net; network
- gɯncaj hm.pooj : mosquito net
- pjaŋ hm.pooj : arrange the mosquito net for the night

hmuu *in:*
- nɛŋ hmuu : all; group of people
- di pruk ʔa noŋ nɛŋ hmuu : come, all of you!
- ʔah ɟum nɛŋ hmuu : all of us
- ʔah ɟum jɤɤm nɛŋ hmuu : we are all here

hmucgoc *idiolectal variant of* hmitgoc

hmujthɔj *(often reduced too* muj-, mɯj-, mi-*)* : run
- hmujthɔj di reew : run as fast as one's legs can carry one
- hmujthɔj ɟa reew : run as fast as one's legs can carry one
- hmujthɔj ɟur-ɟur : run with heavily stamping feet
- ʔoh hmujthɔj ɟur-ɟur, ʔoh chi liŋgeew : I run too heavily, I have a stitch in my side

hmuŋ : Hmong; Meo
- glaʔ hmuŋ met bɤɤn : cannot

speak Hmong

hmup ʔup : on one's stomach (resting position)
- ʔem hmup ʔup : to sleep on one's stomach

hmurɟuur : be pouring down in a thin jet (e.g. water from a spout)

hna I *(possibly a reduced form of* hnɛʔ*) in:*
• hna bɛɛr hna ɟum : our kinsmen over there

hnaa II *(mostly with vowel shortening) in:*
• lɔŋ hna buuk : forwards; straight ahead
- ɟak lɔŋ hna buuk : walk straight ahead

hnʌm : year
• ban hnʌm rɔɔj hnʌm : many, many years ago
• chɛʔ hnʌm : for many years
• hnʌm gʌh : this year; these (past) years
• mɔ hnʌm : one year from now (forwards or backwards in time)
- mɔ hnʌm bn.nah : last year
- mɔ hnʌm ɟruɯ paaj : the next few years
- mɔ hnʌm ɟruɯ paaj laaj kwɛk : for the next many years
- mɔ hnʌm pruk : he will come next year
- mɔ hnʌm tak bn.nah : last year
• tak hnʌm prɪm : many years back; for many years (in the past)

hnʌr : wing (of bird or insect)

hn.cok : (1) inflorescence; stalk
• ʔat hn.cok pleeʔ : the stalk carrying a fruit or vegetable
— : (2) *in:*
• thrɛɛŋ hn.cok : canine tooth

hn.dɤl : heel
• hn.dɤl ɟɤɤŋ : heel *(Ferlus has* dəl ɟəŋ*)*

hn.doom *(also heard as* hn.toom*)* : ripe
- prɛʔ hn.doom : ripe chili
- ʔat pleʔ ʔa hn.doom : the fruit is ripe now
- ʔi ʔɛl hn.doom : it (the fruit or vegetable) is not ripe yet

hn.drɤɤʔ *frequent pronunciation of* hn.rɤɤʔ

hnep : fold
- hnep glɤh : roll up the legs of one's trousers
- chɯr.ʔbat hnep : trouses Northern Thai or Hmong style (fastened by folding and tightening)

hnɛl : lower leg
• chuʌk hnɛl : tie a string around one's ankle (ritual formula)

hnɛɛp : pack and fold something into a lump
- hnɛɛp hmiʌŋ gɯm : make a lump of miang and chew it

hnɛʔ *(cf.* hna; *third person respectful pronoun)* : He; the Creator

hnɯl.hnɯl : mythological giant ant which killed people by biting them

hnop : the folded edge of the

ear lobe

hn.rɤɤʔ *(also heard as* hn.drɤɤʔ*)* : a girl who is old enough to marry (*Ferlus:* nrə)
- ʔɛɛw hn.rɤɤʔ : little girl

hn.taaʔ : tail; rump section (+*Ferlus*)
- gɯrpɯr hn.taaʔ : tail (e.g. of a dog)
• hn.taʔ cewcew : short-tailed
• hn.taʔ lɛn : coccyx; caudal vertebrae; the lower tip of the spine
• hn.taʔ ʔjɛt : loincloth with a strip hanging down

hn.toom *see:* hn.doom

hn.tor : (1) hole; the opening of something hollow (*"male lg."*)
- hn.tor kə.plah lam : a gap in a plank floor
- lo.ʔuh ʔa pen hn.tor : it (the fabric) has a hole in it
• hn.tor keet : hole in ear lobe
• hn.tor kɛp : cave (in rock)
- ʔdoʔ blʌk hntor kɛp : the porcupine enters a cave
• hn.tor kl.dɯl (or kn.dɯl) anus
• hn.tor mɔh : nostril (*"male lg."*)
• khawnom hn.tor thəbɯr : "hollow rolled cookie": a kind of biscuit
— : (2) entrance (opening) in house
• kn.lap hn.tor : door (plate) of a village house
• kralip hn.tor : close the door

hn.theer : be pierced

hnum : young man

hɲaaʔ (*cf.* jaaʔ) : female relative of elder generation; aunt

hɲim.hɲɛɛm : gill; antenna (as a zoological term)
• hɲim.hɲɛɛm mɔh : the horns of a snail

hɲ.ɟʌt *in:*
• mɛʔ ʔa hɲ.ɟʌt : it has stopped raining

hɲuc.hɲec : be lying in a heap
- dɔɔk hɲuc.hɲec : leave something (e.g. a rope) in a heap

hɲuʔ-hɲɔʔ : have a wrinkled face
• hɲuʔ-hɲɔʔ chak-kom.ruujh : old, wrinkled person

hŋ.kah *in:*
• keh (ta) hŋ.kah : break (something)
- toc lam keh ta hŋ.kah : break a stick

hŋ.keeʔ : dry branches or twigs (used as firewood) (*"female lg."*)

hook : (1) hole; gap (*"female lg."*)
• hook dɯm.rɛɛŋ : a gap in a plank floor
• hook mɔh : nostril
— : (2) entrance (opening) in village house (*"female lg."*)
• kn.lap hook : door (plate) of a village house
• kralip hook : close the door

hot : (1) fall (*Ferlus has the word in the meaning* 'to de-

scend')
- dɤŋ ʔi hot : look out, you are about to fall!
- hot tu lam : fall down from a tree
• loon hot : "the spirit falls off" (causing the person to be ill)
• mɛʔ hot : it rains
• tac hot : be torn off
• twec hot : throw
— : (2) set (said about sun, moon or stars)
- tawɪn ʔa hot : it is (just after) sunset
- ʔat ɟjooŋ ʔaar hot, ʔat ʔuuj ɟak klɤɤŋ : the star Venus sets first, and the Moon follows
• tawɪn hot : west
- ɟak lɔŋ tawɪn hot : go west

hɔɔ *in:*
• gr.wɛɛn hɔɔ : left side; left hand

hɔɔt : reach (somewhere)
- ʔa hɔɔt : has arrived
• gɯt hɔɔt : miss (somebody); have (somebody) in one's thoughts

hr.lɛʔ : laugh

hr.liiŋ : forget
- gʌm hr.liiŋ : don't forget it!
- met hr.liiŋ : I have not forgotten
- ʔa hr.liŋ kɯm : has completely forgotten

hr.looj *see* hurlooj

hr.lɔh : five days from now

hr.wah *in:*
• ɟrʌʌk kɯr hr.wah : a narrow stream of water which is almost dried out

huɤk *see* hwɤk
huŋ *see* pleeʔ
hurlooj (*or* hr.looj) : float along
- hurlooj ɟak : float in water; swim
- hurlooj ruʌŋ reew : be carried away by floods of water
• hurlooj gwitgwɛɛc ɟak : swim by moving one's arms

hwɤk (*or* huɤk) : rat (+*Ferlus*)
• hwɤk chəʔuʌk : bamboo rat
• hwɤk dəlawʌk : rat, big species
• hwɤk juuk : rat species living in the cultivated field

hwɤɤŋ *in:*
• ɟrʌʌk lɯŋ hwɤɤŋ : puddle; pool of water

j-

ja(a) I (*cf.* jaaʔ) : title of senior woman; Mrs.

jaa II *see* ʔjaa

jah : we (dual)
- jah bɛɛr mlaaʔ hlooj : we three people
- jah ɟak bɛɛr mlaaʔ : we two go together

jajh : start (suddenly move, e.g. in sleep)

jaɲ : push
• dɯk jaɲ glɤh : raise oneself on tiptoe while pushing a load upwards

jaaw : Yao (ethnic term)

jaaʔ (*cf.* hɲaaʔ) : female relative of elder generation; aunt

jʌk I : (1) thus; like this

- jɤɤm jʌk : sit like this; sit in this posture
- ʔɤh jʌk : do like this
• chi jʌk : something of this kind
• chɯŋ jʌk : in this way
• də jʌk : like this
- ʔɤh ɟak də jʌk do like this!
• lə jʌk : like this
- ɟak lə jʌk mɛh chɯŋ ɲʌʔ : go this way!
- ʔɤh ɟak lə jʌk : do like this!
— : (2) *(Connective, poorly attested:)* like
- choʔ jʌk purdur ʔuulh : hurt like a burn

jʌk II *in:*
• jʌk wʌl jʌk : long ago
• tak jʌk wʌl jʌk : in the past
- bɔ tak jʌk wʌl jʌk : several years ago

jʌk-jʌk : this is how everything should be done
- ʔbɔɔk maʔ mɛh jʌk-jʌk : I tell you what to do

jʌr : have stretched legs *(V)*
• ʔem jʌr : sleep with stretched legs

jʌw : because; since; as
- jʌw chi glɤʔ chi gɯm hmiʌŋ : as I have a headache I wish to chew miang
- jʌw jʌk wʌl jʌk : it happened long ago, you see
- ʔɛɛw beec jʌw chi glɤɤʔ : the child cries because it has a headache
- ʔɛɛw beec jʌw ŋaʔ : the child cries because it itches

jeek *see* gook jeek

jen *in:*
• boŋ dok boŋ jen : eat poor food
• jɤɤm dok jɤɤm jen : live a miserable life
• mlaʔ dok mlaʔ jen : very poor people

jɤɤl *see* dɤl

jɤɤm : (1) *(also with locative complement or object:)* be seated; sit
• jɤɤm bɛʔ : sit down on the ground; be seated on the floor
• jɤɤm nɛh : be seated here
- jɤɤm nɛh, jɤɤm nɛh : come and sit here!
• cʌt jɤɤm : be seated
• chʌr ʔa jɤɤm : sit down (after standing)
• jɤɤm ɟuur : sit down (after standing)
• jɤɤm thɛh : sit in upright position
• jɤɤm ʔa chʌr : rise (after sitting); stand up
— : (2) *(with locative complement or object)* stay somewhere; be somewhere; be an inhabitant of
- boŋ tipiaʔ jɤɤm chugwʌʌʔ : what did you eat while you were down there?
- gɛjh jɤɤm ruʌŋ : the crab lives in creeks
- meh jɤɤm ginɛŋ : where do you live?
- kɛp jɤɤm ɟuuk : that stone was in the rice
- wʌl jɤɤm chrɔɔɲ : come and stay where it is dry (i.e. take shel-

ter)
- jɤɤm briiʔ : live in the forest
- jɤɤm kluɯr : be up in the sky (said of celestial bodies)
- jɤɤm lɔŋ - : stay (outside) in -
- jɤɤm lɔŋ briiʔ : stay in the (deep) forest
- jɤɤm lɔŋ luɤt : stay out (overnight)
- jɤɤm ʔa lɔŋ luɤt : be outside
- jɤɤm nɛh : live here; stay here
- tawɯn nɛh mɛh jɤɤm nɛh : you stay with us today
- ʔoh jɤɤm nɛh : I live here
- jɤɤm nɛŋ - : be together with -
- jɤɤm nɛŋ ʔoh : stay with me
- jɤɤm tʌ(k) tr.dɯŋ : be together
- jɤɤm tr.dɯŋ : be together
- jɤɤm wec : be far away
- jɤɤm ʔa ti nɛj : be inside
- met jɤɤm : there is/are none
- ʔɛɛw met jɤɤm, ʔa bɯɯl : I have no children left, they have died
- wʌl jɤɤm kap chak kap chruʌt : come and stay inside me! (invoking a spirit)
— : (3) live under certain conditions or in a certain state
- jɤɤm bɛɛr mlaaʔ : live together as a couple
- jɤɤm chɛʔ : be many together
- jɤɤm dok jɤɤm jen : live a miserable life
- jɤɤm hn.rɤʔ : be still a young unmarried girl
- jɤɤm kibi ɲaŋ ʔɛɛw : have no children
- jɤɤm tareeŋ : be still an unmarried man *("female lg.")*

- jɤɤm ʔbaw : be still an unmarried man *("male lg.")*
— : (4) be at home; be idle at home; rest; stay here; stay on
- gʌm mɤn ɟak, jɤɤm hɛh : don't go yet, wait a moment!
- jɤɤm chɯ.chɯɯ : take the time off
- jɤɤm ɲʌn kibi thɛh : stay at home not feeling well
- met jɤɤm : is not at home; is not there any longer
- ʔoh chak ɟak ʔoh jɤɤm : I don't go anywhere, I stay at home
- jɤɤm gɛɛŋ : be at home
- ʔot ʔuuj ʔot ɟjooŋ jɤɤm gɛɛŋ : my parents are at home
— : (5) *Postverb encoding state or progressive aspect:*
- mɤm ʔem jɤɤm : father is still asleep
- ʔoh pɯh jɤɤm : I am up already!
- chʌr jɤɤm : be standing upright
- ki boʔ jɤɤm : be still a baby
- met thɛh jɤɤm : be unwell
- rɛɛm jɤɤm : become more alone; become solitary

jɤʔ *see* pajɤʔ

jɛt *see:* ʔjɛt

jirjɛɛr : cicada species (edible)

joc *see* ʔjoc

joh : tear out; tear up; lift something out of its fixed position
- joh mujmuj mɔh : tear hairs out of the nostrils
- joh run juuk : tear up weeds

- joh run kɯm : tear up weeds and dispose of them
- toc cok klukklɔk joh run : use a hoe to remove weeds
- toc tiʔ joh pruk : pull something (e.g. a thorn) out with the fingers

joh.joh : pick at something
- joh.joh bɔŋ : eat meat off a bone by picking it with the fingers

jooŋ : (1) father (mostly about the father of somebody other than the speaker) *(cf. ɟjooŋ, mɤm)*
- jooŋ ʔɛɛw ɟak ʔem : both father and child shall go to sleep

— : (2) man, *in:*
• ʔuj jooŋ : woman and man (as a procreating couple)

— : (3) a very bright star (supposed to be in conjunction with the moon), apparently: Venus *(cf. ɟjooŋ)*
• jooŋ kiiʔ : the star belonging with the moon (= ʔat ɟjooŋ)
• ʔuj jooŋ : the Moon and the star Venus

juh.juh : comfort a child by rocking it (with small vertical movements)

juuk : rice *(also cf. rɔɔj, run) (+Ferlus)*
• bɔŋ juuk : eat rice; eat village-type food *(see bɔŋ)*
• juuk lɯmpɯt : sticky rice
• juuk prijh.prɛjh : biscuit made of rice grains
• juuk thɯrbaaʔ : husked rice
• ɟr.wɤɤl juuk : boil rice

jum *in:*
• ʔah jum : we *(see ʔah)*

ɟ-

ɟa *(distinctly: ɟaa)* I *in:*
• ɟa reew : forcefully
- glaʔ ɟa reew : speak loudly
- hmujthɔj ɟa reew : run as fast as one's legs can carry one
- tɛk ɟa reew : beat; box *(V)*

ɟa II *Imperative Particle, in:*
• ɟa ɟak : go!
• ɟa pruk : come!

ɟak *(emphatically also ɟaak)* : (1) go; walk *(+Ferlus)*
- ɟak di grɯŋ : walk in the middle (of the group)
- ɟak klɤɤŋ : walk behind (somebody)
- ɟak lɔŋ klɤɤŋ : walk in the backward direction
- ɟak met bɤɤn : is disabled: cannot walk
- ʔaar ɟak : walk in front

— : (2) leave; go off in some direction; travel
- gʌm ɟak : don't go!
- ɟak gʌh ɟak ɲʌʔ : stray *(V)*
- ɟak lə jʌk mɛh chɯn ɲʌʔ : go this way!
- ɟak ŋɔɔr met thɛh : go the wrong way
- ɟak prim : go away for a long time
- ɟak rə.ʔʌh : go for a moment
- ɟak wec : go far away
- ʔa rɛʔ ɟak : be escaping
• ɟa ɟak : go!
• ɟak di thɛh : have a good jour-

ney!
• ʔa ɟak : be off; let's go!
— : (3) *(Preverbal:)* go and -; go out to -; shall -
- ɟak gɯɯn leh : go out and return
• ɟak gwaa : stroll; go for a visit; go out (e.g. hunting)
- ɟak loh : go and look for (something)
- ɟak ʔjak : go off to defecate
- mɛh nɛŋ ʔoh ɟak ʔem : we shall both sleep
— : (4) *(Preverbal:)* you had better -; do - please!
- bah ɟum ɟak boŋ juuk ni ʔot gɛɛŋ : come and eat in my house, all of you!
- mɛh ɟak kɯm : you had better throw it away
— : (5) *(Preverbal:)* how/where can one -?
- ɟak toc ginɛŋ, ʔa noɲ : where could one get some, it's all gone!
— : (6) be; become *(Preverbal Auxiliary:)*
• ɟak chɛʔ : be(come) plentiful; abound
— : (7) *(Preverbally, conveying the meaning of near future in special expressions:)*
• ɟak rə.ʌh : in a moment
— : (8) *(Postverbally, conveying the meaning of 'intent or realization of action', also in commands:)*
• kɯm ɟak : throw it away!
• poon ɟak : go far away

• ʔa rɛʔ ɟak : I will run away! *(also cf. (9) below)*
- kheet ʔa rɛʔ ɟak : I am scared, so I'm running away!
— : (9) *(Postverbally, with Preverbal ʔa, conveying the meaning of 'completion' either in the past or in a hypothetical statement:)*
- kan ʔoh bɔ glaʔ ɟak mɛh di tɔɔ : when I have spoken (to you), you should answer
• ʔa bɯl ɟak : is long since dead; would have died
• ʔa rɛʔ ɟak : has run away *(also cf. (8) above)*

ɟakɟak *in:*
• ɟakɟak wʌlwʌl : travel back and forth

ɟakɔn : sit with the palms of the hands stretched forward
- ɟakɔn ʔuulh : warm one's hands at the fireplace
- ɟakɔn thalɛɛl ʔuulh ʔjen : warm one's hands at the fireplace because one is cold

ɟalaaw : Laos
- ti ɟalaaw : in Laos

ɟaʔ *see* toŋ

ɟʌl *see* ɟjʌl

ɟʌt : while
- ɟʌt jɤɤm nam ɲaaw bɯl : died while staying at Nam Jaaw

ɟen *(or* ɟin*)* : experienced
- ʔɤh ɟen : is difficult to do
• ki ɟen : that's OK, I have tried that before

- met ɟen : be unexperienced; be no good at doing something
- met ɟen glaʔ : cannot speak it (that language)
- ʔoh glaʔ met ɟen : I am no good at talking; I cannot recite it
• ʔa ɟen : be experienced; be clever
- mɛh ʔa ɟen : you are very clever

ɟeŋ : sew (V)
- toc cɪmbeelh ɟeŋ : sew with a needle
- toc priilh thapɛɛt ɟeŋ chɯr.ʔbat : use bast fibres of thapɛɛt to mend trousers
- toc tiʔ ɟeŋ : sew by hand

ɟɤɤŋ (unclear vowel length) : foot (+Ferlus)
• ʔat ɟɤɤŋ chɯr.ʔbat : the legs of a pair of trousers

ɟɤɤp : walk slowly; stalk (V)

ɟɤr in:
• ɟɤr ɟrʌʌk : bamboo section for drinking water

ɟi.ʔdɤɤ : anything; any; anywhere
- ɟi.ʔdɤɤ kɔ boŋ : I can eat anything
- kibi ɲaŋ ɟi.ʔdɤɤ boŋ : there is nothing to eat
- kibi ɲaŋ ɟi.ʔdɤɤ ʔbɔɔk maʔ mɛh : I have nothing more to tell you
- met ɲaŋ ɟi.ʔdɤɤ ba.thuul : we have no meat or vegetables
- toc pruk ɟi.ʔdɤɤ : you may bring anything whatsoever!
• ɟi.ʔdɤɤ ʔa dɔ bɤɤn : anything whatsoever will do
- boŋ ɟi.ʔdɤɤ ʔa dɔ bɤɤn : can eat anything
• ɟi.ʔdɤɤ ʔa dɔ thɛh : anything will do

ɟiʌj : chew

ɟin- see ɟn-

ɟi.ʔɛɛŋ : (1) bone
- ɟiʔɛɛŋ chɛɛ : ribs
- ɟiʔɛɛŋ krujh : sternum; breast bone
- ɟiʔɛɛŋ mɛɛw : cheek bone
- ɟiʔɛɛŋ ʔdɯt : spine
— : (2) the shell of a snail

ɟɪn see ɟen

ɟɯɯ : name
- dəmɔj chɛʔ ɟɯɯ : a person changing his/her name several times
• ɟɯɯ jɤɤm hn.rɤɤʔ : a girl's name before marrying
• ɟɯɯ toc glaŋ : a girl's name after marriage
• ɟɯɯ ʔbaw : a man's name before marrying

ɟɯk : (1) scoop up; pour
- ɟɯk ɟrʌʌk : drink from a leaf cup
— : (2) colour
• ɟɯk bn.liiŋ : green; grey
• ɟɯk chɛɛŋ : black; dark; dark blue
• ɟɯk phakhaaw : white
• ɟɯk thwɛɲ : red

ɟɯm : heavy
- nikniit ʔi ɟɯm : walk with bent back because the load is heavy

ɟɯn I : cutting edge (of knife)

ɟɯn **II** : Classifier for cutting implements
- kwɛk muuj dəmɔ ɟɯn : one axe
- tɔʔ bɛɛr ɟɯn : two knives

ɟɯn **III** : a candle light
- tr.leet ɟɯn batoʔ ɟjʌl : roll a wax candle and light it at dusk

ɟɯnraaʔ *see* ɟn.raaʔ

ɟɯŋ- *see* ɟŋ-

ɟɯr- *see* ɟr-

ɟɯt : mourn; be unhappy
- ʔoh ɟɯt mɤʔ mɤm bɯl : I am mourning my deceased parents

ɟjʌl (*or* ɟʌl) : dusk (*Ferlus has* ɟɔl)
• ʔa ɟjʌl : it is becoming dark
— : (2) a night's stay
- ʔem bɛr ɟjʌl : sleep (i.e. stay over) two nights

ɟjooŋ (*also* ɟooŋ) : (1) father (*apparently used especially about one's own father*)
• ʔot ɟjooŋ : my father
- ʔot ʔuuj ʔot ɟjooŋ jɤɤm gɛɛŋ : Mother and Father are at home
— : (2) a very bright star, apparently Venus (*cf.* jooŋ)
- ʔat ɟjooŋ ʔaar hot, ʔat ʔuuj ɟak klɤɤŋ : the star Venus sets first, and the Moon follows

ɟm- *also see* ɟem-

ɟm.nuur : down
• ɟak ɟur ɟm.nuur : go downhill

ɟn.raaʔ (*variable pronunciation:* ɟɯn-, -draaʔ) : liquor
- boŋ ɟn.raaʔ thaŋɔɔt : drink liquor and become drunk
- ɟn.raaʔ boŋ bɛr boom : drink two bottles of liquor
- ɟn.raaʔ boŋ bɛɛr ʔboj : comsume two glasses of liquor
- met gɤj ɟrʌk ɟn.raaʔ : has never tried to drink liquor

ɟŋ.gɯɯn (*also heard as* cŋ.gɯɯn) : it becomes dark night
• ʔa ɟŋ.gɯɯn : dark night; it is dark night
• ʔa ɟŋ.gɯɯn ʔdiŋ : midnight; it is midnight

ɟook : suck

ɟooŋ *see* ɟjooŋ

ɟoʔ *see* toŋ

ɟɔɔj (*or* ɟuʌj) : help (V)
- kuuk hmal ɟuʌj ʔoh gʌm choʔ ki greet : oh Spirit, come back and help me not to be in pain!
- wɔk ʔuuj wɔk ɟjooŋ wʌl ɟɔɔj : my parents' spirits, come and help me!

ɟɔɔn : spoon

ɟɔʔ : not much; only a little
- nɔɔm chɛʔ chala nɔɔm ɟɔʔ : do you urinate much or only a little?

ɟraa : be skinny
• ɟraa kʌr-kɛr : be all skin and bone

ɟram **I** : be exhausted
• ɟram chaw ʔeeʔ : be exhausted and hungry
- ʔoh ʔɤh kaan chak bɤɤn, ɟram chaw ʔeeʔ : I can't work in

the field, I'm too exhausted and hungry

ɟraam **II** *see* pleeʔ

ɟrʌh : clear one's throat

ɟrʌʌk : (1) drink (water, etc.); smoke (tobacco, opium) (*Ferlus has:* ɟrɔk, ɟrək)
- bʌt kumbuŋ ɟrʌʌk : scoop up water with one's hands and drink
- ɟɯk ɟrʌʌk : drink from a leaf cup
- ɟrʌʌk ɟn.raaʔ : drink liquor
- ɟrʌʌk ʔjaa ɟrʌʌk : smoke tobacco
• chi ɟrʌʌk : be thirsty
• cɔʔ ɟrʌʌk : cigarette

— : (2) water
- ɟrʌʌk bohboh : boiling water
- ɟrʌʌk brɤɤl : the water is flooding
- ɟrʌʌk pluŋ : hot (but not boiling) water
- ɟrʌʌk thɛh : potable water
- ɟrʌʌk ʔa ɟuur : the water (level) has sunk
- ɟrʌʌk ʔjen : cold water
- thɔɔk ɟrʌʌk : pour water
• chumdɔɔj ɟrʌʌk : aqueduct; open pipe for conducting water
• ɟɤr ɟrʌʌk : bamboo section for drinking water
• ɟrʌʌk kɯr hr.wah : a narrow stream of water which is almost dried out
• ɟrʌʌk lɯŋ hwɤŋ : pool of water; puddle
• thuŋgot ɟrʌʌk : mug; cup

ɟreen *in:*
• glaʔ ʔa ɟreen : have finished talking

ɟrɤŋ : frog (species with long legs)

ɟr.mɯk : be disgusting; be dirty; be unclean
- ʔat ʔjak ŋɔɔk ɟr.mɯk : the intestines (*in casu* of a crab) are unclean (and thus inedible)

ɟrɯw : (1) tomorrow; next (of time span) (*Ferlus has:* ɟru)
- ɟrɯw chem ʔɤh : we continue tomorrow
• ɟrɯw paaj : the next two days; in two days; in a few days
• ɟrɯw tak ɟrɯw : tomorrow morning
• mɔ hnʌm ɟrɯw paaj : the next few years; in a few years
• tawɯn ɟrɯw paaj : the next two days

— : (2) *in:*
• tak ɟrɯw : this morning; in the early morning

ɟruʔ : deep (*e.g.* about water); far down (*e.g.* into deep forest below the mountain peaks)
• bah ɟruʔ : it is pitch dark (at night)

ɟr.wɤɤl : boil something (rice)
- ɟr.wɤɤl ɟuuk : boil rice

ɟuaaʔ : rags
- ɟuaʔ chɯrɛɛ : a shirt which is all rags

ɟualh : strong (*e.g.* of a string or rope)

ɟuʌj *see* ɟɔɔj

ɟuʌk *see* cuʌk

ɟuʌʌŋ : stretch one's hand out (to get something)
- ɟuʌŋ toc : fetch; pick

ɟuʌt : trickle; drip
- ɟrʌʌk ɟuʌt : the water is trickling down (along something)
- mɛʔ ɟuʌt : the rainwater is dripping down

ɟuɤj *see* tɤj
- ʔat tɤj ɟuɤj : southwards

ɟum *in:*
- bah ɟum : you folks (also used when addressing two people as a group)
- hna bɛɛr hna ɟum : our kinsmen over there
- ʔah ɟum : we; our group; my family; we who are residents here; all of us

ɟuuŋ *in:*
- gɛɛŋ ɟuuŋ : a deserted house

ɟup.lup : umbrella

ɟuur : (1) descend; go down; sink (about the water level after a flood)
- ɟrʌʌk ʔa ɟuur, brarulh chibɛʔ : the water has receded and sinks down to the ground
- ruʌŋ ʔa ɟuur : the (flooding) water has sunk
- ɟur ɟm.nuur : go downhill
- klol ɟuur : be happy

— : (2) *(Postverbal)* down
- dap ɟuur : fall into something
- jɤɤm ɟuur : sit down (after standing)

ɟur-ɟur *in:*
- hmujthɔj ɟur-ɟur : run with heavily stamping feet
- ʔoh hmujthɔj ɟur-ɟur, ʔoh chi liŋgeew : I ran too heavily, I have a stitch in my side

ɟurnɔk : beak

ɟweel : lemon grass
- thɛ.ʔɛn ɟweel : it smells deliciously of lemon-grass
- glɤʔ ɟweel : the edible core of a lemon-grass plant
- pleʔ ɟweel : onion

ɟwɛj *in:*
- ɟwɛj cɛɛʔ : have intercourse

ɟwiin I : weave a decoration on something
- ɟwiin ʔat tirwiil : decorate a plate with a weaved band

ɟwiin II : weaved decoration
- (ʔat) ɟwiin klɤp : weaved band on a box

k-

ka *(final particle, occasionally used when addressing an outsider speaking Mlabri)*
- ŋaam ka : yes, she is pretty!
- toc ka : yes, I certainly accept it (the gift)

kabok : bird species (sounding somewhat like a cuckoo)

kac : the crosspiece or flange mounting a knife onto its handle
- kac tɔʔ : the crosspiece of a big knife

kadɯp : stab

kah : water stream

- kah ʔdiŋ : big creek; river
- ʔɛɛw kah : small creek; well

kajek : smile *(V)*

kajh : measure out; check and mark the intended length of a piece

kaliip *in:*
- kaliip mat : close the eyes

kalɯp *in:*
- kalɯp toc : fetch (a ball)
- kalɯp gooj toc : fetch (a ball)

kamiin : light blue

kamnuʌt : policeman

kampoŋ : (1) skull; head *("male lg.")*
- chi kampoŋ : have a headache
- choʔ kampoŋ : have a headache
- mujmuj kampoŋ : hair on (man's) head
— : (2) detachable cover; the lid of a box *(cf. gl*ɤɤ*ʔ, kralit)*

kan I *(also* gan, *clause-initial Connective)* I : if; when
- kan mʌc mɛh kha hɔɔk pabɯl : if they see you, the "spear tribe" will kill you
- kan mɛh choʔ glɤɤʔ mɛh ʔa ɟak ʔem : if you have a headache, you should go and sleep
- kan mɛh wʌl gɛɛŋ, gɔɔj wʌl gɔɔj dɤŋ chɤm : on your way home, take it easy and look where you are going!
- kan ɲaŋ bliiŋ : if he/she is still alive
- kan ʔoh bɔ glaʔ ɟak mɛh di tɔɔ : when I have spoken (to you), you should answer
- ʔoh jɤɤm dəmɔj, ʔɛl toc hmaaj, kan ʔa ɲaŋ hmaaj jɤɤm bɛɛr mlaaʔ : I live alone, I have not married yet, but if I find a wife, we'll live together
- kan di : when (in future or hypothetically)
- kan di bla(a)j kwaan : when one is grown up

kan II *(one speaker insists on* gan*) in:*
- kan ɟak : take (something/somebody) along

kaan II : dig; work on the soil

kaan III : dry field
- ʔɤh kaan : work in the dry field

kaɲeer : narrow one's eyes

kaɲit : (1) dark weather; overcast
- kaɲit, toc darɔʔ batoʔ di tawɪn : it is dark, take a split bamboo stick and make a fire to light up!
- kaɲit kuup : there are thick clouds; it is cloudy and foggy weather
- kaɲit kuup, ɟak ki kheet : it is foggy so I am afraid of going
- mɛʔ hot kaɲit kuup : it rains and therefore it is dark and foggy weather
- kaɲit mɛʔ hot : it is dark because it rains
- ʔa kaɲit : it is dark; it is cloudy
— : (2) *in:*
- kaɲit mat : be blind; close the eyes

- mat kaɲit : cannot see anything (e.g. because it is dark or because one's eyes are closed)

kap I : song
- ʔɤh kap : sing

kap II : at; with; concerning
- wʌl jɤɤm kap chak kap chruʌt : come and stay inside me! (invoking a spirit)

katooŋ (also heard as gatooŋ) : hop up and down; play with something that hops up and down

kawak : cross (V)
- kawak ruʌŋ : wade across a stream

kaaʔ : fish (N) (+Ferlus)

ka.ʔuup : box of square shape (e.g. a cardboard box)

kʌlh : fall apart
- toh pa(a) kʌlh : pull at something so that it falls apart
- ʔa pa kʌlh : has been hit so that it fell apart

kʌr-kɛr see ɉraa

kʌw : horn (e.g. of a goat); antlers
- bɛɛ ɲaŋ ʔat kʌw : goats have horns

keh : break (something: a hard object)
- keh (ta) hŋ.kah : break (something)
- toc lam keh ta hŋ.kah : break a stick

kelreel see klreel

keeŋ : carry a load

- ɉak keeŋ juuk ʔa wʌl : go and fetch a basketful of rice
- keeŋ gruɤɤ : carry one's belongings
- keeŋ ɉak bɔ nikniit : carry something with a bent back
- toc chɯɯk keeŋ ʔuulh lɔŋ ʔdɯt : take a string for carrying firewood on one's back
- keeŋ ʔdɯt : carry on back
- kwɤj keeŋ : basket for carrying on one's back

keet : (1) ear (Ferlus: kek)
- keet hluut : deaf
- taŋ keet : ear ring
— : (2) spout (of a kettle)

kewkew in:
- kewkew rə.ʔɤk : with folded arms

kədah : small; a little bit (of)
- juuk kədah : a little bit of rice

kəki : not (either)
- juuk kəki bɔŋ, ɉi.ʔdɤɤ kəki bɔŋ : we ate no rice, we ate nothing (i.e. we had no food at all)

kə.plah : plank

kərbeeŋ see kɯrbeeŋ

kɤɤ in:
- kɤɤ ʔbɔʔ : guitar

kɤɤp : shoe
- kɤɤp ɉɤɤŋ : shoe

kɤpkɤɤp : (1) involucre surrounding a sprout; thin layer
— : (2) the area around the lower jaw on a fish

kɤɤt : (1) give birth
- ʔot mʏʔ kɤɤt ʔoh : my mother gave birth to me
• kɤɤt ʔɛɛw : give birth to a child
- kɤɤt ʔɛɛw buɯl : give birth to a stillborn child
— : (2) be born
- kɤɤt briiʔ : be born in the forest
• kɤɤt pruk : come out of the mother's womb
- kɤɤt pruk ʔa buɯl : be stillborn; die at birth

kɛɛ I *in:*
• kɛɛ chalɔɔʔ : palm tree species

kɛɛ II *see* kiʔ, tawɪn

kɛj : from
• pruk ɟak kɛj - : come out of -
- hwʏk pruk ɟak kɛj hn.tor : the rat comes out of its hole
- pruk ɟak kɛj gɛɛŋ : come out of the house

kɛl : be in the way; obstruct
• gʌm kɛl : don't stand in the way!; move away, you're in the way!
• kɛl mat : obstruct somebody's view

kɛɛl *in:*
• pleʔ kɛɛl : cucumber
• pleʔ kɛɛl lwɛc : cucumber species

kɛp : stone *(+Ferlus)*

ki I *(Particle occurring just before the sentence verb)* : also; in fact
- ɟak ki kheet ʔi hr.looj ruʌŋ reew : we are afraid of going out because we may be carried away by the floods of water
- kaɲit kuup ɟak ki kheet : it is foggy so I am afraid of going
• ki bɤɤn : that is also OK; you can also say that
• ki bliiŋ *see* kibliiŋ
• ki boʔ ɟɤɤm : being still a baby
• ki chet : be a child
- ʔoh met mʌc cɯɯɯ, ɲʌn ki chet : I don't know because I was still a child then
• ki ɟen : that's OK, I have tried that before
• ki - ki : (one) as well as (the other)
- pak tiʔ ki buŋbɔɔŋ, pak ɟɤɤŋ ki buŋbɔɔŋ : if it sticks into your hand it swells, if it sticks into your foot it also swells
- pr.neelh ki bɤɤn, thɯp ɲup ki bɤɤn, bɔ gɯɯɯn dr.chʏʔ : you can say either pr.neelh or thɯp ɲup, it is the same thing
ʔoh ki biiʔ, mɛh ki biiʔ : we have both had enough to eat!
• ki mɛɛn : that's also possible; that's also correct; you can say that, too
- bɔŋ bliiŋ ki mɛɛn, bɔŋ thʌp tɯjh ki mɛɛn : you can eat it both raw and roasted

ki II *Negative Marker (in certain lexicalized expressions)*
• kan ki : if not
- kan hlɯɯɯ ʔoh toc, kan ki hlɯɯɯ ʔoh chak toc : if there is any left I'll take it, if there isn't any left I won't take any

- gʌm ki *(plus verb)* : don't -!; please let it not -!
- gʌm ki choʔ ki greet : let me not be in pain (ritual formula)
- ɟuʌj ʔoh gʌm choʔ ki greet : help me not to be in pain! (ritual formula)
• ki bə/bi *see* kibi
• ki chɛʔ : few
- juuk ki chɛʔ : just a little rice
• ʔa ki toc *(with question intonation)* : don't you want any more?

ki III : however many *in:*
• ki hnʌm ʔa dɔ thɛh : any number of years (from now on)

kiʌŋ *see* pleeʔ

kibə *see* kibi

kibɛɛ : there are lots of them around; they are everywhere
- kwʌr kibɛɛ : there are many Lua' persons

kibi *(or* kibə*)* : (1) not; if it is not the case that -
- kibi biʔ boŋ di chɛʔ : if you're not full, eat much!
- kibi boŋ thɛh boŋ mɤk : has no proper food to eat
- kibi ʔɤʔ boŋ : has no food; does not eat
• kibi bɤɤn : cannot
• kibi chak *see* ʔdaaj
• kibi chɛʔ : few
- mlaʔ kibi chɛʔ : a few people
• kibi mʌc : hasn't met
• kibi ɲaŋ : there is none; I/we don't have any
- jɤɤm kibi ɲaŋ ʔɛɛw : have no children
- kibi ɲaŋ gɛɛŋ ɲaŋ bɔh : have no house nor ashes, i.e. be homeless
- kibi ɲaŋ gɛɛŋ ʔem : have no house for sleeping
- kibi ɲaŋ ɟi.ʔdɤɤ boŋ : be without any food
- kibi ɲaŋ ɟi.ʔdɤɤ boŋ nɛŋ juuk : we have nothing to eat with the rice
- kibi ɲaŋ thuul : we have nothing to eat with the rice
- kibi ɲaŋ ʔat prɛʔ : there are no spices in it (the food)
- ʔoh jɤɤm dəmɔj, kibi ɲaŋ hmaaj : I live alone, I have no wife
• kibi thɛh : be ill
- kan mlaʔ prɪm kibi thɛh, ʔa bɯl ɟak : if people in old days were ill, they just died
• kibi ʔɛl : not yet
- ʔoh kibi ʔɛl boŋ : I haven't eaten yet
- kibi ʔɛl chi boŋ : I'm not hungry yet
— : (2) can't you (please)?
- kibi dɤŋ ʔot ʔɛɛw ʔot ŋwɛʔ : can't you look after my child (please)?

kibliiŋ : (1) (be) alive

— : (2) raw; unripe

kilkiil I *in:*
• kilkiil diŋ : insect species (small, red, edible)

kilkiil II *see* kl.kiil

kimriiʔ *see* km.riiʔ

kindiiŋ *(or* kn.diiŋ*)* : navel
• chɯɯk kindiiŋ : the umbilical

cord; the navel string

kin-ʔdeep : (1) centipede (red species)
- kin-ʔdeep krɛc : the centipede bites
- kin-ʔdeep ʔat tiʔ ʔat ɟɤɤŋ chɛʔ : the centipede has many legs

— : (2) *in:*
• pleʔ kin.ʔdeep : wild edible gourd species *(see* pleeʔ*)*

kip.lɛp *in:*
• kip.lɛp tiiʔ : nail cutter *("female lg.")*

kir-wɛl *highly distinct pronunciation of* kr.wɛl

kiiʔ : (1) moon *(Ferlus:* ki*)*
- kiʔ blɯt : the "extinguished" moon (before new moon)
- kiʔ hmɛʔ : new moon
- kiʔ kɛɛ : full moon
- kiʔ met grɤj ʔdiŋ moon when of small size
- kiʔ pruk : the rise of the moon; new moon
- kiʔ rɛɛm : waning moon
- kiʔ rɛɛm blɯt : moon shrinking so it becomes invisible
- kiʔ thʌp pompoo : full moon *("old-fashioned expression")*
- kiʔ ʔa bʌr : it is full moon
- kiʔ ʔa biŋ : it is about to be full moon
- kiʔ ʔa blɯt : the waning moon is extinguished
- kiʔ ʔa kɛɛ : the moon is high in the sky; is is full moon
- kiʔ ʔa noɲ : there is nothing left of the (waning) moon
- kiʔ ʔa noɲ ʔa blɯt : the (waning) moon has shrunk and become invisible
- kiʔ ʔa pruk : it is new moon
- kiʔ ʔa rɛɛm : the moon is waning
- kiʔ ʔa thʌp pompoo : it is full moon *("old-fashioned expression")*

— : (2) sun (in expressions about time of the day)

— : (3) month
- mɔ kiiʔ : one month
- bɛɛr kiiʔ : two months

kɯckaac *(unclear vowel length)* : scratch (the ground) with a leg
- chɔʔ ʔjak, chɔʔ kɯckaac : the dog defecates and then scratches the ground

kɯl-dɯh *see* kl.dɯh

kɯl.wʌŋ *idiolectal pronunciation of* kul.wʌŋ

kɯm : throw (away); remove *cf.:* bakɯm, pakɯm
guhgɔh gwicgwɛc kɯm ʔjak keet : remove earwax with one's finger
- pilh.peelh kɯm : wipe something away
- thɔɔk kɯm ɟrʌʌk : throw water out

kɯm-lɯɯr : swarm
- ʔjek kɯmlɯɯr : the bees are swarming

kɯn-caj *idiolectal variant of* gɯncaj

kɯr I : thunder *(Ferlus has the lexeme but not this gloss)*
- kɯr poh bɯl : the thunder

strikes out and causes one to die
- ʔɤhɤɤj, kɯr bɔ ruŋ.mruŋ : oh my, what a thunder!
• kɯr groo? : it is thundering
• kɯr poh : the thunder strikes out
• kɯr prim see prim

kɯr II in:
• ɟrʌʌk kɯr hr.wah : a narrow stream of water which has almost dried out

kɯr- also see kr-

kɯrbeeŋ : large insect species (?)

kɯr-(r)mɯt (cf. kɯr and rəmɯt) : thunderstorm
- kɯrmɯt parɛɛl : hail storm

kɯt see gɯt

kɯtkeet : spout (of a kettle or pot)
- tr.lɔh kɯtkeet : kettle with a spout

kl- also see kil, krl-

klaj (or klɛj) : be shy; be bashful
- mlaʔ chɛʔ klaj : if there are many people one becomes shy
• mat klaj kl.dɯl tawın : screw up one's eyes while looking in the direction of the sun

klaap : hold (something) by squeezing it
- klaap thʌc : hold meat with a split bamboo stick
• toc kr.lap klaap : hold (something) with a split bamboo stick

klaar : sky (obsolete form, cf. klɯɯr

klaw : scrotum

kl.dɯh : the uvula

kl.dɯl (or krl.dɯl, kn.dɯl) : (1) buttocks; rump
- chi kl.dɯl : have a sore behind
• hn.tor kl.dɯl ʔjak : anus
• kl.dɯl rɛɛlh : root tip (e.g. of an onion)
• lɔŋ kl.dɯl : backwards
— : (2) the rear or truncated end of something
— : (3) the stump of a tree
— : (4) the tip of a (snail) shell
— : (5) first-ranking (of kin)
• hma(a)j kl.dɯl : first wife
- toc hma(a)j kl.dɯl : take a first wife
• ʔɛ.w kl.dɯl : eldest (biological) child
— : (5) in:
• mat klaj kl.dɯl tawın : screw up one's eyes while looking in the direction of the sun

kleh : (1) hard (said to be "female lg." but actually much used by men)
- prım ʔa kleh : it (the wood) is old and hence (dry and) hard
• klol kleh : be "hard-hearted" (probably: be wicked)
• ʔdoŋ kleh : have an erection
— : (2) in a loud voice ("female lg.")

klet : scales
• klet kaaʔ : fish scales

klɤɤŋ : the place behind

- ɟak klɤɤŋ : walk behind; follow
- ʔat ɟjooŋ ʔaar hot, ʔat ʔuuj ɟak klɤɤŋ : the star Venus sets first, and the Moon follows
- lɔŋ klɤɤŋ : (1) behind others (as the last in a file); (2) backwards

klɤɤp : box *(N)*
- klɤɤp lʌp juuk : winnowed case used for steamed rice
- klɤp juuk : box for serving sticky rice
- klɤp maak : betel case

klɛj *see* klaj

klɛɛŋ : have something sticking in one's throat; have a dry sensation in the throat
- bɔŋ thʌc klɛɛŋ : ate some meat, which then stuck in the throat

klɛr : a finger-like extension of a forged blade which is inserted into a handle *(obsolete meaning: 'little finger')*
- klɛr tɔʔ : the part of the blade of a knife which is inside its handle

kluh.klɛh : shallow
- ɟrʌʌk kluh.klɛh : very shallow water
- ɟrʌʌk kluh.klɛh kumduŋ ɟak bɤɤn : (if) the water is shallow, you can wade

kluɯr : sky

kl.kiil *(or krl.kiil, kilkiil)* : knee *(+Ferlus)*
- cʌt kl.kiil : rest one's elbows on one's knees
- com dok cʌt kl.kiil : squat by resting one's elbows on one's knees

klooc : too big; loose (garment, bracelet) *("male lg.")*

klol : heart (in expressions of mood and physical condition)
- klol biʌʌc : grieve
- klol hot : be startled
- klol hot butbot thʌkthɤɤk : be startled, tremble and have palpitations
- klol ɟuur : be happy
- klol luaak : be out of breath
- klol pluŋ : be upset
- ʔoh met thɛh ʔem, klol pluŋ : I am so upset that I cannot sleep
- klol thɛh : be happy *(apparently also be kind-hearted, cf. Thai)*
- klol met thɛh : be unhappy
- klol ʔa thɛh : be in a good mood
- klol ʔa ʔjen : be calm
- phit klol : feel sad; mourn

kloolh : (of fruit or nut) not be fully grown

klor : shave *(V)*
- klor mujmuj : shave the face *(V)*

klɔk *see* pleeʔ

klɔl : the base of a sprout

klɔt : close a bag or bundle with a knot; make a knot on a string or rope
- klɔt dɔɔk juuk : keep rice grains in a cloth closed with a knot
- klɔt kr.lɔt : close something with a knot

kl.reel *(allegro variant:* kreel*)* :

short (visible length)
- chɯɯr.ʔbat kl.reel : shorts; short trousers

kluɤjkluɤj : owl species (probably pied hornbill)

kluh : clean (something, *e.g.* a clogged pipe)

klukklɔk : hoe *(V)*
- toc cok klukklɔk joh run : use a hoe to remove weeds

kl.wʌŋ *see* kulwʌŋ

km.lɯɯr *in:*
- ʔjec km.lɯɯr : the flying bee is humming

km.ɲah *in:*
- ʔɛɛw km.ɲah : daughter (of somebody else than the speaker)

km.riiʔ *(idiolectally:* kimriiʔ*)* : (1) hard
- ʔdoŋ k(i)mriiʔ : have an erection

— (2) in a loud voice *("male lg.")*
- glaʔ km.riiʔ : speak in a loud voice
- glaʔ di km.riiʔ : speak up so that I can hear you!
- glaʔ glaʔ km.riiʔ : speak in a very loud voice

kn.diiŋ *see* kindiiŋ

kn.dɯl *variant pronunciation of:* kl.dɯl

kn.lap *in:*
- kn.lap hn.tor : door (plate) of a village house *("male lg.")*
- kn.lap hook : *id.* *("female lg.")*

kn.ʔdɯp the orifice of a snail shell

kooc *in:*
- kooc toc : collect (small items)

koh : cut something into two parts

kook *see* pleeʔ

kookdrooj : pigeon species *("male lg.")*

kokokdrooj : *id.* *("male lg.")*

kol : stick *(N)*
- kol hlek : lighter
- kol lam : pole (of wood)
- toc kol tɛk : take a stick and hit (the dog)

komcooc : sit with crossed arms and hands on shoulders (because it is cold)

kompoʔ *in:*
- kompoʔ loom : pigeon species *("female lg.")*

kom.room : area underneath (e.g. underneath the plank bed in Hmong house)
- blʌk kom.room : place something or oneself underneath

koon : snore

kot I : in a circular direction
- ɟak kot : walk in a circle
- ɟak kot loh kwɛl : walk in a circle

kot II : brood; hatch
- kot ʔat khɛj : hatch

koot III : shave; scrape something off a surface

koʔ : yes

kɔ *(Preverbal, cf.* kə, ki*)* : also;

then; you see
- jɤɤm rɤɤʔ ʔoh kɔ mʌc : I saw her when she was a young girl
- ɟi.ʔdɤɤ kɔ bon : I can eat anything
- mlaʔ kɔ ʔa ki chɛʔ : and at that time we were few
- toc dəmɔj kɔ maʔ hmaaj : I just take one (fruit) and give it to my wife
- ʔat ti nɛj kɔ chɯɯk chɔɔt : what is inside (the neck), that's the oesophagus, you see
- ʔot thrɛɛŋ kɔ ʔa noɲ : I have no teeth left, you see

kɔbliiŋ *(cf.* kibliiŋ) : raw

kɔɔk : pipe

kraalh : squirrel species

kralip *in:*
• kralip hn.tor : close the door *("male lg.")*
• kralip hook : *id. ("female lg.")*

kralit : lid which is attached at one side and can be tipped up *(cf.* glɤɤʔ, kampoŋ)

kraŋ I : dry (something) in the sunshine; roast
- kraŋ ʔat mɯj : roast the bacon rinds of a slaughtered animal
• pjaŋ kraŋ : unfold and dry (the laundry)

kraŋ II : roasted bacon rind
• ʔat kraŋ : crackling; the roasted bacon rinds of a slaughtered animal

kraŋɛl : descend; go down; walk downhill

• kiʔ ʔa hot ʔa kraŋɛl : the moon has set
• tawɪn ʔa kraŋɛl : the sun has set

kraralh : brush something off
- tɛk kraralh : thresh; get the seeds off by holding the plant and beating it against the ground

krareel : board; plank
- glɛj pak krareel : cut and carve a board into shape

krʌw : be afraid; fear
- krʌw bɯɯk ɲʌn krɛc : fears the bear because it bites
- met krʌw kwʌr : is not afraid of outsiders

kreel *see* kl.reel

kreeʔ *in:*
• ʔa kreeʔ : that's right!

krɛc : (1) bite; gnaw
- bɯɯk krɛc : the bear bites
- chiʌɲ krɛc : the mosquito bites
- kin-ʔdeep krɛc : the centipede bites
• krɛc rt.lat : bite one's tongue
• krɛc thrɛɛŋ : bite one's lip
— : (2) cut; slash
• krɛc chŋ.kɛr tiiʔ : cut one's nails
• krɛc juuk : to harvest rice
• krɛc kampoŋ : cut one's/somebody's hair

krɛk *see* krɛc

krɛʔ : be caught by the loop of a snare
- delh krɛʔ kun : the "delh" is caught in the snare

krɯh *in:*
• krɯh bɛʔ : dig the soil with the snout (said of pigs)

kr.kreel : roll along the ground

krl- *also see* kil-, kl-

kr.lah *in:*
- kr.lah kwɤj : (fully developed) cluster of bananas

kr.laap : split bamboo (e.g. used as a forceps)
- kr.laap tiiʔ : nail cutter (*"male lg."*)
- toc kr.lap klaap : hold (something) with a split bamboo stick

krl.dɯl *see* kl.dɯl

kr.lɤɤt : throat; pharynx region; larynx region (+*Ferlus*)
- choʔ kr.lɤɤt : have a sore throat
- kr.lɤt chrɔɔɲ : my throat feels dry (e.g. after drinking liquor)

kr.liip : nail cutter (*"male lg."*)
- toc kr.liip kliip chŋ.kɛr tiiʔ : cut one's nails with a cutter

krl.kiil *see* kl.kiil

kr.lɔt : knot (made of string)
- klɔt kr.lɔt : close something with a knot

kr.najh *in:*
- mlaʔ kr.najh : ordinary people; tribal people

kr.nap (*cf.* kap) : song
- ʔɤh kr.nap : sing (V)
- ʔɤh kr.nap dɤl jɤɤl : sing in the traditional Mlabri way

kr.niil : (1) ridge
- kr.nil mat : the protuding ridges above and below the eye; eyebrow; cheek bone (+*Ferlus*)

— : (2) the big horizontal beam in the roof of a (Hmong) house

krɔɔ : ask for; request
- krɔɔ toc : request to receive
- krɔɔ toc chɯrɛɛ lɯŋ ʔoh : request a shirt from me
- ʔoh krɔɔ mɛh thʌc : I ask you for meat
- ʔoh krɔɔ nɛŋ mɛh : I request it from you

krɔkkrɔk *see* krukkrɔk

krujh : chest
- ɟi.ʔɛɛŋ krujh : sternum; breastbone

krukkrɔk (*or* krɔkkrɔk) : for the hen to cluck
- ʔat ʔuuj krukkrɔk ʔat ʔɛɛw : the hen clucks to its chicken

kru.ʔuŋ (*or* kr.ʔuŋ) : (1) cavity; hole; hollow
- ʔat kru.ʔuŋ keet : the dent in the ear lobe
- ʔat kru.ʔuŋ mat : the hollow of the eye area

— : (2) shelter; camp (in forest) (*sic Bernatzik*)

kr.wɛk : (animal species, apparently:) bear cat

kr.wɛl : a roll or spiral (e.g. a rolled-up rope)
- tom.ʔooʔ rɛʔ ɟak ʔat kr.wɛl : the snake unrolls itself and disappears
- ŋɔr kr.wɛl : a circular path; a circle

kr.ʔuŋ *see* kru.ʔuŋ

kuʌŋ *see* kwʌŋ

kuɤj *see* kwɤj

kuh : tip over; fall

kuuj : insect species (very large)
- kuj ʔɔɔŋ : insect species (big, stinging, wasp-like)
- kuj ʔɔɔŋ thuuc, pruk tum : if the "kuj ʔɔɔŋ" stings you, you begin to swell

kuj-kwʌj : wrap (i.e. to wrap something into a cover, or to wrap a cover around something)

kuuk : *initial word of certain ritual phrases, said in a falsetto voice and referring to the act of invoking (cf.* hmaal, loon)

kukɔɔʔ *(unclear vowel length)* : neck
- choʔ kukɔɔʔ : have a sore neck

kuu.kwap : frog species which lives in the forest

kul.wʌŋ *in:*
- kul.wʌŋ mat : eyeball

kum : grasp; hold in one's hand
- kum dɔɔk : hold in one's hand and keep
- kum pɤjh : (1) hold something while cutting it into shape; (2) grasp something (e.g. stalks of weeds) and cut it off
- kum buŋ : hold some water in the hollow of one's hands
- bʌt kum buŋ : scoop up water with one's hands

kumduŋ : wade
- ɟrʌʌk kluh.klɛh kumduŋ ɟak bɤɤn : (if) the water is shallow, you can wade
- kumduŋ ruʌŋ : wade across a stream

kumɔɔm : (1) somebody else's child; child of a relative; younger relative *("female lg.")*
- kumɔm bɛɛr : married relative(s) of next generation
- kumɔɔm chak : you (address term to younger relative)
— : (2) top of the head; crown (of the head)
- kumɔɔm glɤɤʔ : top of the head; crown (of the head)

kun I : snare *(N)*
- krɛʔ kun : be caught in a snare
- ʔɤh kun : fabricate a snare

kun II : relating to the past *(also see* tak) *in:*
- mlaʔ kun naaj : our forefathers

kundoʔ : armpit
- kundoʔ waʔ : armpit

kunkwaan *in:*
- ʔem kunkwaan : be sprawling on the ground

kuup : cloud(s); steam in the forest after rain

kur- *also see* kr-

kur.ʔwɔk.ʔwɛk : crooked

kutkwat : embrace

kwaac : sweep *("female lg.")*
- kwac ɟrʌʌk : sweep a water surface clean

- kwac gɛɛŋ : sweep the floor
- ɟak toc kr.waac ɲʌʔ, kwac gɛɛŋ ɲʌn rɤʔ : take that broom and sweep, it is dirty!
- kr.waac kwac gɛɛŋ : sweep with a broom

kwaaj : taro

kwaan : (1) be big (of body size); grown-up
- chɔɔʔ kwaan lɯɯ mɛɛw : dogs are bigger than cats
- kwaan glɤh : grow up
- kwaan glɤh, kwaan glɤh : grow up (over time)
- ʔɛl kwaan : is not grown up yet
- bla(a)j kwaan : big; full-grown
- ʔa kwaan : has come of age; is grown-up
- ʔat kwaan : the three middle fingers (excluding thumb and pinkie)

— : (2) in:
- tak kwaan : long ago

kwʌh : open something; break something apart
- kwʌh hn.tor : open the door ("male lg.")
- kwʌh hook : id. ("female lg.")

kwʌŋ : (1) something of a round shape; the round interior part of something
- naŋ mat pok ʔat kwʌŋ : the eyelid hangs down over the eye

— : (2) Classifier for compact (essentially round) objects
- kɛp bɛɛr kwʌŋ : two rocks/pebbles
- klɤp mɔ kwʌŋ : one box
- piʔ dəmɔ kwʌŋ : one rice grain
- trlɔh bɛɛr kwʌŋ hlooj : three pots

— : (3) in:
- bla(a)j kwʌŋ : large; roomy (said of bags, etc.)

— : (4) in:
- kwʌŋ tiiʔ : a handful (about a considerable number) (sic?)

kwʌr : the Lua' (Tin) people; people living outside the forest (now often referring to all non-Mlabri except the Hmong and Mien)

kwɤj I : banana
- kwɤj tr.lok : wild banana species

kwɤj II : foetus ("male lg.")

kwɤj III : winnowed basket (made of split bamboo strips)
- kwɤj keeŋ : basket for carrying on one's back

kwɤn : play like a child does; play with something
- dik theeŋ ɟak gwaa kwɤn : the children go over to the neighbours to play
- mɛh gʌm wʌl kwɤn ʔot gruɤɤ : don't you start playing with my things! (said to child)
- glaʔ kwɤn : say something for fun; say obscene things
- gʌm glaʔ kwɤn, glaʔ di thɛh : stop these bawdy remarks!

kwɛk I : axe (+Ferlus)
- gɯr kwɛk : axe handle
- kwɛk muuj : axe for chopping firewood
- thrɛɛŋ kwɛk : the sharp edge of

an axe

kwɛk II : Classifier for years
- ɟrɯw paaj laaj kwɛk : for the next many years

kwɛl : to be rolled up in a spiral
- tom.ʔooʔ kwɛl, ʔi mʌc mlaʔ ʔa lɔɔr ɟak : the snake lies rolled up; as it sees the person it crawls away
- ʔat chak ʔi kwɛl jɤɤm : the (snail's) body is rolled up in a spiral (i.e. inside the shell)
• ɟak kot loh kwɛl : walk in a circle

kwiiŋ : plant species (thorny stalks with long, oblique leaves, used for thatching)

kh-

khaa I *in:*
• khaa hɔɔk : "the Spear Tribe", another Mlabri group *(Thai word)*
- kha hɔɔk ʔdɛj ɲaŋ khɔt : the Spear Tribe does have spears
- kha hɔɔk ʔah jum mʌc met bɤɤn pabɯl : the Spear Tribe we cannot meet, they kill us

khaa II : can *(N);* tin
- khaa kaaʔ : can containing canned fish
- khaa prɪm : an old can

khaaj khaw : the Milky Way

khalɯp : put somthing into the mouth
- khalɯp boŋ : take a mouthful and eat

khaw *see* khaaj

khawnom *(sic when spoken distinctly; when spoken more rapidly also* khanom, *as in Thai)* : cookie; biscuit
• khawnom hn.tor thəbɯr : "hollow rolled cookie": a kind of bisquit
• khawnom pleʔ grul : sweet pear-shaped cookie (not made by the Mlabri themselves)
• khawnom prijh.prɛjh : biscuit made of rice grains

kheet : be afraid of; fear; be shy
- chak kheet : he (the little child) is not afraid of you
- kaɲit kuup ɟak ki kheet : it is foggy so I am afraid of going
- kheet ʔa rɛʔ ɟak : I am scared, so I'm running away
- mlaʔ kheet wɔk paŋ : people fear the dragon spirit
- ɲʌn ruʌŋ reew, kheet hr.looj : because there are heavy floods we are afraid of being carried off
- ʔoh kheet mɛʔ hot : I'm afraid that it will rain
• kheet ʔi - : fear that -
- ɟak ki kheet ʔi hr.looj ruʌŋ reew : we are afraid of going out because we may be carried away by the floods of water

khɛj : egg
- kot ʔat khɛj : hatch
• khɛj mat : (1) eyeball; (2) bulb in a flashlight
• khɛj ʔjoc : egg of hen

- khɛj ʔac : egg of a bird
- khɛɛn : mouth organ (which superficially resembles a big Pan flute)
- khɛɛp : rubber sandal (like bath slippers)
  • chɯɯk khɛɛp : the rubber string on a sandal
- khɯɯ : namely
- khɯɯp *in:* edible creeper species (vine)
- khɯʔ ʔdɯɯn : earthworm
- khot : with bent or crossed legs
  • jɤɤm khot : sit with one's legs crossed
  • ʔem khot : sleep lying on one's side with bent legs
- khɔɔŋ I *in:*
  • khɔɔŋ briiʔ : of the forest
  • khɔɔŋ tɤl : cultivated (vegetables)
- khɔɔŋ II *see* lɔŋ
- khɔt : spear (+*Ferlus*)
- kha hɔɔk ʔdɛj ɲaŋ khɔt : the Spear Tribe does have spears
- khrwaʔ : water snail
- khun : muddy (of water) ("*male lg.*")
- ɟrʌk khun met thɛh ɟrʌʌk : muddy water is no good for drinking
- ruʌŋ khun : muddy flooding water
- khwat : drill a hole with a rotating stick; hollow out ("*male lg.*")
- khwat lam : drill or scrape in a piece of wood

l-

la *(Copulative or Sentence Adverb which occurs after the subject NP, cf.* lə*)* : namely; and; it is...
- gʌh la chɯrɛɛ : this is a shirt

laac : (1) be finished; reach completion
- gɛɛŋ met grɤj laac, ɟruw ʔa laac : the house is not yet finished, it will be finished tomorrow
— : (2) *(with perfective* ʔa, *Postverbal:)* have finished doing something; have finished a transitional state
- bɔɲ ʔa laac : have finished the meal
- glaʔ ʔa nɔɲ ʔa laac : have finished talking
- mlaʔ bul ʔa laac : everybody died

ladooŋ : high up; up above
- jɤɤm ladooŋ : sit high up (e.g. in a tree)
- toc dɔɔk ladooŋ : put it in a place high up (e.g. on a shelf)
- ʔac pɤr ɟak ladooŋ : the bird flies high up

lagʌʔ *(or* lagɔʔ*)* : up there (on a hill)

lah *see* lʌh

laaj I : stripes
- chɯrɛɛ laaj wiŋkɛl : shirt with

some stripes across as ornamentation

laaj II : many, *in:*
• mɔ hnʌm ɟrɯɯ paaj laaj kwɛk : for the next many years

lak : sweet gourd species (the inside of which is of orange colour)
- tom bɔŋ pleʔ lak, bɔŋ gɔj pleʔ lak : boil and eat the sweet gourd, and eat the "soup" in which the gourd has been boiled
• ɟrʌʌk lak : water in which the sweet gourd has been boiled (used as a sweet soup)
• pleʔ lak : sweet gourd

lakʌh : up there (in the air)

lam : (1) tree; the trunk of a tree; the stem of a plant (+*Ferlus*)
- dɛl lam : cut down a tree
- glɤh lam : climb a tree
- hot tu lam : fall down from a tree
• lam pleʔ braaw : coconut tree
• lm.bʌr lam : leaf
— : (2) stick; log
- toc lam tɛk chɔɔʔ : hit a dog with a stick
• lam bɯlbɯl : dry firewood
• lam dɯr : bamboo tube used as a pipe

laŋ *(postnominal epithet to kinships terms)* : male relative of somebody else than the speaker
• miɲiŋ ʔa bɤɤn laŋ : married woman
• ʔɛw laŋ : (your/his/her) son
- ʔat ɟjooŋ gɯt hɔɔt ʔat ʔɛɛw laŋ : the father misses his son
• rooj laŋ : (your/his/her) little brother; (your/his/her) younger male sibling
- dɤŋ mɛt rooj laŋ : look after your little brother!

lat I : lick; use the tongue in eating something soft
- lat bɔŋ : eat something soft and juicy
- lat kwɤj : eat bananas
- lat pleʔ chreelh : eat mango fruit
- mɛɛw lat : the cat licks itself

laat II *see:* reet

laaw *(in names for Laos), see* ɟalaaw, mɤŋ law

laaʔ : shoulder
- chabaaj laaʔ : carry on the shoulder

la.ʔɔɔk : thorn (*"female lg."*)
- la.ʔɔɔk gm.tɯl : thorn

lʌh *(also heard as* lah*)* : up; up above; high up
• jɤɤm lʌh : be up above
• pjɯr lʌh : look up into the air

lʌʌp : put somewhere; store; insert
- ʔbuŋ lʌp juuk : basket for rice
- lʌʌp ɟrʌʌk : dip into water (to flush)
- toc ʔjaa lʌʌp druuʔ : take tobacco and put it into a leaf (to make a cigarette)
• lʌʌp gʌh : put it there!
• lʌʌp ti - : put into -
- lʌʌp ti cot : put (something) into one's bag

- lʌp ti trlɔh : put something into the pot
- toc lʌp ti kwɤj : put (something) into the basket
• lʌp tih : put it in here!

lʌʌr : swallow *(V)*
• lʌr brwatbrwat : swallow *(V)*

leh : (1) come; come out; come forward *(considered by some to be "female language")*
- ɟruɯ ʔa leh ʔa pruk : will come tomorrow
- leh ʔbuʔ : come late
• leh muɯr : mucous comes out of the nose *("female lg.")*
• toc leh : take (something) out; bring (something) along
- met toc leh : didn't bring it along
— : (2) (the sun or the moon) rises
• tawɯn leh : east *("female lg.")*
• tawɯn leh : sunrise *("female lg.")*

lemeet *see* ləmeet

leew : scold; abuse
- mɛɛw leew mlaʔ di glɤɤʔ : the Hmong man abuses the Mlabri
- mɛɛw leew ʔoh : the Hmong man abuses me

lə *(cf.* la*) in:*
• lə boh : of that size
• lə jʌk : like this; thus
- ʔɤh ɟak lə jʌk : do like this!
- ɟak lə jʌk mɛh chɯŋ ɲʌʔ : go this way!

ləboh *see* lə

ləbooʔ *(or* lɤbooʔ*)* : (1) *(with a numeral as determiner)* : unspecific Classifier *(+Ferlus)*
• bɛɛr ləbooʔ two items
- chɯrɛɛ bɛɛr ləbooʔ : two shirts
- khɛɛp bɛɛr ləbooʔ : two slippers
• bɛɛr ləboʔ hlooj : three items
- chɔɔʔ bɛɛr ləboʔ hlooj : three dogs
- kaaʔ bɛɛr ləboʔ hlooj : three fish
— : (2) *(with a non-numeral modifier, also as a Noun Classifier:)* person
• ləboʔ gʌh : this person; this one
• ləboʔ ɲʌʔ : that person; that one
- mlaʔ ləboʔ ɲʌʔ : that person; that Mlabri

ləgʌʔ : over there *(?)*

ləgɛʔ *see* lɯgɛʔ

ləjʌk *see* lə

ləm- *see* lm-, lɯm-

ləmbuuŋ : (my) own child
• ʔot ləmbuuŋ : my child
• ʔot ʔɛɛw ləmbuuŋ : my child

ləmeet *(or* lɤmeet, lemeet*)* : of male sex; man
- ləmet chɛʔ mlaaʔ : many men
• ləmeet biʌʌc : young man
• ləmeet ʔa bɤɤn hmaaj : married man
• ɛɛw ləmeet : son
- ʔot ʔɛɛw ləmeet : my son

ləmɯr : soaked; soaking wet

lɤ- *see* lə-

lɛh *(spoken on lowered pitch)* utterance final Question Particle

- mɛh ʔa biʔ lɛh : are you full (with food)?

lɛɛl I = la + ʔɛl ?? *(particle of unidentified meaning)*

lɛɛl II *in:*
- ceet lɛɛl : taste something with the tongue-tip

lɛn : (1) *in:*
- hn.taʔ lɛn : coccyx; caudal vertebrae; the lower tip of the spine

— : (2) *in:*
- glaʔ ʔa lɛn : have finished talking
- glaʔ ʔa lɛn ʔa noɲ ʔa tɯk : no more talking!

lɛŋ *in:*
- gaɲ lɛŋ : early evening (*"female lg."*)
- ʔa gaɲ lɛŋ : the sun has set
- ʔa gaɲ lɛŋ ʔa ɟjʌl : it's already evening
- lɛŋ dooŋ : evening glow (*"female lg."*)
- ʔa lɛŋ dooŋ : sunset

lɛʔ *see* mʌʌʔ

licpɛɛc : muddy
- bɛʔ licpɛɛc : muddy soil

lik.liik *idiolectal variant of* lɯk.liik

liŋeew : the spleen area
- chi liŋeew : have a stitch (in one's side)
- ʔoh hmɯjthɔj ɟur-ɟur, ʔoh chi liŋeew : I ran too heavily, I have a stitch

lɯɯ *(in comparative constructions, apparently marginal in the language)* : than
- chɔɔʔ kwaan lɯɯ mɛɛw : dogs are bigger than cats

lɯgɛʔ : branch; spray (branching from the stem of a plant)
- lɯgɛʔ pleeʔ : branch or spray which bears (a cluster of) fruits

lɯk.liik (*or* likliik) : be burnt (*e.g.* about food or holes in garments); something that has been partly burnt
- lam bɯlbɯl lɯk.liik thɯʔ.thaʔ : the charred stump of a burned tree
- lɯk.liik ʔuulh : firewood that has partly become charcoal

lɯkpaak : body (i.e. what is left when the soul departs at death)

lɯmak : deer (big species)

lɯmbaaʔ : cow; ox

lɯmbʌr *variant pronunciation of* lm.bʌr

lɯmŋɔɔr : insect species (small, with a sting, sits on the leaves of trees)

lɯmpɯt *in:*
- juuk lɯmpɯt : sticky rice

lɯŋ (*or* lɔŋ) : (1) (obtaining something) from (somebody) (*cf.* lɯŋ, nɛŋ)
- mɛh krɔɔ toc lɯŋ ʔoh : you want something from me?
- ʔoh krɔɔ toc chɯrɛɛ lɯŋ mɛh : I request a shirt from you

— : (2) (*cf.* nɛŋ) together with

- jɤɤm lɯŋ mɤm : come and sit with Dad! (said to a little child)

— : (3) *in:*
• lɯŋ ɲʌʔ : over there
- ɟak lɯŋ ɲʌʔ : go over there

lɯɯt *in:*
• ʔa lɯɯt : often; many times (already)
- mɤm pruk ʔa lɯɯt, chak kheet : you ("Father") have come here many times already, he (the little one) is not afraid of you

lm.bah **I** : cabbage
- boŋ juuk gn.rɛɛ lm.bah : I eat rice with cabbage curry
• lm.bah phakaat : cabbage

lm.bah *(also heard as* lm.bʌh*)* **II** : flood

lm.bʌr : (1) leaf
- lm.bʌr kwɤj : banana leaf (can be folded and used as a spoon)
- lm.bʌr lam : leaf (of a tree) *(Ferlus: ləbɔr-)*

— : (2) a leaf-like object (e.g. a piece of paper)
• lm.bʌr keet : ear lobe

— : (3) Classifier for certain fruits, and cups (*cf. Thai "baj"*)
- ʔɛɛw chn.dɛh bɛɛr lm.bʌr hlooj : three small cups

lm.hoor : too big; loose ("female lg.")

loh : (1) search for; look for
- loh tipiaaʔ : what are you looking for?
- loh toc ti nɛj cot : search for and find something in a bag
- loh ʔuulh : look for firewood
• ɟak kot loh kwɛl : walk in a circle
• ɟak loh : go and look for
- ɟak loh ʔuulh : go and look for firewood
• ɟak gwaa loh : be out looking for somebody or something
- ɟak gwaa loh hmaaj : be looking for a suitable wife
- ɟak gwaa loh ʔɛɛw : go look for the child

— : (2) *in various expressions (meaning unclear):*
- ʔee, ʔoh loh ʔa wʌl hlɔɔp : ooh, I'am afraid of hauntings!
- ʔjoc ʔa drɤh ʔa loh bah : the rooster crowed while it was still dark

lok : tuber species (bitter but edible)

loom **I** : love *(V)*
- ʔoh lom di mɤʔ : I love my mother

loom **II** *see* kompoʔ

lom **III** *in:*
• lom hɤr : be clogged

loon : the personal spirit of an individual (which resides in the whole body)
• chuʌk blɛɛŋ chuʌk loon : tie a string around the wrist for protection
• kuuk hmaal loon : oh, my personal spirit! (invoking the spirit in a ritual)
• loon hot : "the spirit falls off"

(causing the person to be ill)
- ʔɤh loon : perform ceremony for personal spirit
- ʔɤh loon ʔɤh hmɯɯl : perform ceremony for personal spirit
- ʔot loon : my personal spirit

lot : car
- ŋɔr lot : road

lo.ʔuh : tear a hole in something; have a hole pierced through
- chat ʔa lo.ʔuh : make a hole in something (e.g. a belt)
- gʌh də lo.ʔuh : see, it has a hole here
- lo.ʔuh ʔa pen hn.tor : it (the fabric) has a hole in it
- taat keet ʔa lo.ʔuh : pierce a hole in the ear lobe

lɔj I *in:*
- lɔj bohboh : be boiling

lɔj II *in:*
- lɔj ʔboh mat : small; a little *(postnominal)*
- boŋ lɔj ʔboh mat : eat a little

lɔj III *see* met

lɔj IV *see* dɯŋ; nʌh

lɔɔj V *(unclear vowellength) in:*
- lɔj ɟrʌʌk : swim *(V)*

lɔɔm : roll as a wrapping (around something)
- toc ʔjaa lʌʌp druuʔ lɔɔm trleet cɔʔ : put tobacco onto a leaf and fold and roll it into a cigarette

lɔŋ *(also cf.* lɯŋ*) :* (1) to; into
- wʌl lɔŋ gɛɛŋ : return to one's house
- lɔŋ briiʔ : into the forest *("male lg.")*
- lɔŋ briʔ lɔŋ tɛɛn : into the deep forest
- lɔŋ luah : into the open forest

— : (2) in the direction of -; over at -
- thʌc blʌk thrɛɛŋ lɔŋ guul : a shred of meat got stuck between my molar teeth
- lɔŋ gʌh : this side; over here; this way
- lɔŋ hna buuk : forwards; straight ahead
- ɟak lɔŋ hna buuk : walk straight ahead
- lɔŋ kl.dɯl *in:*
- tɯltɤl ɟak lɔŋ kl.dɯl : walk backwards
- lɔŋ klɤɤŋ : backwards
- lɔŋ luɤt : out (not at home)
- gʌm ɟak lɔŋ luɤt, chɯkkɔʔ : don't go out or you will get wet!
- ʔa lɔŋ luɤt : be outside
- lɔŋ ɲʌʔ : yonder; over there
- gɛɛŋ lɔŋ ɲʌʔ : the house over there

— : (3) with; on; using (a body part)
- lɔŋ gr.wɛɛn : with the hand
- toc lɔŋ grween thɛh : fetch (something) with one's right hand
- lɔŋ ʔdɯt : on one's back
- toc chɯɯk keeŋ ʔuulh lɔŋ ʔdɯt : take a string for carrying firewood on one's back

— : (4) *in various expressions:*
- lɔŋ br.nah : thunder

- • lɔŋ pr.nah : long ago
- - lɔŋ pr.nah jɤɤm bɔ chuʌk : long ago I lived at Bo Kluea
- • tak lɔŋ pr.nah : long ago
- • ʔɤh lɔŋ khɔɔŋ : sing the Thai way

lɔɔr : crawl (with a sliding motion)
- • lɔɔr ɟak : move like a snail or snake
- - tom.ʔooʔ kwɛl, ʔi mʌc mlaʔ ʔa lɔɔr ɟak : the snake lies rolled up; as it sees the person it crawls away

lɔt *in:*
- • gurtɔr lɔt : the cricoid cartilage; the area just below the Adam's apple

luah : open forest (*cf.* lɔŋ)

luaak *see:* klol

luɤj *see* ʔɛj

luɤt : the outside; the outer part of something (e.g. the outer set of wings of an insect)
- • lɔŋ luɤt : out; outside
- - ʔa lɔŋ luɤt : be away from home; not at home

lugɔɔ *(mostly with vowel shortening) in:*
- • lugɔ mat : close the eyes
- - chi ʔem lugɔ mat : be drowsy
- - lugɔ mat ʔa ʔem : close the eyes and sleep

lugun : middle fingers (excluding thumb and pinkie)
- - ʔat lugun : the index, middle, and ring fingers

luh **I** : scold
- • pa(a) luh : scold; abuse
- • pa(a) luh pa(a) phit : scold; abuse

luh **II** *in:*
- • luh klol : take a deep breath

lumbuk *in:*
- • pleʔ lumbuk : ball

lumpuk *in:*
- • ʔa lumpuk : it (the food) is tender

luun : take (a shirt) off by pulling it over the head

luŋuh : (1) young girl
- - ʔɛɛw ləmeet ɟak pruk luŋuh : my son is dating a girl
— : (2) sprouts on growing bush or creeper
- - luŋuh tuul biʌʌc : fresh sprout

lwɛc *in:*
- • pleʔ kɛɛl lwɛc : cucumber species

lwɛɲ **I** : big fan-shaped leaves used for thatching
- • tʌp ʔat lwɛɲ : thatch a roof

lwɛɲ **II** *in:*
- • pleʔ lwɛɲ : chestnut-like tree with small leaves

m-

mmm *(when spoken in relatively high pitch)* : mmm!; ah!
- - mmm, tɛ thɛ.ʔɛn : mmm! that smells good!

mmm *(when spoken in falling pitch)* : yes

maa : come

mak **I** : (be) fond of
- mak bɔŋ : like to eat; like (a kind of food)
- kibi mak bɔŋ : don't like (to eat)
- met mak bɔŋ : don't like (to eat)
- ʔoh mak bɔŋ thʌc : I like meat

mak **II** *in:*
- mak pat : pearl; round stone for ornamentation *(Ferlus:* 'collier'*)*
- mak pat chɔj : "pearl" of necklace
- mak tʌm : button
- mak tʌm chɯrɛɛ : button in shirt

maak : betel; areca
- pleʔ maak : areca nut
- klɤp maak : betel case

mat **I** : (1) eye *(+Ferlus)*
- chəkmʔ mat : have something in one's eye
- kaliip mat : close the eyes
- khɛj mat : (1) eyeball; (2) bulb in a flashlight
- kr.nil mat : eyebrow
- kul.wʌŋ mat : eyeball
- kwʌŋ mat : the visible, round surface of the eye
- mat met thɛh : have bad eyesight
- naŋ mat : eyelid
- twaj mat : the pupil of the eye
- tuuj mat : the pupil of the eye
- ween mat : glasses; spectacles
- ʔjak mat : matter in the eyes

— : (2) *(in various expressions with transferred meanings:)*
- mat rwaaj : button *(literally:* "tiger's eye"*)*
- mat rwaaj chɯrɛɛ : breast pocket
- mat ʔjoc : malleolus *(literally:* "hen's eye"*)*

— : (3) abscess; core of an abscess on the body

mat **II** *in:*
- ʔboh mat : small

mathuuʔ : creeper with big round leaves

maaʔ (**I**) : (1) give; give as a gift
- maʔ də mlaʔ briiʔ : give to the Mlabri
- maʔ də tɔɔ mlaaʔ : give to the people (*i.e.* the Mlabri)
- mɛh maʔ ʔoh chɯrɛɛ ʔoh ʔa toc : if you give me a shirt I'll certainly accept it

— : (2) *(Postverbal:)* for (a beneficiary); to (an addressee)
- chɯɯ maaʔ : buy (something) for (somebody)
- chɯɯ chɯrɛɛ maʔ ʔoh : buy a shirt and give it to me
- chɯɯ chɯrɛɛ maʔ taŋ mlaaʔ : buy a shirt for somebody else
- dɔɔk maaʔ : keep (something) for (somebody)
- glaʔ maʔ ʔoh : speak to me
- pajok maaʔ : lift (something) for (somebody)
- ʔbɔɔk maaʔ : tell (about something); order (somebody) to (do something)

— : (3) in:
- maʔ ... di : order (somebody) to (do something)
- mɤm maʔ ʔoh di glaʔ : father orders me to speak

maaʔ II *see:* hmaaʔ

mʌc : see; meet; experience; can; remember
- jɤɤm rɤɤʔ ʔoh kɔ mʌc : I saw her when she was a young girl
• met mʌc : did not see; did not notice
• mʌc cɯɯ : know; encounter
- tak lɔŋ pr.nah mʌc cɯɯ : I knew him/her long ago
• mʌc ʔat tiiʔ glaʔ : I remember that they (the old storytellers) said
• met mʌc cɯɯ : hasn't met; doesn't know
- met mʌc cɯɯ toc : I don't know if I can fetch it
- tak hnʌm prɪm met mʌc cɯɯ : I have not seen him/her for many years
- ʔoh met mʌc cɯɯ ɲʌn ki chet : I don't know because I was still a child (when it happened)
• ʔa mʌc cɯɯ : know; remember

mʌʌk : be happy
- mɛh pruk ʔoh ʔa mʌʌk : I'm happy because you have come

mʌʌlh : name; term
- ʔot mɤʔ di mʌʌlh : my mother's name
• chaj mʌʌlh : give a name
- ʔoh chaj ʔɛɛw di mʌʌlh : I give a name to my child
• mɛt mʌʌlh chɯn.ʔdeh : what is your name?
• ʔat mʌʌlh : that's the term for it!; that's what we call it!

mʌʌr : crawl

• mʌʌr cejdej : crawl with the head bent, looking back between the legs

mʌʌʔ : creeper; liane; vine
• pleʔ mʌʔ lɛʔ : species of big nut (circular, chestnut-like)

megrɤɤj *see* met grɤɤj

met : not (*Preverbal, apparently associated with factive or interrogative predication, not with the expression of intention, cf.* chak)
- met toc leh : I have not brought it with me
- tawɪn nɛh ʔoh met ɟrʌʌk : I have not smoken any tobacco today *or:* I have not had anything to drink today
- ʔoh ɟrʌʌk, mɛh met ɟrʌʌk : I'm smoking, won't you smoke? *or:* I'm drinking, won't you drink?
• met bɤɤn : cannot (*Postverbal*)
- glaʔ met bɤɤn : be mute
- leh met bɤɤn : be unable to come
- ʔɤh met bɤɤn : be exhausted
• met biiʔ : not enough (food/beverage) to be full
- bɔŋ met biiʔ : still feeling hungry after eating
- ɟrʌʌk met biiʔ : still feeling thirsty after drinking
• met chɛʔ : not much; (only) a little
- ɟrʌʌk met chɛʔ : drink a little
- mlaʔ met chɛʔ : a few people
• met chi bɤɤn : don't want; prefer to be without
- met chi bɤɤn glaŋ : I don't want

any husband
- met gɤɤj : not so far; never before *(Preverbal)*
- met gɤj ɟrʌk ɟn.raaʔ : has never tried to drink liquor
- met grɯɯj *(often contracted to* megrɯɯj*)* not yet *(Preverbal)*
- mɤm met grɯɯj bɔŋ : father has not eaten yet
- met gɤj ɟr.wɯɯl : we have not yet boiled it
- met gɤj laac, ɟruɯ (tɛ) ʔa laac : it is not yet finished, (but) it will be finished tomorrow
- met gɤj thɛh : has not yet recovered
- met gɤj bɯl : be alive
- mlaʔ met gɤj bɯl : a living person
- met hr.liiŋ : I have not forgotten
- met jɤɤm : is not at home; is not there any longer
- met ɟɪn : do not know how to; am no good at -
- met ɟruʔ : shallow
- met lɔj : not (at all) *(Preverbal)*
- met lɔj bɤɤn : cannot at all; does not master it at all (*e.g.* a language)
- met lɔj bɔŋ thɛh bɔŋ mɤk : be without proper food all the time
- met lɔj toc leh : did not bring it along
- met lɔj gɤj : not yet *(Preverbal)*
- met mʌc : hasn't met; has not seen
- met mʌc cɯɯ : doesn't know
- met mʌc cɯɯ toc : I don't know if I can get it
- met mɤk : not suitable (e.g. as human food)
- met ɲaŋ : there is/are none
- met ɲaŋ ɟi.ʔdɤɤ ba.thuul, bɔŋ dɔj juuk chɯ.chɯɯ : we have nothing but rice to eat
- met ŋaam : not pretty; ugly
- met plɛɛn *see* plɛɛn
- met pruk : hasn't come here
- met thɛh : (1) *(as Main Verb Phrase)* be bad; be of bad quality
- mat met thɛh : have poor eyesight
- met thɛh klol : be unkind
- met thɛh : (2) *(as Main Verb Phrase)* feel unwell
- met thɛh jɤɤm : be ill
- ʔoh met thɛh, pluŋ chak : I feel miserable, I have a chestburn
- met thɛh klol : feel sad; mourn
- met thɛh : (3) *(Preverbal)* be unfit for, be un-
- met thɛh bɔŋ : be inedible
- met ʔɛl : not yet *(Preverbal)*
- chiiŋ met ʔɛl bɯl : the pig is not dead yet
- mɤm met ʔɛl leh : father has not come yet

məɲiŋ *see* miɲiŋ

mɤɤj *in:*
- mɛʔ mɤɤj : the rain is pouring down
- ɟak nɛŋ mɛʔ nɛŋ mɤɤj : ramble in rain and bad weather

mɤk : suitable; good
- bɔŋ thɛh bɔŋ mɤk : eat good food
- kibi bɔŋ thɛh bɔŋ mɤk : has no proper food to eat
- di thɛh di mɤk : in order to be-

come healthy
- klol thɛh klol mɤk : good-hearted
- met mɤk : not suitable (e.g. as human food)

mɤm : father *(the normal term; also as a respectful term) (+Ferlus)*
- mɤm thaw : father-in-law

mɤn *in:*
- gʌm mɤn ɟak : don't go yet!
- gʌm mɤn ɟak, jɤɤm hɛh : don't go yet, wait a moment!
- gʌm mɤn ɟak dɛɛn ʔdɤɤ : don't go anywhere yet!

mɤŋ *in:*
- mɤŋ law : Laos
- mɤŋ thɛj : Thailand

mɤʔ : mother *(+Ferlus)*
- mɛt mɤʔ mɛt mɤm : your parents
- mɤʔ chet : mother who is/was the father's second wife
- mɤʔ hmɛʔ : stepmother
- mɤʔ mɤm : Mother and Father (e.g. as address term)
- mɤʔ thaw : mother-in-law
- mɤʔ ʔdiŋ : mother who is/was the father's first wife

mɛ **I** *in:*
- grɯɯŋ mɛ cɤh : new things ("female lg.")
- chi bɤɤn grɯɯŋ tɛɛ mɛ cɤh : I would like to have some new things!

mɛɛ **II** : title of senior woman; Mrs.
- mɛɛ choo : woman who has recently given birth to a baby

mɛh : you (singular, non-honorific)
- ʔmɛh ʔoh bɛɛr mlaaʔ : the two of us (inclusive)

mɛj *in:*
- mɛj muut *(see* mɛjmuut*)*
- mɛj ʔboŋ : bamboo species

mɛjmuut : torch (used when collecting honey)

mɛɛm : blood
- pruk mɛɛm : there is blood coming out

mɛɛn : (1) be correct
- chak mɛɛn : that's not correct; you cannot say that (in Mlabri)
- ki mɛɛn : that's also correct *(in α-Mlabri it means the opposite!)*
- ʔa mɛɛn : that's correct; yes

— : (2) be usable
- ki mɛɛn
- gʌh ki mɛɛn, gʌh ki mɛɛn you can use this one or that one

mɛt : (1) your *(cf.* mɛh*)*
- mɛt ʔɛɛw : your child(ren)

— : (2) something on you
- mɛt cheʔ ɲaŋ : you have got lice

mɛɛw **I** : cheek; the hind corners of the lower jaw

mɛɛw **II** : Hmong

mɛɛw **III** : cat

mɛɛʔ : (1) rain
- bla(a)j guul mɛɛʔ : cloudburst
- ɟak nɛŋ mɛʔ nɛŋ mɤɤj : ramble in rain and bad weather
- mɛʔ bla(a)j riiŋ : it rains in large

amounts
- mɛʔ hmitbeec : it rains all day
- mɛʔ hot : it rains (+Ferlus)
- mɛʔ ɟuʌt : it rains in single drops; water is dripping down
- mɛʔ mɤɤj : the rain is pouring down
- mɛʔ prim see prim
- mɛʔ pruɲ.pruuɲ : it rains a little
- mɛʔ ʔa hɲ.ɟʌt : it has stopped raining
— (2) rainwater (collected above the ground for domestic use)
- mlaʔ ɟrʌʌk mɛɛʔ : the Mlabri (i.e. our household) drink rainwater

miʌŋ see hmiʌŋ

micmɛɛc : ant (small black species)

min in:
- chal.ʔbuut bia min : it (the meat) stinks of maggots

miɲiŋ (or məɲiŋ) : woman; female ("modern word", "male lg.")
- miɲiŋ ʔa bɤɤn laŋ : married woman
- ʔɛɛw miɲiŋ : daughter

miit : pointed knife; dagger

mi.thɔj see hmujthɔj

mɯɯ : return (verb used in ritual language)
- di wʌl di mɯɯ : return back (to me)! (invoking a spirit)
- kuuk hmal mɯɯ : return, oh Spirit!
- ʔa mɯɯ : has returned

mɯj : fat (N); grease; oil
- ʔat mɯj chaj takiʌŋ : fill (the) oil on the lamp
- ʔat mɯj chaj ti thoŋgot : fill (the) oil into a cup

mɯlh : woman; female ("old word"; "female lg.")
- rooj mɯlh : little sister

mɯɯr : mucous
- leh mɯɯr : mucous comes out of the nose ("female lg.")
- mɯɯr tɯn mɔh : the nose is clogged
- mɯɯr ʔjak mɔh : mucous (from the nose)
- pruk mɯɯr : mucous comes out of the nose ("male lg.")

mɯw see pleeʔ

mlaaʔ : (1) human being; person; Mlabri (+Ferlus)
- mlaʔ jɤɤm chɛʔ : there are many people
- mlaʔ bɯl : corpse
- mlaʔ briiʔ : Mlabri
- mlaʔ di chak : a person's body
- mlaʔ dok mlaʔ jen : very poor people
- mlaʔ grɤŋ : ordinary people
- mlaʔ kr.najh : ordinary people
- taaŋ mlaaʔ : another person

— : (2) the Mlabri
- ʔat tiʔ ɲajh mlaaʔ : they don't like the Mlabri

— : (3) (with a quantifier:) Classifier for humans
- miɲiŋ bɛɛr mlaaʔ : two women ("male lg.")
- mɯlh bɛɛr mlaaʔ : two women ("female lg.")

- gwaj mlaaʔ : the whole group together

mool *see* thʌc

moblɤp *see* moʔ blɤp

morthor *see* borthor

mot : ant (big species)
- mot tɛj mlaaʔ : there is an ant crawling on one's skin
- mot rɯm.ram : small ant species (which irritates the skin)

moʔ *in:*
- moʔ blɤp *(or* moblɤp*)* shiver; shake
- moblɤp dəkat : shiver with cold

mɔ *(proclitic form)* : (1) one (time unit)
- mɔ hnʌm : one year; next year
- mɔ hnʌm (tak) bɯn nah : last year
- mɔ kiiʔ : one month; in a month
- mɔ nɯk : eight days from now (*cf.* mɔ tɯk)
- mɔ nɯŋ : seven days from now
- mɔ tawɯn : one day; in a day; per day
- mɔ tawɯn bɛɛr pɛʔ pon boŋ mɔ tuptoop : I eat one package (of medicine) in one-two-three-four days
- mɔ thɯɯ : once
- mɔ tɯk : eight days from now (*cf.* mɔ nɯk)
- mɔ tɯŋ : six days from now

— : (2) *(with* hak *or* tɛɛ*) in linked, disjunctive propositions:* one (set) each
- ba thɔɔŋ tɛɛ mɔ mɤʔ mɔ mɤm, ba kham tɛɛ mɔ mɤʔ mɔ mɤm : Ba Thong had one set of parents, Ba Kham had another set of parents

— : (3) *in:*
- mɔ teet : a little *(considered by one informant to be Lua')*

mɔɔ : doctor

mɔh : (1) nose (+*Ferlus*)
- ʔjak mɔh : dry mucous in the nose

— : (2) something protruding; something resembling a nose, e.g. the blunt end of a jungle knife or the front strap of a sandal

mɔj : one; some
- mɔj thɛh mɔj met thɛh : some (people) are good, some not good

mɔɔj : beard on the spikes or ears of plants

muu *in:*
- pleʔ muu : water melon

muuj *in:*
- kwɛk muuj : axe for chopping firewood

mujmuj : body hair (*"male lg."*)
- mujmuj glɤɤʔ : hair on one's head
- mujmuj kampoŋ : hair on one's head
- mujmuj kukɔɔʔ : beard on one's neck
- mujmuj mat : eyelashes
- mujmuj thrɛɛŋ : beard (moustache, pointed beard, goatee)
- mujmuj wɤɤŋ : beard (whiskers)

- mujmuj ʔdoŋ : (1) pubic hair of male
- mujmuj ʔdoŋ : (2) beard on the spikes or ears of plants
— : (3) *(as modifier:)* hairy
- chooŋ mujmuj : trousers of terry cloth

muuk : smell with one's nose
- muuk bakkah cho.ʔuum : smell a flower, which smells good

muk : four days from now

muɲ-mɔɲ : move the lips as when suppressing a smile
- muɲmɔɲ hr.lɛʔ : smile (and laugh)

muŋmooŋ : gong (Hmong style)
- tɛk muŋmooŋ : beat a gong

muːt : mosquito (small species)

n-

nah *see* tak

naaj *in:*
- caaw naaj : officials
- mlaʔ kun naaj our forefathers

nak *(Preverbal, intensifying:)*
- ʔac ʔa nak pɤr ɟak tawɪn ʔa taŋ : the bird flies high up in the sky
- nak bliiŋ : be alive

naŋ : (1) skin; outer layer of bark
- naŋ mat : eyelid
- ʔat naŋ mat pok ʔat kwʌŋ : the eyelid hangs down over the eye

— : (2) *in:*
- naŋ ʔdiiŋ : blue sky
- ʔɛɛ naŋ ʔdiiŋ ʔa gaɲ : look!, the sky is blue and the sun is shining

nɛŋ : (1) together with; in company with *(cf.* nɯŋ*)*
- boɲ nɛŋ -
- boɲ nɛŋ ʔat ʔuuj : eat together with the women (e.g. referring to babies)
- ʔoh boɲ juuk nɛŋ mɤm : I eat together with you ("Father")
- jɤɤm nɛŋ - : stay with -
- wʌl jɤɤm nɛŋ ʔoh : come back and stay with me! *(invoking a spirit)*
- ʔoh jɤɤm nɛŋ ʔɛɛw : I stay with my child

— : (2) and; plus
- mɔ bjaalh nɛŋ mɔ pirpiip laaʔ : one fathom and one yard (of length)

— : (3) combined with
- boɲ juuk nɛŋ tipiaaʔ : what are you eating with your rice?
- kibi ɲaŋ ɟi.ʔdɤɤ boɲ nɛŋ juuk : we have nothing to eat with the rice

— : (4) in (weather); exposed to (weather)
- ɟak nɛŋ mɛʔ nɛŋ mɤɤj : ramble in rain and bad weather

— : (5) (obtaining something) from (somebody) *(cf.* lɯŋ, ni*)*
- ʔoh krɔɔ nɛŋ mɛh : I request it from you
- nɛŋ hmuu : all; group of people

(see hmuu)

nɛɛ : yesterday *(also cf.* tak) *(+Ferlus)*
• buɯn nɔʔ nɛɛ : the day before yesterday

nɛh : here (just where the speaker is); this
• jɤɤm nɛh : sit here; stay with us
- jɤɤm nɛh, jɤɤm nɛh : come and sit here!
• tawɯn nɛh : today
- tawɯn nɛh mɛh jɤɤm nɛh : you stay with us today
• ti nɛh : in here
• ʔah ɟum nɛh : we who are here (versus the rest of the group)

nɛj I *in:*
• ti nɛj : inside
• ʔat ti nɛj : the inside; what is inside

nɛj II : monkey species (?, cf. kraalh)

ni I : (1) in; at; with; *(with verbs of "searching":)* from
- cok toc ni dɛj chɯrɛɛ : take something from the breast pocket
- ʔem ni gɛɛŋ : sleep at home
• ni ʔat prɯŋ : inside (it)
— : (2) *in:*
• jɤɤm ni : stay with; be a member of the same household as
- jɤɤm ni ʔat ɟjooŋ : stay with one's father (not having a spouse)
— : (3) (obtaining something) from (somebody) (cf. lɯŋ, nɛŋ)
- toc ni kwʌr : obtain it from outsiders (i. e. non-Mlabri people)

nii II : this; then *(used in narratives)*

nikniit : walk with a bent back (as when carrying a heavy load)
- keeŋ ɟak bɔ nikniit : carry something with a bent back
- nikniit ʔi ɟuɯm : walk with bent back because the load is heavy

niiʔ : move *(V)* (move to another place) *cf.:* paniiʔ
ʔa niiʔ ɟak jɤɤm lɔŋ luah : has gone to stay in the forest

nɯk *in:*
• mɔ nɯk : eight days from now *(cf.* mɔ tɯk)

nɯŋ I : together with; in company with *(cf.* nɛŋ)
- jɤɤm nɯŋ kwʌr : stay together with villagers
- mɛh ɟak nɯŋ ʔoh : you go with me
• chɛw nɯŋ : wait for
- chɛw nɯŋ ʔoh : wait for me!

nɯŋ II *in:*
• mɔ nɯŋ : seven days from now

nɯɯʔ *see* thaŋ

nomɔ : just a -; a single - *(used by one male speaker, discarded by another who insists on* dəmɔ *instead)*
• nomɔ teet : a little
• nomɔ thɯɯ : once
- ʔoh boŋ nomɔ thɯɯ, ʔoh chak boŋ : I have already eaten

once so I won't eat any more (today)

noɲ : (1) *(with perfective particle)* is gone; has run out; there is nothing left; is no good any more
- ʔa noɲ ʔi bɯl : they are all gone, for they have died
- ʔa noɲ ʔi tac : they (clothes, shoes) were broken and have been scrapped
- ʔat lmbah ʔa noɲ : there is no more cabbage
- ʔjoc noɲ ni gɛɛŋ : there are no chickens (left) in this household
- ʔoh ʔot juuk ʔa noɲ : I have no more rice
- ʔot thrɛɛŋ kɔ ʔa noɲ : I have no teeth left, you see
- ʔot ʔɛɛw ləmeet ʔa noɲ : I have no son any more; my son died
• ʔa noɲ ɟak : it (e.g. the tape on a recorder) has run out

— : (2) *(Postverbal with perfective particle, conveying the meaning of termination of action:)* no more; it is over with
- glaʔ ʔa noɲ : talking is over
- glaʔ ʔa lɛn ʔa noɲ ʔa tɯk : no more talking!
- mɛʔ hot ʔa noɲ : it does not rain any more
- ʔa glaʔ noɲ : we have ended our conversation

— : (3) *(Postverbal with preceding connective:)* all; altogether
• di noɲ : so as to make it complete; so as to include all of it *(purposive)*
• ʔbɔɔk maʔ di noɲ : tell everything; give an exhaustive account
• ʔa noɲ : including all of it *(often perfective)*
- choʔ ʔa noɲ : it hurts all over (my body)
- ʔbɔɔk maʔ ʔa noɲ : have told everything; have given an exhaustive account
• ʔa noɲ nɛŋ hmuu : everybody
- di pruk ʔa noɲ nɛŋ hmuu : come, all of you!
• ʔi noɲ : all of it *(resultative)*
- palʏp ɟuur ʔi noɲ : cram it all "down" (into the bag)

— : (4) no!

— : (5) *Negative Adverbial used to express the second of two disjunctive alternatives:*
• chala noɲ : or not
- choop ni ba chak ʔi tɔp toc glaŋ chala noɲ : ask Ba Chak if I Top has married or not

nɔɔm : urinate *(+Ferlus)*
- hmitgoc nɔɔm mat : the "hmitgoc" (an insect) "pisses" into peoples' eyes

nɔɔʔ : grandchild; nephew

nɔʔ *in:*
• bɯn nɔʔ nɛɛ : the day before yesterday

nuu *in:*
• nuu ʔem : drop off to sleep

nuur : the back of a knife

ɲ-

ɲajh : resent; detest
- ʔat tiʔ ɲajh mlaaʔ : they don't like the Mlabri

ɲaam : (1) time; era
• ɲaam gʌh : now; of our time
- ʔi nɔɔt ki ɟak, ʔi lii ki ɟak ɲaam gʌh : Nort and Li both went out for a while
- dɔ mlaʔ ɲaam gʌh met mʌc cɯɯ : people nowadays have not seem them (i.e. mythological giant ants)
• tak ɲaam gʌh : at that time; that was long ago (?)
• ʔa ɲaam gʌh : now; for the time being

— : (2) season of the year
• ɲaam bɔ.ʔɔɔŋ : the hot and dry season
• ɲaam dəm.hnat : the cold season
• ɲaam glʌŋ : the cold season
• ɲaam juuk hn.doom : the season of rice harvesting

ɲaŋ : (1) *(with object, mostly about permanent possession or attributes, cf. pɤɤʔ)* have; possess
- bɛɛ ɲaŋ ʔat kʌw : goats have horns
- ɲaŋ khɔt : have spears (as part of outfit)
- mɤʔ ɲaŋ rɤɤm chet : Mother has yet another baby
- ruʌŋ ɲaŋ wɔk : there is a spirit living in the stream; there is a water spirit
• kibi ɲaŋ : not have any; lack
- jɤɤm kibi ɲaŋ ʔɛɛw : have no children
- kibi ɲaŋ gɛɛŋ jɤɤm : we have no house to live in
- kibi ɲaŋ ʔat prɛʔ : there are no spices in it (the food)
• met ɲaŋ : not have any; lack
- ʔoh met ɲaŋ gɯncaj, nɔɲ : I have no blanket

— : (2) *(existential predicate, cf. pɤɤʔ)* exist; there is/are
- mɛt cheʔ ɲaŋ : you have lice
• met ɲaŋ : there are none
• ɲaŋ ɲi ... : live in ...
• ʔa dɔ ɲaŋ - : there is/are - everywhere
- jɤɤm lɔŋ briiʔ ʔa dɔ ɲaŋ ʔaŋ praŋ : in the forest you see the "ang prang"-bamboo everywhere

ɲʌn *(or* ɲɔn*)* : because *(Phrase Connective)*
- jɤɤm ɲʌn kibi thɛh : be at home not feeling well
- ɟram ɲʌn glɤh chəboh : exhausted from climbing the mountain
- krʌw biɯk ɲʌn krɛc : fear the bear because it bites
- peelh gɛɛŋ ɲʌn rɤʔ : sweep the floor because it is dusty
- ɲʌn ruʌŋ reew kheet hr.looj : because there are heavy floods, we are afraid of being carried off
- tɛk chɔʔ ɲʌn proh : beat the dog because it barks
- ʔoh met mʌc cɯɯ ɲʌn ki chet : I don't know because I was still a child (when it hap-

pened)

ɲʌʔ *(or* ɲɔʔ*)* : that one; there
- ləboʔ ɲʌʔ : that person
- ɟak toc kr.waac ɲʌʔ kwac gɛɛŋ : take that broom and sweep the floor!
• chɯɯŋ ɲʌʔ : like this
• ɟʌk ... chɯɯŋ ɲʌʔ : it is like this it should be done
- ɟak lə ɟʌk mɛh chɯɯŋ ɲʌʔ : go this way!
• ɟak gʌh ɟak ɲʌʔ : to stray
• lɯŋ/lɔŋ ɲʌʔ : over there; yonder; to that side
- gɛɛŋ lɔŋ ɲʌʔ : the house over there
- ɟak lɯŋ ɲʌʔ : go over there
• tipiaʔ ɲʌʔ : why; why that? *(literally:* what's that there?*)*

ɲi : in
- ɲaŋ ɲi ... : live in ...

ɲoɲ-ɲeɲ *(or* ɲəɲ.ɲeɲ*)* wash clothes by rubbing cloth against cloth
• chapat ɲoɲ-ɲeɲ : wash (clothes) by rubbing

ɲɔn, ɲɔʔ *see* ɲʌn, ɲʌʔ

ɲuul *see* tɯp

ɲun : Northern Thai people; Khon Mueang

ŋ-

ŋaa : tusk
- ŋaa pompoo : elephant's tusk

ŋaj : boar

ŋam I : listen (*"male lg."*)
- ŋam ʔat tiʔ glaʔ : listen to him/her
- ʔoh ʔa ŋam : I am listening

ŋaam II : beautiful; good; that's nice!
- met ŋaam : not pretty

ŋaʔ : itch *(V);* itching feeling *(N)*
- gehgeh ʔot ŋaʔ : I scratch myself, because it itches
- grl.griil ŋaʔ : scratch oneself, because it itches
- ŋaʔ cheeʔ : it itches because of lice
- ʔat thm.bʌc ŋaʔ : the hairs on the stalk cause my skin to itch
- ʔɛɛw beec biaʔ ŋaʔ : the child cries, because it itches
- ʔɛɛw beec ɟʌw ŋaʔ : the child cries, because it itches
- ʔjen ŋaʔ : the veins are itching

ŋɔɔk *in:*
• ʔjak ŋɔɔk : the inedible intestines of a crab

ŋɔk-ŋaak (*"female lg."*) *in:*
• ŋɔkŋaak ʔdɯt : spinal chord

ŋɔɔm : (1) be lonely; feel lonely
- ɟʏʏm dəmɔj ʔoh ŋɔɔm : living alone I feel lonely

— : (2) miss somebody *(apparently sic)*
- ŋɔɔm hmaj : miss one's wife
- ʔoh ŋɔɔm mʏʔ mʏm : I miss my parents

ŋɔɔr *(uncertain vowel length)* : (1) way; path; trail *(possibly the same word as Ferlus's* ŋɔk, *similar meaning)*

- ɟak ŋɔɔr wiŋkɛl : go straight on in a horizontal direction
- ŋɔr hlɛŋ : the path is slippery; a slippery path
- ŋɔr thɛh : a passable trail; a path
- pruk ŋɔr wec : I have come a long way
- ʔoh met mʌc ŋɔr ʔa guɯn pruk : I don't know the way back
• ŋɔr gliŋ : highway; road
• ŋɔr lot : road ("car way")
— : (2) *in:*
• dəmɔ ŋɔɔr : in the same way; sounds alike; means the same thing
- gʌh ki ʔjen, ɟrʌʌk ki ʔjen, dəmɔ ŋɔɔr : this *(pointing at a vein)* is called "ʔjen", water is likewise "ʔjen" *(i.e. cold)*, it sounds the same
- ʔat chak ɟak ginɛŋ, mlaaʔ ɟak ginɛŋ, dəmɔ ŋɔɔr : "where did he go?" or "where did the person go?", that means the same thing

ŋuuk-ŋɯɯk *(cf.* ŋɔkŋɯɯk*)* *("male lg.")* : spinal chord
• ŋukŋɯɯk ʔdɯt : spinal chord

ŋwɛʔ *(cf.* ʔwɛʔ*)* : one's own child *(mostly with* ʔot, mɛt*)*
• mɛt ʔɛɛw mɛt ŋwɛʔ : your child
- mɛt ʔɛɛw mɛt ŋwɛʔ ɟak ginɛŋ : where did your child go?
• ʔot ʔɛɛw ʔot ŋwɛʔ : my child

p-

pa- *Causative Marker (cf.* ba-*), see entries beginning in* pa-

paa *(sic?, mostly proclitic* [pa-] *like* pa- *above, also cf.* paaʔ*)* : do something with swift movements *(?)*
• pa(a) blah *(cf.* pablah*)* : move in different directions
• pa(a) kʌlh : hit and inadvertently break
• pa(a) luh : scold in a loud voice
• pa(a) luh pa(a) phit : scold in a loud voice
- mɛɛw pa luh pa phit glaʔ mlaʔ di glɤɤʔ : the Hmong abuses the Mlabri
• pa(a) pruk rt.lat : stick one's tongue-tip out *("male lg.")*
• pa(a) tɯk.lʌk : tickle with moving hands

pabɯl : kill; slaughter *(V)*

pablah *(also cf.* paa*)*: push *(V)*

pablʌk : put (something) inside (something)
- pablʌk ni ʔat prɯŋ : put it inside

pabooʔ : nurse *(cf.* booʔ*)*
- paboʔ ʔɛɛw : nurse a child
- toc ʔɛɛw pabooʔ : take a child in one's arms and nurse it

padruuʔ : belch *(V)*

pagrɛɛt *(rather* pa(a) grɛɛtʔ, *cf.* grɛɛt*)*: decoy by scratching
- pagrɛɛt chat hwɤk : scratch to decoy a rat and stab it

paaj I : thread; string; the wick of a candle
- toc paaj cuʌk blɛɛŋ : bind a string around the wrist (for protection)

paaj II : the day after tomor-

row; two time spans from now
- ɟruɯ paaj : in a couple of days
- mɔ hnʌm ɟruɯ paaj : the next few years

pajɤʔ : wake (somebody) up
- pajɤʔ di hmaaj : wake one's wife up
- ʔoh pajɤʔ ʔɛɛw : I wake the children!

pajok : lift; raise
- pajok glɤh : lift; lift up
• pajok ɟrʌʌk : lift it and drink!
• pajok lat : (the cat) lifts its paw and licks itself

pak I : Classifier for crops
- chaloo bɛɛr pak hlooj : three corncobs

pak II : penetrate; prick (the way a thorn does)

pak III : cut; clear an area by cutting
• glɛj pak : cut and carve something
- glɛj pak krareel : cut and carve a board into shape
• pak chuʌn : cut down weeds and shrub in the orchard (*"male lg."*)
- ʔa pak chuʌn : have removed the weeds in the orchard

pak IV *in:*
• hmɯl pak : hang the washing up (on a string or a pole)

pakʌlh *see* paa

palɤp : cram something (into a container, e.g. a bag)
- palɤp ɟuur ʔi noɲ : cram it all

"down" (into the bag)

paluh *see* paa

paan : time
• dɔ paan gʌh : just now
• paan gʌh : now
- paan gʌh ʔoh wʌl jɤɤm nɛh : now I am going to stay here!
• pan gʌh pan gʌh : let me see...
• pan ʔdɤɤ : when
- mɛh pruk pan ʔdɤɤ : when are you coming?

panɛŋ *in:*
• chɯɯk panɛŋ : a suspended string

paniiʔ *(cf.* niiʔ*) in:*
• paniʔ ɟak : chase; drive
- mlaʔ paniʔ ɟak chiiŋ : the man drives the pig forwards

paŋ *in:*
• puum paŋ : rainbow
• wɔk paŋ : the spirit "Wok Pang" (associated with rainbow)
• wɔk paŋ chɛɛ *(same meaning as* wɔk paŋ*)*

pap : plant species with edible fruits
• pleʔ pap : *id.;* the fruits of pap

paraat : be wounded; have an incision

parɛɛl : lightning
- kɯr rəmɯt parɛɛl : tempest

paruuʔ : smoke (V)
- paruʔ dɔɔk thʌc : hang meat up to be smoked

pa.rwaʔ : invite
- ʔoh pa.rwaʔ mɛh boŋ juuk : I'm inviting you to a meal

pat *see* mak

paat : cut with a knife
- toc tɔʔ paat cɪmbeelh : remove a thorn from the skin with a knife

patɯk.lʌk *see* paa

paaʔ *(sic?, cf.* paa*) in:*
• paa(ʔ) ʔbom : (for the hen to) move its body so as to cover the eggs
- jɔc ʔi wʌl kot paa(ʔ) ʔbom ʔat khɛj : the hen comes to hatch and moves its body to cover the eggs

pa.ʔem : make (somebody) sleep
• pa.ʔem dɔɔk : put (somebody) to rest

pa.ʔɯm *(or* pa(a) ʔɯm?*)* : bathe (somebody)
- pa.ʔɯm rʉʌŋ : bathe it (the child) in the creek
- pa.ʔɯm ʔi choo : bathe the little baby

pʌk : be on a hilltop

pʌp : break
- biip pʌp : squeeze it (a "pap" fruit) so that it breaks (in order to eat what is inside)

pʌr : fly *(V)*
- ʔjec pʌr : the bee is flying

peec : wasp

peelh : sweep with a broom or the like *("male lg.")*
- ɟak toc pr.neelh peelh : sweep with a broom
- peelh rɤʔ : sweep dust away (with a broom)

• peelh gɛɛŋ : sweep the floor
- peelh gɛɛŋ ɲʌn rɤʔ : sweep the floor because it is full of dust
- peelh gɛɛŋ rɤʔ : sweep the floor free of dust

peelh-peelh *(cf.* pilh.peelh*)* : sweep
- rɯh-rɯh peelh-peelh ɟak : clear the ground thoroughly

pen : (1) that's; it's called
- gʌh ʔat chimbeelh tat keet pen hn.tor : this: that the ear is pinched with a thorn, is called a hole

— : (2) to be in a certain condition; to have a certain status
- gɯh-gɯh-gɯh, pen blaaj gr.nɯh : there are increasingly big flames
- lo.ʔuh ʔa pen hn.tor : it (the fabric) has a hole in it

pen.deeʔ *in:*
• toc tiiʔ pen.deeʔ : point with a finger

peɲ *in:*
- mɛh peɲ chɪn.ʔdeh : what are you doing with the gun?; is that a way to aim!
• peɲ piaʔ ʔdɤɤ : hunt *(V)*

petpet *(used by one speaker, unknown to another) in:*
- tac petpet : have a scar such that some skin or tissue is protruding or hanging loose

pɤjh : cut; cut off; cut into size
- ɟak pɤjh thoom : go out to cut some "thoom"
- kum pɤjh : (1) hold something

while cutting it into shape; (2) grasp something (e.g. stalks of weeds) and cut it off
- pɤjh chuʌn : cut down weeds or shrub in the orchard ("female lg.")

pɤɤl : crossbow (+Ferlus)

pɤɤŋ : tilt; be oblique

pɤɤr : lightning ("female lg.")

pɤɤʔ : (1) (existential predicate, cf. ɲaŋ) there is some of it
- mlaʔ pɤɤʔ : there are (Mlabri) people
- ʔot juuk pɤɤʔ : I have some rice
— : (2) (with object) have; possess
- ʔoh pɤɤʔ juuk : I have some rice (meaning diff. from ʔot juuk pɤɤʔ above?)
• pɤʔ ʔat ʔɛɛw : (1) have children
- met pɤʔ ʔat ʔɛɛw : she has no children
• pɤʔ ʔat ʔɛɛw : (2) be pregnant
• pɤʔ ʔɛɛw : id.

pɛʔ : three

piaaʔ (perhaps varying with pjaaʔ) : something edible; good food
• chi piaaʔ : want something nice to eat
- chi piaaʔ ʔa noɲ : there is no good food left
- chi piaaʔ thʌc boŋ ʔa noɲ : I would like some meat but there is none left
• piaʔ ʔdɤɤ : edible animals
- thʌc piaʔ ʔdɤɤ : meat
• piaʔ ʔdiŋ : game; big animal

piʌk : light (not heavy) ("male lg.")

piʌkpiʌw : light (not heavy) ("male lg.")

pijh in:
• bɛʔ pijh : the universe collapsed (mythological event)
• pijh bahaaʔ : (there is a) landslide

pilh.peelh (cf. peelh-peelh) wipe
- pilh.peelh kɯm : wipe something away

pin (sic, with a short vowel in Mlabri) : let something spin

pirpiip (or pr.piip) : the span of an outstretched arm; a yard
- mɔ bjaalh nɛŋ mɔ pirpiip laaʔ : one fathom and one yard (of length)

piiʔ : rice grain; husked rice
- piʔ bɛɛr kwʌn : two grains of rice

pɯh : rise; stand up; wake up (in the morning)
- pɯh jɤɤm : be up (i.e. not asleep)
- pɯh tawɯn ʔa kɛɛ : stand up, the sun is high in the sky!
- ʔoh chak ʔem, ʔoh pɯh jɤɤm : I am not asleep, I am up already!

pɯɯn I : Classifier for clothes
- chɯrɛɛ bɛɛr pɯɯn : shirt and blouse

pɯɯn II in:
• bla(a)j pɯɯn : tall; high

pɯŋcɛɛr : have almost closed eyes

pɯr- *see* pr-

pjaŋ : open; unfold
- pjaŋ hm.pooj : arrange the mosquito net for the night
- pjaŋ kraŋ : unfold and dry (the laundry) in the air
- pjaŋ kraŋ gaɲ : unfold and dry (the laundry) in the sunshine
- pjaŋ kraŋ ʔi di chrɔɔɲ : unfold and expose (the laundry) to air in order for it to dry

pjaaʔ *see* piaaʔ

pjee : monitor (edible lizard)

pjɯppjaap : twitter
- ʔjoc pjɯppjaap : the bird twitters

pjɯɯr : open one's eyes widely
- pjɯɯr pjɯɯr dɤŋ ʔoh : he is staring at me
- pjɯr lʌh : look up into the air

pjɯr.pjɯɯr : be staring incessantly

pjooŋ *in:*
- pleʔ pjooŋ : bitter, nut-like fruit species (mak khom)

pjɔɔlh : stretch oneself (by lifting one's arms)

plʌk : hiccough

plʌlh : play (the guitar) with the nails; strum

plʌm : wax that has been melted and cast in a bamboo tube

pleeʔ : (1) fruit; gourd-type vegetable; nut; seed
- pleʔ booʔ : papaya
- pleʔ braaw : coconut
- pleʔ cʌr : sweet, edible fruit species (resembling lychee)
- ple chaŋ : bitter, nut-like fruit species
- pleʔ chat : orange (fruit)
- pleʔ chreelh : mango
- pleʔ gm.nat : pineapple
- pleʔ hlak.hlek : melon-like gourd species
- pleʔ huŋ : papaya
- pleʔ ɟraam : bean species
- pleʔ kɛɛl : cucumber
- pleʔ kɛɛl lwɛc : cucumber species
- pleʔ kiʌɲ : cherry-like edible fruit
- pleʔ kin.ʔdeep : wild gourd species (green with lengthwise white stripes) = pleʔ tr.loŋ poŋ
- pleʔ klɔk : chestnut-like tree with big leaves (+*Ferlus*)
- pleʔ kulrul : fruit species
- pleʔ lak : sweet gourd species (the inside of which is of orange colour)
- pleʔ lam : fruit (+*Ferlus*)
- pleʔ lwɛɲ : chestnut-like tree with small leaves (+*Ferlus*)
- pleʔ maak : areca nut
- pleʔ mathuuʔ : (inedible) fruits of a creeper with big round leaves
- pleʔ mʌʔ lɛʔ : species of big nut (circular, chestnut-like)
- pleʔ mɯw : honeydew melon
- pleʔ muu : water melon
- pleʔ pjooŋ : bitter, nut-like fruit

species (mak khom)
- pleʔ tr.loŋ poŋ : wild gourd species (green with lengthwise white stripes) = pleʔ kin.ʔdeep
- pleʔ thuʌʌ : beans (species)
— : (2) ball; button; *(first part of collocations:)* any round thing
  - chapat pleeʔ : hit a ball
- pleʔ chɯrɛɛ : button in shirt
- pleʔ lumbuk : ball
- pleʔ tʌm : button
- pleʔ ʔjaa : medicine; pills
— : (3) *(as first part of collocations:)* ball-shaped body-organ
- pleʔ chuʌk : the glands under the lower jaw
- pleʔ klol : heart
- pleʔ kook : Adam's apple; larynx
  - pleʔ kook glaʔ : the larynx speaks, i.e. you speak with the larynx
- pleʔ ʔdɯt : kidney
— : (4) *(with a numeral as determiner)* Classifier for round things
  - bɛɛr pleeʔ : two items, e.g. two kidneys

plɛc : = plɛk

plɛk : pick with one's nails; pinch *(e.g.* one's skin)
- plɛk dɯɯn glɤh : pick something (e.g. a thorn) and pull it out

plɛɛn *in:*
- dɤŋ met bɤɤn met plɛɛn : cannot see anything
- ʔa kaɲit, dɤŋ met bɤɤn met plɛɛn : it is dark, one cannot see anything
- dɤŋ met plɛɛn met mʌc : cannot see anything
- ʔa thm.rɯm, dɤŋ met plɛɛn met mʌc : it is dark, one cannot see anything

plil : vagina

pliin : (be) inside out; (be) upside down
- ruʌŋ pliin : on the wrong side; turning something inside out

plɯɯŋ : trough
- plɯɯŋ chiiŋ : pigs' trough

pluŋ *(also heard as:* pruŋ*)* : hot (the sensation of heat); burning hot
- ɟrʌʌk pluŋ : hot (but not boiling) water
- trlɔh pluŋ : the pot is hot
- klol pluŋ : be irritated
- pluŋ chak : have a chestburn
- pluŋ ʔɔn ʔɔk : warm; hot but not burning hot
- tom pluŋ ʔɔn ʔɔk : heat the food

pluut : (1) fall off
- chŋ.kɛr tiiʔ pluut : the nail of the finger falls off
— : (2) peel; remove the outer layer (e.g. of a fruit)

pmpoo *see* pompoo

pn.deeʔ *see* pendeeʔ

poh : split
- kɯr poh : the thunder strikes out
- kɯr poh bɯl : the thunder

strikes out and causes one to die

pok : cover *(V); house (V)*
- mɛɛw pok mlaaʔ : the Hmong let the Mlabri stay with them
- naŋ mat pok ʔat kwʌŋ : the eyelid hangs down over the eye

poolh : barking deer *(+Ferlus)*

pompoo : elephant *("male lg.")*
• kiʔ (ʔa) thʌp pompoo : it is full moon

pon : four; five (pon is number four in counting but mostly translated by the Thai word for "five")
- pon tawɯn : "five" days
- pon thɯɯ : four times
- pon thwɛɲ : "five hundred baht" *(literally: "four red")*

poon : be far away
• poon ɟak : go far away
• ʔa poon : have gone a long way; be far away (from home)
- ɟak ʔa poon : have walked a long way
- ʔoh ʔa poon : I have gone far already

poŋ *in:*
• pleʔ tr.loŋ poŋ : wild edible gourd species *(see* pleeʔ*)*

poʔ : cup

pɔk : woodpecker (bird species) *(Ferlus:* bird*)*

pɔɔc : rub/wipe one's fingers (to clean them)

pɔɔl : turn upside down *(V)*

prak : open one's hand (which is clenched around something)
• prak bahot : open the hand and let something fall

pralit : glass (e.g. front glass of a flashlight)

praŋ *see* ʔaaŋ

pr.daw *in:*
• chɔɔŋ pr.daw : a married couple
- ʔɛɛw chɔŋ pr.daw : daughter and son-in-law

prɛʔ : spices
- kibi ɲaŋ ʔat prɛʔ : there are no spices in it (the food)
• chapaʔ prɛʔ : lack spices; be bland
- chapaʔ ʔat prɛʔ : it (the food) lacks the appropriate spices

pr.gʌɲ : sharpen; whet
• pr.gʌɲ tɔʔ : sharpen a knife
- toc kɛp ɲʌʔ pr.gʌɲ tɔʔ : take that stone and sharpen the knife!

prijh.prɛjh *(perhaps only in fixed expressions)* : crisp
• glaʔ prijh.prɛjh : speak in a shrill and hoarse voice
• juuk prijh.prɛjh : biscuit made of rice grains
• khawnom prijh.prɛjh : biscuit made of rice grains
• prijh.prejh naŋ chiiŋ : crackling

priilh *in:*
• priilh thapɛɛt : bast fibres of thapɛɛt
toc priilh thapɛɛt ɟeŋ chɯr.ʔbat : use bast fibres of thapɛɛt to mend trousers

priin *(cf. pliin, pɤɤn)* : to be oblique; to tilt

prii? : be obliging; be eager to help
• pri? ɟak : run errands willingly

prɪm : (1) for a long time *(Postverbal)*
- ɟak prɪm : go away for a long time
• ʔa prɪm : since long ago
- mɛt pruk ʔa prɪm : has not come (here) for a long time
- buɯl ʔa prɪm : died long ago; has been dead for a long time

— : (2) former; of the past; going back a long time
• hma(a)j prɪm : former wife
• mlaʔ prɪm : person living in the past
- kan mlaʔ prɪm kibi thɛh ʔa buɯl ɟak : if people in old days were ill, they just died
- mlaʔ prɪm mlaʔ ʔa hɤ-hɤɤj : somebody who lived long ago
• tak hnʌm prɪm : many years back; for many years (in the past)

— : (3) old; aged; obsolete
- guɯncaj prɪm : an old blanket
- mɛt ʔuuj ʔa prɪm, chak-kom.ruujh : your mother is old
• mlaʔ prɪm : obsolete language; word which is obsolete in Mlabri
• ʔa prɪm : to have become old
- ʔa thwɛɲ ʔa prɪm : it (the sugar cane) has turned red, so it's old

— : (4) *(of weather:)* incessant
• kɯr prɪm, mɛʔ prɪm, kɯr mɛʔ mɛʔ mɛɛʔ : it is bad weather with thunder and incessant rain

pruɯk.hʌʌk *(cf. rɯ.hʌʌk)* : gasp (V)

pruɯŋ *(vowel length uncertain)* : interior; cavity
- pruɯŋ diiŋ : the interior of a bamboo section
- ʔat chuɯɯk ʔa pablʌk ni ʔat pruɯŋ : the strap (of the bag) has been put inside it

pr.lɔn : have a deep scar

pr.luut : membranous skin or layer on plant

pr.nah *in:*
• lɔŋ pr.nah : in old days
• tak pr.nah : long ago
- tak lɔŋ pr.nah : long ago

pr.neelh : broom *("male lg.")*
- ɟak toc pr.neelh peelh gɛɛŋ : take a broom and sweep the floor

prɲ.pruuɲ *see* pruɲpruuɲ

proh : bark (V)
- chɔʔ proh : the dog barks

proolh : have saliva squirting out of the mouth

pr.piip *see* pirpiip

pruk : (1) come here *(considered by some to be "male language")*
- glaʔ ba khit di pruk chɤm : tell Ba Khit to come!
- ɟa pruk : come! *(imperative)*

- ɟrɯw ʔa leh ʔa pruk : will come tomorrow
- pruk ŋɔr wec : come a long way
- ʔa pruk di jɤɤm nɛh : has come in order to stay here
- ʔee, rə.ʔʌh thahaan ʔa pruk : oh, the soldiers will be here in a moment!
— : (2) *(after action verbs:) denoting movement toward the salient location*
- mlaʔ kheet ʔa rɛɛʔ pruk, rɛɛʔ pruk lɔŋ briiʔ : the Mlabri were afraid and fled, they escaped into the forest
• gɯɯn pruk : return back
• ɟak pruk : visit; date (somebody)
- ɟak pruk grɛh : go visit the Lua'
- tareeŋ ɟak pruk luŋ.guh : the young man dates a girl
- ʔɛɛw ləmeet ɟak pruk luŋguh : my son is dating a girl
- ʔɛɛw miɲiŋ ɟak pruk tareeŋ : my daughter is dating a guy
• toc pruk : bring
- toc bɛɛ pruk : brought a goat
— : (3) come out; appear
- pruk mɛɛm : there is blood coming out
— : (4) *(after action verbs:)* out
- toc tiʔ joh pruk : pull something (e.g. a thorn) out with the fingers
• pa(a) pruk rt.lat : stick one's tongue-tip out
• ʔbit pruk : unscrew (something)
— : (5) (the sun or the moon) rises (*"male lg."*)
• tawɪn pruk : east

- ɟak lɔŋ tawɪn pruk : go east
• tawɪn ʔa pruk : sunrise
— : (6) (the moon) is in the first quarter (*"male lg."*)
• kiʔ hmɛʔ pruk : it is new moon
pruɲpruuɲ (*or* prɲ.pruuɲ) *in:*
• mɛʔ pruɲ.pruuɲ : it rains a little
pruŋ *in:*
• pruŋ ʔɯm : mumble
pruuŋ : a wild bird species ("big size, says cáwkoo, cɔ́kcɔ́k")
prɯɯcprwʌʌc : stroke softly with one's hand; smoothe the hair; comb the hair
- toc chn.rɛɛt chrɛɛt prɯɯcprwʌc glɤɤʔ : comb and set the hair orderly
pr.ʔɔʔ : bag made by folding a leaf or sheet (*cf.* ʔɔʔ)
puʌc : the moon is in the last quarter
- kiʔ puʌc : the waning moon has almost shrunk to nothing
- kiʔ rɛɛm ʔɛl puʌc : the moon is waning but not yet small
- puʌc blɯt : it (the moon in its last quarter) vanishes
puj : (1) stomach (also interior)
— : (2) the piston of the air pump (bellows) used when forging
pum-pam : play and fight for fun
• gʌm pum-pam : don't play (you're disturbing us)!
puum paŋ : rainbow

pumpoo *idiolectal variant of* pompoo

puuŋ : blow
- puuŋ khɛɛn : play the mouth organ
- puuŋ tii? : whistle by using one's hands as a resonating cavity
- puuŋ ʔuulh : blow into the fire; make the fire ablaze

purdur *in:*
- purdur ʔuulh : a burn (on the skin)

put(-)puʌt *in:*
- put(-)pu̱ʌt darɔɔʔ : split bamboo; spill made of split bamboo (used to singe a pig)

pwɛt : three days from today

ph-

phak *see* khɯɯp

phakaak : vegetable species (*"female lg."*)

phakaat *in:*
- Imbah phakaat : cabbage

phakɯɯk : vegetable species (*"male lg."*)

pha.khaaw : white (*"male lg."*)
- ʔa thɛh, ʔa pha.khaaw : it (the laundry) is nice and white
— : (2) the "white" of the eye; the cornea

phalaŋ : foreigner (*not fully accepted as a Mlabri word*)

phalaat : slip; loose one's foothold
- teen ŋɔr hlɛŋ, phalaat chʌm : slip and fall on a slippery path

phalɯʌm (*also recorded as:* phaljɯ(ɯ)m) : lightning (*"male lg."*)

pha.ʔjaaŋ : raincoat

phit *in:*
- pa(a) luh pa(a) phit : scold; abuse
- phit klol : feel sad; mourn

phɯɯt : feel oppressed

r-

raalh : cut; make perpendicular cuts in something

rahot : throw

rakɤɲ : in close bodily contact with something
- jɤɤm rakɤɲ : sit leaning against something
- ʔem rakɤɲ tr.dɯɯŋ : sleep one just behind the other, each lying on his/her side

reh : tear across; torn into pieces (*"female lg."*)

reet *in expressions about the vaning moon:*
- kiʔ thʌp reet : the moon is beginning to wane
- reet laat : the moon is strongly waning

reew : (1) (*Main Verb*) strong; forceful
- rəmɯɯt reew : strong wind; storm
- ruʌŋ reew : heavy floods of water on the ground

- ʔa thɛh ʔa reew : be healthy and strong
— : (2) *(Postverbal Intensifying Modifier:)* very much
- ʔoh chapat reew ʔi choʔ : I hit myself badly and it hurts!
- ruʌŋ thwɛɲ ɟak reew : muddy water is rushing along the ground
• di reew : forcefully (in some sense)
- glaʔ di reew : speak loudly
- hmujthɔj di reew : run as fast as one's legs can carry one
• ɟa reew : forcefully
- glaʔ ɟa reew : speak loudly
- hmujthɔj ɟa reew : run as fast as one's legs can carry one
- tɛk ɟa reew : beat; box *(V)*
• ʔa reew : very (much)
- chaw ʔeʔ ʔa reew : be very hungry

rəmɯt *(also* rɯmɯt*)* wind *(+Ferlus)*
• rəmɯt reew : strong wind; storm

rəmooj *see* rɯmooj

rəpaaʔ *see* rɯp.paaʔ

rəp.hɛp *see* rip.hɛp

rə.ʔʌh : soon; in a short time
- ɟak boŋ juuk hɛh rə.ʌh ʔa pruk : I go and eat first, I'll be back soon
- rə.ʔʌh thwɛɲ dɔŋ ʔa wʌl : it is soon evening and he'll be back
- rə.ʌh ʔa gɯɯn wʌl : I'm back in a moment
- rə.ʔʌh ʔoh chɛm boŋ : I'll eat again in a little while
- ʔee, rə.ʔʌh thahaan ʔa pruk : oh, the soldiers will be here in a moment!
• ɟak rə.ʔʌh : in a moment
- ɟak rəʔɤh ʔa wʌl : I'll be back soon

rə.ʔɤk *(or* r.ʔɤk*)* : chest (upper part)
• kewkew rə.ʔɤk : with folded arms

rɤʔ : (1) dust
- peelh rɤʔ : sweep dust away (with a broom)
— : (2) be dusty; be covered with loose dirt (referring to the ground or floor)
- peelh gɛɛŋ ɲʌn rɤʔ : sweep the floor because it is full of dust

rɛjwɛj *(also heard as* riwɛj*)* : fruit fly

rɛɛlh : root (of trees as well as smaller plants)
• kl.dɯl rɛɛlh : root tip (e.g. of an onion)

rɛɛm : (1) be diminishing
• kiʔ rɛɛm : waning moon
- kiʔ ʔa rɛɛm : the moon is waning
• rɛɛm jɤɤm : become more alone; become solitary
- hak rɛɛm jɤɤm : I become solitary
- ʔot hma(a)j ʔa bɯl ʔoh rɛɛm jɤɤm dəmɔj : when my wife died I was alone
— : (2) (in certain expressions of age in life:)
• rɛɛm chet : small child (below puberty)

- mɤʔ ɲaŋ rɛɛm chet : Mother has a small child
• rɛɛm hluak (see rɯm hluak) grown-up person

reeʔ : avoid; move away from
- mlaʔ kheet ʔa rɛɛʔ pruk, rɛɛʔ pruk lɔŋ briiʔ : the Mlabri were afraid and fled, they escaped into the forest
• rɛʔ ɟak : escape; run away
• ʔa rɛɛʔ : has disappeared
• ʔa rɛʔ ɟak : has run away; will run away
- kheet ʔa rɛʔ ɟak : I am scared, so I'm running away

rih : here/there (close to the speaker, but cf. nɛh); this way
- ɟak rih : go this way
- ɟak rih chala rih : shall we go this way or that way?
- ɟɤɤm rih : sit over there; stay around here

ril.wel : the natural parting of the hair on top of the head

rim : water level
• ɟrʌʌk rim ruʌŋ : there is a flood; the water level is high

riiŋ in:
• mɛʔ bla(a)j riiŋ : it rains in large amounts

rip.hɛp (or rəp.hɛp) : reddish brown cockroach-like insect

riwɛj see rɛjwɛj

rɯc.rʌc : sift down; fall out through small holes (e.g. grains from an old sack)

- juuk rɯc.rʌc : the rice grains are leaking out

rɯh : (1) clear the ground; clean the floor
— (2) in:
• rɯh gɛɛŋ : tear a house down and move it to another place

rɯh-rɯh (reduplication of rɯh) in:
• rɯh-rɯh peelh-peelh ɟak : clear the ground thoroughly

rɯjh : wash clothes by rubbing them against a stone or the like

rɯm I in:
• mɛʔ rɯm : it rains for several days

rɯm II in:
• rɯm hluak : grown-up person
- chɛw rɯm hluak boŋ hɛh : you (the children) must let the adults eat first!

rɯmɯɯt see rəmɯɯt

rɯmooj : dents in the ground; irregular indentations in a dirt floor

rɯm.ram : small ant species (which irritates the skin)
• mot rɯm.ram : id.

rɯp.paaʔ : wash (by rubbing or stroking with the hands)
- rɯp.paʔ buuk : wash one's face
- rɯp.paʔ chiiŋ : wash a pig (as part of slaughtering process)
- rɯp.paʔ tiiʔ : wash one's hands

rɯp-thɯp : pump (consisting

of two bamboo cylinders with pistons and a shared outlet) which supplies air to a forge
• ʔɤh rɯp-thɯp : operate the air pump

rɯt : tear across; torn into pieces ("male lg.")

rɯw *in:*
• rɯw bɯw : spacious; wide
- rɯw ʔa bɯw : it (the house) is spacious
- ʔɤh rɯw bɯw : make it spacious; build a spacious house

rm.paalh : stroke softly with one's hand

roh : the husband of one's niece

rooj : (1) younger sibling; younger in-law (of same generation) or friend
• rooj bɛɛr : married younger sibling and his/her spouse (also used about nephews and nieces)
• rooj km.ɲah : younger sister ("male lg.")
• rooj laŋ : your/his/her little brother
• rooj mɯlh : younger sister ("female lg.")
— : (2) you (used when addressing one's junior(s))

room : surround; encircle and push together

rompooʔ *in:*
• ʔem rompooʔ : dream *(V)*
- ʔem rompoʔ mʌc : dream *(V)*

rooŋ : elevated floor; plank bed
- gɛɛŋ rooŋ : house with an elevated floor or a plank bed
- jɤɤm rooŋ jɤɤm thɛh : make yourself comfortable on the plank bed!

rɔɔj *(vowel length variable)* : fly (generic term)
• rɔɔj bliiŋ : fly species
• rɔj juuk : fly species *(+Ferlus)*

rɔɔj *in:*
• ban hnʌm rɔɔj hnʌm : many, many years ago

rɔɔɲ : chew with the hind molars

rɔŋ *see* ruʌŋ

rt.lat : tongue *(Ferlus has a form khlat; I have heard rt.klat as a variant form in α-Mlabri)*
• krɛc rt.lat : bite one's tongue
• pa(a) pruk rt.lat : stick one's tongue-tip out

ruʌŋ **I** : creek; brook; water which floods the soil
- ruʌŋ chɛʔ, ɟak met bɤɤn : there is much water, we cannot walk
- ruʌŋ ɟak bɛʔ : the water streams along the soil
- ruʌŋ ɟruʔ : deep water
- ruʌŋ ʔa ɟuur : the (flooding) water has sunk
• buŋ ruʌŋ : pool of water
• ɟrʌʌk rim ruʌŋ : there is a flood; the water level is high
• ruʌŋ chr.kʌl : muddy flooding water *("female lg.")*
• ruʌŋ khun : muddy flooding

water *("male lg.")*
- ruʌŋ reew : heavy floods of water on the ground
- hr.looj ruʌŋ reew : be carried away by floods of water
- ruʌŋ thwɛɲ : muddy water
- ʔɯm ruʌŋ : bathe in a creek

ruʌŋ II *in:*
- ruʌŋ pliin : on the wrong side; turning something inside out
- bɯk chɯrɛɛ ruʌŋ pliin : put the shirt on inside out

ruuc I : together (jointly) *(Preverbal)*
- ruuc boŋ nɛŋ hmuu : eat together

ruuc II *in:*
- ɟrʌʌk ruuc : the water is dripping

ruujh : hide *(V)*

rujkoj : tail feathers

rumgum : finger (or toe), not including the nail
- rumgum chet : (1) little finger; pinkie; (2) crab's claw (referring to the small claws)
- rumgum grʏŋ : the "middle fingers" (i.e. neither thumb nor pinkie)
- rumgum ɟʏʏŋ : toe
- rumgum tiiʔ : finger
- rumgum ʔdiŋ : (1) thumb; (2) crab's claw (referring to the two front claws)

run : weeds
- joh run kɯm : tear up the weeds and dispose of them
- ʔʏh run : weed *(V)*
- run juuk : weeds (in rice field) *(Ferlus translates it as 'grass')*
- joh run juuk : tear up weeds

ruŋ.mruŋ *(sound-imitating) in:*
- ʔʏhʏʏj, kɯr bɔ ruŋ.mruŋ : oh my, what a thunder!

rwaaj : tiger *(+Ferlus)*
- mat rwaaj : button *(literally: "tiger's eye")*

r.ʔʌh *see* rəʔʌh

r.ʔʏk *see* rəʔʏk

t-

ta I *Preverbal Particle (of unidentified meaning, with stative verbs)*
- ta braliiŋ : be green (said of young sprouts)
- ta kun ta kwaan *(?, probably reduction of* tak kun tak kwaan, *vide* tak*)* : of the past
- ta lɔj ʔboh mat : small

ta(a) II *(cf.* taaʔ*) male title* ("Mr.")

tac : break by pulling; tear *(e.g. garments)*
- tac hot : be torn off
- tac petpet : have a scar such that some skin or tissue is protruding or hanging loose
- ʔa tac : broken; torn
- ʔa tac ʔa thalɯɯc : completely worn

— : (2) cut oneself *("female lg.")*

tak : (1) past; before now
- tak bn.nʌʔ : some time ago; in the past

- tak dr.naʔ dr.nɤɤm : long ago
- tak hnʌm prɪm : many years back; for many years (in the past)
- tak jʌk wʌl jʌk : in the past
- tak ɟrɯw : this morning
  - mɛʔ hot tak ɟrɯw bɔ tɔw ɟjʌl : it rains constantly from dawn to dusk
  - ʔɤhɤɤj, mɛʔ hot bɔ tak ɟrɯw : oh my goodness what a rain this morning!
- tak kun *(in rapid speech contracted to* takun*), in expressions of past time:*
  - bɔ tak ʔa hɤɤj bɔ tak kun : long, long ago
  - ʔat tiʔ tak kun : people in the past
- tak kun tak bɛʔ biʌʌc : "long ago when the earth was young" i.e. in the remote past
- tak kun tak naaj : (somebody or something) of the past
  - mlaʔ tak kun tak naaj glaʔ : that's what the elders said
- tak kun tak kwaan *(normally pronounced* takun tak kwaan *or* takun takwaan, *vide* ta) : of the past
  - ʔat tiiʔ tak kun tak kwaan : people in the past; our forefathers
- tak kwaan : long ago
- tak lɔŋ pr.nah : long ago
- tak naaj *see* tak kun
- tak nɛɛ : yesterday
- tak ɲaam *(often with reduction and assimilation to* təc.ɲaam*)* : some time in the past
  - tak ɲaam gʌh : at that time; that was long ago (?)
- tak pr.nah : some time ago; in the past
- tak ʔa hɤɤj : long since
— : (2) early, *possibly only in:*
- tak ɟrɯw : in the early morning
- bon juuk tak ɟrɯw : eat breakfast
- ɟrɯw tak ɟrɯw : tomorrow morning

takiʌŋ : lamp
- ʔat mɯj chaj takiʌŋ : fill (the) oil on the lamp

takun *see* ta, tak

talɤr *in:*
- gɔj mat talɤr : tears are running down one's cheeks

taliir : be introvert; be sluggish

taaɲ : weave (a basket etc.)

taŋ I *in:*
- ʔa taŋ : be high in the sky
  - kiʔ ʔa taŋ ʔa ɟŋ.gɯwn : the moon is high up, it's midnight
- tawɪn ʔa taŋ : high up; the sun is in zenith
  - pɤr ɟak tawɪn ʔa taŋ : fly high up in the sky

taaŋ II : another; a different one *(prenominal)*
- taaŋ mlaaʔ : somebody else
  - chɯɯ chɯrɛɛ maʔ taŋ mlaaʔ : buy a shirt for somebody else

taaŋ III *in:*
- taaŋ keet : ear ring

tareeŋ : young man; guy ("female lg.")

- ʔɛɛw miɲiŋ ɹak pruk tareeŋ : my daughter is dating a guy
• jɤɤm tareeŋ : be still an unmarried man *("female lg.")*

taat : perforate
- tat keet : make a hole in the ear lobe

tawɪn *(also* tawin*)* : (1) sun (used in many expressions for time of the day) *(Ferlus:* ta wɛn*)*
- buɯl dəmɔ tawɪn : died yesterday
• tawɪn ʔa leh : at sunrise *("female lg.")*
• tawɪn ʔa pruk : *id.* *("male lg.")*
• tawɪn ʔa wiic : at sunset *("female lg.")*
• tawɪn ʔa wiik : *id.* *("male lg.")*
• tawɪn ʔa hmɯndɯɯr : at noon
• tawɪn ʔa hɔt : (just after) sunset
• tawɪn ʔa kɛɛ : at noon

— : (2) something that lights up like a sun (e.g. a bulb or light-emitting diode in a radio)
- ʔat tawɪn ʔa bluɯt : the light (bulb) doesn't work

— : (3) *in expressions for geographical directions:*
• tawɪn hɔt : west
• tawɪn kɛɛ : zenith
• tawɪn leh : east *("female lg.")*
• tawɪn pruk : *id. ("male lg.")*

— : (4) day
• dʌlh ʔdɤɤ ʔat tawɪn : in how many days
• tawɪn gʌh : on this day (today) *(sic Ferlus:* taven gəh*)*

• tawɪn nɛh : today
- tawɪn nɛh tak ɹruɯw : this morning

— : (5) daylight; *(as a Verb:)* light up; it is daylight
- batoʔ di tawɪn : make a fire to light up!

tawlii : oil lamp

taaʔ : grandfather; old male relative; male relative of older generation; uncle

tʌk I : lean one's head against something
- ʔem tʌk tr.duɯŋ : sleep with the heads touching each other

tʌʌk II : pour (a liquid)
- tʌʌk ɹrʌʌk : pour water into something

tʌl : throw (while aiming)
- tʌl khɔt : throw a spear

tʌm *see* mak

tʌp *(or perhaps* tɔp*) in:*
• tʌp ʔat lwɛŋ : thatch a roof

tel : listen *("female lg.")*
- kan mɛh glaʔ ʔoh tel : if you speak, I'll listen
- ʔoh glaʔ mɛh di tel chɤm : I'm talking to you, please listen!

teen : step *(V)*
- gʌm teen : don't step there!
- teen ŋɔr hlɛŋ : walk on a slippery path
• teen ɹak : walk away

teet *in:*
• mɔ teet : a little *(acc. to one informant this is* Lua' = Tin*)*
- ʔoh boŋ mɔ teet rə.ʔʌh ʔoh

chɛm bɔŋ : I eat a little, and in a little while, I'll eat again
• dəmɔ teet : a little
- bɔŋ dəmɔ teet : eat a little

tə *see* tɯ

tə- *see* təkʌh, təni, ti

tɔc *see* toc

tɔc.ɲaam *see:* tak ɲaam

təguk *see* toguk

təkʌh (*cf.* ti) : over there (far away); up there on yonder hill

təkɛɛʔ : big gekko species (*"female lg."*)

təkɔjh : *id.* (*"male lg."*)

tələgɤk *see* tr.ləgɤk

təni (*probably contraction of* ti *and* ni) : inside (Preposition)
- jɤɤm təni gɛɛŋ : sit in the house

təpiaaʔ *see* tipiaaʔ

tə.plaaʔ : bark (including inner layers)
- tə.plaʔ ʔuulh : dry bark used as firewood

təptoop (*vowel of first syllable very variable*) : (1) wrap something into a cover of some kind
- təptop druuʔ : wrap into a banana leaf
— : (2) flat package made by wrapping (*e.g.* for medicine)

tɤc *variant pronunciation of* toc

tɤj *in:*
• ʔat tɤj ɟuɤj : southwards
- ɟak ʔat tɤj ɟuɤj : go south

tɤl : cultivate; grow (crops)
- chooc chak tɤl : the "chooc" (plant fibres for making brooms) are not cultivated (*i.e.* they grow in the forest)
- mɛɛw tɤl ʔeʔ lam : the Hmong cultivate "ʔeʔ lam" (a tuber species)

tɤlhɤɤ : mat (of bamboo on floor) (*"female lg."*)
- thampɯl tɤlhɤɤ : lay out the mat

tɤŋ *in:*
• met tɤŋ : not manage to do something before it is too late
- met tɤŋ chaj mʌʌlh : we had no chance to give it (a stillborn child) a name

tɛɛ I (*or* dɛɛ) : however; in fact (*generally placed after the first NP of the clause*)
- chinaat ʔoh tɛɛ bah : it is in fact not my own gun
- mlaʔ ki chɛʔ ... kwʌr tɛɛ chɛʔ : there were only a few Mlabri ... but there were many outsiders around

tɛɛ II (*mostly with vowel shortening; clause initially*) : certainly; indeed
- mmm, tɛ thɛ.ʔɛn : mmm, that smells good!

tɛj : crawl (the way an insect does); walk with very small steps (the way a bird does)
- mot tɛj mlaaʔ : there is an ant crawling on one's skin
- ʔjoc tɛj glɔɔŋ : the chicken walks

along the log
tɛk I : hit; hammer *(V)*
- tɛk ɟa reew : beat; box *(V)*
- tɛk kraralh : thresh; remove the seeds by holding the plant and beating it against the ground
- tɛk muŋmooŋ : beat a gong (Meo style)
- tɛk tuŋtuuŋ : beat the open end of a bamboo section (used as a drum) with the hand
- toc tr.nɛk tɛk hlek : beat iron with a hammer
• tɛk tr.dɯŋ : fight each other with fists

tɛɛk II : (terrestrial) snail

tɛɛn : jungle *cf.* thɛɛk
 lɔŋ briiʔ lɔŋ tɛɛn ɟak wec : go far into the jungle

ti *(cf.* tə-*)* : (1) at; in; into; *(with verbs of "searching":)* from
- bɯl ti puɤɤ : (she) died at Pua
- lʌʌp ti tr.lɔh : put something into the pot
- ti ɟalaaw chuh : down (south) in Laos
- ʔat mɯj chaj ti thoŋgot : fill the oil into a cup
• ti grɤŋ : in the middle (in a group, a row, or a pile)
• ti nɛh : in here
- ʔat chɯɯk ʔa pablʌk ti nɛh : the strap (of the bag) has been put in here (i.e. inside the bag)
• toc ti - : fetch from -; fetch something at/in -
- toc ti cot : fetch (something) from one's bag

— : (2) *in:*
• ti nɛj : inside
- loh toc ti nɛj cot : search for and find (something which is) in a bag
• ʔat ti nɛj : the inside; what is inside; the inner part (e.g. the inner set of wings of an insect)

ti- *also see* tɯ-

tih : (1) along this/that route (around an obstacle)
- ɟak tih chala tih : shall we go this way or that way?
- ɟak dɔɔ tih : we go that way!
- tih ki wec, tih ki wec : it is far if we go that way, it is also far if we go that way (pointing at two alternative routes)

— : (2) in (through a partition); out (through a partition)
- leh tih : come inside; come out (depending on speaker's location or perspective)
- ʔoh ɟak tih met bɤɤn, tawɯn ʔa kɛɛ : I cannot go outside, the sun is in zenith

tiktɛk : beat repeatedly
- toc ʔat nuur tiktɛk chuuʔ : use the back of a knife to crush ginger roots (before boiling)
• tiktɛk ɟirɟɛɛr : make tapping sounds with bamboo strips to attract (and catch) the cicadas

tiin briin : civil servant; person in charge of an administrative unit (a village, a district, a school)

tipiaaʔ *(or təpiaaʔ; ti-/tə- perhaps from tɯ as in ʔitɯ, also cf.* piaaʔ*)* : (1) what
- boŋ juuk nɛŋ tipiaaʔ : what are you eating with your rice?
- boŋ tipiaaʔ : what have you eaten?
- glaʔ tipiaaʔ : what shall we talk about?
- toc tipiaaʔ : what do you want?
• gʌh tipiaaʔ : what's that?
• tipiaaʔ gʌh : what's that?
• tipiaaʔ ʔɤh : are you too busy (to do something or other)?
— : (2) anything; with anything
• boŋ juuk tipiaaʔ : have something with the rice
- ʔoh chak boŋ juuk tipiaaʔ, boŋ juuk chɯ.chɯɯ : I didn't have anything with my rice, I ate only plain rice
— : (3) why; for what purpose
- ʔat tiʔ ɟak tipiaaʔ : why did they go?
• tipiaaʔ ɲʌʔ : why?; why that?
• tipiaaʔ ʔɤh : why is he/she doing that?
tirwiil : large round weaved plate
tit : stick; be adhesive
- bɛʔ tit gɯr cho ʔeeʔ : there is dirt on the handle of the digging stick
- ɟɤɤŋ tit bɛʔ : my feet stick in the mud
tiiʔ : (1) hand (+ forearm) (+*Ferlus*)
• puuŋ tiiʔ : whistle *(V)* (by using one's hands)
• toc tiiʔ : use the hand; with the hand; with the fingers
- toc tiʔ joh pruk : pull something (e.g. a thorn) out with the fingers
— : (2) foreleg of an animal
- ʔat tiʔ ʔat ɟɤɤŋ : its forelegs and hind legs
— : (3) thin stalk carrying flowers
— : (4) eight *(only when counting to ten, not in quantifying expressions)*
— : (5) *in pronominal expressions, (mostly) denoting plurality:*
• bah tiiʔ : you (several)
• ʔah tiiʔ : we
• ʔat tiiʔ : he/she/they (probably mostly plural); the elders; our forefathers
- ʔat tiiʔ glaʔ : that's what they (the old story-tellers) said
- ʔat tiʔ grɔk gɛɛŋ : those in the household
- ʔat tiiʔ pruk : our kinsmen are coming
- ʔat tiʔ ɲajh mlaaʔ : they don't like the Mlabri
tɯ : trousers, Northern Thai style (+*Ferlus*)
- chɯ.ʔbat tɯ : trousers
-tɯ *(interrogative bound pronominal morpheme), see* ʔitɯ, *also cf.* tipiaaʔ
tɯgʌʔ *see* dɯgʌʔ
tɯjh : hit; pound *(V)*

- bɔŋ thʌp tɯjh : eat it (the food) roasted and pounded
- lam tɯjh glʏʏʔ : one's head is hit by a tree

tɯk I *in:*
• mɔ tɯk : eight days from now *(cf.* mɔ nɯk*)*

tɯk II *in:*
• glaʔ ʔa tɯk : have finished talking
- glaʔ ʔa ɟreen ʔa tɯk : that's all I have to say; no more talking!
- glaʔ ʔa lɛn ʔa nɔɲ ʔa tɯk : no more talking!

tɯk.lʌk : tickle
• pa(a) tɯk.lʌk : tickle with moving hands

tɯltʏl *in:*
• tɯltʏl ɟak lɔŋ kl.dɯl : walk backwards

tɯn I : be clogged; obstruct
• mɯɯr tɯn mɔh : the nose is clogged

tɯn II *see* tun

tɯŋ I : boil; steam (some food)
- met ʔɛl tɯŋ kɔ bliiŋ : it is raw, it hasn't been boiled yet
- tɯŋ juuk : make sticky rice

tɯŋ II *in:*
• mɔ tɯŋ : six days from now

tɯŋtʌŋ : ant species (big, black)

tɯp : cover; cover with wickerwork
- goh tɯp : smash and cover (e.g. of a falling tree which hits a person)
• cuʌk tɯp : dig a hole and hide (it) there
- cuʌk tɯp ʔat bontuʔ : bury in a grave
• tɯp bɛʔ : cover with earth
- cuʌk tɯp bɛʔ : bury

tɯp-taap : narrow

tɯptoop *see* tuptoop

tɯr-lʏgʏk *see* tr.lʏgʏk

tɯrnɛk *see* tr.nɛk

tm.ʔooʔ *see:* tom.ʔooʔ

tŋ.tuuŋ *see* tuŋtuuŋ

too : (1) species (of animals)
- thawaaʔ mɔ too, thɛɛŋ mɔ too, chajh mɔ too : one species (of monkeys) is thawaaʔ, another thɛɛŋ, a third chajh

— : (2) *(only if modified by a non-numeral determiner or predicate:)* person; individual
• too gʌh : this person
• too ɲʌʔ : that person; that one
- ʔoh mak too gʌh, too ɲʌʔ met mak : I like this person, I don't like that person
• too ʔa nɔɲ : all of them; everybody
- too gʌh, too ɲʌʔ, too ʔa nɔɲ : this person, that person, all of them!

— : (3) Classifier for living creatures *(in the case of human beings only with a non-numeral quantifier)*
- kaaʔ bɛɛr too hlooj : three fish
- miɲiŋ too gʌh ŋaam : this girl is beautiful

toc *(also* təc*)* : (1) *(mostly in se-*

rial constructions) : fetch; pick
- toc pajok glɤh : fetch and lift up
- toc ʔɛɛw pabooʔ : to nurse a child
- toc ʔuulh keeŋ wʌl : gather firewood and carry it home
• cok toc : take something out; produce something
- cok toc ni dɛj chɯrɛɛ : take something from the breast pocket
- cok toc ti cot : take something from the bag
• kalɯp toc : fetch (a ball)
• toc leh : bring along; take something out
- met toc leh : I didn't bring it along
• toc pruk : bring along
- toc pruk ɟi.ʔdɤɤ : you may bring anything whatsoever (for us)!
- toc pruk met bɤɤn : I could not obtain it

— : (2) use; *(as first V in serial constructions with instrumental complement:)* with
- com dok toc blɛɛŋ cʌt kl.kiil : squat while resting one's the arms (the elbows) on one's knees
- toc kr.lap klaap : use a split bamboo stick to hold something (e.g. meat over fire)
- toc lam tɛk : take a stick and hit (the dog); hit it with a stick
- toc tɔʔ paat cɪmbeelh : remove a thorn from the skin with a knife
- toc tr.nɛk tɛk hlek : beat iron with a hammer
• toc tiiʔ : use the hand; with the hand; with the fingers
- toc tiʔ joh pruk : pull something (e.g. a thorn) out with the fingers
- toc tiʔ ɟeŋ : sew by hand
- toc tiiʔ pn.deeʔ : point with a finger
• toc thrɛɛŋ : use the teeth
- toc thrɛɛŋ chraɲ boɲ : eat using the teeth to scrape the food off

— : (3) obtain; receive; accept; want
- mɛh maaʔ ʔoh ʔa toc : if you give it to me, I shall accept it
- toc tipiaaʔ : what do you want?
- ʔoh chak toc : I don't want it
• krɔɔ toc : ask for; wish to receive; request
- mɛh krɔɔ toc lɯŋ ʔoh : you want something from me?
- ʔoh krɔɔ toc chɯrɛɛ lɯŋ mɛh : I request a shirt from you
• wʌl toc : be reunited with (somebody)
- ʔat ɟjooŋ gɯt hɔɔt ʔat ʔɛɛw laŋ di wʌl toc : the father misses his son and wants him back

— : (4) choose (as one's spouse or as one's labourer)
- mɛɛw chak toc mɛh : the Hmong did not choose you (for the work)
• toc glaŋ : marry; take a husband
- toc glaŋ kwʌr : marry a man outside the tribe

- toc hmaaj : marry; take a wife
- toc bɛɛr hmaaj : have two wives
- toc hma(a)j hmɛʔ : have a new wife; remarry
- toc hma(a)j mlaʔ briiʔ : marry a Mlabri girl
- toc hma(a)j tuul : take a second wife

toctoc : clutch at something
- gɯpgɯp toctoc ɟak : grope and clutch at something while walking

toguk (or təguk) : frog species (living in water)

toh : pull; pull out
• toh glɤh : pull something out of something else (e.g. a case or sheath)

tok : fall (used in ritual lg.)
- gʌm ki lon hot lon tok : don't fall (off me), oh spirit!

tok-tok in:
• tok-tok klol : have palpitations

tom : boil (transitive V)
- tom di biʌʌc : boil until "soft"
- tom gʌm bohboh, tom pluŋ ʔɔn ʔɔk : don't let it boil, just heat the food!

tom.ʔooʔ (or tm.ooʔ) : snake (cobras, not pythons) (+Ferlus)
• tom.ʔoʔ beelh : snake species (said to be moderately poisonous)

toon : Classifier for wood (logs and branches)
- lam bɛɛr toon : two pieces of wood
- lam ton dɯ gʌʔ : the trees around here
- ʔuul bɛɛr toon : two pieces of firewood

toŋ : vertical supporting pole; house pole (in village house)
• toŋ ɟoʔ toŋ ɟaʔ : tripod for fireplace (in Hmong house)

torlok see tr.lok

tɔɔ I (cf. tɔw) : for; to
- maʔ tɔɔ mlaaʔ : give (things) to the Mlabri
• tɔɔ tr.dɯŋ : together (reciprocally)
- glaʔ tɔɔ tr.dɯŋ : talk together

tɔɔ II (cf. tɔɔp) : answer (V)
- kan ʔoh glaʔ mɛh di tɔɔ : if I speak (to you), you should answer

tɔɔ III in:
• wʌl tɔɔ : bind a knot

tɔɔn : Classifier for sections of something
- diiŋ dəmɔ tɔɔn : one bamboo section
- diiŋ ɟrʌʌk dəmɔ tɔɔn : one bamboo section with drinking water

tɔɔp (one speaker consistently says tɔɔ) answer (V)
- ʔat glaŋ crɤw, ʔat hma(a)j tɔɔp : the husband calls, the wife answers
- ʔoh choop mɛh, mɛh tɔɔp : I ask you, and you answer

tɔ.pruʔ gɛjh : middle-aged

tɔw (cf. tɔɔ) in:

- tɔw ɟjʌl : until evening
- mɛʔ hot tak ɟrɯw bɔ tɔw ɟjʌl : it rains constantly from dawn to dusk
- ʔoh choop mɛh, mɛh choop ʔoh tɔw ɟjʌl : we put questions to each other (i.e., we converse) until evening

tɔʔ : jungle knife; big knife with an angular or rounded tip
- tɔʔ gɯr dalɛʔ : knife with a wooden handle
- tɔʔ tuul : pointed knife (+*Ferlus*)
- tɔʔ ʔbɔɔŋ : knife with an iron handle

tr.dɯŋ (or trl.dɯŋ) : together; reciprocally (*Postverbal*)
- batit tr.dɯŋ : close together
- ʔem batit tr.dɯŋ : sleep beside each other
- glaʔ tr.dɯŋ : talk together
- jah glaʔ tr.dɯŋ : we talk with each other
- tɛk tr.dɯŋ : fight each other with the fists
- tɔ tr.dɯŋ : together (reciprocally)

trɤɤl : bird (a species)

trɯh *in:*
- lam trɯh : tree that has fallen to the ground

trɯp : cover oneself; put on
- toc gɯncaj trɯp : use a blanket to cover oneself with
- trɯp gɯncaj ʔem : cover oneself with a blanket and sleep

trl.dɯŋ *see* tr.dɯŋ

tr.leet : (1) rotate; spin; roll (e.g. about an orange spinning or rolling on the ground)
— : (2) rub or roll something between the hands
- lɔɔm tr.leet : fold (a leaf with tobacco) and roll it (into a cigarette)

tr.lɤgɤk (*or* tɯr-lɤgɤk) : a mythical deity

tr.lok (*or* torlok) bird species (small)
- kwɤj tr.lok : wild banana species

tr.loŋ *in:*
- pleʔ tr.loŋ poŋ : wild edible gourd species (*see* pleeʔ)

tr.lɔh : pot
- lʌʌp ti trlɔh : put something into the pot
- tr.lɔh kɯtkeet : kettle with a spout

tr.luuʔ (*or* turluuʔ) : bamboo species

tr.nʌlh : collarbone

tr.nɛk (*idiolectally:* tɯr-nɛk) : hammer (*N*)
- toc tr.nɛk tɛk : use a hammer
- toc tr.nɛk tɛk hlek : beat iron with a hammer

tr.nɔlh : vertical house pole

trŋ.tuuŋ *see* tuŋtuuŋ

tu : from (down from)
- hot tu lam : fall down from a tree

tuuj (*cf.* twaaj) : the pupil of the eye

- tuj mat : *id.*

tuul : (1) a pointed tip (e.g. of a knife, an onion, or a corn-cob)
- blaaj tuul : big, pointed implement
- blaaj tuul tɔʔ : big knife
- ʔɛɛw tuul : small, pointed implement
- ʔɛɛw tuul tɔʔ : small knife
— : (2) junior (in kinship terminology)
- hma(a)j tuul : second wife
- ʔat ʔɛ.w tuul : the youngest (biological) child

tum : swelling (of the skin)

tun *(idiolectally: tɯn) in:*
- tun wʌt : lashing/string (made of split bamboo or plant fibres)
- tun wʌt wʌt gɛɛŋ : tie parts of a house together

tuun : mouse

tuŋtuuŋ *(also* tŋ.tuuŋ, trŋ.tuuŋ*)* : bamboo "drum" (a bamboo section which is made to resonate by hitting its open end with the hand)
- tɛk tuŋtuuŋ : beat the bamboo drum

tuptoop *see* təptoop

tur-lɔh *idiolectal variant of* tr-lɔh

turluuʔ *see* tr.luuʔ

tuut : gourd
- pleʔ tuut : gourd
- tuut ɟrʌʌk : calabash (+*Ferlus*)

tut-tuut : knot (made by folding the upper part of a bag or bundle into itself)

twaaj *(cf.* tuuj*)* : the pupil of the eye
- twa(a)j mat : *id.*

twec *in:*
- twec hot : throw (to the ground)

th-

thapɛɛt : plant species (a vine with strong fibres)
- priilh thapɛɛt the bast fibres of "thapɛɛt"

thahaan : soldier *(probably regarded as a Thai word)*

thakat : be tight
- ʔbiip di thakat : press it (*e.g.* a bracelet) together so that it fits
- thakat klol : feel oppressed; have heart pain

thaal : six

thalɛɛl : heat (from the fireplace)
- ɟakɔn thalɛɛl ʔuulh, ʔjen : warm one's hands at the fireplace because one is cold

thalɯc *in:*
- ʔa tac ʔa thalɯc : completely worn (about clothes)

thalʌm : clench one's fists (as when trembling of cold)

thaluh : flat (land)
- bɛʔ thaluh : flat land
- ɟak thaluh : walk in horizontal direction

thampɯl : roll out; arrange
- thampɯl chaat : lay out the mat
- thampɯl tɤlhɤɤ : lay out the mat

thaŋ *in:*
• thaŋ nɯɯʔ : north; northwards
• ʔat thaŋ nɯɯʔ : north; northwards

thaŋaap : yawn *(V)*
- thaŋaap chi ʔem : yawn out of sleepiness

thaŋɔɔt : become drunk
- boŋ ɟn.raaʔ thaŋɔɔt : drink liquor and become drunk

thapaɲ : bug species ("small, bites at night")

thapuul : (1) abdomen; the hind part of the body of an insect; stomach (+Ferlus)
- chi thapuul : have a stomach-ache
- choʔ thapuul : have a stomach-ache
- thapuul choʔ : my stomach hurts
— : (2) palm of hand

tharac : (1) bowels
— : (2) rafters in the roof of a (Hmong) house

thaw *in:*
• mɤm thaw : father-in-law
• mɤʔ thaw : mother-in-law

thawaaʔ : monkey species *(Ferlus has final -k)*

thʌc : meat; flesh (+*Ferlus*)
- gn.rɛɛ thʌc : thick soup with lumps of meat in it
- thʌc blɛɛŋ : the flesh of the arm
• thʌc mɔɔl : tenderloin
• thʌc piaʔ ʔdɤɤ : edible meat

thʌkthɤɤk *(Expressive, probably = thɤkthɤɤk below)* : have palpitations

thʌp I : roast *(V)*
- boŋ thʌp tɯjh : eat it (the food) roasted and pounded
- thʌp chaloo thʌp boŋ : roast corncobs and eat them

thʌp II *in:*
• thʌp pompoo : (the moon) is full *(old expression)*
- kiʔ (ʔa) thʌp pompoo : it is full moon
• thʌp reet : (the moon) is full
- kiʔ thʌp reet : it is full moon

theeŋ *in:*
• dik theeŋ : adolescent child
• ʔɛɛw dik theeŋ : child that is just able to crawl or walk

thep.ʔjeep : scowl with narrowed eyebrows

thəbɯr : something flat and thin which has been made into a roll
• khawnom hn.tor thəbɯr : "hollow rolled cookie": a kind of biscuit

thɤkthɤɤk *(cf. thʌkthɤɤk above)* : wake up and sit up abruptly (after bad dreams)
- ʔee, ʔi choo ʔa thɤkthɤɤk : oh my, the baby is suddenly awake!

thɤɤl : belch; vomit

thɤɤŋ *(one informant says* thɯɯŋ*)* : (1) five

— : (2) *see* bah, ʔat

thɤŋ *in:*
- ʔɤh thɤŋ bɤɤn : find it easy to do

thɛh : (1) good
- dɤŋ di thɛh ʔi hot : be careful or you'll fall!
- ŋɔr thɛh : a passable trail; a path
- gr.wɛɛn thɛh : right side; right hand
- klol thɛh : kind-hearted
- met thɛh : bad; evil
- wɔɔk met thɛh : evil spirit
- ʔa dɔ thɛh : that's all right; never mind!

— : (2) good-looking
- luŋ.guh thɛh : a beautiful girl
- met thɛh : ugly
- ʔa thɛh, ʔa phakhaaw : it (the laundry) is nice and white

— : (3) be in good health
- ʔa thɛh : recover
- boŋ ʔjaa pleʔ ʔa thɛh : eating pills, he/she will recover

— : (4) *(with* klol, *in expressions of mood:)*
- klol met thɛh : be unhappy
- ʔa thɛh klol : be glad

— : (5) *(Postverbal)* well; properly; suitably
- boŋ thɛh boŋ mɤk : eat good food
- kibi boŋ thɛh boŋ mɤk : has no proper food to eat
- glaʔ thɛh : say the truth
- jɤɤm thɛh : sit in upright position

— : (6) *(Preverbal, in certain expressions, often with preceding* met *'not') be fit for -; be able to*
- met thɛh boŋ : is inedible
- met thɛh ʔem : cannot sleep
- ʔoh met thɛh ʔem, klol pluŋ : I am so upset that I cannot sleep
- thɛh ʔem : to sleep well; to have a good sleep

— : (7) *(with preceding* di, *in expressions of best wishes:)*
- jak di thɛh : have a good journey! *(greeting)*
- jak di thɛh chɤm : *id.*
- ʔem di thɛh : sleep well!

thɛj *see* mɤŋ thɛj

thɛɛk : thicket; scrub

thɛɛŋ : a white monkey species *(according to Ferlus' list: 'langur')*

thɛɛw : honey
- thɛɛw ʔjek : bees' honey

thɛ.ʔɛn : smell good
- mmm, tɛ thɛ.ʔɛn : mmm, that smells good!
- thɛ.ʔɛn jweel : it smells deliciouly of lemon-grass

thit ɲuʔ : wireless set; portable radio

thɯɯ : time (as in "three times")
- bɛr thɯɯ : twice
- bɛr thɯɯ hlooj : three times
- chɛʔ thɯɯ : several times
- boŋ chɛʔ thɯɯ : eat several times

- dəmɔ thɯɯ : once
- ʔɤh dəmɔ thɯɯ : do it once
- mɔ thɯɯ : once
- nomɔ thɯɯ : once
- ʔoh boŋ nomɔ thɯɯ, ʔoh chak boŋ : I have already eaten once so I won't eat any more (today)

thɯbɯr : termite

thɯh.prah : bast

thɯm- *see* thm-

thɯp ɲuul : broom *("female lg.")*
- thɯp ɲuul bakkah chooc : (standard type of) broom made of "chooc" fibres

thɯr-baaʔ *in:*
• juuk thɯrbaaʔ : husked rice

thɯt : wipe; wipe something away; wipe (one's hands) dry
- thɯt chak : wipe one's body

thɯʔ.thaʔ *in:*
• lam bɯlbɯl lɯk.liik thɯʔ.thaʔ : the charred stump of a burnt tree

thm.bʌc : hairs on a hairy stalk
- ʔat thm.bʌc ŋaʔ : the hairs on the stalk cause my skin to itch

thm.rɯm : (1) late in the evening when dark
- thm.rɯm ʔa pruk : will come late tonight
• ʔa thm.rɯm : it is late evening; it is dark
- pan gʌh ʔa bɯl.joon.jeem, rə.ʔʌh ʔa thm.rɯm : now it is twilight, it will soon be dark
- ʔa thm.rɯm, dɤŋ met plɛɛn met mʌc : it is dark, one cannot see anything
— : (2) be unable to see

thɯwɛɲ *(cf.* thwɛɲ, *same etymon??) in:*
• gɔj thɯwɛɲ : a burning hot liquid (mentioned in Mlabri mythology)

thoh-thoh *(also heard as* thu.thoh*)* : lungs

thoj : bowl *(not recognized as a Mlabri word by all speakers)*

thoom : plant species (with edible marrow)

thoɲ : sting (N, *e.g.* of bee)

thoŋgot : (1) cup made out of a bamboo section; mug; bucket
- brɛŋ thoŋgot : cut the edge of a bamboo cup into shape
- chaj ti thoŋgot : fill it into a cup
• thoŋgot ɟrʌʌk : water mug; bucket (also used about plastic buckets)
— : (2) something the shape of a cup; the concave mirror of a flashlight

thɔɔk : pour
- toc ɟn.raaʔ thɔɔk ni poʔ : pour liquor into a cup
- thɔɔk ɟrʌʌk : pour water
• thɔɔk kɯm : throw (some liquid) out
- thɔɔk kɯm ɟrʌʌk : throw water

out
thrɛɛŋ : (1) tooth (*sic also Ferlus; also:* lower lip ??)
- ʔot thrɛɛŋ kɔ ʔa noɲ : I have no teeth left, you see
• krɛc thrɛɛŋ : bite one's lip
• thrɛɛŋ hn.cok : canine tooth
— : (2) the edge of a cutting implement
• thrɛɛŋ kwɛk : the sharp edge of an axe
thrih : unwrap; open
- thrih dɤŋ : open (the package) and have a look
thrit.threet : lift the eyebrows (as in surprise)
throoʔ : put on (pulling a piece of garment over one's legs)
thruut : edible tuber species with a yellow root (+*Ferlus in the meaning of* 'yellow')
thuʌʌ *see* pleeʔ
thuuc : sting (said of insects) (V)
- kuj ʔɔɔj thuuc, pruk tum : if the "kuj ʔɔɔj" stings you, you get a swelling
- ʔjek thuuc, lɯmŋɔɔr kɔ thuuc : bees sting, and so do the "lɯmŋɔɔr"
thuul (*cf.* bathuul) : meat or vegetables eaten with the staple food
- ɟak boŋ juuk, thuul noɲ : we must eat our rice plain, there is nothing else
thup pruuʔ : betel leaf

• thup pruʔ haat : lump (mouthful) of betel
thurthuur : smoke (N)
thu.thoh *see* thoh-thoh
thu.ʔuɲ : warm (said of clothes)
thu.ʔuur : hot (of weather)
- chiiŋ ʔɤh thu.ʔuur : the pig snorts, because it is hot
- chɔʔ hɯl.hal thu.ʔuur : the dog puts out its tongue, because it is hot
- tawɪn kɛɛ ʔa thu.ʔuur : it is noon and very hot
thwɛɲ (*or* thwɛɛɲ, *uncertain vowel length*) : (1) red (deep red)
- prɛʔ thwɛɲ : red chili fruit
• mɔ thwɛɲ : "a red one": one 100-Baht note
• ruʌŋ thwɛɲ : muddy water
• ʔa thwɛɲ : has turned red (said e.g. of dry sugar cane)
— : (2) a red layer (e.g. the mucous membrane under the eyelids, or the reddish inner cortex of a "thoom" stem)
— : (3) red pimple
— : (4) *in:*
• ʔɛɛw thwɛɲ : small baby
- ʔɛɛw thwɛɲ beec : the baby cries
— : (5) *in:*
• thwɛɲ dooŋ : evening glow; sunset colours in the sky ("*male lg.*")
- tawɪn ʔa thwɛɲ dooŋ ʔa ɟjʌl : it is dusk now

w-

wʌl : (1) be back home; return to me/us (*Ferlus has the perfective form ʔa wal*)
- ɟak gwaa ʔa wʌl : will go for a visit first and then be back
- ʔa pruk wʌl ʔem ni gɛɛŋ : has arrived home in order to sleep at home
• di wʌl di mɯɯ : return back (to me)! (invoking a spirit)
• wʌl jɤɤm kap chak kap chruʌt : come and stay inside me! (invoking a spirit)
• ʔa gɯɯn wʌl : is back; will be back here
• ʔa wʌl gɛɛŋ : has come home

— : (2) (*Preverbal*) come and -; start -ing
- ɟak glɤh wʌl jɤɤm nɛh : come up and sit here (with me on the platform)
- klɯɯr wʌl dap bɛʔ : the sky came (down) and hit the earth (a mythological event)
- mɛh gʌm wʌl kwɤn ʔot gruɤɤ : don't you start playing with my things! (said to child)
- wʌl jɤɤm chrɔɔɲ : come and stay where it is dry (i.e. take shelter)
- wʌl ʔbɔɔk maaʔ : come and give orders
- ʔat ɟum wʌl boŋ juuk : come and eat with me, wife!
- ʔii, ʔa wʌl beec : oh my, he/she has started crying
• wʌl dɤŋ : we'll see each other again!

— : (3) *in*:
• ʔat chɯɯrmɯɯl wʌl pruk : his/her soul haunts the place

— : (4) *in*:
• bɔ tak jʌk wʌl jʌk : several years ago

wʌt : lace up (a bag); tie; bind
• tun wʌt : lashing/string (made of split bamboo or plant fibres)
- tun wʌt wʌt : use a lashing or string to lace something up

wec I : (1) far away; far; distant
- gɛɛŋ wec : a distant house
- ɟak wec : go far away
- mɛh jɤɤm rih ʔi wec : you had better stay here, because it's far (to go)
- pruk ŋɔr wec : come a long way
- tih ki wec, tih ki wec : it is far if we go that way, it is also far if we go that way (pointing at two alternative routes)
- ʔot gɛɛŋ jɤɤm wec : my house is far away

— : (2) long (of visible size)
• bla(a)j wec : long (of visible length)
• wec ɟuur : hang down; stick out below

wec II : a length; a piece (of something oblong)
- pɤjh lam dəmɔ wec : cut off one piece of wood

ween *in*:
• ween mat : glasses; spectacles

wɤɤŋ : chin (*Ferlus has wəl*)
wɛj : hurriedly; fast

- bɔŋ di wɛj : eat quickly!
wɛjh : tuber (edible species)
wɛk.wɛm : edible plant species
wiʌŋ : city
wiic *("female lg.")* = wiik *("male lg.")* : for the sun to set, *in:*
- tawɪn ʔa wiic/wiik : sunset
wiik *see* wiic
wiŋcɛɛr : look through narrow eye slits
wiŋkɛl : in horizontal position; in horizontal direction
- laaj wiŋkɛl : horizontal stripes
- chɯrɛɛ laaj wiŋkɛl : shirt with some stripes across as ornamentation
- ɟak ŋɔɔr wiŋkɛl : go straight on in a horizontal direction
- toc wiŋkɛl : take a crying baby and rock it in one's arms
wɪŋ : auditory canal (auditory duct)
- ʔat wɪŋ keet : the auditory canal
wɔk : (1) spirit of nature; the spirit of a deceased person (+Ferlus)
- lam ɲaŋ wɔk : there is a spirit in the tree(s); there is a tree spirit
- ruʌŋ ɲaŋ wɔk : there is a spirit living in the stream; there is a water spirit
- wɔk blʌk jɤɤm mlaʔ di chak : spirits enter people's bodies
- wɔk bɛʔ : earth spirit
- wɔk gɛɛŋ : house spirit (+Ferlus)
- wɔk ɟjooŋ : (deceased) father's spirit
- wɔk klɯɯr : sky spirit
- wɔk lam : tree spirit
- wɔk met thɛh : evil spirit
- wɔk paŋ : a spirit associated with the rainbow
- wɔk paŋ chɛɛ : *id.*
- wɔk paŋ chɛɛ jɤɤm ruʌŋ : the "wɔk paŋ" spirit lives in the water
- wɔk rwaaj : tiger spirit
- wɔk rwaaj met thɛh : the tiger spirit is evil
- wɔk ruʌŋ : water spirit
- wɔk tawɪn : sun spirit
- wɔk thwɛɲ dooŋ : sunset spirit
— : (2) *(euphemistically:)* deceased person
- mɤʔ wɔk, mɤm wɔk, ʔa bɯl : my mother and father are dead
- wɔk ʔa bɯl : the person is dead
- wɔk ʔuuj : (deceased) mother's spirit
wul.wal : hip *("female lg.")* (+Ferlus in the meaning of 'buttocks')
- wul.wal bluuʔ : hip
wul.wɯɯl : hip *("male lg.")*

ʔa-

ʔa : (1) *Aspectual Marker signifying (recent or past) transition to a state*
- mɛh pruk ʔoh ʔa mʌʌk : I'm happy because you have come
- mɛh ʔa bɔŋ juuk tak ɟruɯ : have you had your breakfast? *(intended though not syntactically marked as a question)*

- tawın kɛɛ ʔa thu.ʔuur : it is noon and very hot
- ʔoh ʔa bɔŋ : I have eaten; *(as answer to a question:)* yes, I have eaten
- ʔoh ʔa chi ʔem : I am sleepy
• ʔa bɯl : is dead; has died
- ʔa bɯl chɛʔ tawın : died many days ago
• ʔa blɯt : is extinguished (said of fire)
- ʔuulh ʔa blɯt : the fire is extinguished
• ʔa chak-kom.ruujh : is old
• ʔa hluak : is grown up; big (of person)
• ʔa kaɲit : it is dark
• ʔa mɛɛʔ : it has started raining
• ʔa nɔɲ : is finished; there is nothing left; completely
- ʔa glaʔ nɔɲ : we have ended our conversation
• ʔa prım : is old and worn
• ʔa tac : is broken

— : (2) *in expressions of positive judgment or attitude:*
• ʔa dɔ *see* dɔ
• ʔa mɛɛn : that's correct; yes

— : (3) *in expressions for the time of the day or night:*
• tawın ʔa hɔt ʔa thwɛɲ dooŋ : (it is) just after sunset
• ʔa ɟŋ.gɯɯn dıŋ : (it is) midnight
• ʔa thɯɯm.rɯɯm : (it is) late in the evening

— : (4) *Marker on adverbial phrases signifying elapsed time*
- ʔa bɛɛr kiiʔ : it is two months ago
• ʔa prım : long ago
- bɯl ʔa prım : died long ago

— : (5) *Preterite Marker in narratives*
- mlaʔ kɔ ʔa ki chɛʔ : and at that time we were only a few

— : (6) *Marker of habitual past*
- ʔa ɟɟʌl ʔa ʔem (...), ʔa bah ʔa ɟak : at dusk we would go to sleep (...), at dawn we would be off

— : (7) *Marker signifying certainty of effect, fulfillment or intent*
- bɔɲ pleʔ ʔjaa ʔa thɛh : one eats pills and recovers
- gɛɛŋ met grɤj laac, ɟrɯw ʔa laac : the house is not yet finished, it will be finished tomorrow
- mɤm pruk, ʔa bɔɲ thʌc chiiŋ : if you ("Father") come, we'll eat pork
- mɛh maaʔ ʔoh ʔa toc : if you give it to me, I'll certainly accept it
- rə.ʔʌh thahaan ʔa pruk : the soldiers will be here in a moment!
- ʔoh ʔa ɟak : I'm off!
• met ʔa - : I'm not going to -!
- ʔoh met ʔa leh : I'm not coming!

— : (8) *Perfective Future Marker in hypothetical statements*
- ʔoh jɤɤm dəmɔj, ʔɛl toc hmaaj, kan ʔa ɲaŋ hmaaj jɤɤm bɛɛr mlaaʔ : I live alone, I have not married yet, but if I find a wife, we'll live together

— : (9) *Hortative Marker (also reciprocal)*
- kan mɛh choʔ glɤɤʔ mɛh ʔa ɟak ʔem : if you have a headache, you should go and sleep
- mɛh ɟak ʔa ɟak, ʔoh jɤɤm : you just go, I stay!
• ʔa chak - : please don't -
- mɤm ʔa chak luh : please don't scorn me, "Father"!
• ʔa di - : let's -!
- ʔa di boŋ : come and eat!
— : (10) *(Verb Connective)* until -; in order to -
- gɔj boŋ ʔa biiʔ : just eat until you are full!

ʔaa : oh! (expressing annoyance)
- ʔaa, ʔuulh blɯṭ, grawɯlh ʔuulh : oh, the fire has died out, fan at it!

ʔac : bird (generic term)

ʔah : we
- ʔah bɤr mlaaʔ : the two of us
- ʔah nɛŋ hmuu : we (several people)
• ʔah ɟum : we; our group; our tribe (also said to be the word used about this clan by the "Spear Tribe")
• ʔah ɟum : we; our group; my family; we who are residents here; all of us (often, but not necessarily, used as exclusive 1.p.pl.)
- mɛh nɛŋ ʔah ɟum : you and the rest of us
- ʔah ɟum nɛh : we (those of our group) who are here
- ʔah ɟum nɛŋ hmuu : all of us

ʔaaj I : (speaker's) elder brother
- ʔaaj ɟak ginɛŋ : where are you going? (said to one's brother)
• ʔaaj bɛɛr : (speaker's) two brothers
- ʔaaj bɛɛr ɟak ginɛŋ : where are you going? (said to one's brothers)

ʔaaj II : breath (as felt close to the mouth)
• ʔat ʔaaj chimbɛp : one's breath

ʔan : and; well, you see... ("filler" in narrative discourse)

ʔaaŋ : wood
- ʔaŋ praŋ : bamboo (a species used for making split bamboo mats or walls) ("female lg.", *cf.* dəlaaw)

ʔaar *(mostly shortened to ʔar)* : first; in front; in advance *(always followed by translocational verb)*
- ʔat ɟjooŋ ʔaar hot, ʔat ʔuuj ɟak klɤɤŋ : the star Venus sets first, and the Moon follows
• ʔar ɟak : (1) walk in front; (2) I leave now

ʔat : the *(Definite Article; +Ferlus)*
- dʌlh ʔdɤɤ ʔat tawɪn : "how many the days", *i.e.* in/for how many days?
- ʔat ɟjooŋ gut hɔɔt ʔat ʔɛɛw laŋ : the father misses (the *i.e.:*) his son

ʔʌ-

ʔʌh : oh well! (expressing resignation)

ʔb-

ʔbaa : dumb (as a speech handicap)
- mlaʔ ʔbaa : dumb person

ʔbac : cut (with sidewards movements)
- ʔbac lam : cut in wood

ʔbaw : unmarried man (*"male lg."*)
• jɤɤm ʔbaw : be still an unmarried man

ʔbɛɛk (*also heard as* bɛɛc) : carry (on shoulder)

ʔbin *in:*
• hɯʌ ʔbin : aeroplane

ʔbiip : press; apply pressure

ʔbit : (1) rotate something along its longitudinal axis; screw
• ʔbit blʌk : screw (something) in
• ʔbit pruk : unscrew (something)
— : (2) wring out (the clothes)
- ʔbit ʔi di chrɔɔɲ : wring something (the washing) out in order for it to dry

ʔbiʔ (*also heard as* biʔ) : caterpillar species (poisonous)

ʔboh : size; this size
• bɔɔ ʔboh (*often reduced to* baboh) this size
• ʔboh mat : small

ʔboj : glass; cup (measure word for amounts of liquid)
- ɟn.raaʔ bon bɛɛr ʔboj : consume two glasses of liquor
- ɟrʌʌk dəmɔ ʔboj : drink one glass

ʔbok : bend the toes so as to keep contact with a surface; use the toes as claws
• teen ʔbok : walk while bending the toes (*e.g.* up a steep or slippery slope)
- ŋɔr hlɛŋ teen ʔbok : walk with bended toes because the path is slippery

ʔbom *see:* paaʔ

ʔboŋ *in:*
• mɛj ʔboŋ : bamboo species

ʔbor : scaly anteater

ʔboʔ *in:*
• kɤɤ ʔboʔ : guitar

ʔbɔɔk : tell; give orders
• bɔɔk maaʔ : (1) tell; inform; order (somebody) to (do something)
- ʔoh ɟak ʔbɔɔk maʔ mɛh jʌk-jʌk : I'll tell you what to do
- ʔoh ʔbɔɔk maʔ ʔa noɲ : I have told you all I know

ʔbɔɔŋ : iron handle of knife

ʔbuk.ʔbuuk : bird species (its description resembles pigeon but it is said to be smaller)

ʔbuŋ : basket
- ʔbuŋ lʌp juuk : basket for rice

ʔbuʔ : slowly
- leh ʔbuʔ : come late

- ʔat tiʔ ɟak ʔbuʔ : he walks slowly
ʔbuuʔ : close by

ʔd-

ʔdaaj *in:*
- kibi chak ʔdaaj : be pregnant
- ʔot hma(a)j kibi chak ʔdaaj : my wife is pregnant

ʔdɤɤ *Indefinite or Interrogative Modifier*
- dʌlh ʔdɤɤ : how many
- dɛɛn ʔdɤɤ : any place
- ɟi.ʔdɤɤ : anything; any
- pan ʔdɤɤ : when
- mɛh pruk pan ʔdɤɤ : when are you coming?
- piaʔ ʔdɤɤ : edible animals
- ʔdɤɤ ʔa dɔ thɛh : some (whatever)
- dɛɛn ʔdɤɤ ʔa dɔ thɛh : any place (will do)
- hnʌm ʔdɤɤ ʔa dɔ thɛh : some year (in the future)
- ɟi.ʔdɤɤ ʔa dɔ thɛh : anything will do

ʔdɛɛ *(Clause-final Adverb in paired clauses:)*
- ... ʔdɛɛ, ... ʔdɛɛ : both - and
- glaʔ briʔ ʔdɛɛ, glaʔ ɲun ʔdɛɛ : speak Mlabri as well as Northern Thai
- toc hmiʌŋ ʔdɛɛ, toc thʌc ʔdɛɛ : get some fermented tea and also some meat

ʔdɛj : indeed *(Preverbal)*
- kha hɔɔk ʔdɛj ɲaŋ khɔt : the Spear Tribe does have spears

ʔdiŋ **I** : big; major
- thapuul ʔdiŋ : big belly
- ɟŋ.guɯɯn ʔdiŋ : midnight
- ʔa ɟŋ.guɯɯn ʔdiŋ : it is midnight
- mɤʔ ʔdiŋ : mother who is/was the father's first wife
- rumgum ʔdiŋ : thumb

ʔdiiŋ **II** : mountain ox; water buffalo
- naŋ ʔdiiŋ : blue sky
- ʔdiiŋ briʔ : wild cattle; gaur

ʔdɯɯn : lazy
- miɲiŋ ʔdɯɯn chak toc : I won't marry a lazy girl

ʔdɯt : (1) the back of the upper part of the body)
- toc ʔuulh keeŋ lɔŋ ʔdɯt : gather firewood and carry it on back
- chi ʔdɯt : feel pain between the shoulders
- ŋokŋɯk ʔdɯt : spinal chord
- pleʔ ʔdɯt : kidney
- ʔem ʔdɯt : sleep on one's back
— : (2) the back side of something; the upper side of the hand

ʔdoŋ : penis; outlet tube (*e.g.* of an air pump)

ʔdoʔ : porcupine

ʔdɔlh *in:*
- dɔ ʔdɔlh : together

ʔdɔɔʔ : banana sprout containing the undeveloped banana cluster (used as a vegetable)
- gn.rɛɛ ʔdɔɔʔ : a curry containing banana sprouts
- ʔdɔʔ gɛɛŋ : sprout of cultivated

banana
- ʔdɔɔʔ kwɤj tr.lok : sprout of wild banana species

ʔdum.ʔduum *in:*
- ʔdum.ʔduum thrɛɛŋ : plaque (on teeth)

ʔe-

ʔee : hey!; see!; listen!; oh my!; ooh (expressing a sudden impulse, surprise, or fright)
- ʔee, diiŋ juuk bə.chih : look, the bamboo section in which we are boiling the rice, is cracking!
- ʔee, gʌm mɤn ɟak, mɛh jɤɤm hɛh : hey, don't go yet, you should stay on for a little while!
- ʔee, ɟak dɔɔ tih : let's go this way together!
- ʔee, rə.ʔʌh thahaan ʔa pruk : oh my, the soldiers will be here in a moment!
- ʔee, ʔa groʔ kabook : listen!, the kabok bird is singing
- ʔee, ʔi choo ʔa thɤkthɤɤk : oh my, the baby is suddenly awake!
- ʔee, ʔoh loh ʔa wʌl hlɔɔp : ooh, I'am afraid of hauntings!

ʔek : take *(infrequent word in β-Mlabri, cf.* toc*)*
- ʔek pruk : bring (along)
- ʔa ʔek pruk : have brought something
- ʔek pruk ʔa dɔ thɛh : it is certainly a good thing to bring something
- toc ʔek leh : take out

ʔem : lie down; sleep (+*Ferlus*)
- ɟak ʔem hma(a)j laŋ : we, wife and husband, are going to bed
- kibi ɲaŋ gɛɛŋ ʔem : be homeless
- lugɔ mat ʔa ʔem : close the eyes and sleep
- ʔem dəmɔj : sleep alone
- ʔem gɛɛŋ : sleep at home
- ʔem chi thapuul : lie in bed with a stomach ache
- ʔem chŋ.ker : sleep on one's side
- ʔem gr.lɤɤŋ : sleep on one's back
- ʔem hmaap : lie on one elbow
- ʔem hmɯp ʔɯp : sleep on one's stomach
- ʔem jʌr : sleep with stretched legs
- ʔem kunkwaan : be sprawling on the ground
- ʔem khot : sleep lying on one's side with bent legs
- ʔem rakɤɲ tr.dɯŋ : sleep one just behind the other, each lying on his/her side
- ʔem rompooʔ : dream *(V)*
- ʔem rompoʔ mʌc : *id.*
- ʔem tʌk tr.dɯŋ : sleep with heads touching each other
- ʔem ʔdɯt : sleep on one's back

ʔeeʔ : (edible) tuber *(generic term and in certain specific terms:)*
- ʔe(e)ʔ lam : cultivated white edible tuber species (resembling the stem of a tree)

ʔɤ-

ʔɤɤ : (1) hey, tell me…!
- ʔɤɤ, gla? tipiaa? : hey, what are they talking about?

— : (2) yes; well

ʔɤh I : (1) do (in a certain manner)
• ʔɤh chɯndeh : how shall I do it?
• ʔɤh də jʌk : do like this
• ʔɤh jʌk : do like this!
• ʔɤh ɟɯn : is experienced
• ʔɤh lɔŋ khɔɔŋ : sing the Thai way
• ʔɤh thɤŋ bɤɤn : find it easy to do

— : (2) work; work as a peasant
• ʔɤh met bɤɤn : be exhausted
• ʔɤh ʔa laac : finish working
• ʔɤh chuʌn, bɔŋ juuk : live as a villager
• ʔɤh kaan : work in the dry field
- ʔoh ʔɤh kaan chak bɤɤn, ɟram : I can't work in the dry field, I'm exhausted

— : (3) occupy oneself with something specific
• tipiaa? ʔɤh : are you too busy (to do something or other)?
• ʔɤh chreʔ : copulate; have sex
• ʔɤh kap : sing
- ʔɤh kap met ɟɯn : I am no good at singing
• ʔɤh kr.nap : sing
• ʔɤh loon : perform ceremony for personal spirit
- ʔɤh loon ʔɤh hmɯɯl di thɛh ɟɤɤm : I perform the ceremony for you, my personal spirit, to be at ease!
• ʔɤh rɯp-thɯp : operate the air pump

— : (4) react to physical sensation (?)
- chiiŋ ʔɤh thu.ʔuur : the pig snorts because it is hot

ʔɤh II : oh!

ʔɤh III in:
• tak ʔɤh hɤɤh/hɤɤj : long ago (with final /-h/ or /-j/ according to different speakers)

ʔɤhɤɤj I : oh!; oh my!; phew!
- ʔɤhɤɤj bɔ.ʔɔɔt : phew, what a smoke!
- ʔɤhɤɤj, kɯr bɔ ruŋ.mruŋ : oh my, what a thunder!
- ʔɤhɤɤj, ʔa ɟŋ.gɯɯn ʔdiŋ : oh, it's midnight!
- ʔɤhɤɤj, ʔjek thuuc : oh, the bees sting!

ʔɤhɤɤj II see ʔɤh III

ʔɤɤʔ : eat (very restricted use, cf. bɔŋ)
• kibi ʔɤʔ bɔŋ : has no food; does not eat

ʔɤh-ʔɤh in:
• ʔɤh-ʔɤh ɟak : wail
- gʌm ʔɤh-ʔɤh ɟak kan mlaʔ ʔa bɯl : don't wail if somebody dies!

ʔɛ-

ʔɛɛ (or with extra lengthening: ʔɛɛɛ) : hey!; look!; great!
• ʔɛɛ, naŋ ʔdiiŋ ʔa gaɲ : look!, the sky is blue and the sun is

shining
- ʔɛɛɛ, ʔoh pagrɛɛt chat hwɤk : hey!, I managed to decoy and stab a rat!

ʔɛh *see* chɯŋ

ʔɛl *(Preverbal, often with preceding* met*)* : (not) yet
- chɛw hɛh ʔɛl biʌc : we must wait because the food is not yet ready ("soft")
- kiʔ rɛɛm ʔɛl puʌc : the moon is waning but not yet small
- ʔoh jɤɤm dəmɔj, ʔɛl toc hmaaj : I live alone, I have not married yet
- ʔoh ʔɛl boŋ : (no,) I haven't eaten yet
- ʔɛl kwaan : is not grown up yet
- ʔɛl toc glaŋ : she has not married yet
• ʔi ʔɛl : no, not yet (in answering)
- ʔi ʔɛl boŋ : no, I haven't eaten yet
• kibi ʔɛl : not yet
- ʔoh kibi ʔɛl boŋ juuk, ʔoh chɛw hɛh : I haven't eaten, I am waiting
• met ʔɛl : not yet
- chiiŋ met ʔɛl bɯl : the pig is not dead yet
- met ʔɛl tuŋ kɔ bliiŋ : it hasn't been boiled yet so it is raw
- mɤm met ʔɛl leh : father has not come yet
- ʔoh met ʔɛl boŋ juuk : I haven't eaten yet

ʔɛɛw : (1) child = offspring (son, daughter); son-in-law (+*Ferlus*)

• ʔat ʔɛɛw grɤŋ : the middle child
• ʔat ʔɛɛw kl.dɯl : the eldest child
• ʔat ʔɛɛw tuul : the youngest child
• ʔɛɛw bɛɛr : married child and/or his/her spouse (?)
• ʔɛɛw hn.rɤʔ : little daughter
• ʔɛɛw jooŋ : son
• ʔɛɛw km.ɲah : daughter (of somebody else than the speaker)
• ʔɛɛw laŋ : son (of somebody else than the speaker)
- ʔat ɟjooŋ gɯt hɔɔt ʔat ʔɛɛw laŋ : the father misses his son
• mɛt ʔɛɛw mɛt ŋwɛʔ : your child
• ʔot ʔɛɛw ʔot ŋwɛʔ : my child
• ʔɛɛw ləmbuuŋ : child (the speaker's own child)
• ʔɛɛw ləmeet : son
• ʔɛɛw məɲiŋ : daughter (*"male lg."*)
• ʔɛɛw mɯlh : daughter (*"mostly female lg."*)
— : (2) child = infant
- ʔɛɛw boʔ ʔat ʔuuj di booʔ : the child sucks its mother's breast
• ʔɛɛw dik theeŋ : child that is just able to crawl or walk
• ʔɛɛw hn.rɤʔ : little girl
• ʔɛɛw thwɛɲ : little baby
— : (2) *(Prenominal)* small; of small size
- ʔɛɛw chn.dɛh : small cup
- ʔɛɛw dɛj : small bag
- ʔɛɛw joc : small chicken
- ʔɛɛw kwʌŋ : a small round thing
- ʔɛɛw thuɤj : small cup

ʔi-

ʔi I : (1) *(Preverbal Conjunction, purposive:)* in order to
- boŋ ʔi biiʔ : eat until you are full!
- gm.hɤɤjh ʔi ɟram : be out of breath
- palɤp ɟuur ʔi noɲ : cram it all "down" (into the bag)
- ʔa noɲ ʔi bɯl : they (my relatives) are all gone, for they have died
• ʔi di : in order to -; in order for something to -
- bit ʔi di chrɔɔɲ : wring something (the washing) out in order for it to dry
- pjaŋ kraŋ ʔi di chrɔɔɲ : unfold and stretch the washing in order for it to dry

— : (2) *(Clause-Connective which signifies contemporality and some kind of causal or explanatory relation between two predications:)* since; because; when; and thus; so (that)
- nikniit ʔi ɟɯm : walk with bent back because the load is heavy
- ʔoh chapat reew ʔi choʔ : I hit myself badly and it hurts!
- tom.ʔooʔ kwɛl, ʔi mʌc mlaʔ ʔa lɔɔr ɟak : the snake lies rolled up; as it sees the person it crawls away
• ʔi ʔɛl : no, not yet (in answering)
- ʔi ʔɛl boŋ : no, I haven't eaten yet

— : (3) *(introducing a clause which expresses fear or warning:)* or else -; for it will be -
- dɤŋ di thɛh ʔi hot : be careful or you'll fall!
- gʌm ɟak wec lam ʔi goh tɯp : don't go far away (in thunder) or a tree may hit you!
- gʌm ɟak ʔi hot : don't go there or you will fall down!
- ɟak ki kheet ʔi hr.looj ruʌŋ reew : we are afraid of going out because we may be carried away by the floods of water
- mɛh jɤɤm rih ʔi wec : you had better stay here, because it's far (to go)
- ʔi hot : you will fall down (if you do it)!

ʔii II *(mostly with vowel shortening)* Marker on the names of junior females and of small children
• ii choo : newborn baby
- ʔee, ʔi choo ʔa thɤkthɤɤk : oh my, the baby is suddenly awake!

ʔii III : oh my!; well!
- ʔii, ʔa wʌl beec : oh my, he/she has started crying
• ʔii, ʔoj : oh... (expressing resignation and/or sarcasm)

ʔit *in:*
• ʔit ɟram : be exhausted

ʔitɯ *(cf. tɯ) in:*
• ʔitɯ mlaaʔ : who (interrogative)
- ʔitɯ mlaaʔ pruk gʌh : who is/are coming there?

- ʔitɯ mlaʔ wʌl ʔɤh gɛɛŋ ɲʌʔ :
who are the builders of this
house?

ʔɯ-

ʔɯh : hey!
- ʔɯh ʔoh maʔ mɛh : hey, I'm giving it to you!

ʔɯɯj : (speaker's) elder sister
• ʔɯɯj bɛɛr : (speaker's) two elder sisters
- ʔɯɯj bɛɛr ɟak ginɛŋ : where are
you going? (said to one's sisters)

ʔɯm : bathe; wash by pouring
water over oneself
• ʔɯm ruʌŋ : bathe in a stream

ʔɯŋ-ʔaaŋ : yawn; open one's
mouth wide
• ʔɯŋ-ʔaŋ chimbɛp : sleep with
an open mouth

ʔj-

ʔjaa *(with unstable glottalization: often heard as* jaa *but here generalized as* ʔjaa*)* : (1)
medicine; drug
• chiit ʔjaa : have an injection
• ʔjaa chuʌk : "salt medicine"
(e.g. injected salt water)
• ʔjaa met : medicine (small pills)
• ʔjaa piaaʔ : medicine
• ʔjaa pleeʔ : medicine (pills)
• ʔjaa pleʔ piaaʔ : medicine
(large pills)
— : (2) tobacco
• ʔjaa ɟrʌʌk : tobacco; cigarette

ʔjak : (1) excrements; waste *(N)*
(Ferlus: ʔiak*)*
• ʔjak ŋɔɔk : the inedible intestines of a crab
— : (2) generic term for substances; wax
• ʔjak bɔh : ashes; dust from fireplace
• ʔjak keet : ear wax
- guhgɔh kɯm ʔjak keet : remove
wax from the ear
• ʔjak mat : matter in the eyes
• ʔjak mɔh : dry mucous in the
nose
• ʔjak ʔjek : beeswax; raw wax
— : (3) defecate
• hn.tor kl.dɯl ʔjak : anus
• ɟak ʔjak : go off to defecate
- mlaʔ ɟak ʔjak lɔŋ briiʔ : the
Mlabri goes into the forest to
defecate

ʔjaɲ : walk with slipping
movements of the feet
(e.g. on a steep gravel surface)
• teen ʔjaɲ ɟak : walk with slipping feet
• ʔjaɲ glɤh : move upwards with
slipping feet

ʔjek *(also heard as* ʔjec*)* : bee
• ʔjak ʔjek : beeswax; raw wax

ʔjen **I** : be cold (of objects or
substances)
- dɔɔk juuk di ʔjen : put the
(boiled) rice somewhere in
order for it to cool
- ɟakɔn thalɛɛl ʔuulh ʔjen : warm
one's hands at the fireplace
because one is cold

- ɟrʌʌk ʔjen : cold water
• klol ʔa ʔjen : be calm

ʔjen II : vein

ʔjen III *in:*
• choʔ ʔjen : have a stitch in one's side
• gr.lijh ʔjen : have a stitch in one's side

ʔjɛt *(also heard as jɛt)* : (1) women's skirt *("female lg.")*
• hn.taʔ ʔjɛt : loincloth with a strip hanging down
— : (2) the plate on the lower side of a crab

ʔjiŋ-ʔjɛɛŋ : mongoose
- ʔjiŋ-ʔjɛɛŋ krɛc kr.hɤɤt biip mɛɛm : the mongoose bites the throat and sucks blood

ʔjɯɯk : banana (wild edible species) *("female lg.")*

ʔjɯŋ.ʔjɛŋ *see* ʔjiŋ.ʔjɛɛŋ

ʔjoc : hen; chicken
• mat ʔjoc : malleolus; "hen's eye" *(+Ferlus)*

ʔjɔh : spit *(V)*
• gom.ʔwak ʔjɔh : collect saliva in the mouth and spit

ʔo-

ʔoo : oh!; see!; great!
- ʔoo, ta braliiŋ : oh, it (the rice field) is green now!
- ʔoo, ʔa bɤɤn tawlii : that's great, now we have lamps!

ʔoh : I/me; my

ʔoj *in:*
• ʔii, ʔoj : oh… (expressing resignation and/or sarcasm)

ʔot : (1) my
- ʔot glaŋ : my husband
- ʔot gruɤɤ : my personal belongings
- ʔot juuk ʔa noɲ : I have no more rice
- ʔot ʔɛɛw : my child(ren)
— : (2) something on me
- chapat ʔot chiʌɲ : swat that mosquito on my skin!

ʔɔ-

ʔɔk *see* ʔɔn ʔɔk

ʔɔɔm : bottle
- ʔɔɔm ɟrʌʌk : bottle with drinking water

ʔɔɔn *in:*
• kuj ʔɔɔŋ : insect species (big, stinging, wasp-like)

ʔɔn ʔɔk *in:*
• pluŋ ʔɔn ʔɔk : hot but not burning hot
- tom pluŋ ʔɔn ʔɔk : heat the food

ʔɔʔ : bag made by folding a leaf or sheet *(cf.* pr.ʔɔʔ*)*

ʔu-

ʔuʌʔ : butterfly (various species but apparently not moths)

ʔuuj : (1) mother; *(restrictedly:)* woman
- ʔɛɛw bɔʔ ʔat ʔuuj di booʔ : the child sucks its mother's breast
- ʔot ʔuuj ʔot ɟjooŋ jɤɤm gɛɛŋ :

Mother and Father are at home
- ʔuuj gʌw : female ancestor (?)
- ʔuj jooŋ woman and man (as a procreating couple)
- ʔuuj prɪm : female ancestor (?)

— : (2) female animal
- ʔat ʔuuj krukkrɔk ʔat ʔɛɛw : the hen clucks to its chicken
- ʔuj ʔjoc : hen

— : (3) the Moon
- ʔuj jooŋ : the Moon and the star Venus

ʔuulh : (1) fireplace; firewood (big logs) (+Ferlus)
- ʔuulh batoʔ : fireplace with firewood
- gr.nɯh ʔuulh : flames from the fireplace
- ʔɤhɤɤj, gr.nɯh ʔuulh : see, the firewood is ablaze!
- puuŋ ʔuulh : blow into the fire; make the fire ablaze

— : (2) in:
- chɯɯk ʔuulh : electrical wire

ʔup see hmup

ʔw-

ʔwɛʔ (sic?, cf. ŋwɛʔ) in:
- mɛɛ ʔwɛʔ (sic?) newly married girl
- ta bɔɔ ʔwɛʔ (sic?) newly married man

Chapter 8

English-Mlabri Word Index

(Note: the listing of words under generic headings such as "insect species" is not exhaustive; species which could be given more specific glosses are listed under the appropriate English gloss.)

A

a little: ɟɔʔ, mɔ teet, nomɔ teet
abdomen: thapuul
ablaze: gɯh
able *see* can
abscess *see* core of an abscess
abound: chɛʔ
abuse *see* scold
ache: choʔ, greet
acquire: bɤɤn
Adam's apple: pleʔ kook
adult: rɛɛm hluak, rɯm hluak
adult man: tareeŋ
aeroplane: hɯʌ ʔbin
afraid *see* be afraid of; fear
afterwards (*i.e.* and then): gwɤɤj
again: chɛɛm
aged: chak-kom.ruujh
air pump: rɯp-thɯp
alang-alang leaves: chr.leeŋ
alive: bliiŋ, kibliiŋ, met gɤj bɯl
all: nɛŋ hmuu, ʔa noɲ
all over: ʔa noɲ
alright: ʔa dɔ thɛh
alone: dəmɔj
also: kɔ, ki
altogether: ʔa laac
and: nɛŋ (*also see* with)

and then: gwɤɤj
animal species (unidentified): baruul, dr.mɔʔ
another: taaŋ
answer: tɔɔ, tɔɔp
ant species: hnɯl.hnɯl, micmɛɛc, mot, rɯm.ram, tɯŋtʌŋ
anteater: ʔbor
antenna: chɯɯk thit ɲuʔ, hɲim.hɲɛɛm
anus: hn.tor kl.dɯl
any number of: ki - ʔa dɔ thɛh
anything: ɟi.ʔdɤɤ, tipiaaʔ
anywhere: ɟi.ʔdɤɤ
appear: pruk
aqueduct: chumdɔɔj ɟrʌʌk
area underneath: kom.room
areca nut: pleeʔ maak
arisen *see* awake
arm: blɛɛŋ
arm ring: chuʌk blɛɛŋ
armpit: kun.doʔ
arrest: gɯp
arrive: hɔɔt, pruk, leh
as: jʌk, jʌw
ascend: glɤh
ashes: bɔh
ask for: krɔɔ, choop

astringent: chat
at: kap, ni, ti
auditory duct: wɯŋ
aunt: hɲaaʔ, jaaʔ
avoid (by escape): rɛɛʔ
awake: pɯh
axe: kwɛk

B

baby: ʔɛɛw chilaɲ, ʔɛɛw thwɛɲ, ʔii choo
back: ʔdɯt, nuur
backwards: lɔŋ kl.dɯl, lɔŋ klɤɤŋ, tɯltɤl
bacon: kraŋ
bad: mɛt thɛh
bag: cot, dɛj, ʔɔʔ, pr.ʔɔʔ
ball: pleʔ lumbuk
bamboo: chə.ʔuʌk, dalɛʔ, dəlaaw, dɯr, mɛj ʔboŋ, tr.luuʔ, ʔaŋ praŋ
bamboo section/tube: diiŋ
banana species: kwɤj (tr.lok), ʔjɯɯk
banana leaf (big species): druuʔ
banana sprouts: ʔdɔɔʔ
bark (N): tə.plaaʔ, naŋ
bark (V): proh
barking deer: poolh
base: kl.dɯl, klɔl
bashful: klaj
basket: ʔbuŋ, kwɤj
bast: thɯh.prah
bathe: ʔɯm, pa.ʔɯm
battery: ga.chah
be back: wʌl
be silent!: gʌm chi.ʔih
beak: ɟɯrnɔk
beans: pleʔ ɟraam, pleʔ thuʌʌ
bear (N): biɯk, bɛɛk

bear (V): kɤɤt (ʔɛɛw)
bear cat: kr.wɛk
beard: mujmuj, mɔɔj
beat: chapat, tɛk, tiktɛk
beautiful: ŋaam
because: biaʔ, dɔ, jʌw, ɲʌn, dɔ
bee: ʔjek
beeswax: ʔjak ʔjek
behind: klɤɤŋ
belch: padruuʔ, thɤɤl
bellows: rɯp-thɯp
belt: gɯm-naat
bended legs: khot
beside each other: rakɤɲ
betel case: klɤp maak
betel leaves: thup pruuʔ
big: blaaj, bla(a)j gʌw, kwaan, ʔdiŋ
bind: klɔt, tɔɔ, wʌt
bird (generic term): ʔac
bird species: kabok, pɔk, pruuŋ, trɤɤl, tr.lok, ʔbuk.ʔbuuk
biscuit: juuk prijh.prɛjh, khawnom
bit: kədah
bite (V): cɔk, krɛc
black: chɛɛŋ
bladder: gɛŋ nɔɔm
blade: cɯn, chooʔ
bland: chapaʔ
blanket: gɯmcaj
blind(ed): kaɲit
blink: cip-cɛp
blood: mɛɛm
blow: puuŋ
blow one's nose: ga.theer
blue (shades of –): bn.liiŋ, chɛɛŋ, hlɯɯŋ, kamiin
blunt: mɛt bɯp, mɛt ɲaŋ thrɛɛŋ
boar: chiŋ briiʔ, ŋaj
board (plank): krareel
body: lɯkpaak, chak
boil: bohboh, ɟr.wɤɤl, tɯŋ, tom

boiled: ʔa biʌʌc
bone: ɟi.ʔɛɛŋ
born: kɤɤt
both – and: ʔdɛɛ
both of them: ʔat bɛɛr
bottle: boom
bowels: chi.ʔjʌj, tharac
bowl: chindɛh, thoj
box *(N)*: diiŋ, ka.ʔuup, klɤp
box *(V) see* beat
boy: baaw, lemeet
bracelet: hlɤŋ
brain: dʌm
branch: lɯgɛʔ
break *(V)*: batac, goh, hŋ.kah, keh, kwʌh, pʌp, tac
breast: booʔ
breast bone *see* sternum
breath: ʔaaj
breathe: rɯ.hʌʌk, rɯmthɤɤk
breathless: gm.hɤɤjh
bring: toc pruk, ʔek pruk
broad: rɯɯ bɯɯ
broken: ʔa tac
brood: kot
brook *see* creek
broom: pr.neelh, thɯp ɲuul
brother, *see* elder brother/sibling, younger brother/sibling
brush *(V)*: kraralh
bucket: thoŋgot
bug (species): thapaɲ
bulb: khɛj mat, tawɯn
burning firewood: chɯŋgaɲ
burnt: lɯk.liik
bury: cuʌk tɯp
butterfly: ʔuʌʔ
buttocks: kl.dɯl *(or:* kn.dɯl*)*
button: mak tʌm, mat rwaaj, pleeʔ, pleʔ tʌm
buy: chɯɯ

C

cabbage: lm.bah
calabash: tuut ɟrʌʌk
call: crɤw
calm: klol ʔa ʔjen
camp: kru.ʔuŋ
can *(N)*: khaa
can *(V)*: bɤɤn, mʌc
candle: ɟɯɯn
canine tooth: thrɛɛŋ hn.cok
cannot: chak bɤɤn, kibi bɤɤn, met bɤɤn
cannot eat it: met thɛŋ boɲ
cannot fall asleep: chak grɤj ʔem
car: lot
carefully: gɔɔj
carry: chabaaj, chiw, keeɲ, ʔbɛɛk
carve: glɛj
cat: mɛɛw
catch: gɯp
caterpillar species: ʔbiʔ
caudal vertebrae: hn.taʔ len
cave (in rock): hn.tor kɛp
cavity: kur.ʔuŋ, prɯŋ
cease *see* stop
centipede: kin-ʔdeep
certainly: tɛɛ, ʔa dɔ -
cessation of speech: tɯk
chaff *see* husks
chalk: gompuur
champ *(V)*: gɯɯntak
charcoal *see* burning firewood
chase *(V)*: paniʔ ɟak
cheek: mɛɛw
cheek bone: ɟi.ʔɛɛŋ mɛɛw, kr.nil mat
chest: chruʌt, krujh, rə.ʔɤk
chew: gəm.tɤɤm, gɯɯm, glɛw, ɟiʌj, rɔɔɲ
chew betel: glɛw haat

345

chicken: ʔɛw ʔjoc *(also see* hen*)*
child: dik theeŋ, kumɔɔm, ŋwɛʔ, rɛɛm chet, ʔɛɛw
chili: preʔ
chin: wɤɤŋ
chipped: gɯn-wak
chirp: cɯpcaap, pjɯppjaap
choose: toc
chop: geet, glɛj
cicada: dil-dɛl
cigaret: cɔʔ
circa: ʔa dɔ thɛh
circle: kr.wɛl
circular (movement): kot
city: wiʌŋ
civil servant: tiin briin
classifier *see* noun classifier
claw: rumgum
clean *(V)*: rɯh, kluh
clear one's throat: hlɯŋ, ɟrʌh
clear the ground: pak
clench one's fists: thalʌm
climb: glɤh
clogged: lom hɤr, tɯn
close *(V)*: kralip
close by: ʔbuuʔ
close together: batit
close the eyes: kaɲit mat, lugɔ mat
cloth: gɯn-caj
cloud(s): kuup
cloudburst: bla(a)j guul mɛɛʔ
cloudy *see* dark; sky
cluck: krukkrɔk
cluster: hn.cok, kr.lah
clutch: toctoc
cock's spur: gr.wɛc ʔjoc
coccyx: hn.taʔ lɛn
coconut: pleʔ braaw
cold: dəkat, dəm.hnat, ʔjen
collapse: dɯk
collarbone: tr.nʌlh

collect: kooc toc
collide: dap
colour: ɟɯk
comb *(N)*: chn.rɛɛt
comb one's/somebody's hair: chrɛɛt, prwɯcprwʌʌc
come: leh, maa, pruk, wʌl
comfort a child: juh.juh
comfortably: di thɛh
completed: ʔa laac
completely: noɲ
constantly: bɔ tɔɔ
converse: glaʔ gr.laʔ
cookie: khawnom
copulate: ʔɤh cɛɛʔ
core of an abscess: mat
core of a medulla: blɛɛŋ
corn: chalii, chaloo
corncob: hlaguur
cornea: phakhaaw
corpse: mlaʔ bɯl
correct: chɯŋ chi.ʔɛh, koʔ, kreeʔ, ʔa mɛɛn
cortex *(also see* bark*)*: pr.luut
cough *(V)*: hlɯŋ
country: mɯʌŋ
couple *see* married couple
cover *(N)*: kralit
cover *(V)*: pok, ʔbom
cover grave: tɯp bɛʔ
cover oneself: trɯp
crab: gɛjh
crackling: kraŋ, prijh.prejh naŋ chiiŋ
cram: palɤp
crawl: lɔɔr, mʌʌr, tɛj
crazy (?, *cf.* dumb): mlaʔ ʔbaa
creek: kah, ruʌŋ
creeper (liane): mʌʌʔ
creeper species: chɯrkaan, mathuuʔ, phak khɯɯp

cricoid: gurtɔr lɔt
cricket: cinbriin
crooked: kur.ʔwɔk.ʔwɛk
cross (V): kawak
crossbow: pɤɤl
crossed legs: khot
crow (V): drɤh
crown (= top of head): kumɔɔm
cry (weep): beec
cultivate: tɤl
cup: chindɛh, poʔ, thoŋgot
curry: gn.rɛɛ
cut (N) see wound
cut (V): brɛŋ, dɛl, geet, glɛj, koh, krɛc, raalh, ʔbac
cut off: paat, pɤjh
cut oneself: tac
cutter: kr.liip
cutting edge: ɟɯn
cylinder: diiŋ

D

dance (V): bɔɔn
dark(ness): bah, kaɲit, thm.rɯm
date a girl: ɟak pruk luŋguh
daughter: ʔɛɛw məɲiŋ, ʔɛɛw mɯlh, ʔɛɛw km.ɲah
day: tawɪn
day after tomorrow: paaj
day before yesterday: bn.nʌʔ
daylight: tawɪn
dead: ʔa bɯl
deaf: ket hlɯɯt
deceased person: wɔk
decorate, decoration: ɟwiil
deep: ɟruʔ
deer species: ciaak, delh, lɯmak, poolh
defecate: ʔjak
delapidated: bukbuk

dent: rɯmooj
descend: ɟuur, kraŋɛl
deserted: ɟuuŋ
desiccated: bə.chih
desire: chi bɤɤn
detest: ɲajh
developped: dʌlh
diarrhoea: bet.rec bet.rac
die: bɯl
different: hak, taaŋ
dig: cuʌk, chaʔ bɛʔ, cheh, gɯr, kaan, krɯh bɛʔ
digging stick: chooʔ
diminish: rɛɛm
dirt: bɛʔ, rɤʔ
dirty: ɟr.mɯk, rɤʔ
disabled: ɟak met bɤɤn
disappear: rɛɛʔ
discard: bakɯm
distantly: dəkah
distinctly: ɟa reew
distribute: gr.wah
disturb: cuɤl, hlin
divorce (V): bakɯm
do: ʔɤh
doesn't know: met mʌc cɯɯ
doesn't like: chak bɤɤn, ɲajh
dog: chɔɔʔ
domesticated: - gɛɛŋ
don't: gʌm, ʔa chak
don't know: met mʌc cɯɯ
door: kn.lap hn.tor, kn.lap hook
down: ɟm.nuur, ɟuur
down there: chugwʌʌʔ, chuh
dragon fly: kər.beel
dragon spirit: wɔk paŋ
dream (V): ʔem rompooʔ
drill: khwat
drink (V): ɟrʌʌk
drip: ɟuʌt, ruuc
drop off to sleep: nuu ʔem

drug *see* medicine
drum: tuŋtuuŋ
drunk: thaŋɔɔt
dry: chrɔɔɲ, kraŋ
dry field: chuʌn, kaan
dry firewood: lam bɯlbɯl
dumb: glaʔ met bɤɤn, ʔbaa
dusk: ɟjʌl
dust: rɤʔ, ʔjak bɔh
dusty: rɤʔ

E

ear: keet
ear lobe: dop, lm.bʌr keet, hnop
ear ring: taaŋ keet
early evening: gaɲ lɛŋ, gaɲ thwɛɲ
earth: bɛʔ
earthworm: khɯʔ ʔdɯɯn
east: tawın ʔa leh, tawın ʔa pruk
easy to do: ʔɤh thɤŋ bɤɤn
eat: boŋ, ʔɤɤʔ, chot
edge: thrɛɛŋ
edible meat: thʌc piaʔ ʔdɤɤ
egg: khɛj
eight: tiiʔ
elbow: gr.tʌl
elder brother: ʔaaj
elder female relative: hɲaaʔ, jaaʔ
elder male relative: taaʔ
elder sibling: diŋ
elder sister: diŋ mɯlh, ʔɯɯj
elephant: chaaŋ, pompoo
elephant's tusk: ŋaa pompoo
embers: chɯŋgaɲ ʔuulh
embrace: kutkwat
encounter *(V)*: mʌc
enter: blʌk
entirety: noɲ
entrance: hn.tor
epidermis: kɤpkɤɤp

erection: ʔdoŋ km.riiʔ, ʔdoŋ kleh
escape: rɛɛʔ
evening *see* dusk, early evening, twilight
evening glow: lɛŋ dooŋ, thwɛɲ dooŋ
eventually: gɔɔj
everybody: ʔa noɲ nɛŋ hmuu
exclamatory particles: ʔaa, ʔʌh, ʔee, ʔɤɤ, ʔɤh, ʔɤhɤɤj, ʔɛɛ, ʔii, ʔɯh, mmm, ʔoo, ʔoj
excrement: ʔjak
exhaled air: cuŋ chimbɛp
exhausted: ɟram, ʔit
exist: ɲaŋ
experience: mʌc
experienced: ɟen
extinguished: ʔa blɯt
extra: hlɯɯ
eye: mat
eyeball: kul.wʌŋ mat, khɛj mat
eyebrow: kr.nil mat
eyelashes: mujmuj mat
eyesight *see* have bad eyesight

F

face *(N)*: buuk
fall *(V)*: chʌm, hot, kuh, tok, trɯh
fall apart: kʌlh
fall off: pluut
fan: grawɯlh
far (away): dəkah, poon, wec
far down: ɟruʔ
fashion: dɛɛn
fast: wɛj
fat *(N)*: hlawaac, mɯj
father: jooŋ, ɟjooŋ, mɤm
fathom: bjaalh
fear *(V)*: krʌw, kheet
feel pain: chi, choʔ, thakat

fell (a tree): dɛl
female skirt: chin
female title ("Mrs."): jaa
ferocious: chɛʔ
fetch: kalɯp, toc
few: cɔʔ
fibre: buʔ.bɔʔ, chɯɯk, priilh
fight (for fun): pum-pam
fill on: chaj
finger: rum.gum
finger nail: chŋ.kɛr tiiʔ
finger tip: gr.wɛc tiiʔ
finished: hɲcʌt, tɯk, ʔa ɟreen, ʔa laac, ʔa lɛn, ʔa noɲ
fire fan: grawɯlh ʔuulh
fireplace: ʔuulh
firewood: ʔuulh, hŋ.keeʔ
first: hɛh, ʔar
first wife: hmaaj kl.dɯl
fish (N): kaaʔ
five: thɤɤŋ
five days from now: hr.lɔh
fix: chaj
flames: gr.nɯh
flange: kac
flashlight: gɔɔŋ chooŋ
flat end: dʌl
flesh: thʌc
float: hurlooj
flood: ɟrʌʌk brɤɤlh, ɟrʌʌk rim ruʌŋ, lm.bah
floor compartment: gɛɛŋ chibɛʔ
flower: bakkah
flowing water: buŋ ruʌŋ
flush with water: lʌp ɟrʌʌk
fly (V): pʌr
fly (N): rɔɔj
foetus: kwɤj
fold: hnep
folded arms: kewkew rə.ʔɤk
fond of: mak

foot: ɟɤɤŋ
for a long time: ʔa prɪm
for example: jʌk
for the benefit of: maaʔ
forcefully: ɟa reew
forceps: kr.laap
foreleg: tiiʔ
forest: briiʔ, luah (also see jungle)
forget: hr.liiŋ
former wife: hmaaj prɪm
forwards: lɔŋ hnaa buuk
four: pon
four days from today: muk
four times: pon thɯɯ
frog: ɟrɤŋ, kukwap, toguk
from: kɛj, tu (cf. ti, nɛŋ)
front end: dʌl
fruit: pleeʔ
fruit fly: riwej
fruit species: pleʔ cʌr, pleʔ chat, pleʔ chreelh, pleʔ gm.nat, pleʔ kiʌn, pleʔ kulrul, pleʔ lam, pleʔ pap, pleʔ pjooŋ
full (= not hungry): biiʔ
full-grown: bla(a)j kwaan
full moon: kiʔ thʌp pompoo, kiʔ ʔa bʌr, kiʔ ʔa bɪŋ, thʌp reet

G

game (big animals): piaʔ ʔdiŋ
gap: hn.tor, hook
gasp: gm.hɤɤjh
gaur: ʔdiiŋ
get hold of see fetch
get up see rise
girl: hn.rɤɤʔ, luŋguh
gill: hɲim.hɲɛɛm
give birth: kɤt (ʔɛɛw)
give up on something: bakɯm
give: maaʔ

glad: ʔa thɛh klol
glass: ʔboj, pralit
glasses (= spectacles): ween mat
gnaw: krɛc
go: ɟak
go down: ɟuur, kraŋɛl
goat: bɛɛ
gong: muŋmooŋ
good: thɛh
good-looking: thɛh
gourd species: calamaaʔ, pleʔ
    hlak.hlek, pleʔ kin.ʔdeep, pleʔ
    lak, pleʔ tr.loŋ poŋ
grandchild: nɔɔʔ
grandfather: taaʔ
grasp: ciɣɣk, kum
grave: bontuʔ
grease (N): muɯj
green: bn.liiŋ, braliiŋ, hluɯuŋ
grey: bn.liiŋ
grieve: klol biʌʌc
grind one's teeth: krɛc thrɛɛŋ
grope: guɯpguɯp
ground: bɛʔ
group of people: nɛŋ hmuu
grow (transitive): tɤl
grow up: kwaan glɤh
growl: blot, grooʔ
grown up: ʔa hluak
grub see dig
grunt (V): grooʔ
guitar: kɤɤ ʔboʔ
gullet see oesophagus
gun: chinaat
guy: tareeŋ

H

hail storm: kuɯrmuɯt parɛɛl
hair: borthor, mujmuj, thm.bʌc
hairy: mujmuj

hammer (N): tr.nɛk
hammer (V): pal, tɛk
hand: tiiʔ
handful: kwʌŋ tiiʔ
handle (N): guɯr, ʔbɔɔŋ
hang up: hmuɯl pak
happy: klol ɟuur, mʌʌk, thɛh klol
hard: kleh, km.riiʔ
harvest: krɛc
hatch see brood
haunt: hlɔɔk
have: ɲaŋ, pɤɤʔ
have in one's eye: chəkuɯʔ
have intercourse: ɟwɛj/ʔɤh cɛɛʔ
he see pronoun 3rd person
head: glɤɤʔ
healthy: mɤk
heap (in a h.): hɲuc.hɲec
heart: klol
heat: thalɛɛl
heavy: chwal, ɟuɯm
heel: hn.dɤl
help (V): ɟɔɔj
hen: ʔuj ʔjoc (also see chicken)
here: cuɯj, gʌh, nɛh, rih
hey, see exclamantory particles
hiccough: plʌk
hide (V): gujh, ruujh
high see tall
high up: ʔa taŋ, ladooŋ, lʌh
highway: ŋɔr gliŋ
hip region: guɯmgoʔ
hip: wul.wal, wul.wuɯul
hit: cam, chapat, chat, dap, pal,
    tɛk, tuɯjh
Hmong: mɛɛw, hmuŋ
hoarse whisper: prijh.prɛjh
hoe (N): cok
hoe (V): klukklɔk
hold (V): dumduum, kum, toc
hole: hn.tor, hook, kur.ʔuŋ

hollow out: gwɛɛt, khwat
honey: thɛɛw
honeydew melon: pleʔ mɯw
hoof: chur.bok
hookah (pipe): dɯr
hop: katooŋ
horizontal(ly): wiŋkɛl
horn (of a goat): kʌw, (of a snail) hɲim.hɲɛɛm mɔh
hot: pluŋ, thuʔuur
house *(N)*: gɛɛŋ
house *(V)*: pok
house pole: tr.nɔlh (*also see* pole)
household: grɔɔk (gɛɛŋ)
how?: chɪn.ʔdeh
how many: dʌlh ʔdɤɤ
hum: km.lɯɯr
human being: mlaaʔ
hungry: chaw.ʔeeʔ
hunt *(V)*: peɲ piaʔ ʔdɤɤ
hurry: wɛj
hurt (it hurts) *see* ache
husband: glaŋ, laŋ
husband of niece: roh
husk rice grains: chawoj
husked rice: piiʔ

I

I: ʔoh
identical: gɯɯn dr.chɤʔ
if: kan
ill: choʔ, kibi thɛh, met thɛh
imperative marker: di, ɟa, ʔa, ʔa di
in: nɛj, ni, ti
in order to/that: di
in-law: bɛɛr, thaw
incessant: prɪm
indeed: tɛɛ, ʔa dɔ -
indentation: rɯmooj
induce: maaʔ

inedible: ɟr.mɯk
infant: dik theeŋ
inflorescence: hn.cok
inform: ʔbɔɔk
insect species: hmitgoc, kilkiil diŋ, kɯrbeeŋ, kuuj, kuj ʔɔɔŋ, lɯmŋɔɔr, peec, rɛjwɛj, riphɛp, rɔɔj bliiŋ, rɔj juuk
insert *(V)*: chaj, chɛɛm, lʌʌp
inside: təni, ti nɛj
interior: prɯŋ
intercourse, *see* have intercourse
intestines: ʔjak ŋɔɔk
into: blʌk, lɔŋ, ti
introvert: liir
invisible: blɯt
invite: pa.rwaʔ
invoke: kuuk
involucre: cɯʔ-caʔ, kɤpkɤɤp
iron: hlek
iron handle (of knife): ʔbɔɔŋ
itch *(V)*: hmɯʔ.rɯʔ, ŋaʔ
items: grɯɯŋ

J

joint *(N)*: gr.lɛj
jungle: tɛɛn, thɛɛk
just (Adv): chɤm
just a moment ago: cɤh
just over there: ʔbuuʔ

K

kidney: pleʔ ʔdɯt
kill: pabɯl
kinsmen: hna bɛɛr hna ɟum
kitchen: bɔh ʔuulh
knee: kl.kiil
knife: miit, tɔʔ
knock in: cam
knot: kr.lɔt, tut-tuut

know: hmɯɯn, ʔa mʌc cɯɯ

L

lacking: noɲ
lamp: takiʌŋ, tawlii
landslide: pih bahaaʔ
Laos: ɟalaaw, mɤŋ law
large: bla(a)j kwʌŋ
larynx: pleʔ kook
lashing: tun wʌt
last (former): bɯn nah
late: ʔbuʔ
late evening: thm.rɯm
laugh: hr.lɛʔ
layer: kɤpkɤɤp
lazy: ʔdɯɯn
leaf: chalɔɔʔ, lm.bʌr
lean: glɯn
lean-to house: gɛɛŋ
left side: gr.wɛɛn hɔɔ
leg *see* foot, lower leg, thigh
lemon grass: ɟweel
length: wec
let fall: bahot
liane *see* creeper
lice: cheeʔ
lick: bloom, lat
lid: ghɤɤʔ, kampoŋ, kralit
lie (down): hmaap, ʔem
lie on one's side: chŋ.ker
lie rolled up: kwɛl
lift: pajok
lift the eyebrows: thrit.threet
light (N): tawɪn
light (of weight): bɯrh.ralh, piʌk, piʌkpiʌw
light bulb: khɛj mat, tawɪn
light up: tawɪn
lighter: kol hlek
lightning: parɛɛl, pɤɤr, phalɯʌm

like (= similar to): jʌk
lips: chimbɛp
liquor: ɟn.raaʔ
listen: ŋam, tel
little *see* a little; small
live (V): jɤɤm, ɲaŋ
liver: com
lizard *see* monitor
log: glɔɔŋ, lam dɯlkul
loincloth: hn.taʔ ʔjɛt
loins: gomgoʔ
lonely (feeling): ŋɔɔm
long: wec
long ago: tak -, ʔɤh hɤɤh/hɤɤj
long time: prɪm
look (V): dɤŋ, dɤwdɤw, wiŋcɛɛr
look for: loh
loose: boc, klooc, lm.hoor
lots of –: kibɛɛ
loudly: kleh, km.riiʔ
love (V): hlah, loom
low: chibɛʔ
low down: chuh
lower leg: gur.mɔr, hnɛl
Lua': grɛh, kwʌr
lungs: thoh-thoh

M

maize *see* corn
major: diŋ
major wife *see* first wife
make a fire: batooʔ
male: ləmeet
male title ("Mr."): taa
malleolus: mat ʔjoc
man: jooŋ, ləmeet, mlaaʔ, tareeŋ
manage: tɤŋ
mango: pleʔ chreelh
married couple: – bɛɛr, chɔɔŋ pr.daw, hmaaj glaŋ

marry: toc glaŋ, toc hmaaj
mat: chaat, dɯŋmrɛɛŋ gɛɛŋ, tɤlhɤɤ
matter in the eyes: ʔjak mat
mean the same thing: gɯɯn dr.chɤʔ
meat: thʌc
medicine: ʔjaa
medulla: chak
membranous skin: pr.luut
meet: mʌc, lɔŋ mat
Meo see Hmong
"miang" (fermented tea leaves): hmiʌŋ
middle: grɤŋ
middle-aged: tɔ.pruʔ gɛjh
midnight: ɟŋ.gɯɯn
Milky Way: khaaj khaw
mine: br.ʔoh
minor: chet
minor wife see second wife
miserable: dok, jen
miss somebody: gɯt hɔɔt, ŋɔɔm
missing see lacking
mist: cuŋ
Mlabri: mlaʔ briiʔ
moderately: gɔɔj
molar: guul
mongoose: ʔjɯŋ.ʔjɛŋ
monitor (edible lizard): pjee
monkey species: thawaaʔ, thɛɛŋ, chajh
month: kiiʔ
moon: kiiʔ, ʔuuj
more (of something): chɛɛm
morning: tak ɟrɯw, ʔa bah
mosquito: chiʌŋ, muut
mosquito net: hm.pooj
mother: mɤʔ, mɛɛ choo, ʔuuj
mountain: chiboh, choh.boh
mounting: gr.wɤŋ

mourn: ɟɯt, met thɛh klol, phit klol
mouse: tuun (*also see* rat)
mouth (of crab): biʔ-bɛʔ, *also see* lips
move (leave): bralit, niiʔ
move (the house): rɯh
move swiftly: paa
much: chɛʔ
mucous: mɯɯr, ʔjak mɔh
muddy: chr.kʌl, hlɛŋ, khun, licpɛɛc
mug: thoŋgot
mushroom: het
mute: glaʔ met bɤɤn
my (*also see* mine): ʔot
mynah (bird species): ciaŋ

N

nail (1) (on finger/toe): chŋ.kɛr
nail (2) (of iron): hlek cam, hlek pal
nail cutter: kip.lɛp tiiʔ. kr.laap tiiʔ, kr.liip
name: ɟɯɯ, mʌʌlh
namely: khɯɯ
narrow: tɯptaap
natural parting of hair: ril.wel
navel: kin.diiŋ
neck: kukɔɔʔ (*also see* throat)
necklace: chɔj
needle: cɩm.beelh
nephew: nɔɔʔ
net: hm.pooj
never before: met gɤɤj
new: hmɛʔ, mɛ cɤh
new moon: kiʔ hmɛʔ, kiʔ met grɤj ʔdiŋ, kiʔ pruk
newborn child: dik theeŋ
newly married: – ʔwɛʔ (*sic?*)
next (of time spans): ɟrɯw

night: ɟŋ.gɯɯn
nine: gajh
nipple *see* breast
no (= not correct): bah, noɲ
no more to say: ʔa tɯk
noon: tawɪn ʔa hmn.dɯɯr, tawɪn ʔa kɛɛ
north(wards): thaŋ nɯɯ
Northern Thai person: ɲun
nose: mɔh
nostril: hn.tor mɔh, hook mɔh
not: chak, gʌm, kəki, ki, kibi, met
not much: met chɛʔ, ɟɔʔ
not yet: met grʏʏj, ʔɛl
Noun Classifiers: ɟɯn, kwʌŋ, kwɛk, ləboʔ, lm.bʌr, mlaaʔ, pak, pɯɯn, pleeʔ, too, toon, tɔɔn, ʔboj
now: ɲaam gʌh, paan gʌh
nowadays: ɲaam gʌh
numerous: chɛʔ
nurse a child: pabooʔ ʔɛɛw
nut: pleeʔ

O

oblique: pʏʏn, priin
obstruct: kɛl, tɯn
occupy oneself with: ʔʏh
oesophagus: chɯɯk chɔɔt, chɯɯk kr.hʏʏt, chɯɯk puj
of: bʌr
officials: caaw naaj
often: ʔa lɯɯt
oh, *see* exclamatory particles
oil: mɯj
oil lamp: takiʌŋ, tawlii
old: chak-kom.ruujh, prɪm
on: lɔŋ
on a hilltop: pʌk
on one's back: gr.lʏʏn

on one's side: chŋ.ker
on one's stomach: hmup ʔup
on the ground: batit bɛʔ
on top of: br.kiiŋ
once: dəmɔ thɯɯ, mɔ thɯɯ
one: dəmɔ(ɔ), mɔ, mɔj
oneself: chak, hak
onion: pleʔ ɟweel
only: chɯ.chɯɯ
onwards: dʌm
ooh!: ʔee
open (*transitive V*): kwʌh, thrih
open one's eyes widely: pjɯɯr
open one's hand: prak
open one's mouth: ʔɯŋ-ʔaŋ
opening: blɔn, hn.tor, kn.ʔdɯp, kru.ʔuŋ
oppressed: thakat klol
or: chala, glʏʔ
orange (fruit): pleʔ chat
order to do: maʔ di, ʔbɔɔk maaʔ
ordinary: grʏŋ, kr.najh
orifice, *see* opening
other: taŋ
out (not at home): lɔŋ luʏt
out of breath: klol luaak
outer ear: lm.bʌr keet
outlet tube: ʔdoŋ
outside: luʏt
outstretched arm: pirpiip laaʔ
over here: lɔŋ gʌh
over there: dɯgʌʔ, ləgʌʔ *(?)*, təkʌh
overcast: kaɲit
owl (species): kluʏjkluʏj

P

pack: hnɛɛp
package: təptoop
pair of – (relatives): – bɛɛr
palm (of hand): thapuul

palm species: chrʌl, kɛɛ chalɔɔʔ
palpitations (have p.): blɯkdɯk, thʌkthɤɤk, toktok klol
pandanus: pleʔ chreelh
papaya: pleʔ huŋ
path: ŋɔɔr
peak: cəkoo, tuul
pearl: mak pat
peel off: pluut
penetrate: pak
penis: ʔdoŋ
people: ʔat tiiʔ
perfective aspectual marker: ʔa
perforate: taat
perform a ritual ceremony: gʌm-pʌk
person: chak, mlaaʔ
person in charge: tiin briin
personal spirit: loon
pharynx: kr.lɤɤt
pick: joh.joh (also see pinch)
piece of wood: glɔɔŋ
pierce: droojh, hn.theer, lo.ʔuh
pig: chiiŋ
pigeon: kookdrooj, kokokdrooj, kompoʔ loom
pigpen: gɔɔk chiiŋ
pimple (?): thwɛɲ
pinch: plɛk
pineapple: ganat
pipe: kɔɔk, chumdɔɔj
piston: puj
pith: chak
place (N): dɛɛn
place (V): chaj, dɔɔk
plains (flat land): thaluh
plank: dɯm.rɛɛn, kə.plah
plank bed: gɛɛŋ rooŋ
plant species: chooc, gi.chɛŋ, gook jeek, kwiiŋ, phak khɯɯp, thapɛɛt, thoom, wɛk.wɛm
plaque: ʔdum.ʔduum
play: kwɤn, pum-pam
play the mouth organ: puŋ khɛɛn
plus one: hlooj
pocket: dɛj
point (V): pen.deeʔ
poke with finger: gwɛɛc
pole: cɯŋ-rʌŋ, diŋ.rʌŋ, gr.niil, kol lam, toŋ, tr.nolh
policeman: kamnuʌt
polluted: ba.ʔaaʔ
pool: buŋ, hwɤɤŋ
poor: dok, jen
porcupine: ʔdoʔ
possess: ɲaŋ, pɤɤʔ
possessor particle: di
pot: tr.lɔh
pottery: chn.dɛh
pound (V): tɯjh
pour: ɟɯk, tʌʌk, thɔɔk
pregnant: ɲaŋ ʔɛɛw, pɤʔ ʔɛɛw
prick (V): pak
properly: thɛh
property: bʌr
pubic hair of male: mujmuj ʔdoŋ
puddle: hwɤɤŋ
pull (V): ciɔr, crɔɔl, toh
pupil of the eye: tuuj, twaaj
pus: guuŋ
push: jaɲ, pablah
put: chaj, dɔɔk, khalɯp, lʌʌp, pablʌk
put on: bɯk, throoʔ
put out the tongue: hɯl.hal
put to rest: pa.ʔem

Q

question particle: lɛh
quill: borthor, chɯrh.kalh

R

radio: thit ɲuʔ
raft: bɛɛ
rafter: choolh, tharac
rags: ɟuaaʔ
rain *(N)*: mɛɛʔ
rain *(V)*: mɛʔ hmitbɛɛc, mɛʔ hot,
 mɛʔ ɟuʌt, mɛʔ pruɲ.pruuɲ
rainbow: puum paŋ
raincoat: pha.ʔjaaŋ
raise: chɛɛm *(also see* lift*)*
rasp *(e.g.* with the teeth*)*: grɛɛt
rat: hwɤk
raw: kɔbliiɲ *(also see* unripe*)*
rear end: kl.dɯl
receive: toc
reciprocally: tr.dɯŋ
red: thwɛɲ
remember: ʔa mʌc cɯɯ
remove: guhgɔh, kɯm
request *see* ask for
resent: ɲajh
rest *(V)*: cʌt, jɤɤm gɛɛŋ
rest on one's back: gr.hɤɤŋ
return: gɯɯn, mɯɯ, wʌl
ribs: ɟi.ʔɛɛŋ chɛɛ
rice: juuk, piiʔ
right *see* correct
right?: dɔɔ
right side: gr.wɛɛn thɛh
rim: kurnot
rind: kraŋ
rinse: gluh
ripe: hndoom *(also see* soft*)*
rise: jɤɤm ʔa chʌr, leh, pɯh, pruk
ritual *see* perform
road: ŋɔr gliŋ, ŋɔr lot
roast: kraŋ
rock a child: kɯ thwɛɲ,
 dumduum

roll *(N)*: kr.wɛl, thəbɯr
roll *(V)*: kr.kreel, lɔɔm
roll out: thampɯl
roll up: hnep glɤh
roomy: bla(a)j kwʌŋ
root: rɛɛlh *(also see* tuber*)*
root tip: kl.dɯl rɛɛlh
rope: chɯɯk
rose colour: hlɯɯŋ
rotate: tr.leet, ʔbit
round: gir.wɛj
rub: kulrul, ɲoɲ-ɲeɲ, tr.leet, kulrul
rub one's fingers: pɔɔc
rump: hn.taaʔ, kl.dɯl
run: hmujthɔj, talʌr
run away: rɛɛʔ

S

sad: biʌc klol, met thɛh klol
saliva squirting: proolh
salt *(N)*: chuʌk
same: gɯɯn dr.chɤʔ
sandal: khɛɛp
say *(V)*: glaaʔ
scales: klet
scarred: pr.lɔn
school: br.wɛɛc
scold: leew, luh, paa luh
scoop up: bʌt, ɟɯk
scowl: thep.ʔjeep
scrape: chriilh, gɯlh.galh, koot,
 (with the teeth:) chraɲ
scratch: gehgeh, gip-wɛɛc, grɛɛt,
 grl.griil, guur, gwɛɛc,
 gwicgwɛɛc, kɯckac
screw: ʔbit
scrotum: klaw
scrub *(N)*: thɛɛk
search for: loh
season: ɲaam

second wife: hmaaj tuul
see: dɤŋ, mʌʌc (*also see* meet)
seed: pleeʔ
separately: hak
set (sun, moon): hot, kraŋel
seven: gul
sew: ɟeŋ
shade: grum
shake: butbot (*also see* shiver)
shall (planned action): ɟak
shallow: kluh.klɛh, met ɟruʔ
sharp: bɯp
sharpen: pr.gʌɲ
shave (V): klor, koot
she *see* pronoun 3rd person
sheet: druuʔ (*also see* leaf)
shell (of a snail): ɟi.ʔɛɛŋ
shirt: chɯrɛɛ
shiver: moʔ blɤp
shoe: kɤɤp
shop (V): ɟak gwaa talaat
short (of size): kl.reel
short (time): rə.ʔʌh
shorts: chɯr.ʔbat kl.reel
short-tailed: hn.taʔ cewcew
shoulder: laaʔ
shout (V): crɤw
shovel up: chɯkɯh
shrink: rɛɛm
shy: klaj (*also see* fear)
sibling *see* elder/younger sibling
side: hlɛɛm
sieve (N): dr.wiil
sift: heer, rɯc.rʌc
sing: ʔɤh kap, ʔɤh kr.nap, ʔɤh lɔŋ khɔɔŋ
sink (V): brarulh, brulh, ɟuur
sip: chot
sister: *see* elder sibling/sister, younger sibling/sister
sit: caŋ cɯʔ, jɤɤm

six: thaal
size: ʔboh
skeleton (?): ciʌc
skin: naŋ
skinny: ɟraa, kʌr-kɛr
skirt: ʔjɛt
skull: kampoɲ
sky: klaar, klɯɯr
slanting: durdɔr
slash: krɛc
slaughter: pabɯl
sleep (V): ʔem
sleepy: chi ʔem
slip (V): gəmpɤɤlh, phalaat, ʔjaɲ
slippers: khɛɛp
slowly: ɟaa, gɔɔj, ʔbuʔ
sluggish: liir
small: kədah, ʔboh mat, ʔɛɛw
smash: chapat, goh tɯp
smell: muuk
smell good: thɛ.ʔɛn
smile (V): kajek, muɲmɔɲ hr.lɛʔ
smoke (N): bɤttɤɤʔ, bɔ.ʔɔɔtc, cuŋ, thur.thuur
smoke (transitive V): ɟrʌʌk, paruuʔ
smoothe: prwɯcprwʌʌc
snail: khrwaʔ, tɛɛk
snake (generic): tom.ʔooʔ
snake (species): tom.ʔoʔ beelh
sneeze: dɯkʌlh
snore: koon
snort: ʔɤh
snout *see* nose
soak: chɛɛ, ləmɯr
soft: biʌʌc, hmɯrlaŋ
soil *see* ground
soldier: dəmpʌl, thahaan
some: dɔ
son: ʔɛɛw ləmbuuŋ, ʔɛɛw ləmeet
soon: rə.ʔʌh
soul: chɯrmɯɯl

soup: gɔj
sour: chat
south: ʔat tɤj ɟuɤj
spacious: ruɯ buɯ
spade *see* digging stick
span: bjaalh
speak: gla? *(also see* utter*)*
spear: khɔt
"Spear Tribe": khaa hɔɔk
spectacles: ween mat
speech: gr.la?
spherical: gir.wɛj
spicy: gɪm
spill *(N)*: darɔɔʔ
spin: pin, tr.leet
spinal chord: ŋɔk-ŋaak, ŋuuk-ŋɯɯk
spine: ɟi.ʔɛɛŋ ʔdɯt
spiral: kr.wɛl
spirit: hmaal, hmɯɯl, hmɯlbaaŋ, loon, wɔk
spit *(V)*: ʔjɔh
spleen area: liŋgeew
split: poh
split bamboo: darɔʔ, gr.najh, kr.laap *(also see* lashing; spill*)*
split bamboo sheet: dimrɛɛŋ, dɯŋ.mrɛɛŋ
split rattan: blɛt
spoon: ɟɔɔn
spout: keet, kɯtkeet
sprawl: kunkwaan
spray *(N)*: lɯgɛʔ
spread one's arms: lɔɔj
sprout: luŋguh
spur: gr.wɛc ʔjoc
squat: com dok
squeeze: krɛc
squirrel: kraalh
stab: chat, kadɯp
stalk *(N)*: tiw

stalk *(V)* (= walk slowly): ɟɤɤp
stand upright: chʌr
star: chəmɔɲ
stare: dɤŋdɤŋ
start (suddenly move): jajh
startled: klol hot
stay: ɟɤɤm
steam *(N)*: cuŋ, kuup
step *(V)*: teen
stepmother: mɤʔ hmɛʔ
sternum: ɟi.ʔɛɛŋ krujh
stick *(N)*: kol, lam
stick in the throat: bakoot, klɛɛŋ
stick out: paa pruk
stick through: glɔlh
stick to: tit
sticky rice: juuk lɯmpɯt
still *(Adv.)*: ki
sting *(N)* (e.g. of bee): thoɲ
sting *(V)*: thuuc
stink: chal.ʔbuut, cha.ʔɯɯl
stitch (have a st.): chi liŋgeew
stomach: puj
stone: kɛp
stoop *(V)*: com dok
stop: ʔa noɲ, ʔa hɲ.ɟʌt
store *(V)*: dɔɔk, lʌʌp
storm: rəmɯt
straight (not bent): chɯɯ
strap: chɯɯk
stray *(V)*: ɟak gʌh ɟak ɲʌʔ
stream of water: kah, ruʌŋ, wɤɤk
stretch (out): ɟuʌʌŋ
stretch one's hands forward: ɟakɔn
stretch oneself: cɔɔ ciʌc, dɯk, pjɔɔlh
stretched arms: pirpiip laaʔ
stretched legs: ɟʌr
string: chaaj, chɯɯk, gəm.pʌk
stripe: chɔkchɔɔr, laaj

stroke (V): prɯcprwʌʌc, rm.paalh
stroll (V): ɟak gwaa
strong: ɟualh, reew
strum: plʌlh
stumble: chʌm
stump of tree: kl.dɯl
substance: ʔjaak
suck: biip, bloom, gimheep, ɟook
sugar cane: gilmɛʔ
suitably: mɤk, thɛh
sun: kiiʔ, tawɪn
sun has just risen: ʔa bah
sun is in zenith: tawɪn kɛɛ
sun is low down: tawɪn wiik
sunrise: tawɪn ʔa leh, tawɪn ʔa pruk
sunset: tawɪn ʔa hot, tawɪn ʔa wiik
sunset time: ʔa burɔrɛɛl, ʔa lɛŋ tooŋ
supporting pole: dur.dɔr, gr.nɤl
suppress a smile: muɲ-mɔɲ
surface: rooŋ
surround: room
suspended: panɛŋ
swallow (V): lʌʌr (brwatbrwat)
swarm: kɯm-lɯɯr
sweep: peelh, kwac
swelling (N): tum
swim: lɔj ɟrʌʌk
swing: bel.wet
swollen: buŋbɔŋ

T

tail: hn.taaʔ
tail feathers: rujkoj
take: toc, ʔek
take along: gan ɟak
take care!: ʔa dɤŋ chɤm
take (shirt) off: luun
take out: cok toc, toc ʔek leh
talk (V): glaʔ (also see converse)
talk together: glaʔ dɔʔ dɔlh, glaʔ tr.dɯŋ
tall: bla(a)j pɯɯn, chuuŋ
taro: kwaaj
taste (V): ceet lɛɛl
tear (N): gɔj mat
tear (V): joh, lo.ʔuh, rɯt, tac
tell: ʔbɔɔk
ten: gal
tender: lumpuk
tenderloin: thʌc mɔɔl
term: mʌʌlh
termite: thɯbɯr
terry cloth: mujmuj
Thailand: mɤŋ thɛj
that one: ɲʌʔ
that way (direction): lɔŋ gʌh
thatch (V): tʌp ʔat lwɛɲ
thatching material: chr.leeŋ, lwɛɲ
that's (called –): pen
then: gwɤɤj, nii, tak ɲaam gʌh
there: ɲʌʔ, rih, also see down there, over there
there is: ɲaŋ, pɤɤʔ
they see pronoun 3rd person
they two: ʔat bɛɛr
thick: ʔdiŋ
thicket: thɛɛk
thigh: bluuʔ
things: grɯɯŋ, gruɤɤ
think (V): gɯt
thirsty: chi ɟrʌʌk, (of baby) chi booʔ
this: gʌh, nɛh, nii
this size: boh, bɔɔ boh
thorn: cɪmbeelh, gm.tɯl, la.ʔɔɔk
thread: paaj
three: pɛʔ
three days from today: pwɛt

three times: bɛr thɯɯ hlooj
thresh: tɛk kraralh
throat: kr.lɤɤt
through: tih
throw: bahot, bakɯm, dor, kɯm, tʌl, twec hot
thrown aside: gəmpɤɤlh
thumb: rum.gum ʔdiŋ
thunder: kɯr, lɔŋ br.nah
thunderstorm: kɯr-(r)mɯt
thus: jʌk
tickle (V): tɯk.lʌk
tie (V): chuʌk, wʌt
tiger: rwaaj
tight see too tight
tilt: pɤɤŋ, priin
time (period): ɲaam, paan
time (= occurrence): thɯɯ
tin (N): khaa
tip (of a pointed blade): tuul
tip (of a finger or toe): gr.wɛɛc
tip (of a snail shell): kl.dɯl
tip over: bakuh, kuh
title of junior female: ʔi
title of junior male: baa
title of senior female: mɛɛ
title of senior male: bɔɔ
tobacco: ʔjaa
today: tawɪn nɛh
toe (soft part): rum.gum ɟɤɤŋ
toe nail: chŋ.kɛr ɟɤɤŋ
together: dɔɔ, gɯɯn, gwaj mlaaʔ, kʌn, rɤɤm, ruuc, tr.dɯŋ
together with: lɯŋ, nɛŋ
tomorrow: ɟrɯw
tongue: rt.lat
too tight: thakat
tooth: thrɛɛŋ
top (of the head): kumɔɔm
torch: mɛjmuut
torn: bə.chih, reh, rɯt

torso: chak
touch (V): gip-wɛɛc
touch with the tongue: ceet
trail see path
travel back and forth: ɟakɟak wʌlwʌl
tree: lam
tree species: (pleʔ) booʔ, (pleʔ) braaw, (pleʔ) chat, pleʔ chreelh, dɯmpʌl, goh, (pleʔ) huŋ, (pleʔ) kiʌŋ, (pleʔ) klɔk, (pleʔ) kulrul, (pleʔ) lwɛɲ, see further bamboo species, palm species
tribal: kr.najh
trickle: ɟuʌt
tripod: toŋ ɟoʔ toŋ ɟaʔ
trough: plɯɯŋ
trousers: chooŋ, chr.ʔbat, tɪw
trunk (of chest): chɛɛ
trunk (of tree): glɔɔŋ
tuber, generic term: ʔeeʔ
tuber species: dɯw, hmaaʔ, kwaaj, lok, thruut, wɛjh, ʔeʔ lam
turn upside down (V): pliin, pɔɔl
turtle: gə.chooŋ
tusk: ŋaa
twice: bɛr thɯɯ
twig see withered
twilight: bɯl.joom.jeem
twitter: cɯpcaap, pjɯppjaap
two: bɛɛr, chɔɔŋ

U

ugly: met ŋaam, met thɛh
umbilical cord: chɯɯk kindiiŋ
umbrella: ɟup.lup
uncle: taaʔ
under something (V): br.pooŋ
undevelopped: kloolh

unfold: pjaŋ
unhappy: klol mɛt thɛh
unkind: mɛt thɛh klol
unmarried man: tareeŋ, ʔbaw
unripe: bliiŋ, kibliiŋ
"unripe" of colour: hlɯɯŋ
unscrew: ʔbit pruk
unwrap: thrih
up: lʌh, glɤh
up above: ladooŋ, lʌh
up there: lagʌʔ, lakʌh, təkʌh
uphill: choh boh
upper arm: gr.tʌl
upper side: rooŋ
upset: klol pluŋ
urinary bladder: gɛŋ nɔɔm
urinate: nɔɔm
usable: mɛɛn, thɛh
use *(in some contexts)*: toc
used up: ʔa noɲ
utter a sound: grɯʔ
uvula: kl.dɯh

V

vagina: plil
vegetable (fruit-like): pleeʔ
vein: ʔjen
very: ʔa reew
very much: chɛʔ
vine *see* creeper
visit *see* stroll
vomit: thɤɤl
vulva: cɛɛʔ *(also see vagina)*

W

wade: kawak, kumduŋ
wail: ʔɤh-ʔɤh ɉak
wait for: chɛw
wake up: pajɤʔ
walk: ɉak, ɉɤɤp, tɛj, teen

waning (moon): puʌc, reet, rɛɛm
want to: chi
warm: thu.ʔuŋ *(also see hot)*
wash *(V)*: baɉah, chapat, ɲoɲ-ɲeɲ, rɯjh, rɯp.paaʔ
wasp-like insect species: gumpuur, peec
watch *(V)*: dɤŋ
water: ɉrʌʌk, ruʌŋ
water level: rim
water melon: pleʔ muu
wax: plʌm, ʔjak ʔjek
way: dɛɛn, *also see* path
we: ʔah
we two: jah
weed *(N)*: run juuk
weed *(V)*: ʔɤh run
weep: beec
well *(N)*: ʔɛɛw kah
west: tawɯn hot
wet *(V)*: chɯkkɔʔ
what: tipiaaʔ
when: pan ʔdɤɤ
where: ganɛŋ, ginɛŋ
whet: pr.gʌɲ
which: ʔitɯ
whistle *(V)*: glɔɔc, puuŋ tiiʔ
white: bəlaak, pha.khaaw
who: ʔitɯ mlaaʔ
whose: bʌr ʔitɯ mlaaʔ
why: tipiaaʔ
wick: paaj
wicked: klol kleh
wide *see* broad; spacious
wife: hmaaj
wild dove (?): pruuŋ
wind: rəmɯt
wing: hnʌr
wink *(V)*: cip-cɛp, kaɲeer
winnowed basket: kwɤj
winnowed wall: chɯŋtɯŋ

wipe: pilh.pɛɛlh, pɔɔc, prwɯcprwʌʌc, thɯt
wireless set: thit ɲuʔ
with: kap, nɛŋ, ni
with a bent head: cej-dej
withered: gur.ʔuur
withered twig: bn.rajh
within: kap, ni
woman: mɯlh, ʔuuj
wood: dalɛʔ, ʔaaŋ
woodpecker: pɔk
word(s): gr.laʔ
work *(V)*: ʔɤh
worn (clothes): ʔa tac, ʔa thalɯc
wounded: paraat
wrap *(V)*: kujkwʌj, təptoop
wring: ʔbit
wrinkled: hɲuʔ-hɲɔʔ
wrist: gr.lɛj

Y

yams *see* tuber
yard (measure): pirpiip laaʔ
yawn: thaŋaap, ʔɯŋ-ʔaaŋ
year: hnʌm
yellow: hlɯɯŋ
yes: koʔ, ʔɤɤ, mmm
yesterday: nɛɛ
yet: ʔɛl
yonder: lɔŋ ɲʌʔ
you (singular): bn.hnɛʔ, mɛh
you (dual): bah
you (plural): bah ɟum, bah thɤɤŋ, bah tiiʔ
young (of age): biʌʌc
young (= offspring): ʔɛɛw
young girl: hn.rɤɤʔ
young man: burbur, hnum, ʔbaw
younger brother: rooj laŋ
younger sibling: dadrooj, kumɔɔm, rooj
younger sister: rooj mɯlh
your(s): br.mɛh, mɛt

Z

zenith: tawɪn kɛɛ

REFERENCES

Bernatzik, Hugo 1938: *Die Geister der gelben Blätter.* Bruckmann, München (also – with certain modifications of the text – Leipzig 1941). In English translation 1951: *The Spirits of the Yellow Leaves.* London: Robert Hale Ltd.

Benedict, Paul K. 1943: "Studies in Thai Kinship Terminology", *Journal of the American Oriental Society* 63, p. 168-175.

Bisang, Walter 1992: *Das Verb im Chinesischen, Hmong, Vietnamesischen, Thai und Khmer (Vergleichende Grammatik im Rahmen der Verbserialisierung, der Grammatikalisierung und der Attraktorpositionen).* Tübingen: Narr.

Boeles, J. J. 1963: "Second Expedition to the Mrabri of North Thailand ('Khon Pa')", *Journal of the Siam Society* 50, 2, p. 133-160.

Conklin, Harold C. 1964: "Hanunóo Color Categories", in *Hymes 1964*, p. 189-192.

Davidson, Jeremy H.C.S. ed. 1991: *Austroasiatic Languages: Essays in Honour of H.L. Shorto.* London: School of Oriental and African Studies.

Diffloth, Gérard 1977: "Mon-Khmer Initial Palatals and 'Substratumized' Austro-Thai", *Mon-Khmer Studies* VI, p. 39-57.

Diffloth, Gérard 1980: *The Wa Languages = Linguistics or the Tibeto-Burman Area Vol. 5, Number 2.*

Diffloth, Gérard 1984: *The Dvaravati Old Mon Language and Nyah Kur* (= Monic Language Studies, Vol. I). Chulalongkorn University Printing House.

Egerod, Søren and Jørgen Rischel 1987: "A Mlabri-English Vocabulary", *Acta Orientalia* 48, p. 35-88.

Ferlus, Michel (1964): [Word list from a Mlabri dialect, taken down in Laos in 1964; unpublished].

Ferlus, Michel 1974: "Les langues du groupe austroasiatique-nord", *Asie du Sud-est et Monde Insulindien (ASEMI)* V,1, p. 39-68. Paris: CNRS.

Filbeck, David 1975: "A Grammar of Verb Serialization", in *Harris and Chamberlain 1975*, p. 112-129.

Filbeck, David 1978: *T'in: A Historical Study* (= Pacific Linguistics Series B. No. 49). Canberra: Australian National University.

Filbeck, David 1991: "Keeping Things Up Front: Aspects of Information Processing in Mal Discourse Structure", in *Davidson 1991*, p. 161-182.

Harris, Jimmy G. and James R. Chamberlain eds. 1975: *Studies in Tai Linguistics*. Central Inst. of English Language, Office of State Universities, Bangkok.

Headley, Robert K. 1978: "An English-Pearic Vocabulary", *Mon-Khmer Studies* VII, p. 61-94.

Hymes, Dell ed. 1964: *Language in Culture & Society.* Harper & Row. New York, Evanston, London.

Jahr, Ernst H. ed. 1992: *Language Contact* = Trends in Linguistics, Studies and Monographs 60. Mouton / de Gruyter.

Lindell, Kristina 1974: "A Vocabulary of the Yùan Dialect of the Kammu Language", *Acta Orientalia* 39, p. 191-207.

Matisoff, James A. 1983: "Linguistic diversity and language contact", in *McKinnon and Bhruksasri 1983*, p. 56-86.

Matisoff, James A. 1991: "Endangered Languages of Mainland Southeast Asia", in *Robins and Uhlenbeck 1991*, p. 189-228.

McKinnon, John and Wanat Bhruksasri 1983: *Highlanders of Thailand.* Kualalumpur, Oxford, New York and Melbourne: Oxford University Press.

Nimmanhaeminda, Kraisri 1963: "The Mrabri Language", *Journal of the Siam Society* 50.2, p. 179-184 with appendices.

Polibyenko, T.G. and Buy Kxany Txe 1990: *Jazyk Ksingmul*. Moskva: Nauka.

Pookajorn, Surin and Staff 1992: *The "Phi Tong Luang" (Mlabri): A Hunter-Gatherer Group in Thailand*. Bangkok: Odeon Store. (A previous edition appeared in 1988 in Thai published by the Fine Arts Department of the National Museum, Thailand.)

Premsrirat, Suwilai 1991: "Aspects of Inter-Clausal Relations in Khmu", in *Davidson 1991*, p. 123-139.

Proschan, Frank 1992: "Ethnonymy, with Special Reference to the Kmhmu", paper for the Mon-Khmer Workshop (International Conference on Sino-Tibetan Languages and Linguistics), Berkeley, 1992 (67 pp. plus appendix).

Rathcliffe-Brown, A.R. 1941: "The Study of Kinship Systems", *Journal of the Royal Anthropological Institute of Great Britain and Ireland* 71, p. 1-18.

Rischel, Jørgen 1982: "Fieldwork on the Mlabri Language: a Preliminary Sketch of its Phonetics", *Ann. Rep. of the Inst. of Phonetics, Univ. of Copenhagen* 16, p. 247-255.

Rischel, J. 1989a: "Fifty Years of Research on the Mlabri Language. A Re-appraisal of Old and Recent Fieldwork Data", *Acta Orientalia* 50, p. 49-78.

Rischel, J. 1989b: "Can the Khmuic Component in Mlabri ('Phi Tong Luang') be Identified as Old T'in?", *Acta Orientalia* 50, p. 79-115.

Rischel, J. 1989c: "What Language Do 'The Spirits of the Yellow Leaves' Speak?: A Case of Conflicting Lexical and Phonological Evidence", *Ann. Rep. Inst. Phon., Univ. of Copenh.* 23, p. 87-118.

Rischel, J. 1992: "Isolation, Contact, and Lexical Variation in a Tribal Setting", in *Jahr 1992*, p. 149-177.

Rischel, J. 1993: "Lexical Variation in Two 'Kammuic' Languages", *Pan-Asiatic Linguistics, Proceedings of the Pan-Asiatic Conference on Languages and Linguistics*, vol. III, p. 1451-1462. Bangkok: Chulalongkorn University.

Rischel, J. and S. Egerod 1987: "'Yumbri' (Phi Tong Luang) and Mlabri", *Acta Orientalia* 48, p. 19-33.

Robins, R. H. and E. M. Uhlenbeck eds. 1991: *Endangered Languages*. Oxford/New York: Berg Publishers.

Smalley, William A. 1963: "Notes on Kraisri's and Bernatzik's Word Lists", *Journal of the Siam Society* 51,2, p. 189-201.

Smalley, William A. 1994: *Linguistic Diversity and National Unity. Language Ecology in Thailand*. Chicago and London: Chicago University Press.

Smith, Kenneth D. 1972: *A Phonological Reconstruction of Proto-North-Bahnaric* (= Asian Pacific Series, Number 2). SIL. Santa Ana, California.

Suebsaeng, Nipatwet 1992: "The Mlabri family and kinship system", in *Pookajorn and Staff 1992*, p. 75-91.

Svantesson, Jan-Olof, Damrong Thayanin, and Kristina Lindell 1994: *Kammu-Lao Dictionary* [in Laotian]. Vientiane.

Thomas, David and Robert Headley 1970: "More on Mon-Khmer Subgroupings", *Lingua* 25, p. 398-418.

Thongkum, Theraphan L. 1983: "'To eat' in the Mlabri (Phi Tong Luang) language" (in Thai; mimeographed, 5pp.).

Thongkum, Theraphan L. 1984: *Bibliography of Minority Languages of Thailand*. Faculty of Arts, Chulalongkorn University.

Thongkum, Theraphan L. 1985: "Minority Languages of Thailand", *Science of Language Papers, Fasc. 5, August 1985: Languages and Dialects*, p. 29-69. Faculty of Arts, Chulalongkorn University, Bangkok.

Tongkum *(sic)*, Theraphan L. 1992: "The language of the Mlabri (Phi Tong Luang)", in *Pookajorn and Staff 1992*, p. 43-65.

Trier, J. 1986: "The Mlabri People of Northern Thailand: Social organization and Supernatural Beliefs", *Contributions to Southeast Asian Ethnolography* 5, p. 3-41.

Vongvipak, Chanan 1992: "Economic and social change among the Mlabri", in *Pookajorn and Staff 1992*, p. 92-103.